# THE CRAFT OF PUBLIC ADMINISTRATION

## 12TH EDITION

John E. Rouse
*Ball State University*

C. Kenneth Meyer
*Drake University*

Lance J. Noe
*Drake University*

Jeffrey A. Geerts
*Drake University*

**Millennium HRM Press, LLC** **Des Moines, Iowa**

Book Design and Layout: Sarah Marshall



For more information, write:

Millennium HRM Press, LLC
P.O. Box 41278
Des Moines, IA 50311

ISBN-13: 978-1-7355023-2-8

*Printed in the United States of America*

# The Craft of Public Administration

### Module One: Public Service—the Essential Profession

- Foreword, Preface, and Introduction
- The Administrative Craft
- The Ecology of the Administrative Craft

### Module Two: Understanding the Essential Organization—Design and Dynamics

- The Anatomy of Public Organizations
- The Physiology of Public Organizations

### Module Three: Making the Essential Organization Effective

- Managing Employees as People and Assets
- Communication and Leadership

### Module Four: Purse, Performance and Policy

- Taxing, Budgeting and Spending: The Distributive Question
- The Productivity Challenge
- Administrative Law—the Legal Foundation of Public Administration

### Module Five: Theory with Practice: Bringing Public Administration to Life

- Introduction: Living the Dream—Collaborative Learning, Problem Solving & Team Engagement
- Case studies
- Professional Portfolios: Showcasing Your Experience

# Table of Contents

**Module Five: Integrate Theory with Practice: Bringing Public Administration to Life**

# Essential Views: Academics/Practitioners at the Street Level

# Dedication

To those who faithfully and unselfishly serve the public and conduct the people's business, mindful of their Constitutional obligations, commitment to the rule of law, and steadfast truthfulness and integrity, and fully embrace democracy as an ideal, enshrined in a culture that embraces a process by which public choices are made, and exacts a form of behavior in society that we call "democratic," *The Craft of Public Administration* is dedicated.

—JER, CKM LJN,JAG

# Instructor Resources

The 12th edition of *The Craft of Public Administration* has been tailored not only to student growth but to support online instruction, compressed class schedules, and instructor delivery of course materials. Resources paired with the 12th edition of *The Craft of Public Administration* to assist instructors and students alike are available at www.millenniumhrmpress.com and include the following.

- Presentation slides, hundreds of presentation slides arranged by module;
- Suggested TED Talks, videos, and readings;
- Case studies;
- Sample syllabus; and
- Discussion of using the case study method of learning (see Module 5).

Instructors are encouraged to visit www.millenniumhrmpress.com routinely to access additional instructional aids as they are added.

# Foreword

## *The Craft of Public Administration* in a World of Dramatic and Extraordinary Change

by Parris N. Glendening

About a half a decade ago, I started the foreword for the 11th edition of this text by noting: "We live in a world of change. Dramatic change. Think of the constant reshaping of our world that charges at us almost every day."

At the international level, then as now, the impact of globalization, world recession and economic instability and the threat of terrorism and decades long military conflicts impacted almost every corner of the globe including the United States.

Overlaying this was the growing realization of the impact of global climate change, a force so great as to threaten the very existence of some nations and severely damage or even destroy many American communities with more and more frequent and fierce weather events.

Domestically, in 2016 I wrote, somewhat benignly, that change manifests itself in a growing anti-government, anti-tax movement at the national level and increasingly in many of our states and local governments. The result is a constant series of budget crises, sequestrations, deferred infrastructure investments, growing public debt and pension fund instability, etc.

These changes have been rapidly eclipsed by three major recent phenomena: 1) The COVID Pandemic, 2) The metamorphosis of and our understanding of climate change, and 3) The growing major social and economic inequities in America and much of the world.

These three dramatic and extraordinary changes are a real threat to America. At a minimum they are a test of our political, policy making, and administrative systems.

Look, for example at the very poor functioning of our federal system during the Pandemic with states actively opposing national government health standards and proposed solutions such as testing for COVID and vaccinations. Many states governors at the same time were vigorously attacking their own local governments, especially local school boards and administrators, and Health Officers often over policy differences as simple as requiring masks or mandating vaccinations.

These three threats are often closely interrelated. Witness, for example, the inequitable disparity in health facilities in many of our communities and the impact on infection and death rates. These differences are a reflection of race and income in many communities. In my home state of Maryland, when virtual school education was implemented at the start of the Pandemic, 25% of the homes in Baltimore City did not have internet sufficient to participate. Most of these homes were in lower income communities of color. Similar disparities exist in rural communities in Maryland and almost all other states.

Climate change was predicted as early as the beginning of the 19th century. Research in the 1970's and 1980's clearly demonstrated the danger to our nation and the world. Many Americans and policy makers did not believe the threat was real—"climate deniers"—or thought the threat was in the far in the future and did not require action now.

After watching the impacts of climate change induced major storms, continuing droughts, massive fires, coastal flooding, etc., over three-fourths of Americans understand the reality of climate change. The seriousness of the Climate Change onslaught is best understood by following the reports of the National Oceanic and Atmospheric Administration (NOAA) which reported 2021 as the second worse year on record for climatic disasters: 11 severe storms, 4 hurricanes, 2 periods of massive flooding, severe draught and fires, etc. The worst year was 2020.

While there have been some policy changes in sustainability, mitigation and resiliency, meaningful real change is still hard to achieve. A clear illustration of this reality was the very limited results from the COP 26 International Conference on climate change in 2021.

It is now clear that Climate Change is real! It is pervasive, dangerous and immediate!

Central to the uncertainty and instability produced by the Pandemic and Climate Change crises is the growing social and economic inequity in America. As wealth is increasingly concentrated in the top five percent, the rest of the population struggles to maintain their place in the economic system. Many work extra jobs or simply find themselves falling out of the middle class and into poverty.

The growing inequity has produced not only anti-government feelings and movements, but also an increasing distrust of the political and governmental systems. Indeed, it can be argued that this growing inequity and mistrust of government is one of the root causes of breakdowns in police community relations and outbursts of large-scale violence in cities such as Ferguson, MO, and Baltimore, MD. Unemployment among black males, for example, was 51 percent in the immediate area of Baltimore where the riots started.

While many of the riots and protests in recent years were about police violence, e.g., Seattle, Philadelphia, Minneapolis, and Ferguson, others were dominated by the extraordinary and dangerous political divide in America today, most notably the "Unite the Right" Charlottesville August 2017 deadly riot and the January 6, 2021 "insurrectionist" attack on the U.S. Capitol.

The passionate anger of a political divide burning in the dudgeon of growing social and economic inequalities creates almost unprecedented threats to our political, governmental and administrative systems. Special challenges face those who administer these systems.

All of this takes place in a cauldron of extraordinary population changes. The aging of the 77 million "baby boomers" with their changing lifestyles and impact on social service programs is increasingly overshadowed by the emergence of over 80 million millennials. These 25- to 35-year-olds impact building and locational decisions, modes of transportation (transit and walkability over the automobile), the application of technology and the views about the structure, process and role of government itself.

The impact of the millennials, which the U.S. Census Bureau calls the largest population cohort in American history, is immediate, dramatic and long term. Illustrative of the latter point, a growing percentage of millennials are electing not to have children or to have only one child. The impact on education systems and future work forces is great, similar to what countries like Germany or Japan are facing today.

Perhaps most visible of the population changes impacting our society is the growing diversity. There are now far more Hispanics and Latinos than African Americans, along with other growing populations, e.g., 7% Asian. Often the impact is even more dramatic for a particular region (e.g., African Americans in the South or Hispanics in the West) with even more significant concentrations of diverse populations in a particular community (e.g., Somali Americans in the Twin Cities of Minneapolis-St. Paul or Muslims in Dearborn, MI, or recent settlement of Afghans in Fairfax, VA).

The growing diversity has placed a great strain on the political, governmental and administrative systems. Controversial and hostile reactions to immigrants and people of different religions, often inflamed by extreme political rhetoric, are likely to continue in the near future.

The emerging recognition of the rights of the gay, lesbian, transgender population is another area of change that has unsettled many parts of the political and governmental systems. While many communities welcome this change as long overdue, others vigorously oppose it to the point of refusing to carry out legal mandates. Heated debate at all levels of government about this topic are commonplace, even in presidential elections.

Change comes at us in so many other areas as well. The impact of technology on our society is sometimes overwhelming. This is true for administrative systems as well, as they struggle with maintaining a balance between work and family when employees are "connected" 24/7. This is particularly true during the work at home, virtual meetings, Zoom culture of Pandemic years, a time of significant physiological illnesses.

The pace of innovation can have enormous impact. What is often called the "disruptive economy" is one very visible example. Witness the worldwide ongoing struggle as communities try to seek a balance between traditional regulations and emerging economic forces such as Uber or Facebook, or the on-line economy, or green energy sources as examples.

The impact of these dramatic changes on our administrative systems is huge. For some this may seem daunting. There is often a disheartening, even frightening, fear that much of the administrative process cannot withstand the onslaught of these massive, complex and fast-moving changes, most of which are so interrelated as to defy simple solutions.

In this context we should remember the words of John F. Kennedy, "Change is the law of life. And those who look only to the past or present are certain to miss the future."

Understanding the need for administrative systems that can work effectively in this sea of change is the strength of this edition of *The Craft of Public Administration*. This text is designed to help young practitioners do well in public administration in a time of great change and stress. It recognizes that for a system of public administration to do good for the public it must be built on the knowledge, training and experiences of generations past. It understands that students of public administration must be nimble, flexible and creative to deal with change but still work in a traditional framework of stability, fairness and equality that is expected of our administrative structures and processes.

*The Craft of Public Administration*, 12th edition continues to provide a classic collection of the essential leadership and administrative "notions," theories, issues and techniques that have formed the academic basis for a generation of students majoring in public administration and public policy. Building on this sound tradition, this edition is thoroughly revised, and updated to reflect the growing demand for an introductory textbook that joins in a relevant and practical manner the content of the increasingly mutually reinforcing areas of public administration and nonprofit administration.

The artfully crafted case studies provide the learner with a chance to better understand the dynamic nature of public administration today and to integrate theory with practice. The text is guided by the belief that effective public service in a democratic society is hard work and a noble calling. As Charles A. Beard said in his address to the American Political Science Association in 1939 the goal is "good work, honestly done."

*The Craft of Public Administration*, 12th edition will help a new generation of public administrators achieve those aspirations even in this time of dramatic change.

As a concluding thought I offer a personal perspective, especially to the young professionals who may hesitate to enter the practice of public administration, especially in these challenging times.

As a practitioner of more than 30 years in academia, state and local elected leadership for over 30 years and 20 years in non-profit advocacy organizations and occasional work in the private sector, I ask you to join us in meeting these challenges and offering and implementing a new vision of hope, inclusion, fairness and shared prosperity.

This is not just the call of President George H. W. Bush who said: "Public service is a noble calling, and we need men and women of character to believe in their communities, in their states, and in their country."

It is about joining the fight for a better country and a better world. I buffer that invitation with the words of Teddy Roosevelt in perhaps his most famous speech, Citizenship in a Republic (1910):

"It is not the critic who counts; not the man who points out how the strong man stumbles, or where the doer of deeds could have done them better. The credit belongs to the man who is actually in the arena, whose face is marred by dust and sweat and blood; who strives valiantly; who errs, who comes short again and again, because there is no effort without error and shortcoming; but who does actually strive to do the deeds; who knows great enthusiasms, the great devotions; who spends himself in a worthy cause; who at the best knows in the end the triumph of high achievement, and who at the worst, if he fails, at least fails while daring greatly, so that his place shall never be with those cold and timid souls who neither know victory nor defeat."

**Please join us in the arena of public administration and help make a difference.**

Parris N. Glendening is the former Governor of Maryland (1995-2003). He taught at the University of Maryland, College Park for 27 years and currently teaches at Johns Hopkins University's Carey School of Business. He is the former President of the Smart Growth Leadership Institute, part of Smart Growth America.

# Preface

The foreword by Parris N. Glendening epitomizes the strong sense of urgency that we now face as a nation. Today, perhaps more so than in any time in the last century, The United States is again placed on the center stage of world affairs and scrutinized on how well its democratic intuitions and processes deal with the tumultuous hand that it has been dealt: Rising levels of authoritarianism domestically and internationally, climate change, continuing saga of confronting the age old problems of inequality, and meeting the needs of an increasingly large, diverse, and multi-cultural population during a pandemic With the litany of challenges presented by Governor Glendening, the authors have thought through what basic ideas and notions are essential for the understanding and practice of public administration and they are presented in this newest edition of *The Craft of Public Administration*.

The over-arching goal of this book is to enable readers to understand and value the necessity of integrating the notions of work, citizenship, and living in a world that is undergoing change at warp speeds and, therefore, producing added complexity, anxiety, and uncertainty in our lives.

*The Craft of Public Administration*, 12th Edition, presents the most basic and essential concepts, ideas and principles of public administration in a clear, succinct and synthesized way. The environmental in which public administration courses are taught today has been dramatically altered by the COVID-19 pandemic and its many variants. As universities and colleges transitioned from traditional face-to-face, in-class instruction to distance online learning, the structure of the textbook learning material and how it is prepared and presented also changed. As other introductory textbooks in the field of public administration have maintained their many chapters to coincide with a quarter or semester length instruction (normally somewhere between 11 and 15 weeks in length), this book is structured for an intensive online course with only six or eight modules rather than the 14 or so chapters. Accordingly, the modules integrate the information which must be understood and provide a synoptic overview of notions, ideas, facts and trends which are necessary for understanding and practicing public administration today.

Based on popular response to the 11th edition, the Think About It! inserts are continued and enlarged upon. These inserts are designed to give the reader an opportunity to integrate the theory of the field, its historical connections, and importance, etc., with up-to-date contemporary topics, scenarios and trends, which require added understanding and reflection. As such, no other introduction to public administration textbook presents such a cacophony of topics to digest and form, independently, one's own belief and philosophical orientation. That is, the reader is at liberty, indeed prompted and encouraged, to muse about the varied consequences/implications of what is written in the textbook and then do a "compare and contrast" with what they have experienced in real life and what is taking place in general society. Learning is more than being able to repeat facts, figures and notions, etc.; effective learning is associated with the ability to integrate, synthesize and conceptualize and the Think About It! inserts should be of added value in this important area.

The Think About It! Inserts are varied by topic as the many tensions associated with the concepts presented in each module are presented. The reader will find some inserts to deal with traditional topics that further amplify or explain important managerial or economic models, such as the classical vs. neoclassical schools of thought, or deal with subject matter that is mentioned in the text, but not elaborated upon , such as landmark national legislation (Civil Rights Act, 1964 or the Americans with Disabilities Act, 1990), to discussions that summarize the differences between democracy and bureaucracy, efficiency and equity, and treatments of classical vs. neoclassical economic thought, the changing nature of work, right to left brain activities, and the general modernization of government. Added inserts are based on the 2020 national census data and not only elaborate the changing demographic characteristics of our nation, but also how the city and the county have become increasingly the defining units of government today. The inserts enable the reader to take different notions than those presented in the traditional textbook discussion and try them out and see how they resonate with their own experiences and personal philosophies and orientations.

Unique to this edition of *The Craft of Public Administration* are featured essays and articles written by academics and practitioners initially published in *The Public Administration Times* (PAT) and other professional venues that provide insights to the theory and practice of public administration and public policy analysis. Each author's original essay condensed to approximately 800 words are encapsulated in inserts entitled "**Essential Views: Academics/Practitioners at the Street Level**." Collectively, the vast knowledge, skills and experiences of these scholar-practitioners will provide valuable insights to the study of public administration and augment a major orientation of this textbook that enables theory and practice to be combined and embraced as a "craft—neither all art nor all science, but their comingling". As such, the Essential Views inserts deal with topics, such as whistleblowing, development of professional portfolios, performance management, and management from antiquity to the present, facts versus fiction, and the future characteristics of the public workforce.

In this edition of *The Craft of Public Administration*, some of the enduring principles, facts, and notions remain unchanged. This edition continues to show the centrality of basic principles associated with the organization of governmental organizations at the local, state and federal levels presented within the enduring context of the U.S. Constitution, relevant judicial decisions and legislative public policy making. The historical roots of American government are implanted in the theories and notions which govern basic citizen rights and duties, issues of democratic governance, public interests and how they are manifested, and the basic growth of public bureaucracies over time. Essential for those who wish to practice or experience public and nonprofit management, are the elementary concepts and notions associated with the basic makeup of organizations and their associated terminology; organizational theories pertaining to leadership, motivation, and human behavior and the augmentative issues pertaining to the basics of organizations, such as purpose, process, place, and clientele, centralization and decentralization, and a host of other relevant organizational factors. As the modules unfold, the reader will be introduced to the notions of human resources management (personnel), taxing, budgeting and spending, communication and the dilemmas associated with assessing productivity.

**Getting On With the Study and "Business" of Public Administration: Personal Reflections and Challenges**

As authors, during our many years of research and teaching, we have collectively taught thousands of students in the U.S. and around the world. As teachers, we always reassured those with whom we taught and learned that the basic institutions and structures of government would "hold steady" when under a state of siege, for the roots of our government run deep in theory, practice and in tradition, and the leadership would "...support and defend the Constitution against all enemies, foreign and domestic...." We spoke about the tenets of democracy as being only superficially accepted and embraced, and that our civic knowledge of these principles and processes was like a veneer on a table. That is, it was a thinly disguised coated layer that could be easily scratched or deeply marred. And once blemished, it would take great skill and patience to correct what had been damaged. That is also the case with democracy.

Although the U.S. is the longest lasting constitutional republic in history, there is no assurance that it will remain inviolate over a protracted period of history and remain a stable enterprise. That it had survived the Civil War, World Wars I and II, Korea and Vietnam and another nearly 35 other skirmishes and police actions, is acknowledged, but that it could be usurped by those who are not deeply committed to its basic underpinning—those who would give up democracy for autocracy and power and an "unswerving loyalty" to a strong person or a charismatic cult leader. As authors, we wrote extensively about the basic pillars of a democratic order: Knowledge of the actors of government (policy makers), the structure of government, the actual policies of government, and how to effectively communicate with those in representative positions. Today, these fundamentals are in jeopardy and a majority of the citizenry cannot answer any of these questions with accuracy. Further, as we collectively study public administration, and analyze the daily news and political events, etc., we ask if those in the executive, judicial and legislative branches are holding true to the sacred oath, which they have sworn to uphold.

The economic, political and social climate that dominates affairs at all levels of government—national, state and local—are nearly unmatched in the last century. The crisis was accelerated by the spread of a tiny virus, a novel coronavirus (COVID-19) that burst upon the scene and with pandemic consequences has fundamentally affected how policies and administration will be made and conducted in the immediate future. The economic strife faced by state, municipal, and local governments for the next few years (at least) will leave an indelible impact. The corresponding "shut-down" of the American economy and its disruptive effect on traditionally accepted ways of doing things socially and culturally, will leave a lasting footprint on basic societal structures, mores, and human behavior.

The changes taking place are already palpable in the rapid transformation of how things we used to take for granted were done, to new ways of doing things, augmented by technology and public health necessity. These changes are evident in the following areas: Voting, telecommuting, education systems (from K-12 to graduate levels), all manner of shopping (from the mall and main street businesses to Amazon and from clothing to groceries), Tele-everything (medicine, health care, legal activities, conferencing, insurance claims and adjustments, travel, recreation and leisure, dining activities, manufacturing, assembling, production processes and other congregates, to basic citizen-governmental interactions and essential economic exchanges. In addition, there will be an increase in regional collaboration, interest rate uncertainty, and greater indebtedness (later, perhaps higher tax efforts), complicated further by the decline in globalization, and the rise of populism and nationalism, and the growth of the virtual organization.

It is a truism that pandemics bring about tumultuous change, anxiety, uncertainty, and, historically, have always left their imprint on society. To say these are chaotic times would be a pedestrian observation at best. For those in public administration and public policy analysis, we need to think about the future of governance set within the context of a world-wide pandemic and massive civil protests and demonstrations on the streets of the United States. These tumultuous times are characterized by increasing levels of anxiety, uncertainty, depression, fear, tempered with the triple spirits of resilience, opportunity and the development of institutional trustworthiness.

Last, the principles inherent in our federal system of government will be challenged and tested in terms of rightful power, authority, protections, the "rule of law," and the proper role of national and state governments will be debated and litigated during these chaotic times. Also, the democratic principles of this republic will be increasingly threatened by the rise of authoritarianism, attacks against a "free press," and the elemental standards of fairness, equity, justice, and TRUTHFULNESS. It will be difficult to navigate the future and address these existential threats if a nation cannot agree on what constitute the basic facts of our history, culture, and science.

As experienced teachers, we have exhorted undergraduate and graduate learners to think about what they have experienced, what they are learning, and what they are observing on a day-to-day basis, and asked them how they would react if the fundamental ideas of our democracy came under attack—would they sound an alarm or merely comment on the music that the band leader has selected as the ship of state begins to take on water, begins to list, and even sink. The U.S. Constitution does not come in an unabridged edition—we do not have the option to hunt and pick only those items that suit our fancy. Indeed, there is a long and established, somewhat complicated democratic process by which we collectively agree on what is inviolate in this sacred document: The Constitution of the United States of America.

It is our desire, in writing *The Craft of Public Administration* that the basic structures, processes and ideals that undergird our system of governance be understood, valued and embraced, and that the next generation of public servants will hold steady to the Constitution and the rule of law whenever the threats of authoritarianism jeopardize our Noble Experiment.

As customary, the authors take full responsibility for all errors of omission and commission. It is important to acknowledge that many of our associates and colleagues helped prepare materials that appear in this book.

## ESSENTIAL VIEWS:

### ACADEMICS/PRACTITIONERS AT THE STREET LEVEL

**Management is Like Methuselah—Old**
By C. Kenneth Meyer

The idea of public administration, as it is known in contemporary terms. Is rooted in ancient history. The origins of public administration in this sense can be traced to Near Eastern Culture such as Hammurabi in Babylon with a code of 282 laws (Harper, 1904, cited in Wren, 1979). The ancient Chinese established a bureaucracy to administer as early as 1000 B.C. (Wren. 1979). General Sun Tzu in his classic treatise, advocated extensive discussion and sound plans before going into battle: "Thus do many calculations [plans] lead to victory, and few calculation to defeat." (Wren, 1979). And, in many of the earliest dynasties of Korea, there were national civil service tests administered that were essential to gaining positions in either the military or government. The first national examinations were administered in the Kingdom of Silla in 788. Later on, other dynasties administered competitive examinations in the areas of administration, the military, literacy and miscellaneous areas, such as medicine, geography, translation, and astronomy for advancement positions in society.

The Egyptians also understood the principles of management, such as, unity of command, span of management, division of labor, and basic—albeit authoritarian principles of leadership—as shown in extant documents and excavations. Egypt too created a bureaucracy to administer public works as irrigation canals and other public structures are known today. The Biblical Hebrews and Greece also had governmental structures to manage public affairs. For example, in Hebrew thought the vizier was given temporal matters and to the pharaoh the spiritual powers were reserved to himself (Wren, 1979). These are but a few of earliest principles of management recorded in history: Delegation of authority, forecasting, planning, and as Wren notes, the establishment of a professional "...full-time administrator to control and coordinate the state enterprise".

Scholar Ali Farazmand has informed us about administration and management principles beginning as early as 6000 B.C. in his discussion of the Elanites and the Achaeminid Empire (more recent, 59-330 B.C); they are both instructive in the areas of state building and administration. To recap his exhaustive inventory of practices, concepts and principles of management that were precursors to modern management goes well beyond the central thesis of this paper. However, a summation of these practices is shown in the following list: taxation policy (revenue generation), civil service hiring through merit (career) and patronage appointments, long-range strategic planning, emergency management, professionalization of the bureaucracy (rules provided by a "Guild System"), and capital and developmental investment techniques.

The early Persian cultural orientation built a dominant, middle-class, Persian bureaucracy, whose power was checked to ensure equity and efficiency and truth telling. The telling of a lie was a crime subject to punishment and it was more disgraceful than owing indebtedness—one was prone to tell lies if one owed money. The issues of management and administration that were found in antiquity remain today modern administration: The concepts of centralization vs. decentralization (federalism and intergovernmental relations); tax policy, the role of quasi-governmental institutions, the rise and control of bureaucracies and the abuse of power. In addition, time management, anti-waste and corruption policies, infrastructure development and maintenance issues (roads, irrigation systems, water management, natural resources management, harbors, postal services, waterways), self-government and partnership-based arrangements (collaborative government), contracting-out, bringing women into management, and a host of other concerns were on the Persian agenda 2500 years ago.

On a broader contextual basis, many of the management concepts in use today evolved from ancient civilizations—Western, Eastern and African. Although they have evolved to new levels today, they formed the basis for organization (hierarchy of authority, division of labor (370 B.C.), scalar chain, span of control, assurance quality control (City of Ur in Samaria or modern day Iraq), identified leadership traits and skills (innate vs. learned), controlling (accountability, evaluation, quality control), accounting principles (double-entry bookkeeping), etc. Indeed, perhaps the oldest profession is that of management! The roots of administration from these sources can be traced from the Puritans in New England to later developments after the adoption of the Constitution.

The need for administration, even in ancient societies, resulted from complexities of people living together in communities. Institutions such as churches added to the growth of administration as they created hierarchies intended to bring order to the activities they guided. Tribal societies also had forms of administration with roles for members such as chief and lower ranking roles. Ancient Asian and South Asian societies also matured to levels requiring laws, administration of same, and individuals who would administer them. As complexities of societies grew generated in large part by increasing populations, leaders needed "wisdom", intelligence, and some form of administration skill. Persons filling administrators must be primarily born with these characteristics since there was limited education about administration, as it is known today. While some schooling was present in the ancient world, the primary subject matter would have been philosophy as seen in the Greek approach.

Augmentative of this brief historical discussion, Laila El Baradei, provided a more complete discussion of the beginnings of public administration. She acknowledges the development of many administration/management notions mentioned above, and adds topics such as work management systems, performance/work target and their monitoring, and an education system that not only developed the technical skills of civil servants, but an education that developed their "intellectual abilities" in preparation for their government posts. In short, an educated civil servant was deemed necessary in ancient civilizations.

*Sources: Adapted and modified, Meyer, C. Kenneth, et.al., The Emergence of Public Administration as a Tool for Public Management, Journal of Business and Educational Leadership, Vol. 9, No. 1, fall, 2019. Laila El Baradei, "Public Administration: How it All Started in Egypt, China and Rome, PATimes.org/public-administration: how-it –all-started-in-egypt-china-and-rome/11-3-2021*

***— JER, CKM, LJN, and JAG***

# Introduction

### Seven Pedagogical Segments

The framework of this text is cast within seven pedagogical segments–federalism, public personnel administration, budgets, government regulations, nonprofit and public-sector differentiation--succinctly organize the study of partisan, policy, and system politics–and government bureaucracies. The sixth segment deals with major trends that will impact on the future of governmental organizations. To be sure, conflicting, diverse values challenge the craft of public administration in ways not yet envisioned. Despite this clash of civilizations, all cultures must determine how public bureaucracy is to be responsive and act as an effective catalyst for serving people. The last segment presents case studies as a way to experience reality.

*The Craft of Public Administration*, 12th edition, is not just a textbook; it is a pedagogical gathering of pertinent yet limited literature, assembled to inform and interest college students in the dynamics of the public and nonprofit sectors in the United States. The literature selected for inclusion in the book has been carefully selected because we choose not to write a book that is "everything one wants to know about public administration but is afraid to ask," but rather that material essential to learning and practicing the basics of public administration.

### Federalism

*Federalism* covers craft of public administration; relationships to economic development, political and bureaucratic culture; the structure of politics; partisan, policy, and systems politics; equality; efficiency; synergy; formal organization; and human relations. Modules 1 and 2 focus on the structure of American politics, or issues of U.S. federalism. Module 1, Unit 1, concerns "The Administrative Craft"; Module 1, Unit 2, deals with "The Ecology of the Administrative Craft;" Module 2, Unit 1, investigates "The Anatomy of Public Organizations;" while Module 2, Unit 2, studies "The Physiology of Public Organizations."

### Public Personnel Administration

Public personnel administration covers people, patronage, merit, equal opportunity, affirmative action, job classifications, labor relations, leadership, charisma, communication, and technology. Modules 3 addresses matters of public personnel administration. Module 3, Unit 1, explores "Managing People as Employees and Assets;" and Module 3, Unit 2, reviews "Communication and Leadership.

### Budgets

*Budgets* cover taxing, appropriations, spending, productivity, efficiency, effectiveness, motivation, privatization of government functions, planning, and program evaluation. Module 4, Unit 1, explores "Taxing, Budgeting, and Spending: the Distributive Question;" and points out how partisan, policy, and systems politics affect the likelihood of higher taxes but fewer government programs and services. Module 4, Unit 2, deals with "The Productivity Challenge" and outlines the pressures on government employees to do more with fewer resources.

### Regulations

*Regulations* cover administrative law, administrative controls, administrative law judges, ethics, discretion, rules, procedures, administrative responsibility, administrative state, and clientele relations. Module 4 wraps up with Unit 3 and a discussion of "Administrative Law—the Legal Foundation of Public Administration. It explores clientele relations, the impact of administrative growth on democratic ideals, administrative law judges, and how economic, social, and subsidiary regulations are affected by administrative rules and rulemaking.

**Major Trends and**
**The Future of Public Administration is Now**

As we progress in learning the basic theories, ideas, facts, and notions that underpin our system of government—although essential to our understanding of how governments opérate and behave—we will be asked to set our sights higher and reflect on how our basic public and nonprofit organizations, joined with the private economy, will deal with the enduring issues that we face in the early decades of the 3rd millennium. Therefore, it is also important that we move beyond the ability to merely memorize the everyday "nuts and bolts" of American government and organizational theory and think about what we rather confidently understand and what we believe to be some of the harbingers for the future of public management.

This is one of the most exciting times in the history of the United States to learn about the multitude of intricacies and complexities that accompany the transformation of our political, economic, and governmental organizations. Theories, concepts, notions and facts drawn from different disciplines and perspectives prevail, and it is difficult to separate or discriminate between what information is useful and what is not. For those of us who labor daily in the management and administration of our more than 100,,000 state and local organizations, we more often than not understand the organizational structures in which we work, but are often befuddled and even bemused by the difficulties associated with actually conducting the business of the people in an efficient, effective, and equitable manner.

In this segment, we identify a few of the trends and directions that will impact the future of public service administration—which includes both the public and nonprofit sectors—in the United States.

1. Government and governance is rapidly being transformed before our lives, but sometimes we are unable to discern what is changing and what is driving the change. Some academicians invite their colleagues in the many classes they teach to "drill deeper;" to become more explorative and imaginative in their inquiries; and others stress the desire for more entrepreneurialism, creativity and right brain conceptualization. In short, the DNA of government is undergoing a rapid change in this new millennium.

2. The organizational and human resources strategic planning process has become increasingly sensitive to the global dimensions of organizational behavior and we need to understand the importance that diverse political, economic and cultural environments, laws and regulations, etc., play in managing the people's business—the business of government.

3. Organizations increasingly find it beneficial to recruit and hire people who are representative of the categorical or demographic traits of their clientele or customer base, especially by gender, race/ ethnicity, and sexual orientation.

4. A 21st century organization has characteristics that make it distinctively different from its 20th century counterparts, especial in terms of structure, organization design, reach (domestic versus global), resources, job expectations, and style (structured versus flexible). These changes, in addition to others too numerous to mention here, *demand* that our organizations move from being simply resource driven bureaucracies, to performance, mission, and result-based enterprises. The scope of these changes is so transformative and fundamentally accepted that they require no further explanation or comment.

5. Employee health insurance, professional and continuing education, training, wellness programs, Employee Assistance Programs (EAP), telecommuting and workplace flexibility (time, location, tour, shift, and benefits) are viewed as important motivators and job satisfiers, while simultaneously undergoing scrutiny in terms of their effective Return-on-Investment (ROI) HR metrics.

6. Managers at all levels of authority need to continually increase their understanding in crucial areas of non-discrimination, safety and health, energy and environment, ethics and privacy if they wish to be successful in implementing the voluminous number of federal and state laws, rules, regulations and judicial decisions.

7. The workplace of tomorrow will become more heterogeneous, especially in terms of its aging and immigration characteristics. Workplace diversity will continue to grow, especially in the areas of race and ethnicity, gender, age, disability, veteran status, national origin, religion, language and sexual orientation.

8. Increasingly, transactional HR activities will become a part of electronic Human Resource Management (eHRM) in areas such as pay and compensation, benefits (vacation time, personal time-off, health and insurance payments, pensions, 401(k) and retirement, direct payroll deposits, recruitment), and other administrative and record keeping areas. Also, more and more of these transactional activities are being outsourced to organizations that specialize in HR management and development — or Professional Employer Organizations (PEOs). Most modern organizations have moved toward Web based HR systems and employees are encouraged to self-inform and manage their employment portfolio on a system that is always accessible 24 hours a day, seven days per week.

9. Public and nonprofit employees desire certain factors to be associated with their work. These are some of the most important expectations: Challenging work; personal growth and development; pleasant working conditions, good social relations, job autonomy, giving service to society; job security, personal recognition; opportunity for advancement; pay and financial rewards, and prestige

10. Management is torn between the "bi-polar twins" involved in balancing work and family. Workplace flexibility (flex-time, flex-place, telecommuting, etc.) is now commonly found in organizations, although management continues to struggle with the increased employee autonomy, empowerment, and responsibility that these changes imply.

11. There is a cache of managerial and human resource issues that are of enduring importance, yet the efficacy in which line manager's deal with them remains problematic. A sample listing of these concerns include these salient topics: retention, pluralistic workforce, working mothers (nearly 70 percent of mothers with children under 18 are employed), paternity-maternity leave programs, dual career families, glass and bamboo ceilings, limited or low skilled educated employees, gender pay inequities, work/family issues, child and elder care, sequencing mothers (drop out and then reenter employment market), age and disability discrimination, and immigration and work policies. Also, team or group evaluation methods remain unresolved, along with individual performance evaluation, succession planning, bench-marking, broad banding, e-learning, team building and career planning, and the uses of technology. All of these issues, unresolved as they might be, are part of the staple diet of managers today; they also beg for solutions which blend the theory of our multidisciplinary field with known best practices.

12. The movement from left brain to right brain activities in the workplace. Functions of the left brain: critical thinking, numbers, words (verbal), analysis, and sequence; right brain, color, intuition, imagination, creative thinking, images (non-verbal) and daydreaming.

13. Movement toward the use of teams and understanding the nature of teamwork to accomplish specific goals. To accomplish teamwork, we need to understand the people who make up these collective enterprises, know how to motivate and evaluate team performance and productivity.

14. Change is an imperative and therefore we must understand what factors are associated with initiating successful change and what are its many barriers, such as apathy, "old power," rigidity and fear of the unknown.

15. The enduring issues associated with water availability, decline in governmental effectiveness, climate change, wage and wealth income gaps and general global inequality; failure of the present structure of government to adapt to changing social, political and environmental conditions.

16. The existential question that must be asked over and over as we study public administration is: How do we build a culture that encourages cooperation, collaboration between the three sectors and encourages a spirit of civic, social and political cohesiveness and solidarity, versus ones that disunites and dissipates our collective energies and will? Therefore, the issues of food insecurity, economic interdependencies, income and wealth chasms, environmental and ecological enhancements and protections, civil and human rights, and economic development, commitments to majority rule and minority protections based on constitutional principles serve as a good first step in our discussions in class, and since there are competing ideological views, they are sure to be protracted ones.

17. New technology and social media are transforming organizational management and service delivery in the areas of communication, information systems, record management, personnel accountability, and inventory systems.

# THINK ABOUT IT!

**The New Face of Technology in Governmental Agencies**

Governments at all levels have had to make major transformational decisions on how they conduct the people's business due to the exigencies of a global wide pandemic, economic and political turmoil, and declining levels of governmental trustworthiness. Chloe Kirby presents some digital technology trends that will play a prominent role in the future of public services. These trends in digital transformation should enable employees to do their jobs more successfully regardless of work location, expand citizen accessibility to services, and enhance overall efficiency and effectiveness of government agencies. Some of the trends listed below are already evident.

- More automation that facilitates working from home or remote locations
- IT infrastructure upgrades that support working from home and handling emergencies
- The challenge of cyber-attacks as organizations accelerate digitalization
- Increased digital experience for citizen access to services
- Employees working remotely
- Cloud computing for reliability, accessibility, flexibility and scalability in a digital world
- Expanded use of Edge Computing, 5G, and IoT (internet of things) for expanded computer power, wireless digital services, and building "Smart" organizations
- Artificial intelligence used in predictive analytics or identification of issues before they become problematic.

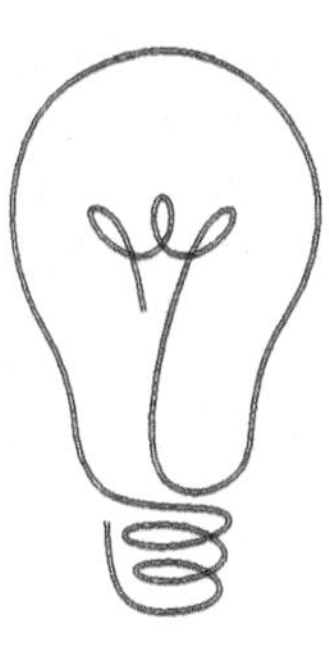

*Source: Chloe Kirby, "10 Public Sector Tech Trends for 2021," PA Times, August 13, 2021.*

**Experiencing Reality through Real-Life Case Studies**

In Module 5, *Integrate Theory with Practice: Bringing Public Administration to Life*, an introduction to the case study method and real-life administrative scenarios are presented to enable class participants to confront a number of complex administrative and public policy issues, and make decisions or recommendations on how they believe the dilemmas, issues, and problems should be handled. In the processes surrounding the case (incident) analysis, the participants will be asked to assume a variety of specific roles such as the role of administrative consultant, program director, department head, policy analyst, staff analyst, administrative colleague, etc., in relation to the specific problems of the case. Typically, individually or in a small group situation, the learners will analyze the problems and present their respective recommendations and evaluations.

The case studies allow students to learn from analyzing the literature in conjunction with specific illustrations. Case studies force us to think about how the general (literature) affects the particular (case study) and how specific illustrations amend our perceptions of public administration literature. Examination of case study facts brings out the dynamic nature of the literature. Laurence E. Lynn Jr., John F. Kennedy School of Government, says it best when he states, "...to be effective in government, students must learn to think on their feet, interact effectively with others in a group, be able to ask and answer questions, and be able to summarize evidence and arguments quickly, clearly, and persuasively." The authors believe these case studies support this vision and that learners will further develop the knowledge base and skills needed for success.

**Summation and a Cautionary Tale**

*The Craft of Public Administration* recognizes that effective teaching of partisan, policy, and systems politics occurs in a global world of images, videos, and films. This edition includes, following the summary at the end of each chapter, suggested TED Talks and readings for instructional consideration. This new feature shows the many faces of public administration in action.

Public administration constitutes the "chemistry" of the United States. The two key principles that have come to embody the American ideal, equality and efficiency, are likewise the crucial determinants of how well the public, or government, sector functions in the United States. Democratic capitalism does not flourish if public infrastructures, such as schools, highways, institutions of public safety, and similar taxpayer-funded government operations, are devalued and rendered ineffective.

Public-sector functions, programs, and activities represent the "bottom line" expectations that society guarantees citizens. A change in domestic and military spending priorities has forced public administration as a field to be more accountable, adjust to economic realities, and evolve in unforeseen ways.

Let us begin our journey to this noble calling of public service by exploring the art, science, and craft of public administration.

# Public Service—the Essential Profession

- **Unit 1:** The Administrative Craft
- **Unit 2:** The Ecology of the Administrative Craft

# UNIT 1: The Administrative Craft

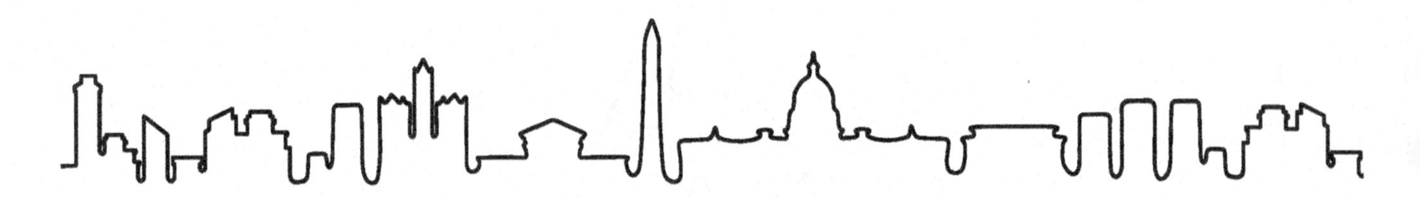

The words *public administration* express a concept that at first glance may seem abstract and nondescript. However, a closer look at the phrase helps relieve the ambiguity.

Public administration is grounded in partisan, policy, and systems politics. It links private and public citizen relations. It is both product and process. It acts on responsiveness and competence. It is administered under the legal auspices of federal, state, and local governments. American constitutional principles dictate its every move. Public administration is an art, uses science, but is mostly a craft.

In its varied activities, the centralization of power is accompanied by the decentralization of governmental function. A diversity of social values skews its uniformity. Its origins are political. It cannot operate without personnel. It is monitored by administrative laws. It regulates private citizens and their many activities. The political cultures of the 50 states penetrate its many behaviors in, of, and for American lives.

*Public* means the citizens of a given area—the people of a town, county, state, or country. If an issue is considered in the public domain, information and discourse about that issue are available to the people and can be known to all. The word *public* also refers to activities the state administers on behalf of the entire community.

Public administrators serve the people. Organized collectives of citizens constitute a variety of public communities in the United States. These publicly organized communities include national, state, and local governments. They include townships, state recreation areas, and public utilities. They include school, sanitary, and water districts. These communities administer public libraries, public parks, public defenders (police, fire, legal), public roadways, and public servants. In the event of war, citizens may be called upon to make the ultimate sacrifice to their national community—their lives. However, in peacetime, Americans are required only to pay taxes and obey the laws. When April 15 rolls around, citizens have a definitive economic opportunity to be patriotic by meeting their financial obligation to society. The one thing all public programs have in common is that they are financed by taxpayers, most of whom want a voice in how those dollars are spent.

U.S. taxpayers often pressure the government to reduce personnel and expenses for services. There is correspondingly less demand to reduce services to citizens. Since most services are delivered by local governments and their employees, the reduction of personnel and expenses must come first at the local level of operations, less so at the state level, and much less so at the centers of federal government operations.

As we study public administration, the abstract, nondescript, colorless images of public bureaucracies will fade away to be replaced by more concrete concerns about the development, evaluation, and implementation of programs that require our tax dollars. Such decisions are usually political in nature; a major function of politics is to allocate importance to numerous and often conflicting values in society. Public administration, then, is the process of implementing those diverse values in our complex and ever-changing society. This process plays a vital role in the daily lives of all citizens.

One issue that affects public administration is the size and role of government. According to Michael Hodges, government spends about half what the nation "earns" each year. Is this amount excessive? The percentage of Gross Domestic Product (GDP) spent by the U.S. government is, in proportion to its economy, smaller than that of nearly any other industrialized nation.[1]

Government spending is more precisely evaluated in the context of population demographics, economic consumption, citizen production, and environmental consequences, all considered over time. To promote standards of a civil society, economic and political systems must proactively respond to population changes. The U.S. population increased from 151 million in 1950 to more than 331 million in 2020. Since the early 1800s, immigration has been a crucial component of America's growth and a periodic source of conflict. In recent years, immigration has surfaced as one of the most contentious issues on the nation's political agenda. The Pew Research Center estimates in recent years that more than one million legal and illegal immigrants settle in the country each year. The projected population increase comes mostly from legal immigration. In 2018, the U.S. population included 44.8 million foreign-born people or 13.7 percent of the overall U.S. population.[2] That is nearly three times the percent of foreign-born in the population in 1970 but is actually less than 14.8 percent of residents in 1890 that were foreign-born. By 2065, it is projected the U.S. foreign-born population will reach 78 million.

Birth and immigration policies affect how the U.S. population grows, as well as affecting demands for limited resources, pollution, deforestation, waste, and habitat choices. The more people, the more demand for government services—and the more government employees, bigger budgets, and higher taxes. Disparity in the tax burden may also increase, with some parts of the population shouldering more of the load.

While the U.S. population has expanded dramatically, federal tax levels have remained relatively stable the past fifty years. Federal tax composition, however, has generally shifted from corporate income and excise taxes toward social insurance taxes, with the individual income tax continuing to produce the most revenue. State and local taxes, unlike federal taxes, have doubled—from 5.3 percent of GDP in 1947 to more than 10 percent today.

## The Heart of the Matter

In a classic textbook, Herbert Simon, Donald Smithburg, and Victor Thompson define administration simply but graphically in this opening sentence: "When two men cooperate to roll a stone that neither could have moved alone, the rudiments of administration have appeared."[3] That illustrates much of what administration is and is not. The first and foremost ingredient of administration is *people*. A stone on a hill is not in itself involved in any form of administration. If that stone rolls down the hill by some act of nature, administration is not involved. People have to be present before administration can take place.

The second ingredient of administration is *action*. Two people looking at the stone are not, in that act alone, involved in administration. They must take some action regarding the stone before administration can enter the picture. There is no such thing as inactive administration (although many who have dealt with administrative agencies sometimes believe otherwise).

The third ingredient is *interaction*. If one person moves the stone, administration does not occur. At least two people must combine their efforts to move the stone for the activity to involve administration. The essence of administration is *people relating to people*.

People interacting with people to accomplish tasks—this is the essence of administration.

## Art, Science, or Craft?

The title of this book clearly proposes that administration is a craft. Why this classification instead of another? Why not consider administration a science or an art?

Science is characterized by precision and predictability. A scientific rule is one that works all the time. In fact, rules in science are so rigid and final that they are not called rules at all, but laws. Two parts of hydrogen combined with one part of oxygen will *always* give us water, steam, or ice, depending on the temperature. While it is true that some sciences, particularly the social sciences, do not achieve such a 100 percent predictability level, it is also true that any scientific theory must stand up to rigorous, repeated tests to be considered valid. Administration uses scientific data, laws, and theories. For example, finance officers use mathematics and computers to keep a government agency's financial records. However, administration itself is not a science.

Although administrators use scientific laws, techniques, and data, they do so in ways that give individual imagination and temperament free rein. Usually, a variety of successful solutions exist for dealing with a particular administrative problem. A creative administrator may even devise a new solution on the spot. Administrative problems are rarely identical, and it is impossible to derive scientific equations that work the same way every time for such problems.

Administration shares traits with the arts as well as the sciences. Administrators often work in highly imaginative ways, employing a mix of methods, including intuition. Like painters and composers, administrators often find their own moods and personalities reflected in their work. There is; however, a vital difference that keeps administration from being characterized as an art. Artists create aesthetic works; administrators attempt to solve problems. The respective end products and the criteria for evaluating them differ.

Although public administration shares traits with both science and art, categorizing the field as one or the other obviously paints an incomplete picture. There is, however, a category more suitable—or at least more comfortable and workable. That category is *craft*.

There is never a precise formula that will invariably work best in all administrative situations. Not only do situations and people vary, but ideas for handling them are almost as infinite as the human mind. Still, we can establish an objective standard for most administrative situations. Did the solution result in more efficient completion of the desired task? Objective standards, a lack of precise formulas, changing situations, and problem solving are traits that best fall under the classification of craft. Whereas science uses unvarying methods to achieve predicted results, and art uses diverse methods to achieve diverse, unpredictable results, a craft uses diverse methods to attain a desired result.

Public administration deals with the ongoing pressing problems of American society. Government administrators—executives, civil servants, and others—may well employ artistry and imagination in dealing with the demands of a variety of interests. However, they are not creating works of art. Administrators rely on hard evidence to resolve dilemmas of consequence to citizens. Yet the possibilities for resolution are virtually limitless—so administration is surely not a science.

Public administration, therefore, is neither art nor science, but can be described as a craft. Working in their craft, executives and civil servants seek to achieve objective goals and standards—with all the creativity, capability, and civility they can muster. In the always evolving American administrative scene, the challenges of the craft of public administration are more demanding than ever before.

One of the toughest political challenges for any current president is shaping the modern government support (welfare) system. The term *welfare* originally referred to government as a "helper of the poor." The benefits the modern government support system offers; however, reflect radical departures from the policy directives Franklin Roosevelt formulated in the 1930s. The current government support system creates widespread dependency on government spending. Yet budget deficits and distrust of government accompany government programs, services, and spending.

According to *Newsweek* columnist Robert J. Samuelson, Americans are bereft of any consistent public philosophy by which to judge the effectiveness of their governments. In other words, no public philosophy spells out what governments should and should not do. Budget deficits and federal debt trace their origins to an inadequate taxing-and-spending philosophy. Though most taxpayers oppose tax increases, they cannot agree on which programs should face revenue cuts. Little consensus exists on which government programs are necessary for the common good.

"Sooner or later," Samuelson argues, "we need to come to terms with the welfare state. We need more rigorous standards for judging whose welfare is being advanced and why."[4] The welfare state emerged in the 1930s as an antidote to the insensitivities of free markets. Today, middle-class government support systems are a subject of increasing anxiety and contention.

## ESSENTIAL VIEWS:

### ACADEMICS/PRACTITIONERS AT THE STREET LEVEL

**Posterity is Centuries Old—So is Public Service**
By Lisa Saye

Posterity is centuries old. We often speak or write about it as if it were something in the future. More accurately, posterity is a record of yesterday's and today's triumphs, grievances, wars, peace and societal advancements that are often more appreciated in the future. Posterity detaches rituals from record. Posterity is then and now.

Public service is also centuries old. The world caught on to its benefits long ago. As public administrators, our role in this drama is continuous, challenging and often thankless. But no one should enter into government service for applause or accolades. Public service is the primary test of government, and the delivery of public goods represents the endless test of the successful structure of government.

Government is where civilization, empathy and duty meet. When we fail to apply the broader meaning of this combination, a mirror can be the worst invention ever created. Posterity's mirror has shown us that government is not a combat sport. Government, for all its starts and stops, is instead a full-time Service Industry.

Public service is not vertical. It is a direct investment in one's community. Public service is a chance to unify the goals of government with the needs of the citizenry. COVID-19 has thrust the world's governments into forced and unforced crises. Some crises have laid bare issues related to the improper handling of power. Populations have become fearful of next week, next month or next year. Public administrators know that fear produces unstable governments and unreliable public service. The examples of how we have gained the means to lessen the unknowns during this pandemic are too numerous to list here. Suffice it to say that although we have been stunned, we have not been defeated.

Our citizens are simply in search of a welcome and acceptance when their structures and lives have been damaged or destroyed. They need action from the promises of tax collection and redistribution. They do not need judgment and ridicule. They most certainly do not need delay and lies or to see someone casually whistling past a cemetery. Government is designed to manage public goods and public service is the immediate vehicle towards that maintenance. Government is compassion when necessary, it is comfort when necessary and it is necessary when necessary. We must help our citizens to heal when they are hurting because forgetting takes too long.

We know that most of the people we serve live in a system of non-justice and exclusion. We must work against the deception of mal-intended processes, policies and procedures by working against the failures that are embedded as normality in our public institutions. We recognize that our most prominent function as administrators is to reorganize abnormal lines of recruitment and management. As such, our current and future academics will have to be different to capture new ideas and interests. COVID-19 is writing the chapters, outlining the theories and producing scenarios and case studies to test and measure how effective we need to be the next time.

Posterity has been a partner of government. When read and watched by tomorrow's children, posterity's stories will present a clear and unaltered picture-narrative of how we steadied the ship of government when it mattered most. COVID-19 is forcing us to transform some government functions from physical to virtual. Local, state and national government schedules may never return to pre-pandemic hours or manpower. As such, current traditions are being written with a pencil and a good eraser. Public administrators are uniquely trained for such an environment as this one.

Valor is defined as someone having great courage in the face of danger. One can see valor manifested in the job that local hospitals and disease centers have performed for the neediest of citizens during the pandemic. Thomas Paine's remark about how times try men's souls remains appropriate. Every day before today and every day after today is an opportunity to meet any crisis as a committed unit of humanity.

NOTABLE QUOTES

Human beings are members of a whole
In creation of essence and soul
If one member is afflicted with pain
Other members uneasy will remain
If you have no sympathy for human pain
The name of human you cannot retain.

*— Sadii*

## Capital, Government, and Myths

Public administration is grounded in capital, bureaucracy, and democracy. Effective government cannot exist without sufficient capital to finance buildings, programs, equipment, skills, knowledge, and expertise.

Some call U.S. democracy a myth. Governments that create myths, sooner or later, are apt to shed them. Myths set ideals and standards governments cannot meet. Self-government does not function effectively when citizens raise skepticism and continuous contest over these fundamental assumptions. Citizens must believe in the system, even when it is imperfect. They must agree to procedural rules for the democracy to function effectively. And no democracy can protect the rights of every individual when those rights conflict.

*The myth of true democratic governance raises several difficulties. First, decreasing accountability of democratic institutions and processes fosters skepticism in the fairness and effectiveness of the system.*

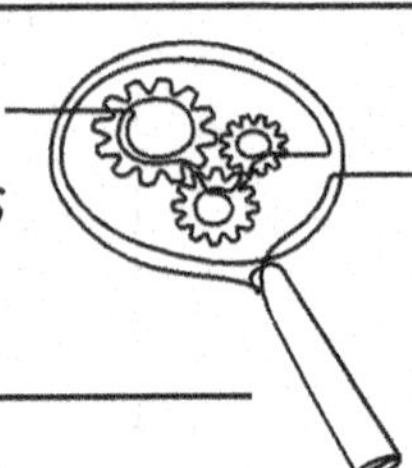

"The myths of our democracy are not delusions," says David K. Shipler. "They may be just part of the truth, or embellishment of an inner reality in our culture's creed. But coupled with our freedom to expose our flaws, the myths have power, because they celebrate the powerful ideas that government belongs to the people, that voting is a universal right, that all citizens are equal, that we are governed by the rule of law, that minority views are protected no matter how abhorrent to the majority."[5]

The myth of true democratic governance raises several difficulties. First, decreasing accountability of democratic institutions and processes fosters skepticism in the fairness and effectiveness of the system.

Second, the American middle class perceives itself as bearing more of the burden and receiving less of the benefits of government than it should. This perceived unfairness is important for public bureaucracy, because the bulk of the money collected to operate, finance, and expand government originates from the middle class. For a variety of reasons, many citizens insist that significant sectors of American society are increasingly excluded from democratic rule. With growing economic disparities comes greater challenges to the integrity of American democracy.

Third, the uniformity of intellectual thought on substantive policy questions closes out many economic and social options. The two political parties are often neither pragmatic nor flexible. They do not cope well with the ongoing, painful economic adjustment of the United States to its challenging role in the post–Cold War world.

Accountability, representation, and intellectual diversity challenge democratic rule. Public administrators are governed by laws, public bureaucracies are limited by the same, and freedom is manifested by a dynamic relationship between citizens and the state. If this relationship is not morally based, representative, and intellectually creative, government programs, services, and expertise suffer. The legitimacy of government functions becomes suspect.[6]

"For two generations, Government elites defined the great issues," writes Garry Wills. "Now, a tidal change in the culture is sweeping away traditional politics." In the title of an article in the *New York Times Magazine,* Wills asks: "Whatever Happened to Politics? Washington Is Not Where It's At."[7] What we think of as political discourse today is in reality celebrity politician scandal and gossip. A stable structure for robust political debate based on substantive knowledge is missing and the nature of expertise is challenged.

However, politics cannot be separated from culture. Creative technologies, markets, and the courts relegate elections to the role of secondary player in political life. Consumerism and political rights emphasize individual prerogatives. Markets are driven by the purchases of consumer goods. Legal rights protect minorities—however they may be constituted—in the marketplace.

Wills argues that family and religion, as American institutions, promoted civic stability. Today, families are being redefined. Many children are born outside of traditional marriage. Divorce is prevalent. These developments reflect definitive structural changes in family organization. Families are the first organized unit of any society. Government programs are only as effective as the political consensus that arises when such social units agree on the common good; therefore, cultural changes effect political changes.

Public administrators respond and act in a cultural context. Whether fighting against terrorism or for more effective health care programs, politicians confront political—and cultural—wars. Television, radio, the Internet, social media, mobile devices and other technologies give citizens access to information for making personal decisions. The average American may feel they need neither priest nor politician to tell them how to conduct their life.

Freedoms make it ever more difficult to mold political consensus. Public administration programs and policies—ideally, at least—are populist concepts built through ideas to which citizens adhere. U.S. citizens enjoy both political and economic privileges. They live in a society that stresses individual rights. They make demands on industries in the public and private sectors. They therefore demand responsiveness and expertise of government employees.

Before the attacks on the World Trade Center, Pentagon, and the nation's capitol what used to be called "the Establishment" was already disappearing. The agenda-setting elite is gone. Wise men, or for that matter wise women, do not exist in a society where sovereignty is less salient and where markets have more immediate impacts.

Marriage and family, as we have stated, are the fundamental institution of any society. In the United States, government and private industry likely come second and third; the media and religion are probably fourth and fifth. Why are the institutions of marriage, family, industry, religion, media, political parties, and governments under assault and constantly in flux?

Family structures and priorities changed once women became formally educated and realized a certain economic status. For two generations, as Wills notes, public policies encouraged citizens to make their own decisions—to not be bound by authorities in civic, religious, or private matters. The spread of egalitarianism has been slow but very persistent.

An Associated Press poll found that the United States is an impatient nation. Americans are demanding— wanting it all *now*. The Department of Motor Vehicles ranks high among places Americans hate to wait. Citizens feel more time poor than money poor. Waiting fifteen minutes in a line is the maximum. Public-sector clients may resort to rudeness if they perceive government inefficiencies.[8]

Despite these changes in culture, citizens still think in terms of public and private sectors. But these distinctions are being called into question. Dwight Waldo offers long-term insights into the notions of *public* and *private*.

The concepts of public and private are very central in the conceptual and emotional structuring of the Western world. A great deal of our thought and action concerning government, law, morals, and social institutions relates one way or another to this distinction, a distinction which the modern experience has taught us to make. But we need to appreciate public and private are not categories of nature; they are categories of history and culture, of law and custom. They are contextual and subject to change and redefinition.[9]

As cultural notions about public and private rights and responsibilities change, pressure is brought to bear on political and governmental systems to change as well. Trust in the public sector soared as our society agreed to tackle the threat of terrorism, but the myth of government as omnipotent provider and protector is collapsing under the weight of political divisiveness and response to events such as the 2020 COVID-19 pandemic. How will we carve out a new sense of the role of government?

## The Emerging American State. Good-bye U.S. Governments?

As Theodore J. Lowi wrote a generation of years ago, the language of the state is economics. Economic analysis, argues Lowi, manipulates the cost rather than the benefit side of the cost-benefit equation.[10] Otherwise, the question arises on how a nation can afford to spend billions for nation building in Afghanistan, but lacks the essential millions of dollars required to fix potholes in our city streets? That scenario posits economics as the language of the state–knowing the price of almost everything, yet the value of nothing? No greater example of this political and economic relationship can be found than that surrounding the passage of the Patient Protection and Affordable Care Act commonly referred to as the Affordable Care Act.

The Affordable Care Act affirms United States governments, all nearly 90,000 of them, to be viewed, appreciated, and understood as the ongoing, developing American 'state.' The Congressional Budget Office projects the net cost of the Affordable Care Act (ACA) to be approximately $1.2 trillion for the 2016-2025 period. The perspectives, notice, and comprehension of the Affordable Care Act turn away from public-sector challenges as the domain of governments to the positive, not reactive, realities of the emerging American 'state.'

In transitioning from governments to state, the ACA employs cost curbing measures that help reduce the growth in health care spending. The purpose is to drive down health care costs over time and increase availability and quality of care. Therefore, the Obama administration took us into the politics of 'state' building domain–not merely orchestrating the dynamics of nearly 90,000 somewhat interdependent governments.

President Barack Obama found sources of skills, knowledge, and expertise to initiate, develop, spend, budget, and reformat the trillions of dollars invested in the wide ranging parameters of this new American state. As there are markets for capitalism, there may emerge markets for demands of socialism. Socialism needs include transportation, education, military, diplomacy, safety [police], and health care.

In the establishment of the new American state, the rule of law is the bottom line common denominator, and commerce, consensus, policies, dollars, bureaucracy take on properties of uniqueness, boldness, and creative political entrepreneurship.

## Local Governments (Cities and Counties) Are the Defining Government Institutions

Each week cities are growing by 1.5 million inhabitants. By 2050, two-thirds of the global population will be city dwellers, up from just one-third in 1950. Nearly two-thirds of energy demand comes from cities while 70% of CO2 is generated in cities, although they, globally, produce 80 percent of the world GDP. In the U.S., 52% of total GDP is created in America's 20 top metropolitan areas, and New York City's metropolitan area produces $1.5 Trillion—about 10% of the United States' total GDP, and The Greater Los Angeles area and Chicago's metropolitan area, add another $866 and $610 billion in GDP, respectively.

Growing urban populations puts more pressure on an already strained infrastructure. The Flint, Michigan water crisis exposed 100,000 residents to lead in their drinking water. Detroit public schools cut off water because of elevated levels of copper and lead. Des Moines, Iowa, Water Works filed a federal lawsuit, claiming drainage districts in rural counties were funneling high levels of nitrates into the local river that serves as a primary source of drinking water for 500,000 central Iowa residents. When Hurricane Katrina struck New Orleans in 2005, Americans witnessed, on their own soil, what looked like an overseas humanitarian-relief operation. The storm destroyed much of the city, causing more than $80 billion in damages, killing more than 1,800 people, and displacing in excess of 270,000.

Like armed attacks, some of the effects of climate change could swiftly kill or endanger large numbers of people and cause such large-scale disruption that local public health, law enforcement, and emergency response units would not be able to contain the threat. For example, a NASA simulation that combined a modest forty-centimeter sea-level rise by 2050 with storm surges from a category three hurricane found that, without new adaptive measures, large parts of New York City would be inundated, including much of southern Brooklyn and Queens and portions of lower

Manhattan. The effects of climate change on America's neighbors could also be severe, with spillover security effects on the United States.

In the Urban world: Mapping the economic power of cites, the McKinsey Global Institute, made a comparison between what the top 600 cities selected from their database of 2,000 cities looked like in 2007 in contrast to what they are projected to show in 2025. The expected change is noteworthy: As a percent of the world's population in 2007, 1.5 billion people, projected 2025, 2.0 billion people, or 22 percent and 25 percent, respectively; $30 trillion GDP (2007), $60 trillion GDP (2025)—60 percent of global GDP; 485 million households with a per-capital GDP of $20,000 in 2007, contrasted with 735 million households with a per-capita GDP of $32,000 in 2025.

Additionally, these statistics only show the dramatic change occurring in urban areas around the world, but for successful urban planning, infrastructure investment, we need to understand the management required for the traditional service areas of safety, security, education, social and human services, healthcare and so on. In combination, the foregoing plethora of activities will need to be managed along with understanding the implications surrounding major demographic changes (aging population, number of children, immigration, poverty levels, and overall dependency levels), and the implication's associated with climate change and migration and immigration patterns. [11]

In addition, very little attention is normally devoted to the county level of government in public administration course work. The county is a general jurisdiction government unit and one that is, like the city, close to its population in terms of function and service deliveries and is another essential governmental unit. In fact, there are roughly 3,100 counties in the U.S. (organized and unorganized), and a mere 31 of them or 1 percent of all counties, make up 32.3 percent of the total U.S. Gross Domestic Product (GDP) in 2018.

These few counties comprise nearly 22.2 percent of the total U.S. population and include about 26.1 percent of all employed Americans. Importantly, there is a major bifurcation between urban and rural counties that reveals an unusually large concentration of the total economy in fewer and fewer jurisdictions.

These are daunting trends and for comparative analysis, Los Angeles County and New York County contributed $735.2 Billion to the U.S. GDP between 2012-2018.[12] Statistically, an examination of the 130 largest counties in the United States, on a per-capita economic output—a mere 4.2 percent—had 49 percent of all county residents and produced 60 percent of all county output in the U.S. in 2018.

The data reveals a wide range between the larger counties and their small county counterparts. For instance, in 2018, San Francisco County per-capita economic output was $184,014, whereas in smaller counties, which comprise 12 percent of all county residents, had a per-capita output of $42,043.[13] The 2020 census revealed that over 50 percent of the counties in the United States experienced a population decline, whereas the population growth was largely centered in metropolitan areas—a growth rate of 8.7 percent since 2010.

Specifically, the world is becoming increasingly urbanized, as is the United States. During this time of unprecedented change, urbanologists and demographers, city planners and economic development professionals, among others, concern themselves with topics such as health care, education, transit, food, clothing and housing. Faced with population change, the notion of how to maintain a sustainable development (social, economic, and socio-demographic) becomes an imperative.

All these factors ideally take place within an ecosystem that is stable and sustainable for generations to come and will include collaborative governance by the three economic sectors as they partner to achieve major social, political, and economic goals, such as building global networks, regenerating urban areas while meeting rural needs, and envisioning the make-up of populations, especially in terms of its demographic characterizations.

**Wrap-Up**

A Summative Demographic Profile of the United States shows the United States has a total population of approximately 331 million and is the third most populous country (below China and India with about 1.3 B each). Some of the major states for immigrants are also the most populous in the United States: California (39.5 M); Texas (29.1 M); Florida (21.5 M); and New York (20.2 M).[14]

A casual walk through the U.S. demographic garden reveals these major population characteristics:
1) Nearly 250 M live in the urban populations contrasted with about 29 M rural inhabitants;

2) The U.S. urban population is already 80.7 percent of the total; and 3) There are now 486 urbanized areas in the U.S. In the 48 contiguous states, there are 1.9 billion acres of land that is segmented into seven categories: pasture/range, forest, cropland, special use national parks, military bases, etc., miscellaneous (cemeteries, deserts, swamps, golf courses, etc.) and urban. Cropland takes one-fifth, but all U.S. towns and cities would nicely fit into the Northeastern region alone or only 3.6 percent of the total land use and this is where 80 percent of all Americans live.[15] Comparatively 75 percent of new workforce entrants will be women and people of color. This should be noted in light of worker shortages where the rate of people leaving the workforce is greater than those entering it.[16]

For comparative purposes, in the 2010 census about one-third of the population identified as other than non-Hispanic White—111.9 million; In 2020, the number had increased to about 140 million or 42 percent of the U.S. population. The South and Nevada had large proportions of minority populations and nearly 50 percent of the West's population was minority such as California, Texas, and Nevada.

Additionally, the District of Columbia and Maryland are now majority-minority populations. For instance, the Hispanic Latino population in California now represents 39.4 percent of all Californians. Indeed, the future is now with over 250 cities with a population size of 50,000 or above, fall into this minority dominant status: New York City, Houston, Oakland, Los Angeles, Miami, Dallas, Atlanta, Sacramento and San Antonio—to name a few.

A deeper dive into the 2020 national census shows the following ethnic/racial distributions: Asian American population, 5.9 percent projected to grow to 9.1 percent of population by 2060; of the 18.9 U.S. Hispanic population projected to grow to 28.6 percent by 2060. The Black or African American growth from 12.0 percent to 12.9 percent by 2060. For the white, non-Hispanic population, a drop from 63.7 percent to 57.8 percent—a 5.9 percent decline.

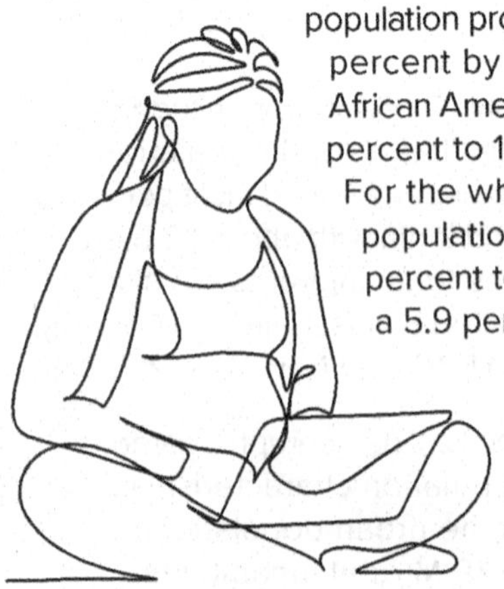

Comparatively, 75 percent of the new workforce entrants will be women and people of color, and this should be noted in light of worker shortages where the rate of people leaving the workforce is greater than those entering it.[17]

Overall, the 2020 census show that there has been a loss in white Americans, the first time since 1790. The nation's growth rate for 2010-2020 was largely associated with people of color who now make-up about 40 percent of the U.S. population. The national growth rate for the period 2010-2020 was 7.4 percent—the lowest since the 1930s. The white population grew almost exclusively in the Sun Belt and Western region of the U.S. For historical trends, keep in mind that in 1980, the white population made up 80 percent of the national population. =

The decline of white youth populations is also of interest since they now comprise less than 50 percent (47.3 percent) of the national under-age 18 population, with Latino or Hispanic youths comprising 25.7 percent and Black youths at 13.2 percent. In 2000, the white youths made up 60.9 percent of the national under age 18 population This trend of further decline in the white youth population is projected to continue over the next decades and will become a potent demographic in the future growth of America's labor force.[18]

Finally, the number of people who identify as having two or more races increased threefold from 9 million in 2010 to 33.8 million in 2020. People who identify as a race other than White, Black, Asian, American Indian, Native Hawaiian or Pacific Islander make up 49.9 million of the population and now eclipses the Black population of 46.9 million–the nation's second largest racial group.[19] It is clear that the United States has become a multiethnic, multiracial democracy.

The population shift from rural to urban areas has political consequences. With the release of the 2020 census data, there are a number of population statistics that are noteworthy for the United States, especially by race/ethnicity. The total population is 331 million comprised of the following racial/ethnic characteristics: White population, 57.3 percent; Black, 11.9 percent; Hispanic or Latino, 19.5 percent; Asian, 5.9 percent and the remaining percentage is made up of Native American, Hawaiian/Pacific Islander, two or more races and the other category.

In short, the country has become less white, more multiethnic and multiracial in 2020. Overall, in 2020, the population numbers will have 226,000 less in rural areas than in 2010, the cities and suburbs grew by 20 million people (8 percent of population) and, inescapably, with population grown in suburban and urban areas, they will gain in representation in both Congress and state capitals. For example, cities growth in Florida, South Carolina, Texas, South Dakota and Texas was over 15 percent, and rural counties declined by 3 percent or only grew slightly by 3 percent. More than 50 percent of all counties in the United States have smaller populations in 2020 than they had in 2010.

This population shift is very important politically since the decennial census data is used in the upcoming redistricting of state legislative and congressional districts. The debate will be largely over the use of "gerrymandering" by state legislatures to create partisan districts (democratic or republican), or the use of commissions in creating fair representation in districts by race and ethnicity and population density. Regardless of the overall accuracy of the 2020 census conducted during a pandemic and period of political turmoil, the data officially reported by the Census Bureau will be used in redistricting decisions, although Hispanic/Latino, transient, lower-income, urban populations may have been undercounted.[20]

## Trust in Government and Politics

When hijacked airliners exploded into the World Trade Center and Pentagon on September 11, 2001, the United States suffered the largest single-day loss of life ever on American soil. Public trust in government surged in the wake of the September 11 attacks. What had government done to earn it?

Perhaps you have heard the old adage: "Trust is something that must be earned. You have to show me you're trustworthy." The post–September 11 confidence level approached that of 1966 when the "Great Society" Democratic Congress, elected on Lyndon Johnson's coattails in 1964, passed the Voting Rights Act, put Medicare on the books, enacted the first large federal education assistance law, and created a host of social and environmental measures designed to improve American lives.

According to *Washington Post* columnist David Broder, government assumes two tasks 1) to protect the people; 2) to promote economic growth.

How much do Americans trust government? Not very much. Trust increased to 61 percent in the early 1960s but plummeted to 24 percent of citizens in the 2020s saying government can be trusted to do the right thing all or most of the time. The very low levels of trust today question the legitimacy of government size, emphasis, and debt.[21]

## Partisan, Policy, and System Politics

American government employees exercise their skills, knowledge, and expertise within the framework of a fast-paced and ever-changing society. Three of the dynamic forces at work in our society are partisan politics, policy politics, and system politics. Partisan politics is concerned with which political party wins office. Policy politics deals with deciding which policies to adopt. System politics examines how administrative systems (decision structures) are set up.[22]

Public administration emphasizes two of the three forms of politics: policy and system politics. However, it originates from partisan politics. Partisan, policy, and system politics are not separate, exclusive applications of the craft in practice—they are highly intertwined. In a nutshell, citizens elect political partisans to public office; partisans establish public policies; and administrative systems implement the policies partisans have established. Consider an example: the administration of Central Park.

Central Park in New York City is a public park. Located in the middle of Manhattan, the park runs from 59th Street to 110th Street, from 5th Avenue to 8th Avenue. In the midst of some of the most expensive private real estate in the world, the park somehow survives the marketplace values of New York City. Central Park affords the citizens of New York a wide variety of playgrounds, bicycle paths, wooded areas, jogging paths, swimming pools, picturesque lakes, and other natural scenery. The facilities of Central Park are offered to the public on a first-come, first-served basis.

Who's in charge of Central Park? Are the politicians in charge? Are the police in charge? Are the bureaucrats from the parks department in charge? These types of questions demonstrate the subtleties of how politics shapes life in the public sector. Similar analogies may be made to federal lands, state parks, and municipal buildings. So, who is really responsible for the upkeep of the facilities of Central Park? In a general sense, the people of New York are responsible. In a more direct way, the New York parks department, the Central Park Conservancy nonprofit organization that manages the park, the police, and the mayor are responsible because they are the custodians of this public interest.

Whereas the concept of political responsibility is often abstract, administrative aspects such as hierarchy, chain of command, unity of command, span of control, due process, regulations, rules, and even bureaucratic ineptness are more definitive and recognizable. Politics, in its varied definitions, may be vague to many citizens; on the other hand, citizens have concrete experiences with bureaucracies.

How is the study of public bureaucracy different from the study of elections, executives, legislatures, or the courts? The study of bureaucracy focuses on obeying authority; the study of elections, executives, legislatures, or the courts relates to the institutionalizing of democratic values. The study of public administration tells us what actually happens as bureaucracies carry out policies enacted by legislatures and approved by executives.

Decisions made by government officials, representing departments and agencies, reflect the policy and system politics that occur in public bureaucracies. Such decisions are monitored by political partisans within the framework of majority rule and minority rights.

## Adversarial Legalism

Compared to other economically advanced democracies, the United States is uniquely prone to adversarial, legalistic modes of policy formulation and implementation, shaped by the prospect of judicial review. While adversarial legalism facilitates the expression of justice—allowing challenges to official dogma—its costs are often neglected or minimized.

A survey of existing research indicates the extent to which adversarial legalism causes (or threatens) enormous dispute-resolving costs and procedural delays, which in turn distort policy outcomes. Adversarial legalism, moreover, has increased in recent decades, as Americans have attempted to implement the ambitious, socially transformative policies of activist government through political structures, forms of legislation, and legal procedures that reflect deep suspicion of governmental authority.[23]

Public administrators rely on, and are vulnerable to, the law. Legalism in general, and laws in particular, tend to limit and influence the operation of a public institution much more than they do a private one. “This pervasive legal context is among the principal distinctions between public and private enterprise,” note John M. Pfiffner and Robert Presthus. “In private management one is assured that he can do anything not specifically forbidden. In public administration, on the other hand, discretion is limited by a great number of laws, rules, and regulations.”[24] To put it more succinctly, in private administration the law generally tells administrators only what they cannot do; in public administration, the law tells them what they *can* do.

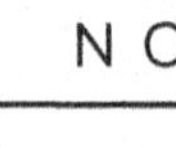

NOTABLE QUOTES

When I am working on a problem, I never think about beauty. I only think about how to solve the problem. But when I have finished, if the solution is not beautiful, I know it is wrong.

— *Buckminster Fuller*

The hiring and firing of employees, the purchase of equipment, and the adoption or even adjustment of a simple operational guideline have produced costly and frustrating litigation. To activist administrators, the law and its practitioners often seem to exist merely to tie their hands. Aggravating the problem for many public administrators is that their craft is becoming increasingly result-oriented. This contrasts sharply with the legalistic approach, which stresses the correctness of procedure. To the legal mind, justice is not a product but a process.[25]

The legal limitations placed on public agencies contribute to or create many of the other differences between them and private enterprise. Government organizations usually operate in a goldfish bowl, subject to scrutiny from politicians, the public, and the press. They must be ready to open their doors and their books to almost any outsider, even though the outsider’s interest in the agency may be prompted by no more than idle curiosity.

The legal context within which the public-sector functions also helps explain why its employees usually enjoy greater rights—and face greater obligations. Public agencies frequently possess less flexibility than private ones. The public organization must hold itself accountable. And new technologies have caused new legal dilemmas to sprout up.

The internet and terrorism threaten to alter public and private boundary delineations. The internet raises questions about applying laws to cyberspace communications; the legal principles surrounding this medium continue to evolve. In the 1960s, the U.S. Supreme Court cited the Fourth Amendment to the Constitution, which protects citizens against unlawful searches and seizures, as providing a "reasonable expectation of privacy" in telephone booths or street conversations. In the 1980s, the court reduced the scope of that protection.

In 1986, Congress passed the ECPA, or Electronic Communications Privacy Act. It outlawed nonconsensual interception and disclosure of electronic communications. Workplace privacy increasingly focuses on the internet and electronic communications.[26]

However, the terrorist attacks of September 11, 2001, or the impacts, results, and implications thereof, now interfere with protections guaranteed by the ECPA. Former Attorney General John Ashcroft called for "sweeping authority" to investigate possible terrorists. Legislation known as the Patriot Act gives the attorney general flexibility to provide broad surveillance over the internet.[27]

Yes, the latter is in contradiction to the former. This is where the issue of "civil liberties" comes to the fore. This is where partisan, policy, and system politics interact as debate continues.

According to Jeffrey Rosen, author of *The Naked Crowd: Reclaiming Security and Freedom in an Anxious Age* (2004), politicians, the media, interest groups, and an adversarial legal system contribute to an unhealthy state of panic. Rosen argues that risk aversion since the September 11, 2001, terrorist attacks erodes our freedoms. "The risk-averse democracies of the West continue to demand ever-increasing levels of surveillance and exposure in a search for an illusory and emotional feeling of security." [28]

In *The Unwanted Gaze: The Destruction of Privacy in America* (2000), Rosen writes that sophisticated surveillance technologies and strategies cannot absorb, analyze, and understand the sheer volume of information. New antiterrorist laws on wiretapping the internet illustrate this point. This legislation vastly expands the FBI's ability to monitor foreign agents. The FBI must hire agents to listen to recordings from start to finish. Filtered or unfiltered, information taken out of context presents challenges for public administrators. Citizen privacy is held at bay.[29] In the interplay of partisan, policy, and systems politics, preservation of freedom, privacy, and security in a post-9/11 world tests the viability of essential American ideals.

## Bureaucratic Legalism and Hidden Law

The establishment of law is one of the greatest achievements of human civilization. However, as Jonathan Rauch asks, what happens if law "starts getting off its leash"? Rauch portrays formal law as "bureaucratic legalism," with a focus on the legalistic bent of law in American society. Bureaucratic legalism posits that if citizens proceed through sufficient legal processes, the resulting outcomes will be procedurally correct and morally right. But does this always hold true when laws are applied to unique situations in American life?

What if the law is applied when an eight-year-old girl brings a nail clipper to school? Rauch points out that etiquette, norms, social codes, and customs exist to avert or resolve such conflicts. He says that these givens are "hidden laws." They are so deeply imbedded in our social structures that we forget they exist. Hidden law, says Rauch, entails everything from table manners to informalities by which neighbors settle land disputes.

Rauch believes that hidden law may be applied to issues such as adultery, pornography, assisted suicide, sexual harassment, and abortion, rather than relying on bureaucratic legalism. Bureaucratic legalism was in play when the Olympic athlete had to give back her gold medal because she took cold medication. It is also in force when a child is suspended or expelled for bringing a plastic squirt gun to school. The weapons policy did not include the word *plastic* when the city council outlawed guns.

When is hidden law relevant? Hidden law can be applied when we ask, "Is this offense worthy of notice? Maybe not. All right, we're going to pretend that it didn't happen." Bureaucratic legalism cannot make these distinctions. As Rauch explains regarding bureaucratic legalism:

By its very nature, its standard of fairness is equal application, to absolutely everybody, all the time. It views Hidden Law as capricious and arbitrary and inequitable in that it makes distinctions between people based on very personal, local judgments. So, with Bureaucratic Legalism, it becomes virtually impossible to make exceptions.[30]

## American Constitutional Principles

The craft of public administration is influenced by factors other than partisan, policy, and system politics and legalism. Our republican form of government, federalism, separation of powers, and constitutionalism—all of which will be discussed in the following pages—help put the craft into a larger perspective. Much is said pejoratively about public bureaucrats and their perceived power to operate without constraints in the American political system. However, a public administrator receives his or her authority for administrative decision making from certain constitutional principles. What are these principles?

C. Herman Pritchett cites four constitutional principles, embodied in the document signed September 17, 1787, that influence the lives of Americans every day.[31]

*First*, the Constitution established a *republican* form of government. Many Americans hold onto their grade-school conceptions of democracy in America, believing that we have a democratic form of government. We do have a democratic *philosophy* of government; however, the *structure* of our government is republican. What *is* a republican form of government? Simply stated, we send representatives— legislators and executives— to city hall, the general assembly, Congress, the governor's mansion, and the White House because it would be impractical for all citizens to vote and decide public policy on every issue. Although Article 4 of the Constitution guarantees "a republican form of government," the definition was left open-ended for future generations of Americans.

*Second*, the Constitution created a *federal system*. The original U.S. government set up in 1776 was a confederation, or a mere league, of states, in which each state retained its sovereign powers. Under the auspices of the 1787 Constitutional Convention in Philadelphia, the delegates formed a stronger central government that was to receive its authority from the people. Powers not transferred to the new national government were to be retained by the states. As the cornerstone of the U.S. governmental system, federalism encompassed a two-level structure of government that divided power between the central government and state governments, allocating independent authority to each level.

The condition of U.S. federalism has been altered by political conflicts and economic crises. The Civil War ended the political aspirations of those who wanted a confederate political system, and the economic collapse of the 1930s brought down a dual form of federalism in which states had been somewhat independent of the central government. Events culminating in the 1860s (Civil War) and 1930s (economic collapse) were steppingstones on the path to a more centralized American political economy.

The Civil War was a crisis in federalism, as its effects encouraged greater centralization and caused the influence of the states to decline. The Great Depression of the 1930s was also a crisis in federalism, as the economic collapse caused the central government to intervene on behalf of the private economy. The Civil War and the economic depression thus had centralizing effects upon federalism. The federal government's influence expanded, as did the expertise, skills, and knowledge of public administrators. However, contrary to what the name implies, the United States are far from united on matters of politics and economics. Federalism, then, is the sometimes changing structure of federal and state politics in the United States.

Demographic federalism, a movement of the mid-1990s, redefined the relationship between the states and the federal government. Demographic federalism makes the federal government accountable for the health and financial security of the elderly and disabled. The states are responsible for human capital and programs for workers, families, and children. These changes will have a significant impact on decision making concerning economic and social policies.[32]

As sovereign communities, states promote their own economic interests, seeking political advantage over each other; this sometimes results in a state public sector being able to offer a better quality of life to its citizens.

*Third*, the Constitution embodies the *separation-of-powers* principle. Each branch of government is assigned a particular task: Congress makes the law, the executive branch administers the law, and the judicial system enforces and interprets the law. The separation-of-powers concept operates in tandem with the goal of limiting governmental powers. Separation-of-powers doctrine restrains one branch from usurping the powers of the others; the limitation of government powers inhibits the national government from overpowering the rights of the states and restricts the intrusion of government into private lives.

A system of checks and balances enables each branch to have some influence on the operation of the others. Congress regulates the kinds of cases the Supreme Court will hear, and the Senate ratifies treaties and approves executive appointments. The president appoints federal judges and vetoes laws, but the Senate must approve his judicial appointments. The courts pass judgment on the validity of executive acts and interpret congressional statutes. With these checks and balances in place, abuse of power is less likely.

Former President George W. Bush declared that he had the power to set aside any statute passed by Congress when it conflicted with his interpretation of the Constitution—disturbing the balance between the branches of government. The Constitution clearly assigns to Congress the power to write laws and to the president the duty "to take care that the laws be faithfully executed." Bush claimed the authority to disobey more than 750 laws enacted while he was in office.

*Finally*, basic to the concepts of republicanism, federalism, and separation-of-powers is the idea of *constitutionalism*. Constitutionalism includes such ideas as the rule of law, representative institutions, and guaranteed individual liberty. Two important elements of American constitutionalism are majority rule and minority rights.

What happens when people disagree? The answer customarily given is "majority rule." It is here, however, that we must exercise caution. If 51 percent of the people voted to put the other 49 percent into concentration camps, we would hardly call this an exercise in democracy.

When we think of constitutional democracy in American political culture, therefore, we must think not only of majority rule, but also of minority rights. This tenuous balance between the wishes of the majority and the rights of the few enormously complicates democracy, especially for public-sector managers who must carry out the majority's mandate while simultaneously safeguarding minority interests. Public administration in a democratic society is a delicate and difficult task, requiring its practitioners to possess generous amounts of tolerance and tact. Those lacking such capacities may well do better in other fields.

*What happens when people disagree? The answer customarilly given is "majority rule." It is here, however, that we must exercise caution. If 51 percent of the people voted to put the other 49 percent into prison, we would hardly call this an exercise in democracy.*

Bush challenged laws on torturing detainees, oversight provisions of the USA Patriot Act, and "whistle-blower" protections for federal employees. He ignored military rules and regulations, affirmative-action provisions, requirements that Congress be told about immigration problems, "whistle- blower" protections for nuclear regulatory officials, and safeguards against political interference in federally funded research.

Political opponents argued that the President was seizing for himself some of the lawmaking role of Congress and the Constitution-interpreting role of the courts. Bush refused to "execute" what he claimed to be unconstitutional laws. He challenged more laws than all previous presidents combined.[33]

Majority rule and minority rights even affect the workings of Congress. Because of the rules, the majority party can work its way more easily in the House of Representatives than in the Senate. In the Senate, regardless of which political party maintains a majority of U.S. senators, the leadership needs sixty senators to cut off debate. Until the magic number of sixty is reached, a minority can stall legislation.

As the loyal opposition, the minority party has responsibilities to offer amendments to the suggested programs of the majority.

A brief synopsis of some of the essential characteristics of the U.S. Constitution that all public administrators should be conversant with are represented in **Figure 1.1.1**, What You Must Know About the Constitution.

**Figure 1.1.1 What You Must Know About the U.S. Constitution**

Federalism Defined: A system of government that constitutionally establishes a national and state level of government and defines the powers given to both; powers are divided between the two levels of government and, thereby, constitute both a political and structural arrangement

Powers held by the federal government (national government) are of Five types:

- Enumerated/Delegated/Listed or outlined in the Constitution (Article 1, Section 8)
- **Implied**—Powers necessary to carry out delegated powers (Art 1, Section 8, Clause 18). The elastic clause states that Congress has the power "...to make all laws which shall be necessary and proper for carrying into execution the foregoing powers..." set forth in Art 1, Sec. 8.)
- **Inherent**—Powers not specified in the Constitution but are reasonable and essential ones required of a sovereign power, such as the power to issue executive orders, to authorize the use of military force, and to deal with immigration policy. Inherent powers enable the president to get the executive job done.
- Reserved or saved for the states (9th and 10th amendments)
- Concurrent or powers given to both the national and state governments.

Supremacy Clause of the Constitution (Art 6, Section 2) applies when the federal and state government's conflict, then, the federal government is supreme to the states. The U.S. Constitution is "...the supreme law of the land."

Denied Powers to national and state governments, such as passing ex post facto laws (punishment for something now that was previously legal); bills of attainder (jailing citizens without trial); denial of writs of habeas corpus (accused people are to be tried in courts). Also, cannot grant title of nobility or tax exports.

Under the federal system of government, the U.S. Constitutions divides powers into three distinct branches with their own responsibilities and powers. This is called the separation of powers and designed to protect liberty and property and serve as a defense against "majoritarianism."

- **Legislative Powers**—Power to enact or make laws or rule making power (Congress or State Assembly)
- **Executive Powers**—Power to enforce the laws (President or Governor)
- **Judicial Powers**—Power to interpret and determine the validity of the law and settle disputes that arise among the people and other jurisdictions (U.S. Supreme Court or State Supreme Court).

Constitution provides a system of checks and balances, for instance between the U.S. Senate and the Presidency treaties are a shared power; Appointments to the U.S. Supreme Court is also a shared power.

Treaties: The President of the United States with the advice and consent of the senate enters into treaties with foreign governments and when approved, they become part of the supreme law of the land.

Constitution was initially amended with the Bill of Rights—first ten (10) amendments--which sets out rights for individuals, such as liberty, speech, religion, assembly, property rights, etc., and sets limits on governmental power and authority. It also establishes the process by which this basic document can be amended or changed. In 1992, the 27th Amendment was adopted.

The Founding Fathers were educated men, experienced with governing, who devised a limited system of Republican (responsible and representative) government, who believed in a powerful national government that would not threaten "liberty or property," and be able to "establish justice, ensure domestic tranquility, provide for the common defense, promote the general welfare, and secure the blessings of liberty."

An illustrated listing of the various powers given to the federal and state governments are briefly summarized in **Figure 1.1.2**. These include powers explicitly granted to the federal government (enumerated, delegated, inherent, and implied powers), those reserved to the states (reserved powers), those denied to both the federal and state governments, and those which are shared between the two levels of government (concurrent powers).

NOTABLE QUOTES

Nothing will change the fact that I cannot produce the least thing without absolute solitude. — *Goethe*

**Figure 1.1.2 Federal System of Government**

**The United States Constitution and Federal System of Government: Powers to the National Government**

- To tax
- To regulate interstate and foreign commerce
- To borrow and coin money
- To establish inferior courts
- To declare war
- To raise and support an army

**Federal System of Government: Concurrent Powers (National and States)**

- Both may collect taxes and borrow money
- Both may establish and maintain a court system
- Both may make and enforce laws
- Charter banks and corporations
- Both may take property for public purposes, eminent domain
- Both may spend for the general welfare

**Federal System of Government: Powers Reserved to the States**

- To regulate intrastate (within the state) commerce
- To establish local governments, such as townships, counties, and municipalities
- To protect the health, safety, welfare, and morals of its citizens
- To ratify amendments to the Constitution
- To conduct elections
- To issue licenses, registrations, and permits (marriage, drivers, hunting, etc.)
- To specify conditions for suffrage except for specific prohibitions set forth in the Constitution
- To change state constitutions and governments
- May exercise powers not Constitutionally given to national government or prohibited to states

**Federal System of Government: National Government Prohibitions**

- Direct taxes must be proportionate to population of states (16th amendment)
- Bill of Rights may not be abridged or denied
- Monies from the Treasury cannot be used without the passage of an appropriations bill
- All states regardless of date of admission, must be treated equally
- Boundaries of states cannot be changed without consent of states involved
- Preference may not be given to one state over another in matters of commerce

**Federal System of Government: State Government Prohibitions**

- May not enter into treaties with other countries
- May not tax imports
- May not coin money (print money), keep troops, or ships of war in time of peace
- May not pass laws impairing obligations of contract
- May not suspend the rights of persons without due process
- May not violate the U.S. Constitution or obstruct Federal laws

**Federal System of Government: Powers Denied to National and State Governments**

- May not tax exports
- May not grant titles of nobility
- Cannot deny right to vote based on gender (19th Amendment)
- Cannot permit slavery (13th Amendment)

These powers are detailed here since many public administrators frequently error in understanding what specifically the national and state governments can or cannot do. For example, one local government sheriff thought he could contract with the country of Mexico for prisoner incarceration and that his county had the power to enter into a treaty obligation with a foreign power.

Similarly, after the November 2015 terrorist attacks on the soccer stadium, restaurants and night club in Paris, France, and the tragic loss of more than 129 "younger" people, at least 30 U.S. state governors indicated that they would not permit refugees from Syria and Iraq to be resettled in their jurisdictions. However, they did not understand that resettlement powers reside with the federal government, not the states and that once refugee status is granted, the refugees are free to travel and reside within any area of the United States. Although the state has the authority to limit access to those programs and services that fall under their exclusive domain.

As students of history and of military tactics and strategy understand, terrorism is designed to instill fear and uncertainty in society! As often stated, when a nation is immobilized by fear, then the terrorists have partially succeeded in attaining their despicable goals. When the people associated with the tragedies whether in France, Egypt, Mali, the United States, Belgium, Spain or Lebanon, came under violent attack, the world developed a greater awareness of the psychological, economic, social, political, and lifestyle ravages affiliated with terrorism. Significant for students of public policy and public administration are the untold and unimaginable sunk costs that will be associated with providing homeland security in the outlying years. These costs will be encumbered in areas as diverse as cyber-security, domestic and international terrorism defeat and destruction, the issues and costs linked to resettling more than 60 million refugees largely from the Middle East other areas of civil war, and the heightened security associated with all transportation types and public venues such as athletic events, parades and days of national celebration. In addition, the unanticipated costs associated with asymmetrical warfare preparation and reconfiguration of the military branch services and related intelligence agencies will take their toll on public budgeting.

As previously emphasized, public administration uses art and science, but is essentially a craft. Considering public administration's grounding in constitutional principles incorporating majority rule and minority rights, the use of the term *craft* seems appropriate and realistic. With the limitations and diversity of constitutional guidelines, public administrators need to be "crafty" to fulfill their responsibilities.

In constitutional terms, then, public bureaucrats exercise power within the framework of a republican form of government, a federal system, the separation-of-powers principle, and constitutionalism. Federalism is the basis of the American constitutional system and American public administration.

William S. Livingston illustrates three ways in which the changing pattern of modern federalism has affected political bureaucracy.[34]

First, he describes a cooperative federalism in which the *centralization of power* is accompanied by the *decentralization of governmental function*. The central government makes policy, then delegates the implementation of this policy to other levels of government. Since the New Deal era, the decentralization of governmental function has followed the centralization of governmental authority and power. State and national governments supplement each other and jointly perform a variety of functions. The federal Supplemental Nutrition Assistance Program (formerly Food Stamp Program) illustrates the centralization of power with the decentralization of administrative function.

Monies to finance the food assistance program are collected under the auspices of the federal purse and the Sixteenth Amendment. Congress authorizes the Department of Agriculture to organize the food assistance program—to pen its varied regulations and to monitor its progress—but depends on the county social services offices in the fifty states for administration. So, the national government, with its enlarged powers, supplements rather than supplants the tasks of the states and local jurisdictions.

State governors deal with issues ranging from education to energy to health care. Governors face tight budgets and rapidly rising costs for the joint federal-state Medicaid program. In regard to energy, President Bush's plan called for the federal government to decide where electrical transmission lines are placed when state and local communities are stricken by the NIMBY ("not in my backyard") illness. According to former Iowa Governor Tom Vilsack (D), "Governors want to maintain control of this."

A familiar question in the federal-state confrontations, at least for the nation's governors, is "How do we keep Washington from messing up our lives?" Governors often agree on education issues; that is, they agree until they must figure out how to pay for new government programs. Conflicts at the various levels of federalism transcend political parties or who occupies the White House. "Governors and mayors don't like to be told what to do," says Connecticut Governor John G. Rowland (R).[35]

Livingston's second illustration of how federalism affects bureaucracy considers the *highly decentralized* nature of the American political party system. Livingston concludes that the decentralization of power within the political parties enhances the decentralization of the political decision-making process and lends strength to federalism. The character of the parties supports federalism, and federalism, in turn, nourishes the decentralized character of the parties.

The third, and final, feature that contributes to the increased vitality of modern day federalism is the diversity of social values in the United States. Livingston argues that the diverse people and values within a society determine the shape and character of political and governmental institutions. Federalism, as an arrangement of political power, responds to the changing values of society. What are the social values of American society? Policies and values differ from state to state. Some states allow lotteries; others do not. Some states are restrictive in cigarette and alcohol sales; others are not. Some states maintain rigorous environmental standards; others do not. Some states have taken firm positions against racial and sexual discrimination; others back off. These illustrations indicate that public bureaucrats will have considerable difficulty enforcing laws mandated by the U.S. Congress if support for such policies does not emerge from the grass roots. From affirmative action to speed limits, public administrators have difficulty implementing laws that people do not support.

Public bureaucrats have been described as timid and ineffectual and at the same time as power-seeking and dangerous. In reality, their influence depends upon the consensus of political support for government laws and programs. Cooperative federalism, the grassroots nature of the political party system, and the diverse social values that Americans hold require public bureaucrats to share power and responsibility with federal, state, and local officials. Administrative federalism is the upshot of these political compromises.

In the next chapter, we will examine the environment in which public administrators practice their craft.

## Summary

- The more people, the greater the demand for government services.
- Administration involves people, action, and interaction. People interacting with people to accomplish a task is what public administration is all about.
- Public administration involves artistry, but it is not an art. It makes use of science, but it is not a science. In these times of declining state, local, and federal budgets, government employees engage in a craft, seeking to achieve goals and meet standards with all the creativity, capability, and civility they can muster.
- Americans have no consensus on a public philosophy by which to judge the effectiveness of government- run, taxpayer-financed public-sector programs.
- Compared to the growth of the United States economy, federal tax levels have remained relatively stable over the last fifty years.
- The percentage of gross domestic product spent by the U.S. government is, in proportion to the U.S. economy, smaller than that of nearly any other industrialized nation.
- Public administration is grounded in capital, bureaucracy, and democracy. In general, the poorer a country is in capital, the less efficient are its government programs, services, and operations.
- Politics cannot be separated from culture. Families are the first organizational unit of American life. Public administrators respond to and act in a cultural context.
- Delineations of public versus private are central to the conceptual and emotional structuring of the Western world.
- Partisan politics is concerned with which political party and personalities win office. Policy politics deals with deciding which policies to adopt. System politics examines how administrative systems (decision structures) are set up to implement policies.
- In private administration, laws generally tell administrators only what they cannot do. In public administration, laws tell them what they can do.
- The internet and terrorism threaten to alter boundaries between public and private sectors.
- The U.S. Constitution established a republican form of government and a federal system. It enacted the separation-of-powers principle and established the rule of law, representative institutions, and individual liberty. Public administration is grounded in constitutionalism.
- The centralization of power in U.S. federalism is not accompanied by the centralization of governmental function. Conflicts at various levels of federalism transcend political parties and who occupies the White House.
- Federalism is tempered by the diversity of social values in the United States.
- The worlds of behaviors, institutions, processes, and policies significantly affect the professional lives of public administrators.

## Videos, Films and Talks

Please visit *The Craft of Public Administration* at www.millenniumhrmpress.com for up-to-date videos, films, talks, readings, and additional class resources.

We the People, and the Republic we Must Reclaim [18 min]
Lawrence Lessig, TED Talk
https://www.youtube.com/watch?v=mw2z9lV3W1g

## Suggested Readings

**The Six Basic Principles of Government**
https://theconstitutionpolik6.weebly.com/6-basic-principles.html

**What Makes Public Administration Art or Science?**
https://ifioque.com/career-workshop/management/public_administration_as_art_science

**Future of Work: Trends transforming the workplace and a blueprint for action**
https://papers.governing.com/Future-of-Work-Trends-transforming-the-workplace-and-a-blueprint-for-action-135967.html

**Citizen-Centered Service Delivery**
https://papers.governing.com/Citizen-Centered-Service-Delivery-7581.html

**3 Events That Shaped Modern Federalism**
https://www.governing.com/archive/gov-modern-federalism.html

## Notes


1. Michael Hodges, "Federal Government Spending Report," *Grandfather Economic Reports*, March 2007, https://grandfather-economic-report.com/fed_budget.htm.

2. Pew Research Center, August 20, 2020, https://www.pewresearch.org/fact-tank/2020/08/20/key-findings-about-u-s-immigrants/

3. Herbert A. Simon, Donald W. Smithburg, and Victor A. Thompson, *Public Administration* (New York: Alfred A. Knopf, 1950), p. 3.

4. Robert J. Samuelson, "Clinton's Nemesis," *Newsweek*, February 1, 1993, p. 51; "Our Love-Hate Relationship with Government," *Washington Post*, January 27, 1993, p. A19.

5. David K. Shipler, "The Myth of Democracy," *Washington Post*, December 3, 2000, p. B7.

6. Jorge G. Castaneda, "Three Challenges to U.S. Democracy," *Kettering Review* (Summer 1997), pp. 8–20.

7. Garry Wills, "Whatever Happened to Politics? Washington Is Not Where It's At," *New York Times Magazine*, January 25, 1998, p. 27+.

8. Calvin Woodward, "AP Poll Finds Americans in a Hurry," *Boston Globe*, May 28, 2006.

9. Dwight Waldo, *The Enterprise of Public Administration* (Novato, CA: Chandler & Sharp Publishers, 1980), p. 164.

10. Theodore J. Lowi, "The State in Political Science: How We Become What We Study," *American Political Science Review*, Vol. 86, No. 1 (March, 1992).

11. McKinsey Global Institute, "Urban world: Mapping the economic power of cites," March 2011.

12. Andre Tartar and Reade Pickert, "A third of America's Economy is Concentrated in Just 31 Counties," Bloomberg.com/graphics/2019-us-gdp-concentration-counties.

13. Teryn Zmunda and Ricardo Aguilar, "County Economic Output Trends," February, 2020, www.naco.org/sites/default/files/documents/County-Economic-Output-Trends_2020.pdf.

14. Census Bureau, 2020.

15. Dave Merrill and Lauren Leatherby, "Here's How America Uses its Land," July 31, 2018, https://www.bloomberg.com/graphics/2018-us-land-use/?sref=q8selhDd.

16. Census Bureau, 2020.

17. U.S. Bureau of the Census and William H. Frey, "New 2020 census results show increased diversity countering decade-long declines in America's white and youth populations," Brooking Institute, August 13, 2021.

18. William H. Frey, "Reducing immigration will not stop America's rising diversity, Census projections show," February 19, 2020, https://www.brookings.edu/research/reducing-immigration-will-not-stop-americas-rising-diversity-census-projections-show/.

19. Census Bureau, 2020.

20. Tim Henderson, "Shrinking Rural America Faces State Power Struggle," Stateline Collection, The Pew Charitable Trusts, August 16, 2021.

21. Pew Research Center, "Public Trust in Government: 1958-2021," May 17, 2021, https://www.pewresearch.org/politics/2021/05/17/public-trust-in-government-1958-2021/.

22. Aaron Wildavsky, *The Politics of the Budgetary Process* (Boston: Little, Brown, 1979), pp. 191–193.

23. Robert A. Kagan, "Adversarial Legalism and American Government," *Journal of Policy Analysis & Management* 10, no. 3 (Summer 1991): 369–407.

24. John M. Pfiffner and Robert Presthus, *Public Administration*, 5th ed. (New York: Ronald Press, 1967). In regard to the subsequent sentence in the text, Donald S. Vaughn, former chair, Department of Political Science, University of Mississippi, points out that the law also tells the public administrator what he or she cannot do. Professor Vaughn cites the first eight amendments to the U.S. Constitution as a case in point.

25. See Alan M. Dershowitz in *The Best Defense* (New York: Random House, 1982). However, the same theme runs through many other legal statements and writings. Oliver Wendell Holmes, for example, once said that his job as Justice of the U.S. Supreme Court did not require him to "do" justice, but merely to see that the rules of the game were followed.

26. Daniel J. Appelman, "The Law and the Internet: Emerging Legal Issues," http:// www.isoc.org/lamp/ paper/222/abst.html.

27. Carrie Davis, "Terrorist Attacks Spawn Greater Surveillance Powers," *Internet Law Journal*, February 2, 2002.

28. Jeffrey Rosen, *The Naked Crowd: Reclaiming Security and Freedom in an Anxious Age* (New York: Random House, 2004), p. 7.

29. Jeffrey Rosen, *The Unwanted Gaze: The Destruction of Privacy in America* (New York: Random House, 2000).

30. Charlotte Hays, "TWQ Interview: Jonathan Rauch Talks about the Value of Hidden Law," *The Women's Quarterly*, Summer 2001.

31. C. Herman Pritchett, *The American Constitutional System* (New York: McGraw-Hill, 1981), pp. 7–8.

32. David Hosansky, "Reshaping the Federal-State Relationship," *Congressional Quarterly Weekly Report* 54, no. 40 (5 October 1996): 2824–2826; Bert Waisanen, "Demographic Federalism: Defining the New Federal-State Relationship," *Spectrum: The Journal of State Government* 69, no. 4 (Fall 1996): 53–58.

33. Charlie Savage, "Bar Group Will Review Bush's Legal Challenges," *Boston Globe*, June 4, 2006; "Bush Challenges Hundreds of Laws: President Cites Powers of His Office," *Boston Globe*, April 30, 2006.

34. William S. Livingston, "Federalism in Other Countries: Canada, Australia, and the United States," in *Federalism: Infinite Variety in Theory and Practice* (Itasca, IL: F. E. Peacock Publishers, 1968), pp. 131– 141.

35. David S. Broder and Dan Balz, "Bush Agenda Concerns Governors Over U.S. Role," *Washington Post*, August 7, 2001, p. A2.

# UNIT 2: The Ecology of the Administrative Craft

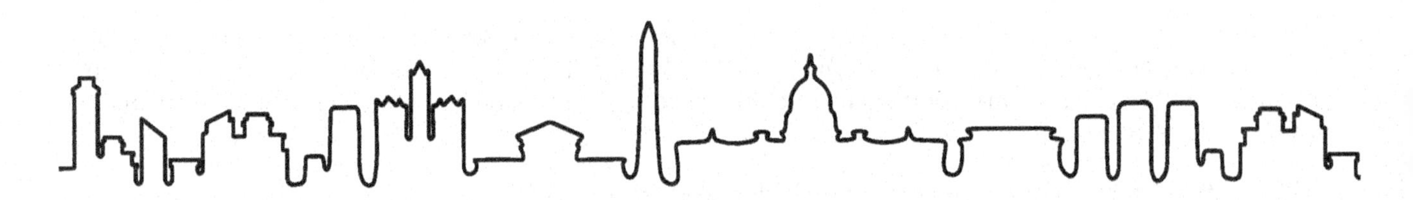

## "Political Economy" Plays an Important Role in the Study of Public Administration

In a historical context, economic theories, accompanied by their dedicated disciples, have been in tug-a-war over many administrative and policy issues which serve as the platform for political discussion and debate. Therefore, it is necessary to understand the tension and debate that is associated with two major competing schools of economic thought: classical versus neoclassical. In the discussion, analysts examine what is proper role of government in the "authoritative allocation of values"—the distributive question—or colloquially, who gets what, when, where, and how much. Coupled with this essential question, is the role that government as a collective enterprise plays in relation to the functions which remain public, or those which are allocated to the private and nonprofit sectors. In this context what does government do and how much should it do to provide an incentive or restraint on the private economy, and how is this reflected in perhaps a Keynesian way with spending and investment policies or in terms of taxation or monetary and fiscal policies.

The debate is not one that either side of the economic coin, classical or neoclassical schools, easily submit and both sides use at times similar metrics to bolster their arguments. For example, how does the size of government affect the efficiency and effectiveness of services and program deliveries. In this area size of the public sector is examined as a percentage of the Gross Domestic Product (GDP). Using this indicator, Japan (29%) and South Korea (36%) demonstrate a lower percentage of economic output than in countries such as Denmark (47%) and Sweden (50%). Using Organization for Economic Cooperation and Development (OECD) data, public spending on social matters ranged from a low of 6.9 percent of GDP in Mexico to high of 29.7 percent in France. (Ben Tafoya, "Pick the Goals, Not the size," *PA Times*, December/January, 2015, p. 3.) These measurements vary depending on how societies provide for education, social services, healthcare, defense, social insurance (social security), and pensions, etc., and their respective costs connected with international terrorism.

NOTABLE QUOTES

Ideas are like rabbits. You get a couple and learn how to handle them, and pretty soon you have a dozen.

— *John Steinbeck*

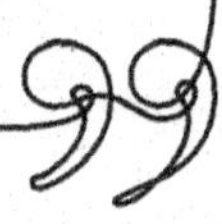

The size of government argument also uses economic measures such as the number of executive branch civilian employees. These numbers are most likely associated with the changing role of government in society over time, and variables such as social inventions (unions and corporations), transportation innovations (automobiles, planes, trains, etc.), agriculture policies, regulatory policies (workplace to banking), social services and assistance needs (SNAP and TANF), growing size of population, number of political jurisdictions (90,100+), preventing economic depressions, and governmental policies that affect defense spending and war.

Between 1962 and 2012, King notes that the "executive branch civilian employees did not exceed 3.064 million in any one year; the average was 2.751 million" during this period. In fact, federal government employment, as a percentage of the total civilian employed population, decreased by 16 percent (Stephen M. King, How Active (Big) Should Government Be to Serve Citizens? *PA Times*, December/January 2015, p.1.). If federal government per capita spending is used, in 1792, the expenditure was below $35 per person; in 1910, $129; in 2013, $7,702; and in 2020, $19,962 nearly155 times the amount spent in 1910.

The debate as to what metrics should be used in political and economic analysis must move beyond the mere numbers associated with size. Jon Raadschelders notes in his new book, *Global Dimensions of Public Administration and Governance*, attempts to defuse the argument that neither smaller nor larger government is more or less effective. He argues that government effectiveness, based on performance, should rule the day. No economist seriously argues that government is not needed, indeed essential to building of civil society and the infrastructure, but the argument rages on between the competing schools of thought offered by those persuaded by John Maynard Keynes on the role that government should play in the nation's economy, contrasted with Frederick von Hayek who takes a more libertarian view on the role of government, such as providing financial and investment incentives and keeping taxes low.

There is now a widespread consensus that mainstream/neoclassical economists failed miserably to either predict the coming of the 2008 financial implosion or provide a reasonable explanation when it actually arrived. Not surprisingly, many critics have argued that neoclassical economics has created more confusion than clarification, more obfuscation than elucidation. Economic "science" has, indeed, become "an ideological construct which serves to camouflage and justify the New World Order."[1]

Also not surprisingly, an increasing number of participants who take classes and/or major in economics are complaining about the abstract and irrelevant nature of the discipline. For example, a group of French graduate learners in economics recently wrote the following open letter, akin to a manifesto, critical of their academic education in economics as "autistic" and "pathologically distant from the problems of real markets and real people":

"We wish to escape from imaginary worlds! Most of us have chosen to study economics so as to acquire a deep understanding of the economic phenomena with which the citizens of today are confronted. But the teaching that is offered... does not generally answer this expectation.... This gap in the teaching, this disregard for concrete realities, poses an enormous problem for those who would like to render themselves useful to economic and social actors."[2]

Except for unfortunate use of a mental development disability, the French learners made their point clearly and unambiguously.

Interestingly, most economists do not deny the abstract and irrelevance feature or property of their discipline; but argue that the internal consistency of a theory—in the sense that the findings or conclusions of the theory follow logically from its premises or assumptions—is more important than its relevance (or irrelevance) to the real world. Nobel Laureate economist William Vickery, for example, maintains:

"Economic theory proper, indeed, is nothing more than a system of logical relations between certain sets of assumptions and the conclusions derived from them. The validity of a theory proper does not depend on the correspondence or lack of it between the assumptions of the theory or its conclusions and observations in the real world. In any pure theory, all propositions are essentially tautological, in the sense that the results are implicit in the assumptions made."[3]

Paul Samuelson, another Nobel Laureate in Economics, likewise writes, "In pointing out the consequences of a set of abstract assumptions, one need not be committed unduly as to the relation between reality and these assumptions."

How or why did economics as a crucially important subject of inquiry into an understanding of social structures evolve in this fashion, that is, as an apparently rigorous and technically elaborate discipline without much usefulness in the way of understanding or solving economic problems?

**Origins of Neoclassical Economics**

Perhaps a logical way to answer this question is to look into the origins of the neoclassical economics, and how it supplanted the classical economics that prevailed from the early stages of capitalism until the second half of the 19th century—supplanted not as an extension or elaboration of that earlier school of economic thought but as a deviation from, or antithesis, to it.

Well-known classical economists like Adam Smith, David Ricardo, John Stuart Mill and Karl Marx sought to understand capitalism in fundamental ways. They studied the substance of wages and prices beyond supply and demand. They also examined the foundations of economic growth and accumulation—that is, the sources of the "wealth of nations," as Smith put it, or "the laws of motion of capitalist production," as Marx put it. They further sought to understand the basis or logic of the distribution of economic surplus, that is, the origins of the various types of income: wages/salaries, interest income, rental income, and profits.

To this end, they distinguished two major types of work or economic activity: productive and unproductive, that is, productive labor and productive enterprise (manufacturing) versus unproductive labor and unproductive enterprises (buying and selling, or speculation). Accordingly, they saw the capitalist social structure as consisting of different classes of conflicting or antagonistic interests: capitalists, workers, landlords, tenants/renters, and the poor.

These classical economists wrote in an era that could still be considered a time of transition: transition from feudalism to capitalism. Although feudalism was in decline, the powerful interests vested in that older mode of production and social structure still fiercely resisted the rising new mode of production, the modern industrial capitalism, and its champions, called the "bourgeoisie."

In the second half of the 18th and first half of 19th centuries, the conflicting interests of these two rival factions of the ruling elites served as powerful economic grounds for a fierce political/ideological struggle between the partisans of the two sides. Whereas the elites of the old system viewed the rising bourgeoisie as undermining their traditional rights and privileges, the modern capitalist elites viewed the old establishment as hindering rapid industrialization, "proletarianization," and urbanization.

In the ensuing ideological battle between the champions of the old and new orders, the writings of classical economists such as Smith, Ricardo and Mill proved quite helpful to the proponents or partisans of the new order. As influential intellectuals who were concerned that the hindering influences and extractive businesses of the old establishment may hamper a clean break from pre-capitalist modes of economic activity, they wrote passionately about what created real values and/or "wealth of nations," and what was wasteful and a drain on economic resources. To this end, their writings included lengthy discussions of the labor theory of value—the theory that human labor constitutes the essence of value—and related notions of productive and unproductive activities.

Accordingly, they characterized the propertied classes that reaped income by virtue of controlling the assets (that the economy needed in order to function) as the "rentier," "unproductive" or "parasitic" classes. Rentier classes collect their unearned proceeds from ownership "without working, risking, or economizing", wrote John Stuart Mill of the landlords and money-lenders of his day, arguing that "they grow richer, as it were in their sleep."[4]

Unsurprisingly, during the early stages of industrial revolution, when the old establishment still posed serious challenges to the relatively new and evolving capitalist mode of production, the view of human labor as the source of real values, expounded by Karl Marx and other classical economists, provided a strong theoretical case for industrial expansion and/or capitalist development. "In its earliest formulations, the labor theory of value reflected the perspective of,

*In place of owners/managers, more and more corporate managers were hired to direct and oversee industrial enterprises and to channel profits automatically as part of a perpetual accumulation process.*

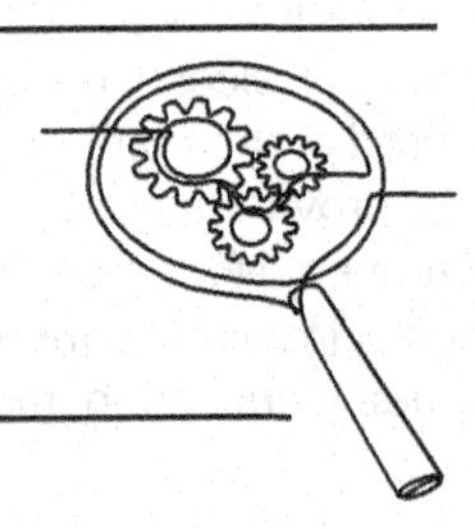

and was serviceable in, the fulfillment of the objective needs of, the industrial capitalist class."[5]

Although the rising capitalist class found the labor theory of value (and its logical implications for class conflicts) potentially "disconcerting," that concern was temporarily set aside, as the main threat at this stage of capitalist development came from the landowning/ rentier classes, not the working class. Indeed, history shows that in nearly all the so-called "bourgeois-democratic" revolutions, signifying the historical transition from pre-capitalist to capitalist formations, the burgeoning working class, the newly proletarianized peasants, sided with the bourgeoisie against its pre-capitalist nemesis.

By the mid-19th century, however, this pattern of social structure and/or class alliances was drastically changed. Concentration of capital and the rise of corporation had by the last third of the 19th century gradually overshadowed the role of individual manufacturers as the drivers of the industrial development. In place of owners/managers, more and more "corporate managers were hired to direct and oversee industrial enterprises and to channel profits automatically as part of a perpetual accumulation process. Increasingly, profits and interest came to be the result of passive ownership," similar to absentee landownership of the feudal days.[6]

Along with agricultural production on an increasingly capitalistic basis, these developments meant a radical reconfiguration of social and/or class alliances: the industrial bourgeoisie and the landowners were no longer adversaries, as they were all now capitalists and allies; and the working class, which had earlier supported the bourgeoisie against the landed aristocracy, was their class enemy. What added to the fears of the capitalist class of the growing and relatively militant working class was the spread of Marx's theory of "labor as the essence of value and economic surplus," which was by the mid- to late-19th century frequently discussed among the leading circles of industrial workers.

The formal theoretical shift from classicism to neoclassicism was pioneered (in the last three decades of the 19th century) by three economists: William Stanley Jevons, Carl Menger and Leon Walras. A detailed discussion of these pioneers of neoclassical economics is beyond the purview of this essay. Suffice it to say that all three categorically shunned the labor theory of value in favor of utility theory of value, that is, "value depends entirely upon utility," as Jevons put it.

At the heart of the theoretical/philosophical shift was, therefore, the move from labor to utility as the source of value: a commodity's value no longer came from its labor content, as classical economists had argued, but from its utility to consumers. The new paradigm thus shifted the focus of economic inquiry from the factory and production to the market and circulation, or exchange.

By the same token as the new school of economic thought abandoned the classicals' labor theory of value in favor of the utility theory of value, it also discarded the concept of value, which comes from human labor, in favor of price, which is formed (in the sphere of circulation or market) by supply and demand interactions. Henceforth, there was no difference between value and price; the two have since been used interchangeably or synonymously in the neoclassical economics.

Once the focus of inquiry was thus shifted from how commodities are produced to how they are bought and sold, the distinction between workers and capitalists, between producers and appropriators, became invisible. In the marketplace all people appear as essentially identical: they are all households, consumers or "economic agents" who derive utility from consuming commodities, and who pay for those commodities "according to the amount of the utility/pleasure they derive from their consumption." They are also identical in the neoclassical sense that they are all "rational," "calculating," and utility "maximizing" market players.

An obvious implication (and a major advantage to the capitalist class) of this new perspective was that in the marketplace social harmony and "brotherhood," not class conflict, was the prevailing mode of social structure. "The supposed conflict of labor with capital is a delusion," Jevons asserted, arguing that "We ought not look at such subjects from a class point of view," because "in economics at any rate [we] *should regard all men as brothers*."[8]

It should be pointed out (in passing) that the utility theory of value did not start with Jevons. The theory had already been spelled out in the late 18th and early 19th centuries by earlier economists such as Jeremy Bentham, Jean-Baptiste Say, Thomas Malthus and Claude Frédéric Bastiat. However, Jevons and his utilitarian contemporaries of the second half of the 19th century added a new concept to the received theory: the concept of marginal utility or, more specifically, diminishing marginal utility. According to this concept, the utility derived from the use or consumption of a commodity diminishes with every additional unit consumed.

"By introducing the notion of marginalism into utilitarian economics, Jevons had found a way in which the utilitarian view of human beings as rational, calculating maximizers could be put into mathematical terms."[9]

Whereas the utilitarian views of the earlier economists had been firmly discredited in the late 18th and early 19th centuries by proponents of the labor theory of value as truisms that did not explain much of the real world economic developments, the math-coded utilitarianism of Jevons (and his fellow neoclassicals since then) has been shielded from such criticisms by a protective cover of mathematical veneer. Despite the fact that, aside from the mathematical mask, the new notion of utility represented no conceptual or theoretical advances over the earlier version, it was celebrated as a "revolution" in economic thought, the so-called "neoclassical revolution." Presenting a body of largely axiomatic principles, or religious-like normative guidelines (such as how "rational" consumers should behave), by means of elaborate and mesmerizing mathematics is like covering weeds with Astroturf.

It follows from the discussion, that a driving force behind the evolution of economics is the role of influential vested interests and/or the dominant ruling ideology. In a critique of mainstream/neoclassical economists' blatant disregard for actual developments in the real world, economics Professor Michael Hudson writes:

"Such disdain for empirical verification is not found in the physical sciences. Its popularity in the social sciences is sponsored by vested interests. There is always self- interest behind methodological madness. That is because [professional] success requires heavy subsidies from special interests who benefit from an erroneous, misleading or deceptive economic logic. Why promote unrealistic abstractions, after all, if not to distract attention from reforms aimed at creating rules that oblige people actually to earn their income rather than simply extracting it from the rest of the economy?."[10]

Contemporaneously, and perhaps coincidentally, as this essay is being written, Thomas Picketty's *Capital in the Twenty-First Century* brings into sharp relief the enduring debate presented above between capital and labor. As long established by the classical economists, the history of capitalism is one that disproportionately rewards capital relative to the value for labor. Accordingly, it comes as no surprise to those who study the nature of inequality, that the demonstrable income and wealth gap between the "have and the have not's," the rich and the poor, the powerful and the powerless is increasing not only in our own backyards, but worldwide. This is a harbinger, at least from Picketty's vantage point, of lowered prospects for future economic growth and progress.

Interestingly, Pope Francis encouraged economists, politicians, corporate, religious, and civic leadership to revisit once more, as the Roman Catholic pontiffs have consistently done through their social doctrine teachings, over a thousand or so years, and evaluate the relations between profit and a so called free-market economy, and global selfishness, poverty and hunger. Not surprisingly, his admonition resonates more clearly with the ethical and moral imperatives of the classical writers than with the neo-classical economists' view on economic structures and remedies.

For instance, do our economic pillars promote happiness and community or loneliness and isolation? Do economic situations promote meaningful, dignified and valuable work that is inextricably connected with the principles of human self-determination, growth and development? Or, is work a means to revenue generation to be used and used up in consumption and mindless materialism?

*By introducing the notion of marginalism into utilitarian economics, Jevons had found a way in which the utilitarian view of human beings as rational, calculating maximizers could be put into mathematical terms.*

NOTABLE QUOTES

Sit, walk, or run, but don't wobble.

— *Zen proverb*

How do our economic policies and structures, such as banking, finance, corporations, the nation state, etc., address the fundamentals of sustainability, such as ecological and environmental policies, a livable wage, access to jobs and economic and social security, public property rights, mountain top removal, endangered species, child welfare, renewable energy, biodiversity, deep ocean drilling, fracking, community stability, climate change, etc., and the promotion of human justice and dignity, and inclusiveness?

In conclusion, aren't these the enduring questions for which we seek answers and solutions, rather than to operationalize logical, mathematical abstractions that are, for the most part, irrelevant to our real-world situations and concerns. And importantly, how do our neo-classical colleagues address these existential problems of real-world human economic and social consequence?

Are they inclined to deal with these protracted issues through sundry seen or unseen regulatory or distributive mechanisms or some kind of new "invisible hand" or "mathematical algorithm," or even one or more new forms of untested citizen economic and political participation? Generally, how can economic theory become a useful field of study and analysis for understanding, forecasting, and resolving concerns that directly correspond to reality, rather than to the products of elaborate and sophistical mental abstractions and untested and untestable assumptions?

With this story of the debate between classical and neoclassical economic theories, it comes as no surprise when pupils get introduced to public administration and public policy studies, that they often get confused as to what should be the proper size, role, functions of government in our society.

## Our Organized Society

Ecology is the study of the relationships between organisms and their environments, and public administrators not acutely aware of how environmental factors influence administration are doomed to failure. This chapter describes the relationship between public administrators and the environment in which they work.

Public administrators do not operate in a vacuum. Countless environmental factors buffet administrators, making their tasks remarkably complex. Public administration occurs within the framework of an organized society. The principal barriers to the effective implementation of public programs are the conflicts between the political principles of democracy and the economic principle of capitalism.

Public administration is also carried out within the political cultures of states and communities. Culture, tangible and intangible, affects the environment in which public administration takes place.

A drive down Main Street, U.S.A., will take you past clinics, banks, dry cleaning establishments, cafes, and retail stores. Keep driving and you'll pass churches, shopping malls, fast food outlets, factories, gas stations, and schools. All are examples of organizations that affect our daily existence. Organizations must be managed or administered. We live in a complex society in which public organizations are needed if the smaller, private organizations are to thrive or operate at all. The alternative is anarchy.

Public organizations receive their lifeblood from legislative, executive, and judicial collectives in our organized society. Legislatures authorize and appropriate revenues to fund public programs. Presidents, governors, and mayors carry out the legislative will of the people. Courts adjudicate disputes between parties contesting, among other things, the delivery of government programs.

With its numerous organizations, modern America is the epitome of the organized society. The legislative, executive, and judicial branches of our national and state governments are the basic units of public organization. For example, Congress enacted the Social Security program for the elderly; the Social Security Administration implements the policy; and administrative judges decide disputed claims.[1]

Questions constantly arise concerning the fairness and efficiency of public organizations—questions that contribute to these organizations' administrative entanglements.

Why focus on equality versus efficiency, rights versus dollars, democratic capitalism versus political economy, and other trade-offs in the organized society? The answer is that public administration enjoys a very conceptual grounding in partisan, policy, and system politics. To comprehend the interplay of these definitive aspects of the field, scholars need to understand how government programs, agencies, and departments operate.

Thinking about the many applications of public administration requires reading, focusing, illustrating, applying, and comprehending concepts, terms, trends, facts, and principles of the field. Before departments and agencies implement goals, directives, and processes, administrators must develop an understanding of what the community wants from these units. Communities direct their public administrators to fight wars on many fronts—terror, poverty, ignorance, sickness, and even incompetence. Government cannot operate effectively if the community is not in agreement with its goals and policies.

Thinking about the many applications of public administration and its varied applications requires a mix of conceptual and analytical thinking, as well as deductive and inductive reasoning. A concept is a general notion or idea; conceptual thinking involves the formation of ideas, the recognition of patterns and relationships. Analytical thinking requires one to examine the parts of some larger concept, to find out their nature, proportion, function, and relationship to one another as one breaks a whole puzzle into separate parts. A deductive thinker reasons from a general, known principle to a specific, unknown conclusion, or from a premise to a logical conclusion. An inductive thinker, by contrast, reasons from a particular fact or individual case to form a general conclusion.

Scholars learn to think by combining conceptual and analytical thought and deductive and inductive reasoning. Units 1 and 2 of this Module 1 are especially conceptual and inductive. In order to understand the principles (and principals) of public administration, learners need to think conceptually and inductively, yet be analytical and, on occasion, deductive, as they think through the diverse challenges confronting public administrators.

Students cannot learn the dynamics of the organized society if they do not work to comprehend how, where, when, and why general concepts explain agency actions and how agency behaviors contribute to emerging conceptual definitions.

## Equality, Efficiency and Equity

American society professes to provide equal opportunities for all citizens. This does not, however, guarantee that citizens will achieve equal results for their efforts. Your contribution in the competitive market depends on your skills, assets, and efforts and also on the supply of and demand for what you have to offer. As free speech does not guarantee an audience, free enterprise does not guarantee a demand for one's services. Effort does not guarantee excellence. Although a pupil studies long and hard for an exam, an "A" is not a foregone conclusion. It is easy to see that these factors, when applied to individuals in the marketplace, can result in unequal individual outcomes.

Our organized society, therefore, exists in an environment of equal rights and unequal outcomes. Conflicts between these two phenomena result in tensions between the *political principles of democracy and the economic principles of capitalism.*

The United States is a democratic society with a capitalistic economic system. In keeping with our democratic political philosophy, we hold elections. In keeping with our economic philosophy, we let supply and demand decide who achieves financial success. Arthur Okun describes contemporary U.S. society as a "split-level institutional structure" because of the combination of democracy and capitalism.[2]

We have a "split-level institutional structure" because private institutions value efficiency, while public-sector institutions favor equality. Efficiency gives the top producers priority, and equality gives everyone priority.

The services provided by public administrators reflect the concept of *equality*. In recent years the voice has grown louder calling on the public sector to not only practice equality but emphasize equity as well.

The concept of *efficiency* comes from letting the marketplace decide what goods and services are produced and purchased. Services and programs that governments produce are available to all citizens. Police, fire, water and sewers are usually provided by government.

Electricity, cable television, internet services, gas, refuse removal, and telephone services, although regulated by government, may be provided privately. Even though these utilities are produced privately, the government regulates their activities to assure "fairness" of delivery.

The rich and the poor have equal rights to travel on our network of interstate highways. The economic realities of the efficient marketplace may determine, however, that certain people lack any car to drive while others cruise along the turnpike in a chauffeur-driven luxury vehicle. A public program is not maintained just for the very poor or the ultra-rich, but for the masses independent of social-economic status (SES).

In that respect, America's highway system serves as an example of an efficient economy—the more we drive, the more road and gasoline taxes we pay. "With the great quarrel between capitalism and socialism in mothballs," says Suzanne Garment, "critics of the free market do not attack it by offering some grand, principled alternative. Instead, they march under the banner of prudence, calling for a pragmatic mixed economy that values markets but avoids the extremism preached by excessively principled free-market ideologues."[3]

In today's world, public administrators must be aware of the issues of equity, equality, efficiency, and justice (see **Figure 1.2.1** on the following page).

Citizens make economic choices, such as buying a car or riding a bus. If we all choose to commute only by car, bus drivers will be out of work, the victims of our equal freedom of choice and the workings of our efficient economy. It is often the role of the public administrator to step in if one of these values begins to supersede the other. This is where the public administrator's regulatory powers come into play.

Citizens make economic choices, such as buying a car or riding a bus. If we all choose to commute only by car, bus drivers will be out of work, the victims of our equal freedom of choice and the workings of our efficient economy. It is often the role of the public administrator to step in if one of these values begins to supersede the other. This is where the public administrator's regulatory powers come into play.

Through these powers, public administrators exercise great influence in determining the role of the marketplace. The public administrator does not, however, have unlimited regulatory power. As regulators of private interactions, public administrators are checked by limits on administrative power spelled out in laws such as the Administrative Procedure Act.[4]

In defending the state of affairs regarding equality versus efficiency, Okun says, "The market needs a place, and the market needs to be kept in its place."[5] The market is kept in its place by the limited regulatory

## THINK ABOUT IT!

**Thomas Picketty's Weighs-in on the Gap Between the Rich and the Poor**

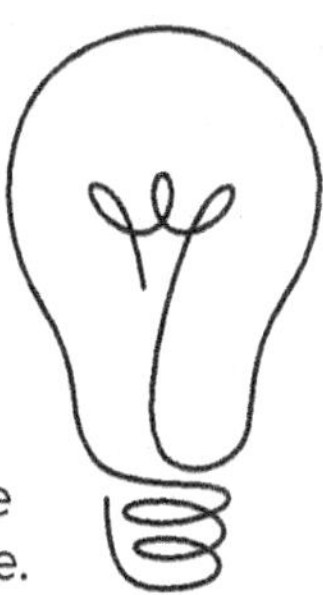

Governments at all levels have had to make major transformational decisions on how Thomas Picketty's Capital in the Twenty-First Century brings into sharp relief the enduring debate presented above between capital and labor. As long established by the classical economists, the history of capitalism is one that disproportionately rewards capital relative to the value for labor.

Accordingly, it comes as no surprise to those who study the nature of inequality, that the demonstrable income and wealth gap between the "have and the have not's," the rich and the poor, the powerful and the powerless is increasing not only in our own backyards, but worldwide.

This is a harbinger, at least from Picketty's vantage point, of lowered prospects for future economic growth and progress.

powers of public administrators, so equality may be sacrificed for the sake of efficiency, and efficiency for the sake of equality. What provisions exist to protect the individual's equal rights in this market-driven economy? Today's administrators are being called upon not only to protect equal rights but to go beyond equality to equity.

The issue of economic decision making late last century focused on ensuring the right mix between government and private-sector participation. A purely government-led or a pure market-dictated economy will not only be ineffective in economic terms but also in social and political terms. The market is usually more

**Figure 1.2.1 Equality, Equity and Justice: Understanding the Differences**

| Equality | Equity | Justice |
|---|---|---|
|  |  |  |
| The assumption is that **everyone benefits from the same supports.** This is equal treatment. | **Everyone gets the support they need** (this is the concept of "affirmative action"), thus producing equity. | All three see the game without supports or accommodations because **the cause(s) of inequity was addressed.** The systematic barrier has been removed. |

*Source:* https://www.solanocounty.com/depts/mhs/cultural_competence.asp

efficient than the public sector, but the latter is needed to ensure that the allocation of resources is balanced.[6]

American society promotes equality by allocating social and political rights equally and distancing these rights from the marketplace of supply and demand. For example, due process is a constitutionally mandated guarantee. Governments in the United States must act with fairness, justice, equity, and reasonableness, irrespective of economic considerations. Accused criminals have the right to seek fairness in prosecution through due process. Equal opportunity is protected in a court of law by constitutionally mandated due process. Due process is the legal cornerstone of the craft of public administration.

There are two types of due process, *substantive and procedural*. *Substantive due process* refers to the content or subject of a law. *Procedural due process*, the more commonly litigated of the two, refers to the procedures used in implementing a law or administrative practice. Deciding whether a law is constitutional is part of procedural due process.

The concept of equality is also demonstrated in the open admissions policies of many state universities. These policies require a university to accept participants from all ethnic and racial groups and income levels. The taxpayers subsidize public education to guarantee fairness, justice, equity, and reasonableness in the admission of participants. The state university must pay careful attention to due process. On the other hand, a private college is not required to follow due process as stringently as a public university. A private college may, with some restrictions, select only those learners who meet certain criteria that may not be used at a state institution. Their adoption of standards of excellence embraces the value of efficiency.

The value of equality is embodied in guarantees grounded in basic citizen rights. The value of efficiency is embodied in market productivity. Public administrators operate in a complex environment in which these two fundamental values often collide. The challenge of public administration must be to maximize efficiency without sacrificing equality and equity and vice versa.

## Rights and Dollars

As we have already pointed out, a trade-off exists between our equal rights as individuals and the unequal distribution of wealth in our society. The United States pursues an egalitarian political and social system, yet it generates gaping disparities in economic well-being.

We acquire and exercise our rights without any monetary charge; rights cannot be bought or sold in the marketplace. Thus, in a sense, rights infringe on economic efficiency, and the marketplace infringes on rights. The poor are disadvantaged in terms of buying and political power. Campaign financing and lobbying regulations favor persons with access to wealth. The Citizens United ruling released by the U.S. Supreme Court in January 2010 affirming the ability of corporations and labor unions to invest in political campaigns is yet another challenge to equal rights and representation for all. Yet the poorest person has the right to challenge the wealthiest business, or even the government, in our system.

The conflicting values of equality and efficiency are manifest in government organizations. Everyone has an equal right to apply for public-sector employment, but certain people will be more efficient in fulfilling the tasks of a given position. On the one hand, we emphasize individualism—rights, self-interest, liberty, freedom, choices, and rewards. On the other hand, we value community—consensus, agreement, sacrifice, altruism, and commitment to the greater good.

This mixture of equality and efficiency is crucial to American economic development. If one does not have the right to enter the marketplace, one is not going to be productive, on an individual basis or for the greater good. Therefore, if women, minorities, or other persons are denied equal opportunities, they have no chance to benefit themselves or society, and our productiveness as a nation suffers. Most citizens support equal access to opportunities. However, many question whether we can or should guarantee equal outcomes.

Equality and rights are the groundings for community consensus. Individual citizens agree on what elements constitute a satisfactory community for all. Markets value efficiency. Communities tax market profits and commit them to public administration programs—schools, streets, transit systems, parks, libraries, and other public services. Capitalistic markets depend upon community consensus, or democracy, and on the efficient use of community resources.

**Table 1.2.1** contrasts equality and efficiency. The terms listed in the table are neither all-inclusive nor mutually exclusive as applied to American politics, governments, parties, or leaders; they are simply meant to provoke thinking, discussion, questions, and commentary in the ecology of American public administration. The mix of these concepts is witnessed in the development, implementation, and evaluation of government programs and functions.

**Table 1.2.1 Contrasting Equality and Efficiency**

| EQUALITY | EFFICIENCY |
|---|---|
| fairness | advantage |
| socialism | capitalism |
| public | private |
| community | individualism |
| government | business |
| inductive | deductive |
| democracy | bureaucracy |
| mediocrity | excellence |
| employees | executives |
| rights | responsibilities |
| chaos | order |
| collective bargaining | merit |
| accessible | restricted |
| common | elite |
| equal opportunity | affirmative action |
| elections | courts |
| horizontal | vertical |
| egalitarianism | authoritarianism |
| tolerant | judgmental |
| incompetence | expertise |
| open | closed |
| level | hierarchical |
| modernization | traditionalism |
| decentralization | centralization |
| average | superior |
| diversity | homogeneity |
| April 15th | July 4th |
| Democrats | Republicans |
| bottom-up | top-down |

Two crucial questions for our democratic and capitalistic society are where and how the organized modern society establishes boundaries between the domain of rights (equality) and the domain of the capitalistic marketplace (efficiency). Conflicts between these domains are inevitable and pose dilemmas for our split-level, political economy.

Our democratic, capitalist society searches continuously for better ways to establish clear boundaries between the domains. The marketplace needs equality to put some *humanity* into *efficiency*; our democracy needs efficiency to put some *rationality* into *equality*. Capitalistic and bureaucratic systems will be more effective if they are more humane. Equality will be more acceptable to those who value efficiency, and hence, less chaotic, if consistent standards are applied to the diverse applications of the democratic principle.[7]

Democracy is characterized by equality, majority rule, due process, fairness, participation, suffrage, and electoral politics. Capitalism implies efficiency, productivity, hierarchy, competition, and entrepreneurship.

Public administration finds its origins in democracy but owes much to the fundamental principles of capitalism.

The modern organized society can also be described as a *political economy*. Our society is *political* in that citizens have the opportunity to organize and set priorities about what is important to them. The *economy* comprises the collective productivity of goods and services our society generates. The split-level structure of the political and economic systems affects public policy and administration. Communities cannot expect to have public services without providing an ample supply of *revenues*, raised by taxing citizens and businesses. Our organized society, therefore, depends upon the political system and the structure of the economic sector. The maintenance of the relationship between political power and economic structure is vital to the future of American democracy. Public administration depends on economic growth and its corresponding revenue to finance the delivery of services to the American people and pay salaries.[8]

The thrust of democratic capitalism comes from the opposing values of political power and economic structure. Middle-class citizens who do not possess the means of economic production agree to the private ownership of capital stock; meanwhile, wealthy citizens, who own the instruments of economic production,

# THINK ABOUT IT!

**Equality as Investment?**

Nations forge trade-offs between income equality and economic efficiency. Scholars and policy makers argue that greater equality reduces investment and dampens the incentive to work. Lane Kenworthy, however, argues that a more egalitarian distribution of income encourages consumer demand—as a greater number of workers become able to purchase consumer goods. If this premise is correct, egalitarian governmental policies would benefit efficiency, not dilute it.

Kenworthy offers evidence based on cross-sectional data from seventeen advanced industrialized economies over the period 1974–1990. He finds no adverse impact of greater equality on investment or work effort. According to his research, higher levels of equality associate with stronger productivity, growth, and trade performance. A national emphasis on equality does not adversely affect productivity, trade balances, inflation, or unemployment.

*Source: Lane Kenworthy, "Equality and Efficiency: The Illusory Trade-off," European Journal of Political Research 27, no. 2(1995): 225–254.*

accept democratic institutions that allow interest groups to press for further allocation of resources and output—and often redistributive policies. The large middle class thus permits members of the economic elite to own capital and organize production (the economy). The economic elite allows the general population to affect the allocation of resources and the distribution of the material effects of economic production.[9]

# THINK ABOUT IT!

**Net Worth by Race and Ethnicity, 1989-2019**

| YEAR | WHITE | AFRICAN AMERICAN | HISPANIC |
|---|---|---|---|
| 1989 | 143,560 | 8,550 | 9,940 |
| 1992 | 124,600 | 17,700 | 12,140 |
| 1995 | 128,200 | 20,870 | 18,230 |
| 1998 | 150,960 | 24,380 | 15,460 |
| 2001 | 177,500 | 27,870 | 16,900 |
| 2004 | 191,110 | 27,660 | 20,800 |
| 2007 | 211,730 | 25,920 | 26,050 |
| 2010 | 152,880 | 18,730 | 19,500 |
| 2013 | 155,830 | 14,360 | 15,150 |
| 2016 | 181,870 | 18,240 | 22,040 |
| 2019 | 189,100 | 24,100 | 36,050 |

Note: White families on average had nearly eight times the wealth of African American families and more than five times the wealth of Hispanic families in 2019.

*Source: Federal Reserve, "Survey of Consumer Finances: 1989-2019," https://www.federalreserve.gov/econres/scf/dataviz/scf/chart/*

The craft of public administration occurs within the general economic shift from manufacturing toward services—in both outputs and employment. The upgrading of skills and gender balancing of the labor force triggered a major revolution in the field of education. A century ago, women received little or no education; now they constitute more than half of most learning populations. Women now account for more than one half of those graduating with undergraduate degrees and their percentage is increasing dramatically for all graduate degrees granted.

The U.S. economy has also shifted from domestic to international competition, removing most forms of protectionism and heightening the importance of international communications through the World Trade Organization (WTO) and the United Nations (UN). Globalization and the removal or reduction of tariff barriers have resulted in the growth of gross domestic product (GDP) and worldwide efficiency. Workers, consumers, and the economy have benefited from competition with other countries.[1]

## THINK ABOUT IT!

**Comparing Statistics on Women and Children: Iowa and National Data**

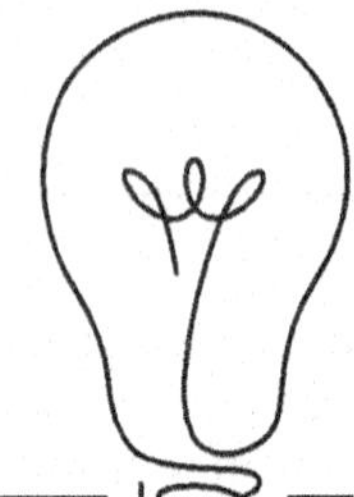

The issue of pay equity is not just a women's issue, it is a family issue. As the Bureau of the Census data reveal one of the fastest growing family types in the United States is a single parent female headed household with children. And, it is also this family type that stands out in its high percent of poverty households.

**How does your own state look by the number?**

| NUMBER | DESCRIPTION |
|---|---|
| 121,044 | The number of Iowa families with a female head of household & no husband present in 2018; in 1970 there were 52,025 families with a female head of household. |
| 22.3% | The percent of families with children under 18 in 2018 living in single-parent households with their mother compared to 9.7 percent living with their father. This compares to 68 percent living with both parents. |
| 38.9% | 38.9%: The percentage of female households, no husband present with related children under age 18, below the poverty level in 2018. The corresponding rate for married-couple families with related children under 18 years was 5 percent. |
| $28,610 | $28,610: The median income for female householders, no husband in 2018. The median income for married-couple families was $97,993. |
| 351.5 | 351.5: The rate of Iowa births to unmarried women in 2018 per 1,000 births compared to 102.4 in 1980. |
| 43.6 | 43.6: Birth rate for Iowa women under 20 years of age in Iowa per 1,000 women in 2018. In 1980 the birth rate for women under 20 was 32.5. |

*Source: Women in Iowa: 2020, Iowa State Data Center and the Iowa Department of Human Rights' Office on the Status of Women*

American participation in politics has declined, often below fifty percent participation rates, as citizens do not perceive their economic well-being as being greatly dependent on political involvement.[12] The U.S. cultural emphasis is on individualism, not political participation. Citizens separate their personal lives and interests from other matters of national life. America is the country of *individualism par excellence*.[13] This culture of individualism negatively affects political participation among lower-income groups, causing an economic class bias to emerge. Citizens of higher economic status are much more politically involved than those of lower economic status.

## The Growth of Public Bureaucracy

The organization of federal, state, and local jurisdictions is evidence of the fragmented nature of public administration in the United States. The concept of federalism, or the structure of politics in the United States, implies a system of authority apportioned constitutionally between the national and state governments.

Frederick S. Lane points out the three principal dimensions of federalism: *political*, *fiscal*, and *administrative*. The political dimension accounts for the ways in which local, state, and national jurisdictions participate in decision-making processes. The fiscal dimension indicates which jurisdictions pay what amount for services. The administrative dimension tells us which level will supervise the administration of various services. Lane concludes: "Federalism is a contradiction: it tries to marry diversity and central direction."[14]

According to U.S. Bureau of the Census Figures for 2017, state, and local governments numbered 90,126, a decrease of 22.9 percent since 1952 when there were 116,807 state and local governments. They provide transportation, public safety, health care, education, public utilities, and an array of court systems. State and local governments employed about 19.7 million workers as of March 2019. Local governments—such as counties, cities, special districts, and towns—employ almost three-fourths of these workers. In many states, citizens are served by more than one local government unit.

- There are 90,126 units of local government. Of these, 38,779 are general- purpose local governments.
- Counties (3,031) may contain cities or towns and often include unincorporated rural areas. There are 35,748 sub-county governments (townships and municipalities).
- Townships (16,253) often encompass suburban or rural areas and may or may not contain municipalities. Townships do not exist in some states.
- Municipalities (19,495) are self-governing bodies or any formally created subnational government. Municipalities enact ordinances or local laws. Municipal courts have exclusive jurisdiction over violations of municipal ordinances.
- School districts (12,754) include elementary, middle, secondary, and postsecondary government institutions. Postsecondary special districts provide academic or technical courses or both in colleges, universities, professional schools, community or junior colleges, and technical institutes. The educational services industry also includes libraries, vocational schools, and specialized training institutes. Over the past half-century, the number of school districts has decreased by 81 percent— from 67,355 in 1952 to 12,754 in 2017.
- Special districts (38,542) are independent, limited-purpose governmental units (see **Table 1.2.2**). They usually perform a single function or activity. Large percentages of special districts administer natural resource usage; examples include drainage, flood control, irrigation, soil, and water conservation services. Special districts have increased by 312 percent—from 12,340 in 1952 to 38,542 in 2017.[15]

**Table 1.2.2 Special District Governments by Function, 2017**

| FUNCTION | NUMBER | PERCENT | FUNCTION | NUMBER | PERCENT |
|---|---|---|---|---|---|
| Total | 38,542 | 100.0 | Soil and Water Conservation | 2,546 | 6.6 |
| Single-Function Districts | 32,834 | 85.2 | Other Natural Resources[c] | 1,518 | 3.9 |
| Education[a] | 184 | 0.5 | Parks and Recreation | 1,440 | 3.7 |
| Libraries | 1,660 | 4.3 | Housing and Community Dev. | 3,344 | 8.7 |
| Hospitals | 640 | 1.7 | Sewage | 1,840 | 4.8 |
| Health | 947 | 2.5 | Solid Waste Management | 450 | 1.2 |
| Welfare | 69 | 0.2 | Water Supply | 3,593 | 9.3 |
| Highways | 1,091 | 2.8 | Other Utility Districts[d] | 584 | 1.5 |
| Air Transportation | 489 | 1.3 | Fire Protection | 5,975 | 15.5 |
| Other Transportation[b] | 167 | 0.4 | Cemeteries | 1,681 | 4.4 |
| Drainage and Flood Control | 3,189 | 8.3 | Indust. Dev. and Mortgage Credit | 214 | 0.6 |
| Multiple-Function Districts | 5,708 | 14.8 | Multiple-Function Districts | 5,708 | 14.8 |

[a] *Includes school building authorities, school insur- ance authorities, educational facilities authorities, etc.*
[b] *Includes parking facilities and water transport and terminals.*
[c] *Includes irrigation, reclamation, and natural resources, not elsewhere classified.*
[d] *Includes electric power, gas supply, and public transit.*

Note: The U.S. Census Bureau produces this data every five years in years ending in "2" and "7."

Demands for government services have multiplied with an expanding population. The population of the United States in 1950 was 157,813,000; by 2000, it had increased to 283,230,000; in April 2021, it was approximately 331,450,000 (out of a world population of 7,875,000,000). The federal government has devolved, or decentralized, turning many services over to state and local governments; devolution is the practice whereby the federal government delegates to state and local governments the development, implementation, and management of government programs. The practice of government support system reform illustrates federal government devolution. The 1996 Welfare Reform Act provided block grants that gave state governments the prerogative to devise programs that meet their needs. The nature of government services provided by state and local governments will continue to change as relationships between federal, state, and local jurisdictions shift in the political economy.

While the demands for government services have multiplied with the expanding population, the growth in government employment does not reflect the growth in service demands and population. In the last 50 years while the U.S. population has increased by about two-thirds, the federal workforce in absolute numbers is actually smaller than it was nearly 50 years ago. In 1967, the federal workforce equaled 1.1 percent of the total U.S. population but in 2018 the federal workforce was equivalent to .6 percent of the U.S. population. Not counting the postal service and the military, approximately 16 million people were employed by state and local governments and two million employed by the federal government.

## Private, Nonprofit and Public-Sector Differences

Public organizations are designed for and required to serve the public interest and, thereby, treat citizens equitably and fairly. In contrast, business firms exist to serve the private and capital interests of their owners. They segment their customers based on the customers' ability and willingness to pay for products and services offered by the firm and, therefore, are not required to treat all customers alike. In addition to public organizations and business firms, about one and one-half million nonprofit entities populate our society. These nonprofits fit between public organizations and business firms. Like public organizations, nonprofits are required to serve a public purpose (e.g., feed and shelter the homeless, conduct medical research, provide for private education) in society in exchange for their tax-exempt status. Yet, similar to business firms, nonprofits must be managed with an eye toward the bottom line to remain in business, and their mission statements determine what clientele they will or will not serve in society.

Despite the fact that there are managerial differences among public organizations serving the public interest, nonprofits serving a public purpose, and businesses serving private interests, there are two things that do create similarities among these three types of organizations. First, across all three sectors, there is an increasing emphasis on the importance of governance, accountability, and the "sunshine twins" of openness and transparency. Second, all three types of organizations must become "learning communities" to effectively and efficiently adapt to their dynamic and changing environments so that they can produce and deliver quality products and services to their citizens, clients, and customers.

## Laws and Procedures: Public and Private

Public and private administration differ in important ways. These differences can be compared in two areas: *substantive* and *procedural*.

*Substantive* issues of public and private administration include questions concerning politics versus profits, the measurement of objectives, and management versus administration. These are all areas of potential conflict.

*Procedural* issues address management as a universal process. Issues for procedural deliberation include open versus closed systems, methods of evaluation, criteria for decision making, personnel systems, planning, and efficiency.[16]

Substantive issues refer to conceptual or abstract concerns such as goals, objectives, means, ends, values, results, and priorities. Nobel Prize-winning author Herbert Simon argued that the means and ends of public administration differ significantly from those of private administration.[17] He maintains that the importance of an end or value should not be ignored and that the process, or means, of management is a value in itself and cannot be separated from other values.

The purpose of a college education, for example, is to seek learning, training, and knowledge about the significant values of life. The *end* is learning, training, and knowledge. Education is the *substance*, and the institution is the *procedure*. The institution provides the procedural means for attaining the specific substantive ends. The *means* are provided by the curricula of the respective disciplines. In other words, the means for achieving the learning, training, and knowledge you seek are to meet the requirements of your discipline's prescribed curricula by attending classes and successfully completing exams.

Justice and the implementation of justice can also illustrate *ends* and *means*. Justice, in the philosophical realm, is an *end* in itself, a commonly held value. Justice can only be found in the United States by a *means*—due process of law. Justice is an example of a substantive issue; the matters of the judicial process constitute processes, authorities, and institutions that enforce procedural concerns. By unpacking the distinctions between substantive and procedural issues in public administration, we can clarify the differences between administration in the private and the public sectors.

## Substantive Issues

1. **Politics versus Profits.** Decision making in public bureaucracies is achieved by meeting the objectives of compromise, consensus, and democratic participation. These objectives are different from the private-sector's emphasis on the concepts of efficiency, rationality, and profit. Although the goals of public administration and private administration both respond to outside clientele pressures, their concepts of bottom-line accountability differ—one's God is a consensus of citizens concerned about the issues confronting an entire community, and the other's god is profit.

2. **Measurement of Objectives.** The private sector ultimately makes rational decisions based upon clear, concise, and quantifiable statements found in the sales ledger. The public-sector deals with social intangibles such as social services and common defense.

3. **Management versus Administration.** In the private sector, the term management commonly refers to those persons in line *positions*, whereas in the public sector, the term *administration* refers to those in line *functions*. Line personnel command, have authority, and are generalists; staff personnel possess knowledge and skills, give advice, and are specialists. The term *management* is characterized by decision making in the private-sector corporate model of hierarchy.

## Procedural Issues

1. **Open versus Closed Systems.** Procedural concerns, such as accountability, reflect the dilemma of the open versus closed system, or the goldfish bowl of public administration versus the closed boardroom of private administration.

2. **Methods of Evaluation**. Community leaders seek consensus, agree to compromise, and advocate citizen participation to find support for policies. In contrast, efficiency, rationality, and concern for profit cause private-sector entrepreneurs to view corporate evaluation differently. The public sector focuses on social good; the private sector emphasizes fiscal control. The two may, in some cases, be incompatible.

3. **Public versus Private Decision-Making Criteria**. Although the formal steps in decision making may be similar in both public and private administration, the criteria managers use to make decisions are not. The definition of the goal or problem, the desired consumer response, and the allocation of resources may apply similarly to both sectors: the logic, or mode of thinking, behind decision making differs. The public-sector university's bookstore is, for example, under very different constraints from a privately-run bookstore across the street. The public-sector bookstore demands a higher standard in procedural process (the manner in which a function is carried out) and maintains certain expectations and guarantees in hiring, firing, promotions, and general conduct of bookstore business. The private-sector bookstore can sell items based upon the supply and demand of the marketplace; the public-sector bookstore must respond to every course, no matter how esoteric or obscure, and to every program offered by the state university.

4. **Personnel Systems**. Several differences exist in personnel systems. Unlike an applicant in the private sector, an applicant for a full-time civil service position governed by a merit system will go through a fixed process, monitored by law. Public-sector employees also enjoy the privileges of administrative due process because laws prescribe guidelines for the recruitment, selection, promotion, and retention of employees. Merit plans that evaluate skills, knowledge, and expertise are a hiring tool, but they may differ greatly from agency to agency and are based on the three "capital Es" of achievement: education, experience, and examination. Private enterprise employees have no guarantees of due process, and in the U.S., employment at will doctrine dominates management and employee relationships.

5. **Long-Term and Short-Term Planning**. Planning may be considered part of the process of decision making. The private-sector manager does not need to seek consensus among employees before acting.

   The manager alone makes decisions, and the company's profit or loss ledger reflects success or failure. For the public-sector employee, planning becomes hazardous if leadership is continuously changing after elections. Public officials need program continuity and political stability to carry out their responsibilities consistently. In the private-sector, planning is easier because there are no automatic demands of due process or legally prescribed guarantees concerning hiring, firing, and promotion.

6. **Efficiency.** Hierarchical control, coordination, planning, meritorious performance, and lines of authority are emphasized in both the public and private sectors. However, the bottom line, or profit concern, of the private sector allows managers to realize success or failure immediately; in the public sector, with its less precise methods of evaluation, it may take longer to evaluate the efficiency and success of a public service.

## Blurring or Bifurcation?

On the substantive issues we have discussed (politics versus profits, measurement of objectives, and management versus administration), a comparison of the public and private sectors reveals more blurring than bifurcation. A comparison of procedural issues (open versus closed systems, methods of evaluation, public versus private decision-making criteria, personnel systems, planning, and efficiency) reveals distinctions in regard to the accountability factor, but similarities in developing participative personnel systems to evaluate the expertise, knowledge, and skills of employees.

The public sector is grounded in *political equality* with consideration for everyone's opinion, seeking consensus, compromise, and democratic participation. The private sector is based on *economic efficiency*, seeking definitive results, rationality in decision making, and the maximization of profit. In practice, the realities of political equality and economic efficiency blend into what many call the "American System."

To a larger degree than most people realize, Alexander Hamilton's "American System" still plays a critical role in American economic development. The government uses investment and trade policies to promote American industry and create jobs. President Dwight D. Eisenhower's interstate highway system was a 1950s version of Hamilton's system of canals. In 1997, U.S. Trade Representative Charlene Barshefsky followed Hamilton's lead when she signed agreements making certain that U.S. companies were able to access world telecommunications markets. Profits for the rich may mean jobs for the rest of us. If so, perhaps special interests and national interests are joined.[18]

Public administration, then, differs in significant ways from private administration. These differences hinge largely on the greater legal accountability of the former and the greater flexibility of the latter. Determining which sector is the most efficient remains a complex question, subject not only to differences in products and procedures but also to differences in purposes, services, and processes.

## Nonprofit and Public-Sector Differences

It is generally thought that there are more similarities than differences between public and nonprofit organizations (NPOs) and that NPOs have historically taken their cues on how to operate, manage, transact, and deliver services from governmental bodies and even for-profit companies.[19] In fact, much of the literature on the public sector will include examples and case study scenarios from government entities and nonprofit agencies interchangeably. Yet, there are nuances between public organizations (e.g., federal, state, and local governments) and NPOs that justify scholarship and research specific to the nonprofit sector.

The key differences between governmental bodies and nonprofits examined in this text are the areas of volunteer employees; the presence and role of a board of directors; and the emphasis NPOs place on strategic planning. These three factors present challenges that must be addressed in order to facilitate effective human resources management in nonprofit organizations. While these same traits could arguably be valuable to the public sector as well, these traits are largely unique to NPOs and not usually present within governmental organizations, literature that takes a combined approach to addressing human resources in both governments and NPOs typically falls short in addressing these defining characteristics.

Indeed, the literature supports the view that volunteerism is a unique trait of nonprofit organizations.[20] The importance of volunteers to NPOs should not be trivialized or discounted due to the wide range of duties they perform, the value they help create, their inclusion in key organizational decisions, and their impact on organizational structure. According to data from the Corporation for National and Community Service (AmeriCorps) approximately 75 million adults volunteer annually worth an approximate dollar value of nearly $200 billion.

Boards of directors serve as another differentiating characteristic of the nonprofit sector. As previously stated, the vast majority of nonprofit organizations feature a board of directors consisting of volunteers, and some consider membership on a governing board to be "the pinnacle of volunteer involvement" because of the "financial, human resource, and physical assets" for which trustees are responsible.[21] While boards of directors are also used in some instances in the public sector such as elected city councils and boards of supervisors or regulatory types of commissions, the boards of directors in the public setting often don't provide the strategic planning and mission focus provided by their counterparts in the nonprofit sector.

NOTABLE QUOTES

Not everythng that counts can be counted, and not everything that can be counted, counts.

*— Albert Einstein*

Volunteer boards of directors fulfill both legal and practical needs. Board members serve as trustees of nonprofit organizations and strive to set the higher-level objectives and overall trajectory with mission and vision in mind. They also bear fiduciary responsibilities and fulfill human resources roles in many organizations. For example, board members work to minimize conflicts of interest by drafting sound policies, hire and evaluate the executive director, help ensure strategic planning and resource allocation processes are in place, develop incentive plans, and maintain internal command so there is no threat of breakdown in organizational control.[22] And similar to the uses of succession planning for other positions in the organization, it should also be used for the board of directors.

The Internal Revenue Service requires tax-exempt organizations to be governed by a board of directors. Practically speaking, a board of directors can provide a wealth of expertise to a nonprofit organization with few resources.[23]

Strategic planning is required for long-term organizational sustainability. From a human resources management viewpoint specifically, strategic planning attempts to "envision a long-term plan of reaching where the personnel system desires to be in 10, 15, or 20 years, while outlining clear goals, objectives, and programs by which to accomplish its mission."[24] Thus, strategic planning is a key element in a systematic approach to public personnel administration.[25] It defines the priorities of an organization and builds the commitment of the people working toward achieving those priorities.[26]

The essence of strategic planning remains consistent whether the organization is for profit, a governmental body, or nonprofit. What differs, however, are internal and external forces that influence inputs and outcomes. An organization's governance affects strategic planning significantly. While government organizations are governed by elected and appointed officials, nonprofits and for-profits are governed by a board of directors. Nonprofit boards represent the interests of the public. A company's board includes or represents the owners. Through market research, customers of for-profit businesses can have a much greater influence on strategic planning than most consumers of nonprofit and government services. Donors and taxpayers, both of whom may or may not utilize the services of a nonprofit or government organization, can significantly influence a strategic plan. The mission and values are key elements of a nonprofit's strategic plan, while usually less important for business and government planning, although this is changing.[27]

Unfortunately, as Borins and Behn have suggested, strategic planning forms and templates have become overused in organizational analysis and have not produced the level of desired performance. Clearly, nonprofits and public entities face many different problems and contexts—organizational, cultural, social, political, and economic. They too have not only different values, beliefs, and orientation, but different stakeholders and legislators whose diverse interests must also be met.[28]

This analysis has shown that there are many similarities that exemplify nonprofit organizations and other public-sector agencies. This analysis further demonstrated that there are many important differences that remain.

## Interest Groups and the Greater Good

The corps of Washington lobbyists has grown steadily since the New Deal, but especially since the early 1970s. This growth parallels the growth in federal spending and the expansion of federal authority into new areas. Voters may appear to demand political reform, but government is unlikely to change except in composition. The unwieldy size and contradictory complexity of modern governments has developed because of the cumulative inertia of entrenched lobbyists and special-interest groups. Reforms continue, but they come only gradually. Substantive change can come from the presidency or the electorate, but not unless individuals are willing to make personal sacrifices for widespread social welfare.[29]

Lobbyists compete vigorously to safeguard traditional spending in their areas of interest. Industries, labor unions, ethnic groups, religious groups, professional organizations, citizen groups, and even foreign business interests all periodically—and some continuously—seek to exert pressure on national and state legislatures to attain legislative goals. *Pressure by interest groups usually has a selfish aim: Their members wish to assert rights, win privileges, or benefit financially.* A group's power to influence legislation is often based less on its arguments than on the size of its membership, its financial resources, and the astuteness of its lobbyists. If there were any doubt about the increasing presence of special interests in American politics, within the Capital Beltway—the interstate highway that circles Washington, D.C.— there were 11,541 federal lobbyists in 2020 spending an estimated $3.53 billion on lobbying according to the Center for Responsive Politics based on data from the Senate Office of Public Records.

Expert articulation of particular citizen interests drives public bureaucracies in the United States. Legislatures write vague laws. Public administrators interpret those statutes with specificity in the Federal Register. The statutes are then codified in the *Code of Federal Regulations*. The public philosophy of the United States in this century is no longer capitalism but *interest group liberalism*, a concept developed by Theodore J. Lowi. Lowi claims that capitalism has declined as an ideology and is dead as a public philosophy. Capitalism, the old public philosophy, has become outmoded since World War II because the elite, such as lobbyists, no longer agree on whether government should play a role in making policies for private citizens or for private-sector businesses. Republicans and Democrats, as participants in interest group liberalism, fully agree that government should be a player in monitoring, if not directing, the relations among private citizens.[30]

Interest groups reflect partisan bearings. Labor unions lean toward Democratic Party candidates, while many, but not all, business groups flock toward Republicans.

As the Great Depression ended and World War II began, U.S. capitalism came to be called "conservatism," but Lowi argues that this description is a misnomer. He states that capitalism never became conservative but declined because it became irrelevant and erroneous. Capitalist ideology, according to Lowi, did not endure as the public philosophy because it could accept only one legitimate type of modern social control—competition. Lowi concludes that the old dialogue between liberalism and conservatism "passed into the graveyard of consensus," spelling the "decline of meaningful adversary political proceedings in favor of administrative, technical and logrolling politics. In a nutshell, politics became a question of equity rather than a question of morality. Adjustment comes first, rules of law come last, if at all."[31] As interest groups clash, the priority becomes equal opportunity for any group to put forth its unique version of how life should be conducted. The values of any particular organization are secondary.

In interest group liberalism, diverse groups check the values, or perspectives, of opposing interests by arguing for their own set of values in the great American marketplace of ideas. Milk producers, tobacco growers, billboard advertisers, moviemakers, bankers, physicians, broadcasters, cable TV operators, farmers, entrepreneurs, and energy interests are represented by a few of the more than two thousand lobbyists who insist that their concerns should be written into law. Whether liberal or conservative, the elite want to use the power and funding of government for their personal ends.

According to Lowi, the most significant difference between liberals and conservatives, Democrats and Republicans, can be found in the interest groups with which they identify. The values of organized interest groups guide Congress members in casting their votes, presidents in shaping their programs, and bureaucrats in exercising their administrative discretion. The only necessary guidelines for framing laws depend upon the validity or legitimacy of interest group demands.[32]

The philosophy of interest group liberalism is pragmatic, with government playing the role of broker, and is optimistic about government's role; that which is good for government is also good for society. The liberal process of private interaction with public officials is accessible to all organized interests and offers no value judgments concerning any particular claim or set of claims. Interest group liberalism defines the public interest as the amalgamation of claims of various interests. The principle of representation extends into public bureaucracy as administrators provide due process and a voice to all citizens.

To represent such diverse political, economic, and cultural interests, legislatures make open-ended, vague laws and issue broad delegations to public administrators to regulate interests in society. Says Lowi: "It [interest group liberalism] impairs legitimacy by converting government from a moralistic to a mechanistic institution. It impairs the potential of positive law to correct itself by allowing the law to become anything that eventually bargains itself out as acceptable to the bargainer. Interest group liberalism seeks pluralistic government in which there is no formal specification of means or of ends. In a pluralistic government there is, therefore, no substance. Neither is their procedure. There is only process."[33] In other words, procedures and processes become vital, and substance and values are at the mercy of the strongest interests.

In recent years, private interests have contributed ever increasing amounts of money to participants fighting either to preserve the status quo of the political system or to change it, subsequently purchasing privilege, power, and profit. It was recently reported that the vast majority of all political action committee (PAC) moneys were contributed by less than 155 donors. It would not be an exaggeration to assert that the American government—President, executive branch, and Congress—has been bought and sold. The Madisonian faction is firmly in the saddle and rides the nation.[34]

*Quid pro quo* (one thing in return for another or this for that) is a pragmatic approach to America's version of democratic capitalism. Access to capital dominates democracy. Do rich people and interest groups give large sums of money to politicians to promote good and just causes? Lee Hamilton, a Congressman from Indiana for more than a generation, reveals that "money, money, money, and the money chase" dominates political talk on Capitol Hill. As columnist Robert Higgs states, "The root of the problem lies not in the takers, who will always find a way to take, but in the givers. Foxes do not voluntarily evacuate the henhouse," Higgs speculates. "The hydra-headed government now dominating this country is inherently corrupt."[35]

In an era when politics seems, increasingly, to be the pursuit of self-interest under the banner of some high-sounding principle, one can be excused for doubting whether the opponents of campaign finance reform are really so passionately devoted to protection of the First Amendment. Nonetheless, the free speech argument is important enough to address on its merits.[36]

## The Information Age and Social Media

### Governing with Social Media: From Novelty to Permanency

It is a truism that the worldwide social media usage has been growing at a phenomenal rate and is expected to increase from around 3.6 billion users in 2021 to 4.1 billion users by 2025. The global social media usage rate is reported at 49 percent in 2021 and expected to surge as more mobile devices are introduced around the world and developing nations rapidly transition to digital platforms.

Modern governments have largely made the transition from the old ways of communication to the newest advances in social media. The transition to a digital platform has been fast and professional. And administrators at all levels of government now consider it "old hat' to think and act on this platform, especially as it embraces the tenets of democratic society: equitable, open, transparent, participative, accessible and accountable programs, services and activities.

The need to proclaim the advantages of two-and-multiple-way, clear and effective communication between political leaders, public administrators and their numerous stakeholders is acknowledged and accepted today, especially in the areas of community service, engagement, revenue generation, delivery of an array of public services, etc., and the routine activities of applying for licenses, registrations, permits and financial services. In addition, social media has found its way into community-based health, natural resources, and urban planning crowd sourcing. To illustrate its prominence, one only has to reflect on its centrality during the recent pandemic as millions of people located health services and signed up for their vaccinations.

Social media assisted by a vast array of technologies is affecting how government conducts the people's business in the areas of crisis and emergency management (wildfires, floods, tornadoes, oil spills, weather assessments, first responders, etc.), improving interagency coordination and collaboration and strengthening partnerships with the citizenry writ large. Although these many positive and transactional features of social media, mentioned above, are present on the administrator's "dashboard of metrics," it would be remiss if some of the troubling aspects of cybersecurity and cyberattacks (data breaches and losses), and ransomware were not mentioned. For example, the average organization cost after a data breach ranged from 3.54 million in 2006 to 8.64 million in 2020, based on estimates associated with the loss of business, costs related to "detection, escalation and notification of the breach," credit report monitoring and, of course, loss of trust and confidence with clientele.

Accompanying the robust increase in the use of digital communication, are the large security breaches and the rapidly increasing cost for insurance and security protection. Virtually no area of business, commerce, industry, education, medical/healthcare, and government remain unscathed: debit and credit cards, insurance data, nuclear power plant data, military records, social security information, bank statements, financial records, electric grids and pipelines of one type or another. For instance, organizations paid about 125 Billion in U.S. dollars in 2019 for protection. Some of the largest data breaches were found in India's, Aadhaar (ID identification data), with 1.1.B records lost; Yahoo's online platform, 500 million user accounts (2017), and Yahoo's loss of 1.1. Billion records in 2013, later updated to 3 billion. The largest data breach was with Apollo—a sales intelligence company—that had 9 billion data points affected. In the United States, 1,506 data breaches in 2019 and 471 million personal records exposed to cyber-attack in 2020. The three business areas, in addition to governmental ones, that were impacted by cyberattacks were healthcare, energy and financial. The average cost per leak for healthcare was 7.13 million, and 6 million per leak in energy and financial sectors.

Comparatively, the United States is the most affected country in terms of financial damage. The U.S. government costs of 13.7 billion in cyberattacks. In 2018, 23,107 cybersecurity incidents reported by U.S. federal agencies alone; and in 2019, the U.S. government reported that nearly 200 million records were compromised. In the same year, the U.S. government IT expenditures were 88 billion, anticipated to go up to 92 billion in 2021. The costs per data breach goes up as the number of employees in the organization rises. For instance, organizations with less than 1,000 employees the average cost per attack was $133,000, compared to $500,000 for organizations with over 1,000 employees.[37, 38, 39]

# THINK ABOUT IT!

**Managing with the Threat of Ransomware**

Cybersecurity has become, at an alarming speed, a major part of the critical infrastructure as cyber-attacks affect all economic sectors. Malicious software is designed to corrupt and exfiltrate (data thief by unlawful movement) computer systems, preventing computer access, and infecting and/or compromising sensitive personal or organizational information, encrypting the data and impeding required organizational activities, jeopardizing privacy rights, and done for profit by the cyber-criminals. In the Kaseya attack, for instance, the Kaseya Virtual System Administrative software (VSA) was invaded and used to compromise approximately 1,500 of their clients in one of the largest supply chain attacks in U.S. history. There are other notorious instances of ransomware attacks, such as Solarwinds and Colonial Pipeline and they represent the "dark side" of cyber-security. Noteworthy, the number of ransomware attacks is increasing dramatically, the public sector is the hardest hit, and the average ransom has increased to $111,600.

Cyber-attacks can destroy entire computer systems and present a prisoners' dilemma for public administrators—either pay the ransom and retrieve the use of the data system or ignore the thieves, rebuild the system and face legal implications from clientele and citizens.

*Source: Malik Dulaney, "Held Hostage: The Threat of Ransomware," PA Times, July 22, 2021.*

## Mission, Money and Manipulation

Pressure groups manipulate the laws by which we live. A generation ago, lobbyists were portrayed as fat, cigar-smoking men who lined the pockets of lawmakers with $100 bills. This stereotypical description no longer applies, but the connotation of corruption persists. Rallying constituents through "grassroots" telemarketing has become as suspect as the old images of backroom bribery. The onslaught of a thousand identical postcards is discounted as a lobbying trick, and a hundred calls originating from a telephone bank arriving in the office on the same day are recognized for what they are. The new lobbying is much more subtle.

Researchers, rather than high-priced lobbyists, now inhabit the offices of Washington's most powerful interest groups. The clout of these groups depends on the sincerity of support they receive from actual voters back home. The ability to "buy" politicians or manipulate a groundswell of last-minute phone calls has less relevance than it used to. The "iceberg" principle of legislative success posits that the powerhouses of interest group persuasion are not very visible at the Washington "waterline" of influence. But these interest "icebergs" are very big and very menacing, and they "run" in deep political waters.

Interest groups are valued more for the votes they can deliver on behalf of certain candidates than for direct monetary contributions. Memberships are geographically dispersed and politically active. Members focus their activities on a narrow range of issues. They are true believers in the organization's cause. They turn out in droves on Election Day. In low voter turnout elections, committed voters may spell the difference between victory and defeat for partisans. And reelection is high on the priority agenda of partisans.

According to the Center for Responsive Politics, Washington's influence industry has increased its spending on lobbying by nearly 243 percent going from $1.45 billion in 1998 to $3.53 billion by 2020 which is a new record topping the record 2010 amount of $3.52 billion (**Table 1.2.3**).

**Table 1.2.3 Total Lobbying Expenditures**

| YEAR | BILLIONS | # OF LOBBYISTS |
|---|---|---|
| 2000 | $1.57 | 12,540 |
| 2001 | $1.64 | 11,851 |
| 2002 | $1.83 | 12,140 |
| 2003 | $2.06 | 12,958 |
| 2004 | $2.19 | 13,211 |
| 2005 | $2.44 | 14,090 |
| 2006 | $2.63 | 14,489 |
| 2007 | $2.87 | 14,819 |
| 2008 | $3.30 | 14,131 |
| 2009 | $3.50 | 13,717 |
| 2010 | $3.52 | 12,911 |
| 2011 | $3.33 | 12,605 |
| 2012 | $3.31 | 12,169 |
| 2013 | $3.24 | 12,081 |
| 2014 | $3.24 | 11,791 |
| 2015 | $2.39 | 11,525 |
| 2016 | $3.16 | 11,200 |
| 2017 | $3.38 | 11,555 |
| 2018 | $3.46 | 11,649 |
| 2019 | $3.51 | 11,892 |
| 2020 | $3.53 | 11,544 |

*Source: OpenSecrets.org:*
*https://www.opensecrets.org/federal-lobbying*

The pharmaceutical, biotechnology, and health products industry lead all industries for the twenty-first straight year spending more than $309 million in 2020, a new high-water mark, up from $165 million in 2006. The top 20 lobbying industries had already invested $1.1 billion to influence legislation in the first six months of 2021 (**Table 1.2.4**). Among individual clients, the U.S. Chamber of Commerce reported spending nearly $30 million on federal lobbying in the first six months of 2021. Top five spenders from 1998-2021 were the U.S. Chamber of Commerce, National Association of Realtors, American Medical Association, American Hospital Association, and Pharmaceutical Research and Manufacturers of America, spending a combined $3.7 billion. The biggest spenders for the first six months of 2021 are shown in **Table 1.2.5**.

**Table 1.2.4 Lobbying: Industries Ranked by Expenditures, First Six Months of 2021**

| INDUSTY | AMOUNT | RANKING |
|---|---|---|
| Pharmaceuticals/ Health Products | $171,262,239 | 1 |
| Electronics Manufacturing & Equipment | $87,196,840 | 2 |
| Insurance | $75,708,089 | 3 |
| Oil & Gas | $55,616,285 | 4 |
| Hospitals/Nursing Homes | $55,365,197 | 5 |
| Electric Utilities | $53,994,293 | 6 |
| Health Services/HMOs | $52,715,013 | 7 |
| Air Transport | $52,412,166 | 8 |
| Securities & Investment | $51,719,372 | 9 |
| Telecom Services | $51,464,510 | 10 |
| Misc. Manufacturing & Distributing | $51,293,389 | 11 |
| Business Associations | $48,541,823 | 12 |
| Health Professionals | $43,992,779 | 13 |
| Internet | $43,874,461 | 14 |
| Real Estate | $41,772,440 | 16 |
| Education | $41,218,949 | 15 |
| Civil Servants/ Public Officials | $38,563,814 | 17 |
| Automotive | $35,202,127 | 18 |
| Misc. Issues | $26,697,533 | 19 |
| Misc. Energy | $27,401,639 | 20 |

*Source:* *https://www.opensecrets.org/federal-lobbying.*

**Table 1.2.5 Lobbying: Clients Ranked by Expenditures, First Six Months of 2021**

| CLIENT | AMOUNT | RANKING |
|---|---|---|
| US Chamber of Commerce | $29,630,000 | 1 |
| National Association of Realtors | $18,133,428 | 2 |
| Pharmaceutical Research & Manufacturers of America | $15,218,000 | 3 |
| American Hospital Association | $12,121,176 | 4 |
| Blue Cross/Blue Shield | $12,018,300 | 5 |
| American Medical Association | $10,880,000 | 6 |
| Amazon.com | $10,190,000 | 7 |
| Facebook Inc | $9,560,000 | 8 |
| Business Roundtable | $8,840,000 | 9 |
| Raytheon Technologies | $8,150,000 | 10 |
| National Association of Manufacturers | $7,710,000 | 11 |
| Lockheed Martin | $7,467,350 | 12 |
| Comcast Corp | $6,720,000 | 13 |
| Northrop Grumman | $6,690,000 | 14 |
| Pfizer, Inc | $6,670,000 | 15 |
| NCTA The Internet & Television Association | $6,570,000 | 16 |
| America's Health Insurance Plans | $6,410,000 | 17 |
| Boeing Co | $6,170,000 | 18 |
| CTIA | $5,930,000 | 19 |

*Source:* *https://www.opensecrets.org/federal-lobbying/top-spenders*

While the amount of money spent on lobbying described above may seem staggering, the Center for Responsive Politics calculates spending on lobbying as defined under the Lobbying Disclosure Act of 1995. Spending by corporations, industry groups, unions, and other interests that is not specifically for lobbying of government officials, but is nevertheless meant to influence public policy, is not reported. This spending may exceed what is spent on direct lobbying. These activities include public relations, advertising, and grassroots lobbying.

In 2020, 4,440 lobbyists worked on issues related to the federal budget and appropriations, more than any other issue. However, that is down from the nearly 5,179 lobbyists that worked on the same issue just eleven short years ago in 2009. Perhaps this decrease is a result of the reduction in federal earmarks since the House Appropriations Committee began implementing rules to ban earmarks in March 2010? Earmarks are back in Congress in 2021. Time will tell if the return of earmarks will result in an uptick in the number of lobbyists. **Table 1.2.6** provides a listing of lobbying activities on selected issues and corresponding number of clients represented.

**Table 1.2.6 Lobbying by Issue, 2020**

| ISSUE | NO. OF CLIENTS [a] |
|---|---|
| Federal Budget & Appropriations | 3,544 |
| Health Issues | 2,610 |
| Taxes | 1,909 |
| Defense | 1,555 |
| Transportation | 1,509 |
| Trade | 1,334 |
| Medicare & Medicaid | 1,080 |
| Energy & Nuclear Power | 996 |
| Environment & Superfund | 969 |
| Education | 921 |
| Government Issues | 907 |
| Agriculture | 818 |

[a] Each client may report lobbying on multiple issues.

*Source: Center for Responsive Politics, http://www.opensecrets.org/.*

## Summary

- Ecology is the relationship between private economic developments, or the marketplace, and the state's responsibility for monitoring, supervising, and regulating personal freedoms and commercial activities. Government employees do not operate in a vacuum, but in a complex environment.
- Modern America is the epitome of the organized society. The organized society exists in an environment of equal rights and unequal outcomes. Conflicts result between the political principles of democracy and the economic principles of capitalism.
- Students learn to think by a combination of conceptual and analytical thought and deductive and inductive reasoning.
- Congestion is the toughest challenge in the nation's transportation ecology.
- *The craft of public administration* is changing as the economy shifts from manufacturing toward services—in both outputs and employment.
- The political economy of the United States is one of democratic capitalism. The thrust of this ideology comes from the opposing values of political power and economic structure.
- Democracy is characterized by equality, due process, fairness, participation, suffrage, and electoral politics. Capitalism rests on efficiency, productivity, hierarchy, competition, and entrepreneurship.
- Rights are acquired and exercised without monetary charge. Rights cannot be bought or sold in the marketplace, but may infringe on economic efficiency.
- Public administration finds its origins in democracy but owes much to the fundamental principles of capitalism.
- The "body politic" of the United States is more pragmatic than ideological.
- Democracy is unpleasant and hard work. It isn't enough to hold the right opinion. You have to speak to those who hold what you believe to be the wrong opinion in such a way as to convince them.
- 90,126 governments were counted in 2017, of which 38,779 were local governments. Counties number 3,031, townships 16,253, municipalities 19,495, school districts 12,754, and special districts 38,542.
- Demands for government services have multiplied with an expanding population.
- The dimensions of U.S. federalism are political, fiscal, and administrative.
- As demands for government services have multiplied with an expanding population, the federal government has devolved, or turned over many services to state and local governments.
- Americans opt for market justice over political justice. Benefits are allocated by the economic marketplace—not by government programs and policies.
- The U.S. cultural emphasis is on individualism—not political participation. Citizens separate their personal lives and interests from matters of national life. America is a country of individualism par excellence.
- Substantive issues of public and private administration raise questions concerning politics versus profits, measurement of objectives, and management versus administration. Procedural issues concern open versus closed systems, methods of evaluation, decision-making criteria, personnel systems, planning, and efficiency.
- Pressure groups manipulate the laws by which we live. The clout each of these groups yields depends on the sincerity and depth of support from actual voters back home.
- Quid pro quo (one thing in return for another or this for that) is the pragmatic approach that defines America's version of democratic capitalism. Access to capital dominates democracy.
- The public philosophy of the United States is interest group liberalism. Whether liberal or conservative, elites utilize the power and purse of government for personal ends.
- The philosophy of interest group liberalism is pragmatic—with government exercising its role as broker. In a pluralistic government, procedure and process may be as important as substance.
- The effectiveness of interest groups among elected officials, consumers, and government bureaucrats depends, in large part, upon the group's number of members, the size of its budget, and the expertise of its staff in Washington and/or any one of fifty state capitals.
- One of the best ways to judge a president's effectiveness is to ask: Did this president solve more problems than he or she created?

Now that we have explored the ecology of the craft of public administration, we are ready to move to another important subject that public administrators must be aware of—the anatomy, or structure, of government organizations.

## Videos, Films and Talks

Please visit *The Craft of Public Administration* at www.millenniumhrmpress.com for up-to-date videos, films, talks, readings, and additional class resources.

3 myths about the future of work (and why they're not true) [15 min]
Daniel Susskind, TED Talk
https://www.ted.com/talks/daniel_susskind_3_myths_about_the_future_of_work_and_why_they_re_not_true

## Suggested Readings

**"Local Politics and the Malaise of the Millennials,"** Governing, https://www.governing.com/gov-institute/voices/col-local-politics-voting-community-engagement-millennials.html.

**"The Next Big Thing in Local Government: Many challenges lie ahead. Cities and counties will need to collaborate and innovate as never before,"** Robert J. O'Neill Jr., September 25, 2015, https://www.governing.com/archive/col-next-big-thing-local-government.html

**"Why Trust in Local Government Should Be Even Higher Than It Is Far more than the public realizes, innovators are making extraordinary efforts in communities across America,"** Stephen Goldsmith, August 18, 2015, https://www.governing.com/archive/col-innovation-trust-local-government.html

## Notes

1. Emmette S. Redford, Democracy in the *Administrative State* (New York: Oxford University Press, 1969), p. 3.
2. Arthur M. Okun, *Equality and Efficiency: The Big Tradeoff* (Washington, DC: The Brookings Institution, 1975), p. 4.; The analysis associated with the classical and neoclassical economic traditions through Thomas Picketty's *Capital in the Twenty-First Century* and our organized society is extracted and modified from "The Evolution of 'Economic Theory' and its Role in Public Policy," *American Journal of Business and Behavioral Sciences*, Ismael Hossein-Zadeh, Stephen E. Clapham and C. Kenneth Meyer, forthcoming, spring 2016. Reprinted with permission from ASBBS.
3. Suzanne Garment, "Making a Case for Regulation," *Washington Post*, February 2, 1997, p. A8.
4. Henry T. Abraham, *Freedom and the Court: Civil Rights and Liberties in the United States* (New York: Oxford University Press, 1977), pp. 110–129.
5. Okun, *Equality and Efficiency*, p. 119.
6. Ralph D. Christy, "Markets or Government? Balancing Imperfect and Complementary Alternatives," *American Journal of Agricultural Economics* 78, no. 5 (December 1996): 1145–1157.
7. Ibid.
8. Lester M. Salamon and John J. Siegfried, "Economic Power and Political Influence: The Impact of Industry Structure on Public Policy," *American Political Science Review* 71, no. 4 (December 1977): 1026–1043.
9. Adam Przeworski and Michael Wallerstein, "Democratic Capitalism at the Crossroads," *Democracy* 2, no. 3 (July 1982): 52–68.
10. John Pollacco, "Old Economy vs. New Economy," *Business Times*, January 31– February 6, 2001, http:// www.businesstimes.com.mt/2001/01/31/focus.html.
11. Robert E. Lane, "Market Justice, Political Justice," *American Political Science Review* 80, no. 2 (June 1986): 383–402. See also Jennifer Nedelsky, *Private Property and the Limits of American Constitutionalism* (New York: Oxford University Press, 1990).
12. Harry Holloway with John George, *Public Opinion*, 2d ed. (New York: St. Martin's Press, 1986), p. 157.

13. William Watts and Lloyd A. Free, eds., *The State of the Nation* (New York: University Books, Potomac Associates, 1967), p. 97.

14. Frederick S. Lane, *Current Issues in Public Administration* (New York: St. Martin's Press, 1982), p. 156.

15. *2017 Census of Governments – Organization.* U.S. Census Bureau, 2017, www.census.gov/data/tables/2017/econ/gus/2017-governments.html.

16. Michael A. Murray, "Comparing Public and Private Management: An Exploratory Essay," *Public Administration Review* 35, no. 4 (July/ August 1975): 364–371.

17. Herbert A. Simon, *Administrative Behavior* (New York: Macmillan, 1957).

18. Walter Russell Mead, "To Tether Big Business to the National Interest, Read Hamilton," *Los Angeles Times*, February 23, 1997, pp. M2, 6.

19. Arthur C. Brooks, 2002. "Can Nonprofit Management Help Answer Public Management's 'Big Questions'?". *Public Administration Review* 62 (3): 259-66.

20. Roland J. Kushner and Peter P. Poole. 1996. "Exploring Structure-Effectiveness Relationships in Nonprofit Arts Organizations" *Nonprofit Management and Leadership* (7): 119-36.

21. Alceste T. Pappas, *Reengineering Your Nonprofit Organization: A Guide to Strategic Transformation*, (New York: John Wiley & Sons, Inc, 1996).

22. Eugene F. Fama, and Michael C. Jensen. 1983, "Separation of Ownership and Control," *Journal of Law and Economics* (26): 327-49.

23. Stephen R. Block, "Board of Directors," *In Understanding Nonprofit Organizations: Governance, Leadership and Management*, editors J. Stephen Ott and Lisa A. Dicke, (Boulder: Westview Press) p. 7-17.

24. Ali Farazmand, *Strategic Public Personnel Administration: Building and Managing Human Capital for the 21st Century*, Vol. 1, (Westport: Praeger Publishers 2007), p. 6.

25. Ibid. 5

26. Michael Allison and Jude Kaye, "Introduction to Strategic Planning," *In Understanding Nonprofit Organizations Governance, Leadership and Management*, editors. J. Steven Ott and Lisa A. Dicke, (Boulder: Westview Press, 2006), 105-110.

27. Ibid. 105-110

28. Robert Behn, 1995. "The Big Questions of Public Management," *Public Administration Review* 55 (4): 313-24.

29. Jonathan Rauch, "The End of Government," *National Journal* 28, no. 36 (September 7, 1996): 1890– 1896.

30. Theodore J. Lowi, *The End of Liberalism: The Second Republic of the United States* (New York: W. W. Norton & Co., 1969).

31. Ibid., 43.

32. Ibid., 51.

33. Ibid., 63.

34. Richard N. Goodwin, "Perspective in Politics," *Los Angeles Times*, January 30, 1997, p. A9. 43. Higgs, Robert. *The Futility of Campaign Finance Reform.* The Independent Institute, 1997. https://www.independent.org/news/article.asp?id=221.

35. Andrew Bard Schmookler, "When Money Talks, Is It Free Speech? PACs Give Big Bucks to Buy Access and Influence," (Christian Science Monitor, November 10, 1997), p. 15.

36. Johnson, Joseph. *Cybercrime: number of breaches and records exposed 2005-2020.* 3 Mar. 2021, www.statista.com/statistics/273550/data-breaches-recorded-in-the-united-states-by-number-of-breaches-and-records-exposed/. Accessed 11 Nov. 2021.

37. Johnson, Joseph. *Number of U.S. data breaches 2013-2019, by industry.* 9 Mar. 2021, www.statista.com/statistics/273572/number-of-data-breaches-in-the-united-states-by-business/. Accessed 11 Nov. 2021.

38. Johnson, Joseph. *Average cost per data breach in the United States 2006-2020.* 25 Jan. 2021, www.statista.com/statistics/273575/average-organizational-cost-incurred-by-a-data-breach/. Accessed 11 Nov. 2021.

# Understanding the Essential Organization—Design and Dynamics

- **Unit 1:** The Anatomy of Public Organizations
- **Unit 2:** The Physiology of Public Organizations

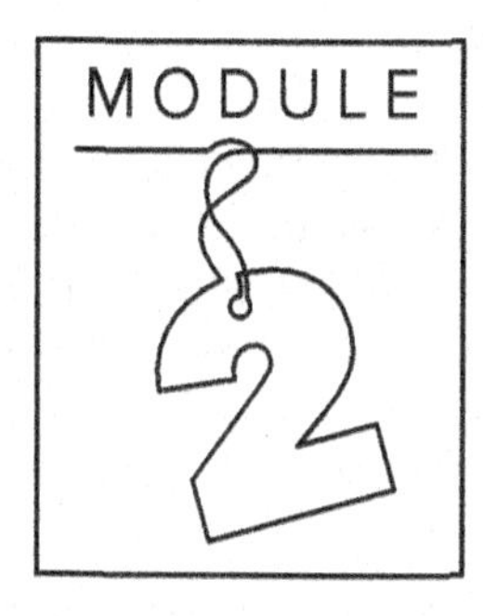


# UNIT 1: The Anatomy of Public Organizations

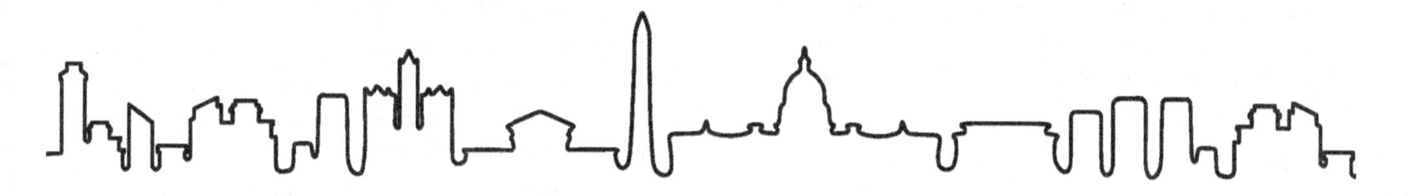

## The Anatomy of Public Organizations

Every public administrator works within an organizational framework. Effective administrators have a solid understanding of general organizational principles and the structure of their particular organization. This chapter examines key organizational principles that have a major impact on public administration.

The Merriam-Webster dictionary defines anatomy as the art of separating the parts of an organism in order to ascertain their position, relations, structure, and function.

The anatomy of U.S. public bureaucracy—its organizational framework or administrative structure—owes much of its development to the 1933–1945 era of the Depression, World War II, and Franklin D. Roosevelt's leadership skills during the New Deal. Since the 1990s, Republicans argued that the government support systems FDR created and nurtured had gotten out of control. Much of what FDR accomplished is thus now under attack. Many agencies in the federal bureaucracy that were created during the New Deal and recent past face privatization, consolidation, or elimination.

For Roosevelt, change was policy. "It is common sense to take a method and try it. If it fails, admit it frankly and try another. But above all try something," FDR said. Through the New Deal, Roosevelt built dams and brought electricity to millions, created farm subsidies and unemployment insurance, regulated a stock market gone out of control, set up a Social Security program for the elderly, and gave unions the right to organize. While many agencies no longer exist as they were created, other federal agencies and departments absorbed many functions in a greatly expanded government support or human services state.

## The Basis of Organization

The structures of most public organizations are rather complex. These complexities can be simplified, however, by taking a look at the fundamental principles of organization outlined by Luther Gulick, who classified organizations into four categories. These categories are based on an organization's raison d'être—the reason it was established. The categories are purpose, process, place, and clientele.[1]

### Purpose

Organizations established on the basis of purpose are oriented toward the accomplishment of specific tasks. Examples of organizations developed on this basis are school systems, fire departments, and the major branches of the military. These organizations engage in purpose-specific activities and seldom extend beyond their purpose.

### Process

A process organization is oriented not so much toward accomplishing specific goals but toward performing certain functions. From our understanding of the law as process, we might guess that a good example of such an agency is a city legal department or planning departments at the state and local levels. Process organizations concern themselves almost completely with the procedural aspects of administration.

### Place

Organizations under this heading serve particular locales. These agencies provide a variety of services to the people in a particular neighborhood, city, county, or other region.

### Clientele

Closely linked to place organizations, clientele organizations are a less common feature of our administrative landscape. These agencies serve particular groups of people, such as seniors, children, or people of a particular ethnic background. Today clientele organizations are often found serving specific groups of people and known as hospices; assisted care facilities; half-way or transitional housing for vocational, and drug and alcohol rehabilitation; group homes for persons with mental disabilities; and prisoner release programs.

Obviously, these categories overlap, and many organizations fall into more than one. Fire departments are not only established for the purpose of putting out fires but are also organized to serve particular geographic areas; yet purpose, not place, is the main reason for establishing a fire department. Most organizations are established not on the basis of just one of Gulick's categories, but through a combination of purpose, process, place, and clientele, regardless of which factor dominates.

Of the three branches of government, the executive, legislative, and judicial, the executive has the widest range of responsibilities. Through the power vested by the U.S. Constitution in the office of the President, the executive branch includes the Office of Management and Budget (OMB), National Security Council (NSC), and Council of Economic Advisers (CEA). OMB oversees administration of the federal budget. NSC advises the President on matters of national defense. CEA offers economic policy recommendations.

Each of the fifteen federal government departments administers programs that oversee an element of American life. The highest official of each cabinet department is a member of the president's cabinet. Each department is described here; **Table 2.1.1** lists the number of employees in each agency as of June 2021.

- **Education**: Provides scholarships, student loans, and aid to schools.
- **Housing and Urban Development (HUD)**: Funds public housing projects, enforces equal housing laws, and insures and finances mortgages.
- **State**: Oversees the nation's embassies and consulates, issues passports, monitors U.S. interests abroad, and represents the United States before international organizations.
- **Labor (DOL)**: Enforces laws guaranteeing fair pay, workplace safety, and equal job opportunity; administers unemployment insurance; regulates pension funds; and collects and analyzes economic data at the Bureau of Labor Statistics.
- **Energy (DOE)**: Coordinates the national use and provision of energy, oversees the production and disposal of nuclear weapons, and plans for future energy needs.
- **Commerce**: Forecasts the weather, charts the oceans, regulates patents and trademarks, conducts the census, compiles statistics, and promotes economic growth by encouraging international trade.
- **Transportation (DOT)**: Sets national transportation policy; operates the Coast Guard (USCG) except in time of war; plans and funds the construction of highways and mass transit systems; and regulates railroad, aviation, and maritime operations.
- **Interior**: Manages federal lands, including the national parks; runs hydroelectric power systems; and promotes conservation of natural resources.
- **Health and Human Services (HHS)**: Sponsors medical research, approves the use of new drugs and medical devices, runs the Public Health Service, and administers Medicare.
- **Treasury**: Regulates banks and other financial institutions, administers the public debt, prints currency, collects federal income taxes and carries out law enforcement in a wide range of areas, including counterfeiting, tax, and customs violations.

- **Agriculture (USDA)**: Promotes U.S. agriculture domestically and internationally and sets standards governing quality, quantity, and labeling of food sold in the United States.
- **Justice (DOJ)**: Enforces federal laws, prosecutes cases in federal courts, and runs federal prisons.
- **Homeland Security**: Works to prevent terrorist attacks within the United States, reduce vulnerability to terrorism, and minimize the damage from potential attacks and natural disasters. It also administers the country's immigration policies and oversees the National Guard.
- **Defense (DOD)**: Manages the military forces that protect the country and its interests, including the Departments of the Army, Navy, and Air Force, as well as a number of smaller agencies. The civilian workforce employed by the Department of Defense performs various support activities, such as payroll and public relations.
- **Veterans Affairs (VA)**: Administers programs to aid U.S. veterans and their families, runs the veterans' hospital system, and operates our national cemeteries.

Numerous independent agencies perform tasks that do not originate within the jurisdictions of executive departments or that are more efficiently executed by an autonomous agency. Some smaller but well-known independent agencies include the Peace Corps, Securities and Exchange Commission (SEC), and Federal Communications Commission (FCC). The majority of these agencies employ fewer than one thousand workers, and many count fewer than one hundred.

**Table 2.1.1 June 2021 Federal Executive Branch Cabinet Level Employment**

| DEPARYMENT/ AGENCY | # OF FULL-TIME POSITIONS |
|---|---|
| Education | 4,116 |
| Housing and Urban Development | 7,818 |
| State | 12,163 |
| Labor | 13,810 |
| Energy | 14,595 |
| Commerce | 50,907 |
| Transportation | 53,795 |
| Interior | 67,799 |
| Health and Human Services | 87,627 |
| Treasury | 95,922 |
| Agriculture | 93,809 |
| Justice | 117,390 |
| Homeland Security | 211,336 |
| Defense | 106,658 |
| Veterans Affairs | 426,014 |
| TOTAL | 1,363,759 |

*Source: Fedscope.opm.gov*

Examples of large independent agencies:

- **Social Security Administration (SSA)**: Operates various retirement and disability programs and Medicaid.
- **National Aeronautics and Space Administration (NASA)**: Oversees aviation research and conducts exploration and research beyond the Earth's atmosphere.
- **Environmental Protection Agency (EPA)**: Administers programs to control and reduce pollution of the nation's water, air, and land.
- **General Services Administrations (GSA)**: Manages and protects federal government property and records.
- **Tennessee Valley Authority (TVA)**: Operates the hydroelectric power system in the Tennessee River Valley.
- **Federal Deposit Insurance Corporation (FDIC)**: Maintains the stability of and public confidence in the nation's financial system by insuring deposits and promoting sound banking practices.

# THINK ABOUT IT!

**Local Government as Plural, Not Singular, Noun**

The concept, local government, incorporates more than cities. The term may include a county, a city, a school district and community college district—plus numerous specialized and politically independent entities whose purposes entail regional mass transit, waste-water treatment, firefighting, mosquito abatement, and flood control. Los Angeles County, for example, includes 88 cities.

Policymakers, periodically, get alarmed by the proliferation and complexity of local government. County-level commissions monitor annexations and formations of new cities and special districts. The effects of highly decentralized land-use powers on growth patterns concern policymakers. Community leaders debate regional reorganizations. Government fragmentation questions the responsiveness of coordinated government action. Cries of "wasteful duplication" and "local control" fail to probe the structure of local governance.

Partisan, policy, and system politics produces political fragmentation—or the geographic and functional division of power among local governments. Political fragmentation affects government services and land use regulation. Proliferation of local governments frustrates policy coordination of transportation, housing, and environmental protection initiatives. Government structures may separate fiscal needs from resources. Citizens become confused and dissensus emerges.

**Four distinct roles suggest differences in local government structure.**

**Service provision.** Local government is the primary provider of routine public services. Trash collection, fire protection, and public education are illustrations. Competitive economic theories function in tandem with political fragmentation. Fragmentation sorts citizens into "communities of interest." Similar tastes for services and tax levels result.

**Land use and economic development.** The so-called "police power" affords cities and counties the power to create zoning ordinances, rules for subdividing land, and building regulations. Partisan politics decide land-use patterns for constructing growth-supportive infrastructures, such as turnpike authorities; pipelines; water, sewer and utility services; and roads. Localities often regulate land use in their narrow self-interests, yet they may slight area-wide concerns. These powers are largely placed under the fifth amendment of the Constitution and fall into the area of eminent domain—or the uses of due process and just taking of property for public purposes.

**Equity.** Political fragmentation may separate fiscal resources from social needs. Equity distributes and redistributes life's chances. Separate taxing-and-spending jurisdictions may lead to service disparities. Unequal service distributions may reflect government fragmentation per se. Or different "tastes" for services may emerge from inequality. Redistributive policies attempt to rectify disparities among local governments.

**Representation.** Government fragmentation emphasizes effective political representations and accountability. Decision making close to home builds faith in government services. However, general purpose governments focus on more global budgeting. Overall taxing and spending levels are set. Tradeoffs are made between competing services. Community service demands competition between services shared by larger populations in an interconnected region.

*Source: Lewis, Paul G. Deep Roots: Local Government Structure in California,* *https://www.ppic.org/wp-content/uploads/content/pubs/report/R_998PLR.pdf.*


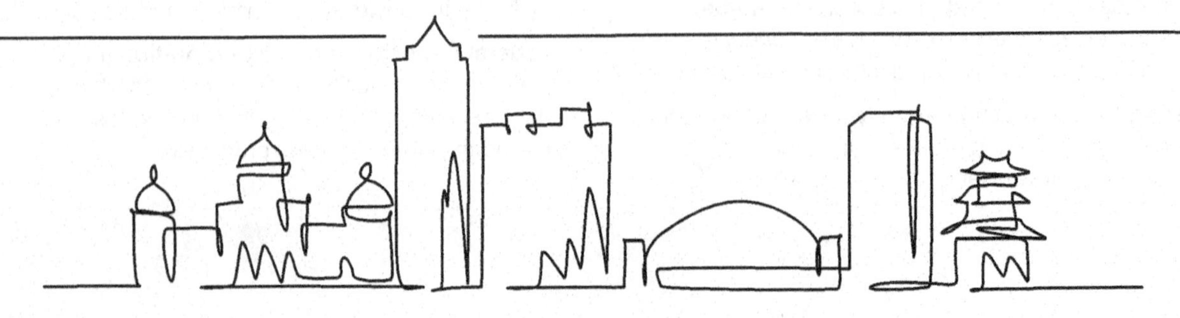

## Points about Pyramids

The organizational structure of most institutions is best thought of as a pyramid. The organization must delegate its work to a number of employees. To make sure that these employees do the work and to see that their efforts are coordinated, the organization appoints supervisors. These supervisors may be numerous enough that they, in turn, require supervisors. As a result, one or more levels of hierarchy tend to emerge in any sizable organization, with the number of persons at each level dwindling until the tip of a pyramid is reached. The pyramid model brings with it the concepts of unity of command, chain of command, and span of control.

Unity of command describes the exclusive relationship between those who follow orders and those who give them orders. No one can serve two masters. This maxim has held true for work organizations, particularly those operating under the bureaucratic norms of delegation, specialization, and accountability, and accounts for much of their success.

Requiring an individual or a group to respond to the orders of two or more superiors may produce conflict, confusion, and even chaos. If unity of command does not exist, conflict and confusion will not only characterize those being commanded but those doing the commanding. In other words, multiple superiors will not only confuse their employees or team members but also each other.

The unity of command principle may conflict with the methods of some boards and commissions. Such multiple-headed bodies are considered suitable only for semi-judicial organizations (such as regulatory commissions) or for certain policy-making or advisory functions. If an organization is administering a program, if it is doing things, then the reins of its authority should converge eventually into one pair of hands. Responsibility can then be pinpointed, and conflicting orders, internecine warfare, and a host of other organizational ills can be avoided.

Unity of command usually requires a chain of command, the second concept in the pyramid model. In any large organization, the person at the top cannot oversee all that is going on below; he or she needs others to help do this. Frequently, these helpers cannot supervise all those beneath them. As a result, several echelons of command may emerge, theoretically allowing commands to proceed downward in a neat, orderly flow. Unity of command means that the captain of A Company does not give orders to the soldiers of B Company. Within a chain of command, the battalion major does not give direct orders to soldiers from either company but works instead through their company commanders.

Even less structured organizations observe, to some degree, the same principle.

The college dean, if he or she has reason to be disturbed by the behavior of a particular professor, will usually first contact the professor's department chairperson before taking any direct action against the faculty member. In this way the chain of command at the university streamlines the administrative process.

A third concept linked to a pyramidal structure is span of control. Span of control refers to the number of units, whether individuals or groups, that any supervising unit must oversee. Unlike unity of command and chain of command, span of control does not constitute a principle of organization; instead, it serves as a frame of reference.

Put another way, span of control is not something that organizations ought to have, but something they do have. Usually, a government organization develops guidelines for span of control based on an organization's mission. A challenge exists in making sure that the number of subunits to be supervised is neither too many nor too few—to make sure that the supervisor's span of control is neither too great nor too small. Unfortunately, public administration provides no hard-and-fast criteria for determining such things, for the span of control (attention) varies by such factors as type of work performed, geographical dispersion, technical and professional qualities of the workforce. As with so many other questions concerning this capricious craft, the only intelligent answer is the highly unsatisfactory, "It all depends," for there is no optimal span of control number.

Public administrators in America have functioned with relatively narrow spans of control. It is rare to find a manager overseeing more than twelve employees or subunits, and it is not rare to find a manager overseeing as few as three or in short, the taller the pyramidal structure, the more layers of supervisory authority.

The tighter the span of control, the more intervening levels between top and bottom, increasing paperwork and procrastination. A tight span of control also leads to decisions made and policies formulated too far from the scene of action. It can lead to difficulties in acquiring and retaining the services of top-notch people in vitally important, but no longer top-rated, positions.

As with so much in public administration, span of control becomes a question of finding a proper balance for each situation. In finding this balance, we must assess the specific circumstances, keeping in mind that a gain achieved by moving in one direction may be offset by some losses.

These losses do not, however, necessarily cancel the gain. If an executive has multiple agencies under their tutelage, some consolidation is almost always needed, even at the expense of creating more administrative levels. However, every consolidation carries a price tag that we must be willing to pay if we wish to reap the benefits.

**Figure 2.1.1** illustrates how the principles of unity command, chain of command, and span of control need to be grounded in political compromise, consensus, and democratic participation.

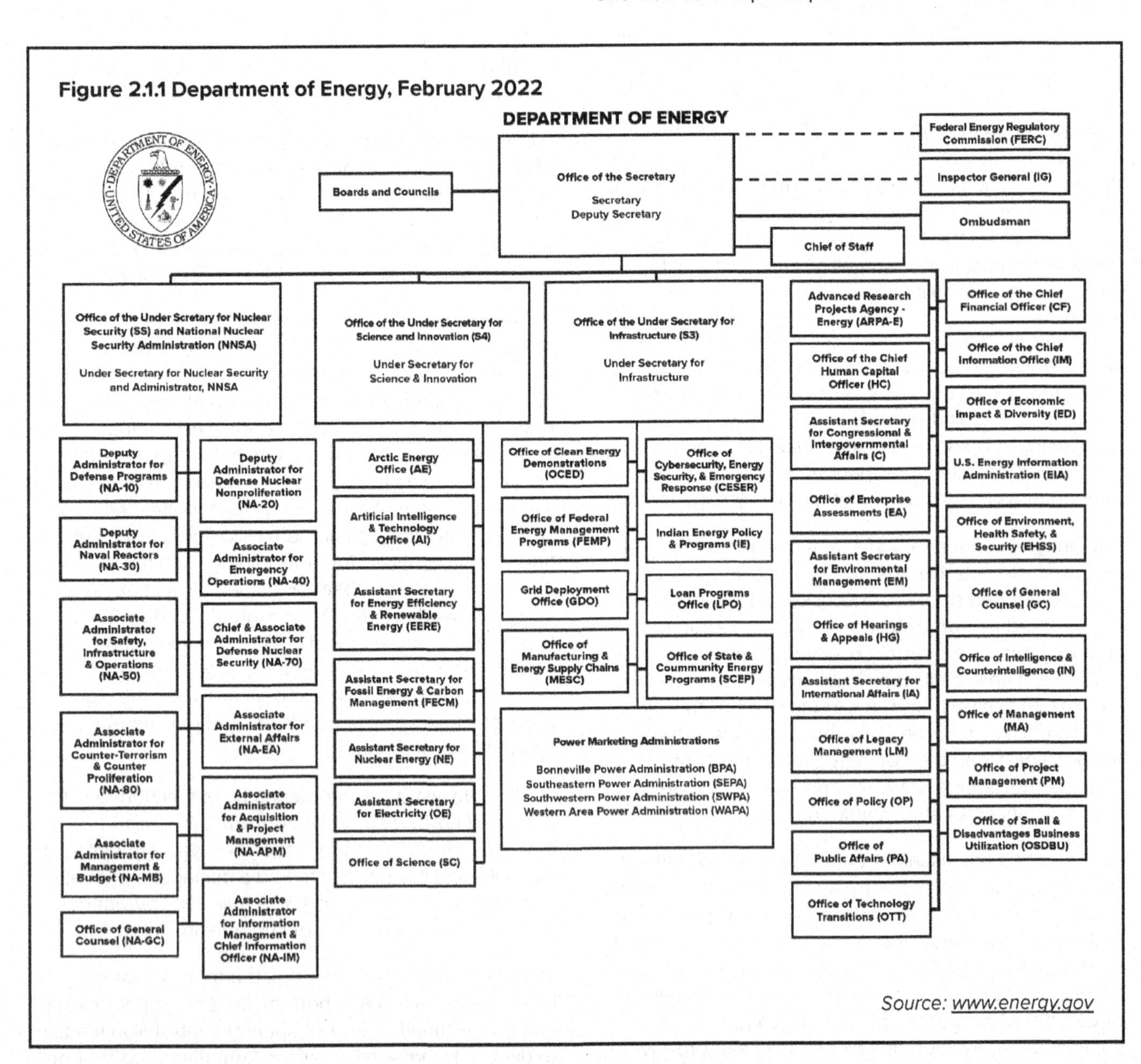


**Figure 2.1.1 Department of Energy, February 2022**

*Source:* [www.energy.gov](www.energy.gov)

## Line and Staff

The individuals working in the pyramid examples discussed earlier—U.S. Army companies and large state universities—are called line personnel. Another group of people to be considered are staff personnel.

While line personnel are primarily concerned with implementing policy, staff personnel are the working members of an organization who do not implement policy. Line agencies and employees are directly responsible for furthering an organization's goals. Staff employees are primarily concerned with assisting senior administrators in the determination of policy and the effective operation of the agency as such they work in departments dedicated to finance, accounting, and budgeting, human resources management, planning and development, and legal assistance.

Line people are generalists who occupy positions of authority in the organization and command implementation of the organization's operations. The Departments of Agriculture, Commerce, Defense, Education, Energy, Health and Human Services, Housing and Urban Development, Interior, Justice, Labor, State, Transportation, Treasury, Homeland Security and Veterans Affairs constitute the major line agencies of the federal government. These organizations administer clientele programs and deal directly with the public.

The United States federal government established the 15 federal executive departments in **Table 2.1.2** in the following order.

**Table 2.1.2 United States federal executive Departments (2021)**

| YEAR ESTABLISHED | DEPARTMENT |
|---|---|
| 1789 | State |
| 1789 | Treasury |
| 1849 | Interior |
| 1862 | Agriculture |
| 1870 | Justice |
| 1903 | Commerce |
| 1913 | Labor |
| 1947 | Defense |
| 1953 | Health and Human Services |
| 1965 | Housing and Urban Development |
| 1967 | Transportation |
| 1977 | Energy |
| 1979 | Education |
| 1989 | Veterans' Affairs |
| 2002 | Homeland Security |

Staff people are specialists who provide skills, knowledge, and expertise to line personnel. For example, staff personnel draw up job classifications, program computers, or provide legal services. These are the employees who are most accurately referred to as the "staff." Staff agencies aid the chief executive and line personnel in developing, evaluating, and implementing public policies. Within the Executive Office of the President of the United States, examples past and present include, Office of Management and Budget, Council of Economic Advisors, National Security Council, Office of Policy Development, Office of the U.S. Trade Representative, Council on Environmental Quality, and Office of Science and Technology Policy.

The essence of staff work is thought, fact-finding, and planning.[3] Staff units are usually formed on the basis of process. An organization's computer center, for example, is typically comprised of people engaged in a process while technically serving a variety of purposes, places, and clientele within the larger organization. In a school system, the computer center prepares attendance figures for principals, correlates statistics on children with learning disabilities for the director of special education, and pinpoints certain cost trends for the budgeting department. This last function illustrates that staff agencies may serve not only line departments, but also other staff units.

The pyramid serves as the "coat of arms" for bureaucratic organizations, and in its pure form, makes no provision for staff units and their personnel. Traditionally, staff units have played only a small and shadowy role in the structure of work organizations. The place they occupied was usually at the hands or feet of the organization's leader, providing advice and assistance. However, staff services and personnel have increased tremendously. They now occupy a greater place in an organization's structure, play a greater role in its activities, and consume a greater portion of its budget. In so doing, they provide the organization with new benefits and new problems.

Problems stem from the model pyramid's lack of provision for staff units. It is difficult, at times almost impossible, to establish the correct niche for staff within an organization's hierarchy. Staff people tend to be specialists whose expertise does not lend itself to a graded ranking except, possibly, within their own ranks. The authority of a line unit is fairly definite. Its personnel know which units are above them and which ones are below. The authority of a staff unit is, by contrast, much more nebulous and elusive. Such authority is determined by whatever need the line units have for the staff group at a particular time, the proficiency the staff can demonstrate in meeting this need, the administrative and political skills the staff demonstrates in its relationships with other units within the organization, and a variety of other factors.

Specialization tends to destroy hierarchy. The more the members of an organization are differentiated from each other in terms of separate, specific skills, the more difficult it becomes to position them on a hierarchical scale. Knowledge, in and of itself, knows no hierarchy.

There is no "higher" or "lower" knowledge. Thus, the increasing presence of staff personnel is disrupting many bureaucratic organizations as specialists, "technocrats," begin to dominate generalists in making agency policies. Staff people are undermining the cherished bureaucratic principles of unity of command, chain of command, and span of control.

Unity of command requires one channel of authority, but specialization creates several channels. The specialists, in one way or another, start giving orders relating to their areas of expertise. That these orders are not labeled as such and stem not from rank but from expertise does not fundamentally alter the situation. If the organization intends to use the energies and abilities of specialists, it must respond to what they say. To the extent that the specialists' capabilities are used, the authority of line personnel, particularly those in a supervisory capacity, is undermined.

The contrasting assignments of line (generalist) and staff (specialist) personnel generate a good deal of conflict and tension in organizations. At times, line people will complain that staff people are not sharing enough responsibility. More often, however, line personnel resent the intrusions of staff people. To line employees, the activities of staff personnel frequently seem more subversive than supportive.

To reduce the rivalry and rancor that may creep into line-staff relationships, organizations try to integrate the two as much as possible. They may make staff people spend time familiarizing themselves with line functions and line personnel, sometimes requiring staff personnel to perform some line functions for a time. They may recruit their staff people from the ranks of the line personnel, giving them special training for their new positions. Whatever is the case, successful line managers develop strong relationships with finance, budgeting, information technology, communication, and human resource management departments and their success is often gauged on whether the interactions are done on a collaborative and cooperative basis or based on competition or adversity. In short, the staff agencies can be your best ally or greatest nightmare.

There is no optimal organizational arrangement of unity of command, chain of command, span of control, and line and staff. These organizational principles vary from organization to organization and are based upon the most satisfactory way to serve the needs of clientele.

## Centralization and Decentralization

One issue that has bewildered public managers since the beginning of public organization is centralization. Arguments have been raised on the devolution affecting the balance between nation and state as states have undertaken policy reforms that work to their individual advantage at the expense of national interest. Devolution is perceived to be an attempt to simplify incentives for common interests. However, reforms should balance multiple interests within the framework of the larger government.[4] In early times, concern focused largely on how to achieve this, for even the simplest communication between headquarters and the field often took weeks, months, or, in a few instances, years. Egyptian pharaohs, Roman emperors, and Chinese mandarins spent a good deal of time wondering how to control and use the energies of "subordinates" in distant subunits. (Note: In modern language of management and organizational theory the terms "superior" and "subordinate" the language of hierarchy and inferiority is no longer commonly used. Instead, we use team members, people, employees, associates, leaders, managers, and supervisors.)

The emphasis has shifted. Now the number one concern often centers on how much centralization should be achieved. Centralization is no longer viewed as an unmixed blessing. Its opposite, decentralization, has become the watchword, if not the battle cry, of many theorists and practitioners involved in the administrative craft. Several movements throughout U.S. history have tried to downsize and decentralize government. Assaults on big government began with Thomas Jefferson and continued with the diverse group of Jacksonian Democrats, the states' rights movement, and the anti-statism movements of the twentieth century.[5]

The "citizen legislator" is a quaint vestige of early American democracy that continues to dominate our state government. A large majority of states have legislatures that meet part-time—some for as little as thirty days a year— and their members spend the rest of the time practicing law, tilling fields, or staffing shops as ordinary citizens. However, the federal government's desire to send power to the states is increasing these legislators' workload and making it tough for them to keep up.[6] Only months after Congress turned control of government support systems over to the states (devolution or load shedding), legislatures around the country began considering whether to hand off responsibility for the poor once again, this time to county and local governments.[7]

We have seen how decentralization has characterized our country's political system since its inception. While such political decentralization may facilitate and foster administrative decentralization, it does not necessarily ensure it—at least not in all instances.

Political decentralization calls for policies to be developed as much as possible at the lower levels (the "grass roots"). Administrative decentralization requires that the organizations charged with carrying out these policies allow their subunits a great deal of autonomy in interpreting and applying them. When a city institutes its own health program, political decentralization is at work. If at the same time the health department refuses to set up neighborhood centers or insists that even the centers' most minor decisions must be made at headquarters, the program is not administratively decentralized.

Centralization and decentralization are relative terms. Nearly every organization of any size and scope must, to some extent, decentralize, for once it sets up subunits, it must grant them some discretion in carrying out their functions. The question, therefore, becomes a matter of deciding how far this independent discretion should go. Many argue that it should be pushed to the maximum limits.

Decentralization, or its lack, is no abstract concept in public organizations. An organization's tasks, values, and organizational structures are related to unique political, administrative, and economic characteristics. And the structural arrangements of an organization are never value neutral. The locations of decisions affect an administrator's objectives and values. The perspectives of federal employees located in Washington are different from the perspectives of those implementing services in Peoria. As Miles' Law states, "Where you stand depends upon where you sit."

States respond to increased marginal expenditure costs and reduced federal aid. States may also have to overcome spending limits and short-term policy perspectives. State finance research should focus on state spending determinants, interactions with local governments, federal aid changes, discretionary tax changes, and whether budgets are structurally balanced.[8] With devolution it is believed that state governments will gain control of many social programs presently run by the federal government. Legislators and other state officials will finally have the flexibility to choose which programs will work best for their situation. Experts believe that no single pattern of government support systems and Medicaid reform will emerge. They also believe that reforms will evolve over time as states learn from their experience and that of other states.[9] As such, states are often called "laboratories of democracy," in which trial and error, experimentation, and demonstration projects and policies may be tries out and evaluated, prior to their more widespread implementation in other jurisdictions.

## THINK ABOUT IT!

**Change in the Nature of Work**

"A shift has been occurring in the nature of work—from individual to collaborative, from process-based to creative, from locally to globally influenced." —David Fik

A 21st century organization has characteristics that make it distinctively different from its 20th century counterparts, especial in terms of structure, organization design, reach (domestic versus global), resources, job expectations, and style (structured versus flexible). The changes listed below, in addition to others too numerous to mention here, demand that our organizations move from being simply resource driven bureaucracies, to performance, mission, and result-based enterprises. The scope of these changes is so transformative and fundamentally accepted that they require no further explanation or comment.

The movement from left brain to right brain activities in the workplace. Functions of the left brain: critical thinking, numbers, words (verbal), analysis, and sequence; right brain, color, intuition, imagination, creative thinking, images (non-verbal) and daydreaming.

Management is torn between the "bi-polar twins" involved in balancing work and family. Workplace flexibility (flex-time, flex-place, telecommuting, etc.) is now commonly found in organizations, although management continues to struggle with the increased employee autonomy, empowerment, and responsibility that these changes imply.

Movement toward the use of teams and understanding the nature of teamwork to accomplish specific goals. To accomplish teamwork, we need to understand the people who make up these collective enterprises, know how to motivate and evaluate team performance and productivity.

The existential question that must be asked over and over as we study public administration is: How do we build a culture that encourages cooperation, collaboration between the three sectors (public, private, nonprofit) and encourages a spirit of civic, social and political cohesiveness and solidarity, versus ones that disunites and dissipates our collective energies and will? Therefore, the issues of food insecurity, economic interdependencies, income and wealth chasms, environmental and ecological enhancements and protections, civil and human rights, and economic development, commitments to majority rule and minority protections based on constitutional principles serve as a good first step in our discussions in class, and since there are competing ideological views, those class discussions are sure to be in-depth and engaging.

Change is an imperative and therefore we must understand what factors are associated with initiating successful change and what are its many barriers, such as apathy, "old power," rigidity and fear of the unknown.

The structure of an organization affects the delivery of services to its clientele. This discussion continues today as organizations struggle with these competing leadership paradigms of management—"top down" leadership or bottom up leadership. The processes involved in these orientations are fundamentally different and are bifurcated by the concepts "controlling of..." or "listening to...."

Public organizations must mobilize resources to perpetuate themselves and their values. Decisions cannot be imposed from the top down if people in the subunits do not subscribe to the values and methods of implementing particular services. Administrators sometimes entertain reorganization plans to gain more control over the structure of the organization's policies and programs. Since any reorganization is implemented by the permanent bureaucracy, or the employees in the field accomplishing the everyday tasks of the organization, any decisions to decentralize or recentralize are of great consequence to the organization. These decisions should be made with sensitivity to the skills, knowledge, and expertise of field employees who must carry out the organization's values and purposes.[10]

The 1981-1988 Reagan administration saw centralization as the best way to put its values into action and to achieve its goals. For most of the 1980s, the administration "devised a strategy for centralizing unprecedented decision- making power in the White House."[11] The Reagan administration centralized the budgetary process, the federal appointments process, decision making in the executive branch, and control of federal regulation.[12]

In contrast, under the 1993-2001 Clinton administration the goal was to reinvent government and move from "resources based monopolistic" structures to a "performance/results based and mission driven" set of enterprises. A future president may take the opposite approach and opt for decentralization as a way of expressing a different set of values and achieving different goals. As these examples illustrate, two types of decentralization exist: political and administrative.[13]

# THINK ABOUT IT!

**Who Affects Security?**

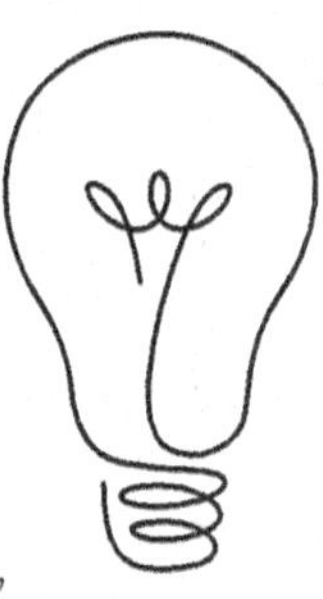

"A shift has been occurring in the nature of work—from individual to collaborative, from process-based to creative, from locally to globally influenced." —David Fik

In creating the Department of Homeland Security, 23 departments and agencies with unique responsibilities were consolidated into a single department. This was done with the intent to improve communication, coordination, and collaboration between the many organizations committed to the efforts of security of the nation. However, from an organization culture perspective, it has been difficult to fully integrate and accommodate nearly two dozen historically separate and independent cultures (values, mores, beliefs, traditions, and practices) that were developed often after decades of time.

## Political Decentralization

Political decentralization describes the allocation of powers among territories, which in this context refers to states, provinces, counties, municipalities, and other local governments. According to this approach to governing, general-purpose government officers residing in a specific territory coordinate public-sector activities, because they are in closer contact with citizens and may alter programs according to particular territorial priorities. Political decentralization advances few real restrictions for guidelines and control, keeping them at a minimum to allow for local discretion. The territories, or subunits, possess considerable power, coordinating and reshaping resources coming into their geographic areas to meet local needs. Manifestly parochial and unable to formulate and act on national goals, politically decentralized systems experience difficulty "vertically" integrating a diverse set of governmental activities. The transfer of political power from nation to state to community constitutes a vertical pass-through of influence at each level. How is this vertical pass-through frustrated in a decentralized system?

Issues such as equal opportunity, the environment, and health and occupational safety illustrate the barriers to vertical pass-through that the parochialism of local jurisdictions poses. Congress may, for example, impose affirmative action criteria for implementing equal opportunity goals for every state in the union. If local groups of citizens are opposed to civil rights, however, equal opportunity policies may be frustrated.

Likewise, when administrative specialists in the Environmental Protection Agency (EPA) interpret U.S. environmental statutes to mean that private industry must control its waste emissions, EPA field officials may be frustrated in their efforts to enforce these laws if a community values the economic status of that industry more than clean air or water. If occupational safety is a concern of federal officers but not of local government, industry, and labor leaders, then Congress and the Occupational Safety and Health Administration may be wasting their time attempting to convince local residents otherwise. Groups of citizens in every political jurisdiction must be voluntarily committed whether in tax collection or environmental protection to the goals of the organization, at least in some fashion, for procedures and processes to be effective in implementing these goals. Although coercion, legal sanctions, and legal penalties may be used to achieve compliance, nothing succeeds as well as voluntary compliance when dealing with the IRS, OSHA, EEOC, or other enforcement and regulatory agencies.

## Administrative Decentralization

Administrative decentralization occurs when a public organization delegates powers to subordinate levels within the same department or agency. The delegating authority may revise or retract such delegations at will. The central office of a bureaucracy in Washington may transfer federal government functions to regional or state offices, for example.

Whereas political decentralization pertains to powers allocated among geographic areas, administrative decentralization emphasizes functions, or specialties, and lines of authority for implementing agency functions. Functional and professional specialties of the central office bureaus and agencies are held in high regard in the field offices.

Politically decentralized jurisdictions grapple with "vertical" integration of governmental activities; administratively decentralized systems experience difficulties with "horizontal" integration of governmental activities. While a city might relate to a vertical hierarchy of state and federal governments for policy determination in political decentralization, federal administrators might horizontally coordinate the activities of several agencies within the same geographic area in an example of administrative decentralization. In such operations, problems are often addressed in a fragmented manner with specialists (staff) dominating the narrowly focused programs, and generalists (line) concerned for the whole project and guidelines emanating from the central office.

For example, the issue of civil rights concerns several federal departments and agencies; specific policies need horizontal coordination for implementation at the grassroots level. Departments challenged to coordinate civil rights regulations based upon the administrative discretion of bureaucrats include the Departments of Commerce, Education, Health and Human Services, Housing and Urban Development, Justice, Labor, and Transportation. Independent agencies also involved include the Commission on Civil Rights, the Equal Employment Opportunity Commission, and the Small Business Administration. The line officials of these departments and agencies could be in agreement on general purposes, desiring to implement civil rights statutes; however, the more narrowly focused specialists within each bureaucracy may disagree on the specifics.

## Geographic Area Versus Administrative Function

Decentralization has its proponents in every political camp. Suspicion of the dangers inherent in a strong, centralized government dates back beyond the American Revolution. Participation, access, and responsiveness are characteristics of decentralized systems that in principle promote flexibility and democracy within federal organizations at the grass roots. By allowing flexibility within federal guidelines, political decentralization helps state and city officials to meet the needs of their constituents. Rigid functional categories of administratively decentralized systems restrict the options of leaders representing general-purpose governments.

Students of political decentralization argue that governors and mayors are better able than nonelected bureaucrats to allocate available resources effectively according to local priorities. But cogent arguments exist against political decentralization as well. Local jurisdictions may be fragmented and ineffective; states sometimes refuse to grant sufficient resources for local bureaucracies to implement functions in a professional and effective manner. Accusations of unprofessional behavior and political graft undermine citizens' confidence in the legitimacy of local governments. Regional and national concerns may be overlooked, ignored by smaller jurisdictions, or may be unmanageable for them.

Conflicts between political and administrative decentralization models pit the values and priorities of geographic area (Peoria) against administrative function (Washington). Local partisans champion the political will of the former; national leaders insist upon the dominance of the latter. A balance between the extremes usually results. The vertical and horizontal mixing of political and administrative decentralization illustrates that values, tasks, and organizational structure interrelate in an effective organization.

However, centralization of functions at the state level may promote more uniform policies, resulting in certain economies of scale, and may eliminate the impact of local fiscal disparities on the quality and cost of services. The ebb and flow of centralizing and decentralizing decisions in individual states is constant.

Decisions to centralize or decentralize public organizations cannot, therefore, be divorced from values, tasks, and organizational structure. An appropriate organizational design facilitates an administrator's values and objectives; an inappropriate organizational structure frustrates his or her purposes.

A variety of political, administrative, and economic characteristics typify public program functions. As new values and technologies emerge, organizational objectives change; new technologies affect community values. Issues affecting governmental centralization and decentralization include political, administrative, economic, and technological factors that may point the agency in conflicting directions as it attempts to integrate its values, tasks, and organizational structure into an effective organization.

*An appropriate organizational design facilitates an administrator's values and objectives; an inappropriate organizatioinal structure frustrates his or her purposes.*

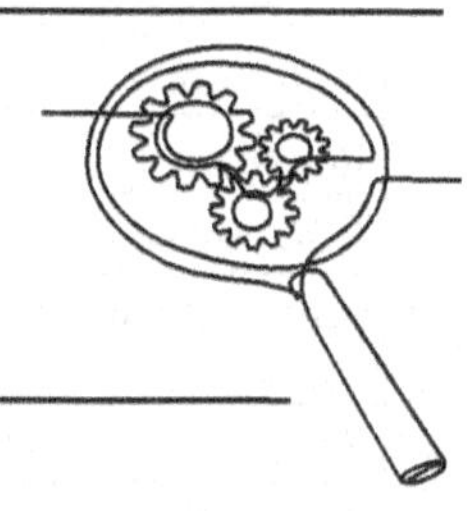

The enduring conflict over which level of government is closest and therefore most responsive to the citizens is never clearly conceptualized and argued. A Google search of government services in your area will reveal many local municipal and county agencies providing a myriad of essential functions as well as a large number of equally important services provided by either the state or federal level of government in the local community.

Structural arrangements selected for implementing a task directly affect the success administrators enjoy in achieving their objectives and values. Decentralization moves government closer to citizens, offering elected officials and voters opportunities to witness more closely the programmatic and fiscal consequences of their decisions. Decentralization also gives decision makers the flexibility to meet local conditions.

The many political and administrative issues discussed here are central to Gaebler and Osborne's study and recommendations found in the *Reinventing Government: How the Entrepreneurial Spirit is Transforming the Public Sector.*[14] In their discussion of things organizational, they visualized a new paradigm shift within the context of a domestic change in the United States, especially with the blossoming of the global economy. The competing organizational and administrative models were labeled alternately as the capital resource model (RM) and the performance model (PM). Correspondingly, the RM may be called the bureaucratic model and the PM is labeled the entrepreneurial model.

Osborne and Gaebler indicated that U.S. government organizations should transition away from the bureaucratic model toward the performance model that focused on creativity, employee empowerment, improvement of customer services, and performance (outcomes or results). In brief, the various models can be efficiently summarized by listing of key words and concepts which characterize the essential elements of these competing models as shown in **Table 2.1.3** below.

**Table 2.1.3 Resource and Performance Model Examples.**

| RESOURCE MODEL (RM) | PERFORMANCE MODEL (PM) |
|---|---|
| Bureaucratic | Entrepreneurial |
| Monopolistic | Debureaucratized |
| Agency centered | Customer centered |
| Accountability oriented | Proactive/anticipatory |
| Serving customers | Flexible |
| Reactive | Empowering customers/citizens |
| Rigid | Competitive |
| Slow moving | Market-driven |
| Inefficient | Fast moving |
| Impersonal | Efficient |
| Risk aversion | Personal |
| Rule and regulation driven | Relevant |
| Spending centers | Government as "steerer" |
| Government as "rower" | Earning centers |
| Centralized | Risk oriented |
| Pyramidal structures | Goals and mission driven |
| | Decentralized |
| | Flattened structures |

*Source: C. Kenneth Meyer*

In summation, if governmental processes, structures, and policies were to undergo this prescribed paradigmatic shift from being monopolistic to competitive and market-driven, from central to decentralized administrative arrangements, and from being agency-centric to customer-focused, alternative service delivery systems would need to be expanded such as the use of quasi-public corporations, franchising, public- private partnerships, vouchers, equity investments, impact fees, co-production, and Quid Pro Quos. Of course, traditional service delivery mechanisms that we have grown accustomed to using would also, when appropriate, be used such as: licensing, subsidies, tax policy, contracting, grants, and deregulation.

In a dynamic society espousing democracy and capitalism, we may ask: an effective organization for whom, what, when, where, and how?

## The Craft and Political Culture

Many are claiming that the United States is in the midst of a culture war over moral values and lifestyles.[15] Therefore, an understanding of culture is of great value to public administrators. To recognize the expectations and guidelines for professional behavior in one's culture is to promote understanding of the organization.

The culture of an organization provides guidelines for member behavior and performance. For example, the composition of the class is one feature of academic culture. The size of the class or languages spoken influences the type and number of assignments professors may require. If the number of participants in your class reaches into the hundreds, you may assume that your professor will emphasize short-answer examinations instead of essays. However, the culture of small classes allows your professor to be more personal in their approach to teaching and gives the professor more flexibility for evaluating your writing skills and critical thinking abilities. An understanding of classroom culture can help you steer toward classes where you are likely to perform best.

For our purposes, culture is defined as "that complex whole which includes knowledge, belief, art, morals, law, custom, and any other capabilities and habits acquired by [a person] as a member of society."[16] An awareness of culture is crucial for understanding the development, implementation, and evaluation of public administration.

Culture, or ways of life common to a society, government organization, or interest group, includes the ideal and the real. Ideal cultural patterns focus on what citizens do or say if they adhere completely too recognized cultural standards. Real behavioral patterns refer to actual citizen observations and behaviors. Various aspects of culture, such as religious rituals, work habits, beliefs, ideologies, and marriage relationships, relate to and affect one another.

Culture may be divided according to:

- Technology, or the ways in which people create and use tools and other material artifacts
- Economics, or the patterns of behaving relative to the production, distribution, and consumption of goods and services
- Social organization, or characteristic relations among individuals within a society, including the division of labor, the social and political organization, and the relationship between a society and other societies
- Religion, or ways of life relative to the human concern for the unknown
- Symbolism, or systems of symbols (such as language, art, music, and literature) used to acquire, order, and transfer knowledge[17]

The nature of our organized society and developments in the history of public administration underscore the importance of political and bureaucratic culture in the public administration environment. Partisan, policy, and system politics operate within a larger framework of political culture. Political culture, according to Daniel Elazár, is "the particular pattern of orientation to political action in which each political system is embedded."[18]

Culture puts limits on individuals in organizational settings. An organization is a subculture. For example, your public administration class is a subculture of your department, which is a subculture of a larger academic unit— usually a college of humanities, a subculture of the university or college. An understanding of the concept of culture is vital because we must recognize that an organization's members or employees are not free agents in any society.

Any organization is part of a larger social system. At least indirectly, its employees are thus subject to a larger set of values. Certain cultural patterns of conduct and belief can be found in any organization. The culture of an organization reflects a consensus of the particular values of that organization, but no organization can be isolated from its cultural environment.[19]

An understanding of culture can provide an advance indication of how people will act in a situation. A keenly developed sensitivity to culture can also be a substitute for experience. If you expect to climb the ladder of managerial success, pay close attention to your organization's culture. Traditions, customs, and patterned modes of behavior run through organizations. If you understand such structuring influences, you may even be able to facilitate changes in the organization.

According to J. Steven Ott, there are three levels of organizational culture and their interaction (**Figure 2.1.2** on the following page).[20] Level 1A involves artifacts, including both technology and art. Level 1B entails patterns of behavior, including familiar management tasks, visible and audible behavior, and norms. Level 2 focuses on values, whether testable in the physical environment or only by social consensus. Level 3 comprises basic assumptions regarding relationship to the environment; the nature of reality, time, and space; the essence of human nature; the nature of human activity; and the nature of human relationships.

On your college or university campus, examples of artifacts (Level 1A) are abundant. The administration building, main library, health center, basketball arena, football stadium, and parking garage all qualify. The technology of the shuttle bus that circulates to and from the dorms and classroom buildings and the artwork of plant life maintained by the grounds keepers also illustrate organizational culture Level 1A.

Certain norms of deportment are expected of students and faculty. Visible and audible expected behavior patterns include arriving at class on time. Familiar management tasks comprise daily routines for college classroom productivity and performance. These types of behaviors illustrate Level 1B.

Level 2 includes values that are testable in the physical environment and by social consensus, providing greater levels of awareness about organizational culture. The classroom limits or promotes effective exchanges between learners and professor. The heating or cooling systems may malfunction, the lighting may be poor, the acoustics may be weird, the chairs may have splinters in them, or the roof may leak. The physical environment of the classroom contributes to the culture of the academic exercise.

**Figure 2.1.2 Levels of Organizational Culture and Their Interaction**

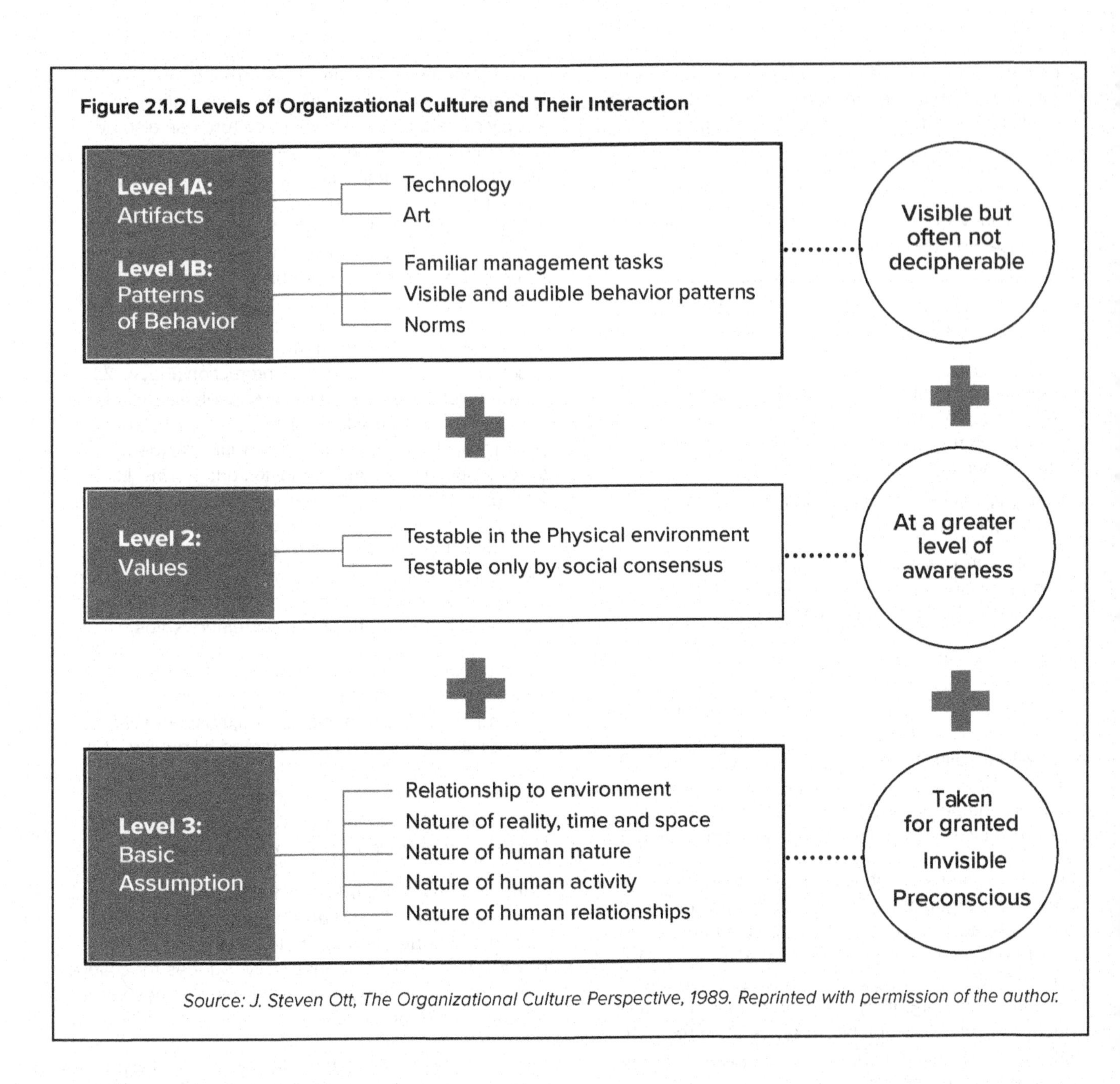


*Source: J. Steven Ott, The Organizational Culture Perspective, 1989. Reprinted with permission of the author.*

Level 3 examines the relationships of students to their cultural environment. The components of culture are material and nonmaterial. As **Figure 2.1.2** shows, the basic assumptions of Level 3 are often invisible and outside of consciousness.

Physical layout and organizational techniques are illustrations of material culture. Both contribute to the environment of public administration by focusing on the interaction between habitat and culture and by emphasizing how and why certain actions occur.

As learners attend different classes, they move from one classroom culture to another. In chemistry, a chart showing the elements is part of the material culture. In biology, a skeleton hangs for the professor's demonstration to students. In architecture, drawing boards are a common feature of material culture.

Not all culture is observable in the same way as material culture. Nonmaterial culture includes beliefs, systems of communications, and modes of conduct. Rituals, taboos, and jargon are modes of conduct that influence important aspects of nonmaterial culture. All organizations follow these prescribed formulas when employees act in ritualistic unison, observe a system of taboos, or speak in a peculiar jargon. One of the rituals of college classes is to arrive on time; cheating on examinations is taboo. Public administrators communicate in an "alphabet soup" jargon of acronyms for departments, agencies, and programs.

Material and nonmaterial culture may conflict if organization members confuse patterns of conduct with changes occurring in the world outside the organization. In other words, your nonmaterial value system, or beliefs, may not line up with the realities of the material world, which can result in cultural lag. Our organized society is constantly changing. Our values and preferences, however, tend to remain the same. The challenge is to respond appropriately to the changes in society without altering core values.

them. Political competition focuses on winning office to reap tangible rewards. Government is viewed as a marketplace, and economic development is favored. The appropriate spheres of activity are largely economic. Bureaucracy is viewed ambivalently. A loosely implemented type of merit system is favored. Indiana, Nevada, New Jersey, and Pennsylvania are states that reflect the individualistic political culture.

**Moralistic**. In a moralistic political culture, the practice of politics is viewed as healthy and as every citizen's responsibility. Everyone can participate. Political parties are vehicles to attain goals believed to be in the public interest. Party cohesiveness is subordinate to principles and issues. Competition is over issues, not parties. Political orientation focuses on winning office to implement policies. Government in a moralistic system is viewed as a commonwealth, answering directly for the general welfare and common good of the people. Appropriate

*Material and nonmaterial culture may conflict if organizational members confuse patterns of conduct with changes occuring in the world outside the organization.*

spheres of activity include any area that will enhance the community through nongovernmental action. New programs are initiated without public pressure if they are believed to be in the public interest. Bureaucracy is viewed positively, bringing desirable political neutrality. A strong merit system is favored. Colorado, Michigan, Minnesota, North Dakota, Oregon, Utah, Vermont, and Wisconsin reflect the moralistic political culture.

Material and nonmaterial bureaucratic cultures reflect a larger political culture. Political culture, as Elazár notes, includes perceptions held by the general public and politicians concerning the nature of politics and the perceived role of government in society.

A statewide political culture gives citizens a framework for what to expect from government and for how they perceive officeholders, bureaucrats, and campaign workers.

Political culture outlines the boundaries and practices of citizens, politicians, and public officials. Elazár carves out three types of political culture in the United States and describes the relation of bureaucracy to each type. The three types of political culture are individualistic, moralistic, and traditionalistic.

**Individualistic**. In this type of political culture, politics is viewed as dirty. Only professionals participate in politics, and parties dole out favors and responsibilities among them. Party cohesiveness is strong; competition arises between parties, not over issues. New programs are not to be initiated unless public opinion demands

**Traditionalistic**. Politics is viewed as a privilege in which only those with legitimate claim to office should participate. Participation in politics is limited to the appropriate elite. Political parties serve as vehicles to recruit people for public offices not desired by established power holders. Party cohesiveness depends upon family and social ties and is highly personal. Competition is between the elite-dominated factions within a dominant party. The orientation to politics depends upon the political values of the elite. Government is viewed as a means of maintaining the existing order. Appropriate spheres of activity are those that maintain traditional patterns. New programs are initiated if the program serves in the interest of the governing elite. Bureaucracy is viewed negatively, as it depersonalizes government. Merit should be controlled by the political elite, so no merit system is favored. Mississippi, South Carolina, Tennessee, and Virginia are states reflecting the traditionalistic political culture.

Some states fall into more than one type of political culture. Those states that are mainly moralistic political cultures yet also have individualistic traits are California, Iowa, Kansas, Montana, New Hampshire, South Dakota, and Washington.

States that are mainly individualistic but have moralistic traits as well are Connecticut, Illinois, Massachusetts, Nebraska, New York, Ohio, and Rhode Island.

States that are individualistic yet traditional are Delaware, Hawaii, Maryland, and Missouri. Those that are traditionalistic yet individualistic are Alabama, Arkansas, Florida, Georgia, Kentucky, Louisiana, New Mexico, Oklahoma, Texas, and West Virginia. States that are traditionalistic yet moralistic are Arizona and North Carolina.[21]

Political culture, then, can be said to encompass a state's orientation to political action. Culture includes knowledge, belief, art, morals, law, customs, capabilities, and habits institutionalized within an organization's environment. Material culture is observable, focuses on relationships of people distributed in space, and includes tools and techniques for fulfilling organizational purposes. Nonmaterial culture is not so obvious because it incorporates belief systems and patterns of conduct. No organization can be isolated from its cultural environment. This means the bureaucratic culture of the government organizations in a particular state cannot be divorced from that state's political culture.

When one examines various aspects of public or government organization, one must look beyond mere facts and seek out factors that define reality or the culture of government, including:

1. The history of government, or how it developed;
2. The role of government as perceived by members of society;
3. The structures and processes considered proper to government; and
4. The values, mores, and habits of the primary people, especially the elected and appointed officials and the bureaucrats working beneath those officials.[22]

Culture affects the everyday operations of a government organization. Culture resides in the ideas, values, norms, rituals, and beliefs of socially constructed realities, or organizations. Patterns of belief or shared meaning cause organizations to adopt their own ways of perceiving problems and resolving them.[23] The dynamics of culture incorporate traditions, perceptions, attitudes, assumptions, perspectives, values, and behaviors.

The next step in understanding the craft of public administration is to examine some key theories about organizations. That is the focus of the next chapter.

## ESSENTIAL VIEWS:

### ACADEMICS/PRACTITIONERS AT THE STREET LEVEL

**Facts Are Stubborn Things**
By Anna Marie Schuh

Friction between federal government career and political managers is normal. This occurs because political and appointed officials bring different perspectives to government service. However, the friction during the Donald Trump administration was unusually turbulent because the difference was over facts, not perspective.

Understanding the context of career employment is necessary to understanding the friction. Career federal employees take an oath to support the Constitution. Their loyalty is to the Constitution, not a person or political party. Career employees see their loyalty to the Constitution operationalized through their focus on providing the best technical expertise to the problem. Career employees typically leave their political perspectives at home and only bring their technical perspective to the workplace. Political leadership can choose to accept the technical recommendations or not. Normally, there has been a bright line between the technical recommendation and the political decision. Career employees are not pressed to alter their technical perspective to fit political needs. The available technical decision, untainted by political considerations, allows the American citizen to evaluate the quality of the political choice.

During the Trump administration, this bright line dissolved. For example, in a 2018 Union of Concerned Scientists survey of 16 federal agencies, 50 percent of scientists identified political considerations as barriers to science-based decisions. In the same survey, 70 percent of Environmental Protection Agency scientists indicated that political appointees had inappropriately affected decisions. In 2019 the National Oceanic and Atmospheric Administration chided the Weather Service because of an accurate hurricane assessment inconsistent with a misstatement by President Trump.

The friction between facts and politics is highlighted by the Trump administration's handling of the pandemic. In April 2020, Dr. Rick Bright was sidelined from director of the Biomedical Advanced Research and Development Authority because he refused to support chloroquine and hydroxychloroquine as a COVID-19 cure. President Trump had touted the drug initially approved by the Federal Drug Administration for emergency use and subsequently revoked because of serious side effects. In May 2020, the Trump administration bypassed the Center for Disease Control guidance on reopening state economies because the administration wanted states to reopen more quickly. In the summer of 2020, respected immunologist

Dr. Anthony Fauci was sidelined because his warnings about the pandemic were inconsistent with President Trump's view.

In a Partnership for Public Service and Princeton University survey more than 4 in 10 federal executives observed that mission delivery problems related to inadequate workforces and involved "political pressure." Most seriously, the Trump administration attempted to force civil service expertise to conform to the President's political perspective through an Executive Order turning high level technical positions into at will political employment which would make technical employees more responsive to political perspectives.

Still, facts and evidence eventually prevail over political posturing. With respect to pandemic mask wearing, in an August 2020 survey 85 percent of Americans said that they regularly wore masks in stores despite President Trump's mocking of mask wearing. In the words of President John Adams: "Facts are stubborn things."

*Source: Adapted from Anna Marie Schuh, "Facts are Stubborn Things" PA Times Online, November 15, 2020.*

# THINK ABOUT IT!

**Thirty (30) Rules for Personal Survival in Bureaucratic Organizations and Hierarchical Living**

Which rules reinforce conformity and which rules produce dysfunctional behavior? You be the judge.

| | |
|---|---|
| • Don't go against the grain | • Show up and stay awake |
| • Don't try to swim upstream | • Nice guys finish last |
| • Don't rock the boat or make waves | • Speak up or shut-up |
| • When uncertain, mumble | • Never volunteer for anything |
| • The nail that stands out gets hammered | • Don't commit to a decision before you must |
| • Don't take it personally | • Never say no! Rather, say thank you for the advice |
| • Don't get caught | • The squeaky wheel gets the grease |
| • Information is power, use it sparingly | • Nod with acceptance and keep your powder dry |
| • Better to scheme than to plan | • Information is power, share it sparingly! |
| • CYA or cover your assets | • An action passed is an action completed |
| • Don't dig up old bones | • Organizations have long memories |
| • Never try to understand | • Don't be an outlier |
| • Don't be a hero | • Don't jump the chain |
| • Stay low and zig-zag | • Don't be smarter than your boss |
| • Feed the monkey | • You must be flexible to avoid getting bent out of shape. |
| • Admit nothing, deny everything, and make counter-allegations | |

## Summary

- The anatomy of public bureaucracy is its organizational framework or administrative structure.
- Purpose, process, place, and clientele explain why an organization was established.
- Of the three branches of government, the executive, legislative, and judicial, the executive has the widest range of responsibilities.
- Principles for building a new agency are to keep it flat, focus on performance, and prepare for quasi-government status.
- Unity of command shows the relationship between those who order and those who follow orders. Unity of command usually requires a chain of command, because in any large bureaucracy, the person at the top cannot oversee all that is going on below. Span of control refers to the number of units— individuals or groups— that any supervising unit must oversee.
- Staff personnel are specialists who provide skills, knowledge, and expertise to line personnel. Staff functions to provide planning, fact finding, and support for line executives.
- Staff units in the Executive Office of the President include the White House Office, Council of Economic Advisers, Office of the U.S. Trade Representative, Office of Management and Budget, National Security Council, Council on Environmental Quality, Office of Policy Development, and Office of Science and Technology Policy.
- Line personnel are primarily concerned with developing, implementing, and evaluating policy. Line administrators are generalists. They legitimize authority and are in command. Line employees are directly responsible for furthering an organization's goals. Staff and line employees sometimes come into conflict. This should come as no surprise because their goals and functions are inherently different.
- Line departments in the federal government include Agriculture, Commerce, Defense, Education, Energy, Health and Human Services, Homeland Security, Housing and Urban Development, Interior, Justice, Labor, State, Transportation, Treasury, and Veterans Affairs.
- Decentralization occurs when an organization delegates powers to subordinate levels within the same department or agency. Political decentralization allocates power among states, counties, cities, and other local governments. Decisions to centralize or decentralize cannot be divorced from the values, tasks, and structure of an organization. Americans seem to agree that governmental power should be shifted to the states. However, a 10 percent increase in efficiency as a result of state control would reduce government costs by less than 0.5 percent.
- Political culture consists of the pattern of political action within a political system. Any organization is part of a larger social system. Indirectly, an organization's employees are therefore subject to a larger social system. Its employees are also subject, indirectly, to a larger set of values. No organization can be isolated from its cultural environment.
- Physical layout, organizational techniques, and technology illustrate material culture. Beliefs, systems of communication, and modes of conduct illustrate nonmaterial culture. Our nonmaterial values or beliefs may not line up with the realities of the material world, which can result in cultural lag.
- Corruption and scandal signify moral unsoundness. Corruption denotes legal violations, or the breaking of laws. Scandal simply offends moral values. Scandal surrounding sexual immorality may be emblematic of personal lies. Poverty, racism, economic disparity, lowering of education standards, and social welfare policies may be symbolic of institutional lies.
- Culture may be divided according to technology, economics, social organization, religion, and symbolism.

## Videos, Films and Talks

Please visit *The Craft of Public Administration* at www.millenniumhrmpress.com for up-to-date videos, films, talks, readings, and additional class resources.

Future of Work: The Workforce I The Future of Work After COVID-19
https://www.youtube.com/watch?v=mMeci_y-Jzg

Future of Work
https://www.pbs.org/show/future-work/

## Suggested Readings

**Groupthink**
https://www.psychologytoday.com/us/basics/groupthink

**The Online Sourcebook on Decentralization and Local Development**
https://resources.platform.coop/resources/the-online-sourcebook-on-decentralization-and-local-development/

**The Five Core Values of Public Administration**
https://www.govloop.com/community/blog/the-five-core-values-of-public-administration/#:~:text=These%20values%20are%20also%20a,ethics%2C%20professionalism%2C%20and%20leadership

**Four Tips for Mission and Values Statements in Local Government**
https://icma.org/blog-posts/four-tips-mission-and-values-statements-local-government

**World Development Report 2019: The Changing Nature of Work**
https://www.worldbank.org/en/publication/wdr2019

**The Future of Work in Government**
https://www2.deloitte.com/us/en/insights/industry/public-sector/future-of-work-in-government.html

## Notes

1. Luther Gulick and L. Urwick, *Papers on the Science of Administration* (New York: Institute of Public Administration, 1937), p. 15.
2. Barbara J. Saffir, "Evolution of Cabinet," *Washington Post*, February 9, 1993, p. A15.
3. John M. Pfiffner and Frank P. Sherwood, *Administrative Organization* (Englewood Cliffs, NJ: Prentice- Hall, 1960), pp. 170–188.
4. John D. Donahue, "The Devil in Devolution," *The American Prospect* 8, no. 32 (May–June 1997): 42–48.
5. Mary O. Furner, "Downsizing Government: A Historical Perspective," *USA Today* 126, no. 2630 (November 1997): 56–58.
6. Dana Milbank, *Wall Street Journal*, January 8, 1997, p. A1.
7. Judith Havemann, "After Getting Responsibility for Welfare, States May Pass It Down," *Washington Post*, January 28, 1997, p. A1.
8. Steven D. Gold, "Issues Raised by the New Federalism," *National Tax Journal* 49, no. 2 (June 1996): 273–287.

9. Hal Hovey, "The Challenges of Flexibility," *State Legislatures* 22, no. 1 (January 1996): 14–19.

10. David O. Porter and Eugene A. Olsen, "Some Critical Issues in Government Centralization and Decentralization," *Public Administration Review* 36, no. 1 (January/February 1976): 72–84.

11. Harold Seidman and Robert Gilmour, *Politics, Position, and Power: From the Positive to the Regulatory State*, 4th ed. (New York: Oxford University Press, 1986), p. 127.

12. .Ibid.

13. Herbert Kaufman, "Administrative Decentralization and Political Power," *Public Administration Review* 29 (January/February 1969): 3–15.

14. David Osborne, Ted Gaebler, "*Reinventing Government: How the Entrepreneurial Spirit is Transforming the Public Sector,*" (New York, Addison-Wesley Publishing Company, 1992).

15. See Rhys H. Williams, "Is America in a Culture War? Yes—No—Sort of," *The Christian Century* 114, no. 32 (November 12, 1997): 1038–1043; Leslie A. White, "The Concept of Culture," *American Anthropologist* 61, no. 227 (April 1959). White reports that there is great divergence of view among anthropologists as to a definition of culture.

16. Thomas R. Dye, *Power & Society: An Introduction to the Social Sciences*, 4th ed. (Monterey, CA: Brooks/ Cole, 1987), p. 39.

17. Ibid., p. 40.

18. Daniel J. Elazár, *American Federalism: A View from the States* (New York: Harper & Row, 1984), p. 109.

19. Pfiffner and Sherwood, *Administrative Organization*, pp. 249–272.

20. J. Steven Ott, *The Organization Culture Perspective* (Chicago: Dorsey Press, 1989), p. 62.

21. Elazár, *American Federalism*, p. 136.

22. Harold F. Gortner, Julianne Mahler, and Jeanne Bell Nicholson, *Organization Theory: A Public Perspective* (Fort Worth, TX: Harcourt Brace, 1997), p. 71.

23. Gareth Morgan, *Images of Organization* (Beverly Hills, CA: Sage, 1986).

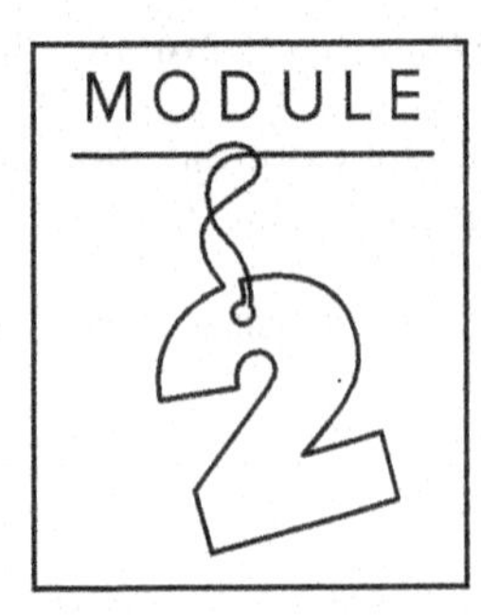


# UNIT 2:
## The Physiology of Public Organizations

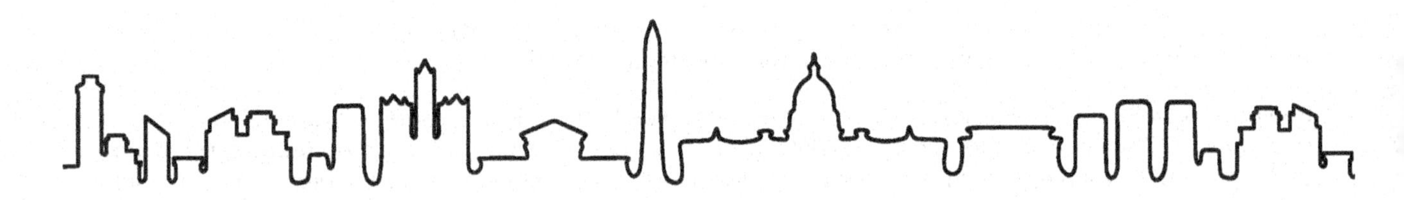

Physiology is the study of life processes, activities, and functions. Just as a medical student must study physiology to understand how the human body works, scholars of public administration must be familiar with organizational theories so they will be prepared to confront the realities of bureaucracy. This chapter provides a look at the most influential and helpful organizational theories and theorists.

### Democracy in Bureaucracy

Bureaucracy and democracy are the central pillars of the public and private organizations of our society. Bureaucratic hierarchy and democratic equality influence the vital processes and functions of all organizations. Despite the apparent paradox, bureaucracy and democracy are both antithetical and complementary.

In partisan politics, we periodically elect presidents, governors, and mayors. In such electoral processes, we take advantage of the fundamental principle of democracy. While in office, however, presidents, governors, and mayors depend upon principles of bureaucracy, which apply formalism, strict rule adherence, impersonality, unity of command, chain of command, span of control, and similar values to the exercise of authority. Authority in a bureaucracy is checked by democratic voting procedures, but only on a periodic basis. As we consider the functions and processes of organizations, therefore, an understanding of the philosophical differences between bureaucracy and democracy is crucial.

The development of our organized society underscores the need for democracy in the administrative state. We, the voting public, come into contact with numerous public and private organizations each day. Government constantly exercises its influence on the public. Legislatures allocate public functions to administrative structures. What input should employees and clientele have in internal decision making within public organizations? Can there be democracy in bureaucracy? How democratic should life in organizations be?

If you are not already employed, in a matter of years, even months, you will probably enter the American workforce. You may be employed by a business, labor, social, or public organization. You may be full of ideas and energy to tackle your employer's challenges and problems, and you will want to be heard. How much democracy will exist in your bureaucratic workplace? The authoritarian tenets of bureaucracy and the egalitarian tenets of democracy are major forces shaping life and the pursuit of happiness in the twenty- first century. These concepts interact with other organizational philosophies, such as capitalism, nationalism, industrialism, and socialism; all historical antecedents to democracy and bureaucracy.

# THINK ABOUT IT!

### Bureaucracy and Democracy Are Not Esoteric

Bureaucracy and democracy—concepts, terms, ways of working life—may seem esoteric, even to government employees. They are key aspects of government-operated, taxpayer-financed, public-sector organizations. Capital is a necessity if public bureaucracy is to function well and if democracy is to realize a diversity of expression.

The respective definitions of capital, bureaucracy, and democracy are economic wealth, employee skills and responsiveness, and the relatively free articulation of opinions. Capital does not necessarily mean money, but it often does. Money is wealth, or economic access to what one wants in life. And, simply stated, wealth is power.

Wealth also implies having good health and access to good health systems, educational and economic opportunities, high expectations for youth, transportation options, viable communities, strong family structures, respect for the aged, and meaningful religious beliefs.

Wealth is very different, of course, from income. Most government workers have incomes. We support ourselves and our families through our incomes. We also contribute to health insurance and retirement plans, as do our taxpayer- based employers. But most government employees—public safety officials, teachers, military personnel, transit workers, and not-for-profit employees, among others—maintain incomes, yet have very limited access to wealth.

Of the three concepts—capital, bureaucracy, and democracy—democracy is the most challenged or threatened, even pleading for its very existence. Most government workers are not likely to speak out or exercise their due process rights if they suspect that their salaries may be affected—even indirectly.

Bureaucracy, according to Max Weber's theories, is structured by hierarchy, chain of command, specialization of task, a specified sphere of competence, established norms of conduct, and records, paperwork, or similar documentation. Government employees are expected to be responsive to citizen-clients. A certain level of competence is demanded.

Any citizen can file to compete for elective office. That's the democratic way. But how many political candidates have access to skilled campaign officials and large bank accounts (wealth) to make their candidacies competitive?

Definitions of public and private regulate the relationships between capital, bureaucracy and democracy. As Dwight Waldo wrote in The Enterprise of Public Administration (1980), "Concepts of public and private are very central in the conceptual and emotional structuring of the Western world. A great deal of our thought and action concerning government, law, morals and social institutions relates one way or another to this distinction. But we need to appreciate public and private are not categories of nature; they are categories of history and culture, of law and custom. They are contextual and subject to change and redefinition." (p. 164)

Professor Waldo suggests redefinition, reevaluation, and restatement of the nature, culture, and context of capital, bureaucracy, and democracy as they are played out on the public and private stages of American governments and politics. Do partisan political leaders advocate space shields or provide a Patients' Bill of Rights? The Departments of Health and Human Services, and Defense, are governed and administered according to laws. Nurses, medical doctors, and other caregivers are private-sector entrepreneurs or employees of not-for-profits. The U.S. government provides soldiers and strategy for military missions. Private-sector groups produce tanks, airplanes, missiles, ships,guns, uniforms, and boots. In both health and defense administration (HHS and DOD), the government produces little or nothing. In wars on disease, in military conquest and economic advantage, citizens make sacrifices for the common good.

On matters of life (health) and death (military power), priorities of capital, bureaucracy, and democracy are vigorously debated. In efforts to redefine, reevaluate, and restate the parameters of public and private life, citizens determine what they owe the state (society), and what the state owes them. In determining such boundaries, democracy is as prevalent—and as effective—as citizen access to incomes and wealth.

*Source: "Bureaucracy and Democracy Are Not Esoteric" by John Rouse, as appeared on ASPA Online Columns, https:// www.aspanet.org, July 17, 2001. Reprinted by permission of the author.*

Defining democracy is not easy. We live in a democracy. In the classical sense, though, our system of political economy, or politics and economics, is not a democracy, but a republic. We have a democratic type of government; however, we have a republican form of government: In our republic, elected officials represent us in our state and national legislatures. Other tenets of democracy call for "rule by the people." However, who are "the people"? How, and by what means, do they "rule"?

Democracy is not an economic, social, or ethical concept, but a political one. It emphasizes the values of liberty, equality, human worth, human dignity, and freedom by guaranteeing the right to secret voting. With these values come free expression of ideas, free association of persons, representation, legislatures, due process of law, and the privilege of assuming our soap box and speaking our minds about virtually anything.[1]

While democracy has a leveling, or horizontal, feature about its application, bureaucracy is vertical. Democracy implies equality and equal opportunity; bureaucracy denotes hierarchy. Every four years American citizens vote for or against a presidential candidate because of the candidate's support of political principles as expressed in the party's platform. The party platform serves as a voters' guide to how its leaders should address the nation's challenges during the next term. Voting, which espouses equality, is a political right in a democratic society.

However, once a candidate becomes president, the direct democratic powers of voters are diluted. Voters may encourage members of Congress to oppose the president's new programs, for example, but the rights of suffrage in our electoral democracy come up only periodically. Except for those periodic elections, the premises of bureaucracy, or hierarchy, assume preeminence in our system. Public institutions—ranging from health to defense—develop, evaluate, and implement public policies.

The oft-used term bureaucracy has two meanings. In its most popular sense, the concept refers to any substantial public organization or group of organizations, as in "federal bureaucracy" or in "welfare bureaucracy." The other meaning is more specialized; it refers to a particular method or manner of administration. A bureaucracy in this sense is an organization or group of organizations that operates in a particular way.

What constitutes the bureaucratic way of doing things? The German sociologist Max Weber (1864–1920) was the first to define it. He saw bureaucracy as an impersonal system operating on the basis of "calculable rules" and staffed by full-time and professional (as opposed to political) employees. Bureaucracy presupposes hierarchy, but this hierarchy is based on organizational rank, not on social status or other considerations.

The chief characteristic of a bureaucracy in Weber's sense of the word is its uniform, non-arbitrary, and non- personal method of administering public affairs. "Bureaucracy," wrote Weber, "is like a modern judge who is a vending machine into which the pleadings are inserted along with the fee. The machine then disgorges the judgment based on reasons mechanically derived from the code."[2]

In Weber's view, bureaucracy is a bloodless mechanism devoid of the capriciousness and color we associate with human activity. Yet the positive features of such an administrative approach, characterized by impersonality and professionalism, must not be overlooked. Impersonality implies impartiality, and professionalism opens the possibility of an employee selection system based less on social status and more on personal skill.

This bureaucratic ideal has made headway in Europe, especially in Germany. As such, it has brought more uniformity, predictability, and equality to public administration.

Because bureaucratic systems rest upon a highly systematized administrative arrangement, they often show resistance to change. The devotion to calculable rules often causes rule-conscious bureaucrats to "go by the book," regardless of the situation. Such routinized organizational behavior may, however, prove advantageous. France, with its long history of unrest and upheaval, has often been held together by its plodding but enduring bureaucracy.

Although the bureaucratic style has conquered the public sector in Western Europe, it has scored somewhat less decisively in this country. The dynamics of U.S. political bureaucracies, especially in state and local jurisdictions, are highly personal. It is often who one knows rather than what one knows that affects the administrative system. Just as personalities often count for more than parties or principles in policy making, so personalities often outweigh "calculable rules" in policy execution. This is not always true, but it happens often enough to differentiate U.S. administration from that of other economically developed democracies such as England, France, or Germany.

Lessened concern for abiding by the rules provides many rewards. Although U.S. administration has often been accused of stodginess, and rightly so, it is perhaps less than its Western European counterparts. It is much easier to bend, if not break, the rules in the United States than elsewhere in the world of modern democratic capitalism. The U.S. administrative setup, reflecting vast differences in bureaucratic cultures, can more easily accommodate individual idiosyncrasies and initiatives.

Before breaking out into cheers, the anti-bureaucratic enthusiast should note some of the benefits that we thereby forego. A system more open to the influence of individual personality is open to caprice and whim. As calculable rules become more easily manipulated, the system is also more vulnerable to corruption. If change can sometimes come more quickly, then such change may spring not only from public demand but from personal desire as well.

The distinctiveness of US administration should not be overstated: The bureaucratic way of doing things is scarcely a stranger to our shores. And the systems of other countries are certainly not incapable of capriciousness or change. Yet for both good and ill, bureaucracy in Weber's sense characterizes the U.S. public sector less than it does that of many other modern developed nations.

## Interpretations of Bureaucracy

According to Dwight Waldo, the term "bureaucracy" has two interpretations. The popular-pejorative interpretation is widely recognized in society: Bureaucracy is bad because bureaucrats are timid, ineffectual, power-seeking, and dangerous.

A second interpretation of bureaucracy is descriptive and analytical. This interpretation says that bureaucracy fosters advanced legal and economic systems and, therefore, advances civilization. Descriptive and analytical terms related to this interpretation include form of government, formalism, rules, impersonality, hierarchy, expertise, records, large-scale, complex, efficiency, and effectiveness.

# THINK ABOUT IT!

### Normative Vectors

The norms or values of public administration are grouped into three general areas, or normative vectors.

Concerns about efficiency and effectiveness. These areas of concern focus primarily on the workings of government and the way its goods and services are distributed and delivered. A public dollar should be expended with as much care and deliberation as feasible. This attitude toward government values the ability to mobilize, organize, and direct resources.

Concerns about rights and the adequacy of governmental process. These themes scrutinize a government's relationship with its citizens. Individual liberties provide a sense of equity; each citizen should be treated as an individual, according to their circumstances. As concerns arose about the manner in which governments treat people, the notion of due process emerged. Rights, due process, and equity focus on measuring the quality of interaction between an agency and its clientele. This focus is rooted in democratic theory. It reaches as far back as Aristotle.

Concerns about representation and the exercise of discretion. These themes point toward controls the citizenry has over the workings of government and its agents. Accountability implies external standards of correct action and is thus institutionalized. Legal, political, and bureaucratic sanctions induce competent and conscientious administrative performance. Administrators must act in accordance with moral obligation. Accountability, responsibility, and responsiveness put representation into operation.

*Source: Michael M. Harmon and Richard T. Mayer, Organization Theory for Public Administration (Boston: Little, Brown, 1986). See Chapter 3, "The Normative Context of Public Administration," pp. 34–53*

In reality, the concept of bureaucracy is neither good nor bad. Bureaucracy simply is; it exists. The concept of bureaucracy encompasses procedures for organizing people within a certain culture in order to achieve a particular set of goals and objectives. Bureaucracy exists for accomplishing tasks. The tasks range from fighting dictators to fighting poverty.

How, then, are the societal values of democracy and bureaucracy antithetical, yet complementary?

According to Waldo, there are two problems in reconciling democracy and bureaucracy. One concern focuses on the definition of the administrative unit. Any organization able to respond to clientele is a unit. The function of a unit of bureaucracy may be defined by the manner in which the organization responds to its clientele. Academic departments, as administrative units at a college or university, are organized depending upon college and student demands for certain skills, knowledge, and expertise.

For example, English and math may be the largest departments on campus because most colleges mandate that learners take courses in these subjects. Meanwhile, the departments of philosophy, anthropology, and foreign language may be smaller because the demand for courses taught by those departments is lower.

Waldo's concern is the status and weight accorded to nondemocratic values. Liberty and equality are democratic values; nondemocratic values include national security, personal safety, productivity, and efficiency. If the chairperson of an academic department is elected by members of that unit, the values of democracy have predominated. However, if the department head is selected by the dean of the college, then the values of bureaucracy—efficiency and productivity—have taken precedence.

## Baseline Originals in Organizational Life

Max Weber, Frederick Winslow Taylor, Elton Mayo, and Chester Barnard form an intellectual baseline of early classical thinkers concerned with the anatomy and physiology of private and public organizations. Thinking of the organization as a "rational machine" provides a useful metaphor in understanding this approach to organizational behaviors.[3]

### Max Weber

Weber's work on the nature of bureaucracy is considered by many the most important of its kind. Weber was trained in law, history, and economics. He viewed action as both individual and social. Weber postulates the ideal-type of bureaucracy, not referring to "goodness" or "badness," but suggesting a standard or model for organizational environment. Characteristics of the ideal-type may be found in any organization.

In the following list, John M. Pfiffner and Frank P. Sherwood summarize components of Weber's ideal-type. These components contribute to our understanding of the functions and vital processes of organizations.

- Emphasis on form. Bureaucracy's first, most cited, and most general feature, according to Weber, is its emphasis on form of organization. In a sense, the rest of the components are examples of this.
- The concept of hierarchy. The organization follows the principle of hierarchy, with each lower office under the control and supervision of a higher one.
- Specialization of task. Incumbents are chosen on the basis of merit and ability to perform specialized functions within a total operation.
- A specified sphere of competence. This flows from specialization of task. It suggests that the relationships between various specializations should be clearly known and observed in practice. In a sense, the job descriptions used in many American organizations are a practical application of this requirement.
- Established norms of conduct. There should be as little unpredictability as possible in the organization. Policies should be clearly enunciated, and the individuals within the organization should see that these policies are implemented.
- Records. Administrative acts, decisions, and rules should be recorded to ensure predictability of performance within the bureaucracy.[4]

Weber emphasized the universality of bureaucracy by emphasizing its rationality. His observations on bureaucracy coincided with the industrial revolution in Germany at the turn of the century. In seeking rationality in human behavior, Weber concluded that the ideal-type is the best means for achieving rationality at the institutional level.

Weber also assumed freedom for bureaucrats. Far from promoting a master-slave relationship, he emphasized that people were free agents, even within nineteenth-century economic bureaucracies.

Finally, Weber forecast a general separation of policy making and administration. The ideal-type organization is grounded in predictable decision-making processes and is staffed by professionals; therefore, its bureaucracies should not be subverted by nonprofessionals, according to Weber. In this view, professionals organize and implement expertise. Nonprofessionals, armed only with opinions about expertise and goals, do not fit into Weber's game plan. Neither the monarch ruling by divine right, nor the elected American president would be part of Weber's ideal-type framework.[5]

## THINK ABOUT IT!

**When Bureaucracies Get Sick the Diseases are Called "Bureaupathologies."**

Max Weber, in his "ideal type," presented bureaucracy as an organizational form in which rational decision making was the coin of the realm, and because of its formalization of rules and processes, routinized behavior, job specialization, etc., was the perfect match for government, business, and the military.

Weber could not have foreseen what happens when the elements of bureaucracy fall into misuse. Now, enter critics of bureaucracy, such as Thorsten Veblen, who coined the concept of "conspicuous consumption," and also "trained incapacity" as a dysfunctional characteristic of bureaucracy.

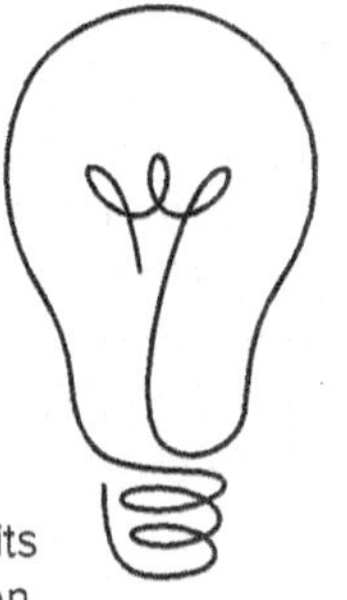

John Dewey termed this incapacity as "occupational psychosis," and Warnotte termed it "professional deformation." No one, however, provided a better listing of its maladies and problems than Gerald Caiden. He simply called them "bureaupathologies."

| | | |
|---|---|---|
| • Abuses (of power, authority, position) | • Fraud | • Lawlessness |
| • Alienation | • Highhandedness | • Malfeasance |
| • Arrogance | • Ignorance | • Meaningless/make work |
| • Bureaucratese | • Illegality | • Mediocrity |
| • Conflicts of interest/objectives | • Inaccessibility | • Misconduct |
| • Corruption | • Inaction | • Misfeasance |
| • Cowardice | • Incompetence | • Nepotism |
| • Criminality | • Inconvenience | • Neuroticism |
| • Deceit and deception | • Ineffectiveness | • Nonfeasance |
| • Delay | • Inferior quality | • Nonproductively |
| • Discourtesy | • Injustice | • Patronage |
| • Discrimination | • Insensitivity | • Red tape |
| • Diseconomies of goals/objectives | • Intimidation | • Reluctance to delegate |
| • Empire-building | • Irresponsibility | • Rudeness |
| • Extravagance | • Lack of imagination | • Spoils |
| • Failure to acknowledge | • Lack of initiative | • Tokenism |
| • Failure to respond | • Lack of performance indicators | • Unprofessional conduct |
| • Foot-dragging | • Lack of vision | |

*Source: Michael M. Harmon and Richard T. Mayer, Organization Theory for Public Administration (Boston: Little, Brown, 1986). See Chapter 3, "The Normative Context of Public Administration," pp. 34–53*

**Frederick Winslow Taylor**

Mass production suffered a long and fitful birth when it appeared in America in the eighteenth century and slowly developed thereafter. Oliver Evans, Linus Yale, Lillian and Frank Gilbreth, and Henry Ford later made huge contributions to its development. But it was Frederick Winslow Taylor who developed the underlying theory of scientific management that gave mass production its enduring form. Scientific management captivated the American consciousness and catapulted Taylor's ideas onto center stage, where they have remained. Yet until the publication of Wellford Wilms's "The One Best Way," little was known about the man who revolutionized the workplace.[6]

Frederick Taylor (1856–1915) is often called the father of scientific management. He recognized the importance of technology, work, and organization to the functions and vital processes of bureaucracies. In the opening of his classic, *The Principles of Scientific Management*, Taylor wrote:

The principal object of management should be to secure the maximum prosperity for the employer, coupled with the maximum prosperity for the employee. The words maximum prosperity are used, in their broad sense, to mean not only large dividends for the company or owner, but the development of every branch of business to its highest state of excellence, so that prosperity may be permanent.[7]

According to Taylor, scientific management is both liberating and economically rational. Employees and employers are assumed to be rational. Through rationality in the work process, labor and management determine the proper way to complete a task.

Taylor, like Weber, assumed the importance of the individual and foresaw the shift of power from both the bourgeoisie (economic elites) and the proletariat (masses) to the expert (possessor of skills and knowledge). Taylor emphasized cooperation in the workplace and spoke of making life better for each employee. He represented a pre–World War II line of thought that there are principles and laws that order our knowledge of the world. By seeking to use the scientific method, organizations become impersonal but rational.

**Elton Mayo**

Elton Mayo stands out in the study of human relations since he and his other notable Hawthorne researchers (F. J. Roethlisberger, Henry Landsberger, W. J. Dickens) at the Hawthorne Works of the Western Electric Company on the outskirts of Chicago (Cicero, IL) were there at its very origin. Many who have graduated from high school and essentially everyone who has ever taken a college course in the social sciences (sociology, psychology, anthropology, political science, leadership, or management, etc.), have read about the famous illumination (lighting) experiment with its accompanying variation in rest breaks or pauses and the bank-wiring room experiment.

These two experiments literally jettison out as some of the most widely taught textbook examples of how the scientific management theory of Frederick Winslow Taylor and especially his motivational theory of "Economic Rational Man," was turned upside down and largely debunked. Of course, now, to be sure Taylor was himself a perceptive researcher, a tireless worker, who rose from the lowest to the highest rungs of success in the steel industry. He understood that the organization was a social system, but his desire was to control and manage the informal social forces which operate within in the workforce or group of workers.[8]

*In short, leadership style, social factors (pride in work, feeling of achievement, personal recognition, praise), different forms of motivation, and so on, affected the performance of individuals of individuals, and accordingly, that of the organization.*

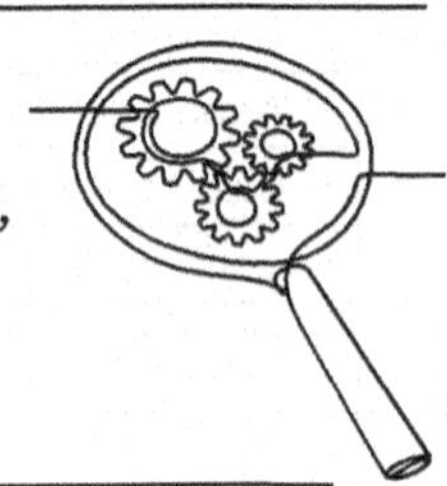

If retention and comprehension in learning is reinforced by redundancy, and they are, then these two experiments deserve repetition because they eloquently reflect the origin of several important theories that have come to undergird the field of human relations. For instance, the lighting or illumination study involved the manipulation of the lighting levels by the researchers and whether the lighting was turned up or down for the experimental group (EG), and left alone for the control group, the rheostat changes produced unexpected behavior in the study group. Simply, productivity increased in the EG regardless of the lighting variation (candlelight power) and productivity also increased in the control group (CG).

What had taken place in the plant is now well known as the "Hawthorne Effect." The experimental group was reacting, as it turned out, as much to the attention that these women were given by the researchers as was their reaction, per se, to the manipulation of the lighting.

The workers felt that the researchers were interested in what was going on with them and in their work environment; they felt a sense of belonging to a social work group; they were being recognized by the researchers as more than interchangeable and replaceable parts of a machine (bureaucracy); and they responded accordingly. In short, leadership style, social factors (pride in work, feeling of achievement, personal recognition, praise), different forms of motivation and so on, affected the performance of individuals, and accordingly, that of the organization.

For the sake of clarity, the "Hawthorne Effect" has been generally understood in the academy since 1929 yet understanding and acceptance of the underlying factors that produced it are still resisted by some in management, supervision and those involved in motivational endeavors.

Secondarily, the bank wiring room experiment deserves its own dramatization in the origins of human relations theory. At the Hawthorne Plant the male workers informally set their own norms (expectations) for producing electrical components (wiring and soldering bank terminals) at a sub- optimal rather than at a maximum level of productivity.

Accordingly, they policed (enforced) the group norms by applying peer pressure ("gang" pressure), and physical sanctions—in reality they had an informal production norm. Thus, was born the idea that the organization was simultaneously comprised both of formal and informal leaders and these informal aspects of organizational theory were at least as important as the formal side of the management and motivational house.

**Moving from Theory to Practice—Hawthorne Experiments 1927-1929**

Moving from theory to practice—The Hawthorne Experiments (1927-1929). The empirical, scientific evidence discovered nearly 100 years ago speaks "knowledge to practice." It is essential to learn human relations theories and gain insights into human behavior from its many companion disciplines and understand and internalize the theory in such a way that we can put it into practice — applications that give meaning to theory; that make theory come alive—that offer solutions to the problems we face. Thus, the following conclusions are based on the Hawthorne studies and the writings of Elton Mayo. Paradoxically, even though our discipline has long-embraced these findings that help us better understand the organizations in which we work and the people who comprise them, they are yet to be fully valued and utilized by many who hold supervisory positions today.

- Organizations are social systems and small group behavior is important;
- Informal organizations develop with their own informal leaders, establish and enforce their own work norms through group sanctions;
- There are a variety of incentives, other than money, which motivate workers to produce, such as recognition by superiors;
- Worker participation in setting goals impacts production in a positive manner and if workers are involved in making decisions that affect them, they treat the task as more important; and
- Identified the Hawthorne effect — that needs to be controlled in experimental studies of human behavior.

In summation, understanding human relations theories is important for those who work in the traditional areas of employment, and it will become nearly obligatory for the newest knowledge and biotechnological occupations that are quickly coming on board. For instance, today it is nearly impossible to imagine working in the fields of distance learning, meeting and convention planning, sustainability, video game design, electronic commerce, survey research, creative writing, interpretation and translation, linguistics, psychiatric and geriatric nursing, genetic counseling, aqua-cultural management, green marketing, Brownfield redevelopment, and informatics, etc., without knowing some the basic ideas in the areas of behavioral science, motivation theory, group behavior, social and technical systems (technology), ethics, multiculturalism, and communication and leadership theory.

It is commonly known, that organizational living and the changing nature of work is not becoming simpler —indeed it is becoming more dynamic as we are expected to address the impact of technology, diversity, knowledge, globalization or internationalism, entrepreneurialism, innovation, creativity, changing demographics and quality management, etc., and at the same time recognize basic civil and human rights and fight against the insidiousness of discrimination (gender, age, ability, appearance, religion, lifestyle, neurodiversity, and so on), when and where it is found.

**Chester Barnard**

Chester Barnard (1886–1961) is the final member of the baseline foursome. Intrigued by the experiments at the Hawthorne plant, Barnard formulated a theory of organizational life that focuses on the organization as a system, formal and informal organizations, and the role of the executive. In Functions of the Executive, Barnard distinguishes between organizational purpose and individual motive. He postulates that each person in the organization reflects a dual personality, one organizational and the other individual. As an individual leaves home and enters the workplace, he or she becomes "the organization man or woman."

An organization is a collection of actions focused on a purpose; an equilibrium is necessary for an organization to sustain itself. A successful equilibrium must exist between the organization and its employees. The organization receives energies and productive capacities from employees, and employees receive compensation, benefits, and meaning from their work.[11]

Although the distinction between formal and informal organization is now commonplace, Barnard introduced these concepts in the late 1930s as new analytic tools for examining organizational life. According to Barnard, formal organization is comprised of the consciously coordinated activities of people, while informal organization entails the unconscious group feelings, passions, and activities of the same individuals. Informal organization is essential to the maintenance of formal structures and relationships. The formal organization cannot exist without its informal counterpart. Not all activity can be structured by a chain of command because of the reality of informal organization.

Finally, Barnard addresses executive functions of organizations. These functions are:

- Maintaining organization communication
- Securing essential services from individuals
- Formulating the purpose and objectives of the organization

Barnard writes that the functions of the executive are "those of the nervous system, including the brain, in relation to the rest of the body. It exists to maintain the bodily system by directing those actions which are necessary more effectively to adjust to the environment. But it can hardly be said to manage the body, a large part of whose functions are independent of it and upon which it in turn depends."[12]

The writings of Weber, Taylor, Mayo, and Barnard form an axis around which the theory and practice of public organizations revolve. Focusing on three early organizational themes—system, hierarchy, and structure—writers who follow these classical thinkers assume that understanding human rationality is central to theorizing about organizational physiology.

The human relations school of thought is based on the belief that it is important to understand those direct as well as subtle forces that are at work in our society. These pressures result from complex economic, historical, political and social factors that are in inextricably linked to disparities (institutional, group and individual) that exist in our society. Also, the relationship between different groups in the United States must be considered and understood. For instance, the relationship between dominant (majority) and minority (subordinate, marginalized) groups are often associated with contemporary problems and societal change.

In the human relations approach, you may have been already acquainted with a number of major human relations problems faced by society, such as the area of social inequality (class, race, and gender), intra- and interpersonal tensions (individual stress, personal relationship in groups, and violence), and intergroup tension (multicultural and multinational). Certain resources of society, such as power, influence, money, income, wealth, status, position, etc., are unequally distributed and these contribute to and fuel the stress and difficulties that are found in resolving problems of human relations in our organizations.

## Neoclassical Theories

The neoclassical perspective on organizational theory is represented by the works of Luther Gulick and Herbert Simon. "Decision-set" organizational theory is characterized by several important themes, including decision making as the heart and soul of administration; administrative capacity as measured by efficiency; an emphasis on organizational roles, not individual roles, as they relate to decision making; and instrumental rationality as the center of operation.

### Luther Gulick

In 1937, Luther Gulick and Lyndall Urwick edited the *Papers on the Science of Administration*, a collection of eleven papers reflecting the predominant thinking concerning organizations in Europe and the United States prior to World War II. Divided into two groups, the papers examined structural aspects and social and environmental aspects of organization.[13]

Gulick's "Notes on the Theory of Organization," in which he introduced the acronym POSDCORB, has influenced teaching and thinking about public administration for more than seventy years. Gulick's POSDCORB (Planning, Organizing, Staffing, Directing, Coordinating, Reporting, and Budgeting) helped shape the Wilsonian separation of politics from administration, the need for a division of work to reach organizational objectives, and the efficiency criterion for judging governmental activities. In POSDCORB, Gulick outlines the work of the chief executive:

- Planning is working out in broad outline the tasks that need to be done and the methods for doing them to accomplish the purpose set for the enterprise.
- Organizing is establishing the formal structure of authority through which work subdivisions are arranged, defined, and coordinated for the defined objective.
- Staffing is bringing in and training the staff and maintaining favorable work conditions.
- Directing is the continuous task of making decisions and embodying them in specific and general instructions as well as serving as the leader of the enterprise.
- Coordinating is the important duty of interrelating the various parts of the work. Reporting is keeping the top executive informed as to what is going on, and keeping subordinates informed through records, research, and inspection.
- Budgeting includes fiscal planning, accounting, and control.[14]

### Herbert Simon

After World War II, in 1947, Simon illustrated the decision-set perspective in "The Proverbs of Administration," later incorporated into his classic, *Administrative Behavior*. Simon viewed the decision as the central act of organization, and instrumental rationality as the basis for decision making. By instrumental rationality, Simon meant that the individual is rational and responsible only within the environment of a particular organization. The organizational environment encompasses the purposes of rational behavior; autonomous individuals behave only within the confines of those organizational purposes.

In emphasizing the decision as the basis for administrative theory, Simon distinguished between value premises and factual premises of public administrators. He wrote, "The process of validating a factual proposition is quite distinct from the process of validating a value judgment. The former is validated by its agreement with the facts, the latter by human fiat."[15] In other words, the facts of any circumstance are validated within a given set of values in which those facts, or actions, occur.

Simon focuses on the means-end sense of rationality as most significant. Administrators weigh the means, ends, and consequences of acting; therefore, Simon suggests, decisions may prove objectively rational, subjectively rational, deliberately rational, organizationally rational, or personally rational. Regardless of adverb, to be rational means to consider only those choices present within a prescribed system of values. Government employees are not autonomous individuals. The organizational environment of the department or agency articulates the values that determine rational behavior. In other words, an employee is rational and responsible only within the environment of a particular department or agency. A government employee acts rationally only within the framework of the department's pre-established goals and purposes.

Values, on the other hand, are arbitrary, regardless of their origins. Human decree, sanction, or authority validates a certain set of organizational values. Executives, legislatures, and judges decide by fiat that a set of values, encompassed in laws and implemented by bureaucrats, are of importance to organizations and to society.

Citizens of public organizations then respond to the rules and regulations and the boundaries these values impose upon them.

All decisions in organizations only satisfy and suffice—that is, they satisfice. Our focus on choices and decision making and our acceptance of organizational premises brings us to the limit of administrative rationality. This final Simon theme, that of satisficing, recognizes that rationality, or human reasoning, is bounded by administrative settings. After analyzing the problem and considering the complexities of the situation, administrators "satisfice," surveying their options and selecting the first one they find at least minimally satisfactory.

With respect to employee "satisficing," Simon concludes that rationality is bounded. In describing bounded rationality, he concludes that an administrator's reasoning options are limited by unconscious habits and skills, values and conceptions of purpose, and degree of information and knowledge.[16]

## Human Relations Theories

As we have seen in the previous passages, Max Weber speaks in bureaucratic terms; writes in productivity terms; Chester Barnard thinks in organizational terms; and Herbert Simon stresses decisional terms. Writing histories of the increasing bureaucratization of society, each of these authors emphasizes efficiency in some form as a potent force in any organization, but also concludes that organizations embody not just task but social purposes. In other words, they believe that if conflict exists within the organization, individuals must subordinate their interests to those of the organization.

For example, if pupils are not learning in a classroom, the onus usually is placed upon the pupils to change their behavior or study habits to respond to the professor's demands. Likewise, if the college's basketball team is losing, the assumption is that the players are not responding to their coach's leadership. Student athletes must subordinate their actions to the coach's instructions for the benefit of the team.

Human relations theories question such assumptions, placing responsibility on the professor to change his or her teaching methods and on the coach to change his or her leadership style and set up a new strategy for winning games. This shift in responsibility makes for several new ways of envisioning organizational structure and function.

# THINK ABOUT IT!

**Miles' Law**

Rufus E. Miles, Jr., proudly claims to have parented Miles' Law. The law states that "Where you stand depends on where you sit." Miles says he discovered the law while serving as a division director of the former Bureau of the Budget. He noted that a budget examiner might be a constant critic of an agency whose budget he oversaw, yet if the examiner were to be later hired away by the agency, he would promptly do a 180° turn and become one of the agency's most adamant advocates. The position a bureaucrat takes thus depends on what position he is in, or "Where you stand depends on where you sit.".

**Mary Parker Follett**

An early prophet of human relations thinking was Mary Parker Follett (1868–1933). While the classical and neoclassical writers were attempting to construct a field of public administration along systematic and somewhat mechanical lines, Follett was marching to the beat of a different drummer.

She had become impressed with the psychological factors she had seen at work in her active life as an organizer of evening schools, recreation agencies, and employment bureaus and as a member of statutory wage boards. Already the author of two books on political science, *The New State* and *Creative Experience*, she embarked on a series of speculations in the 1920s concerning the functions and vital processes of organizations. Her work signaled the advent of a new era in administrative theory.[17]

In various papers and articles, Follett depicted administration as essentially involved with reconciling the agendas of both individuals and social groups. An organization's principal problems, in her view, were not only determining what it wanted its employees to do but guiding and controlling the employees' conduct in such a way as to get them to do it. This, she indicated, was a much more complex task than previous writers had suggested.

Follett not only anticipated what was to become the human relations school of administration, she also foreshadowed the humanistic school that was to grow out of it. She urged organizations to stop trying to suppress the differences that may arise within their boundaries and to seek instead to integrate those differences, allowing them to contribute to the organization's growth and development. She advocated replacing the "law of authority" with the "law of the situation," admonishing organizations to exercise "power with" rather than "power over" their members.

A philosophical analysis of Mary Parker Follett's writings on democratic and organizational theories reveals similarities with the feminist theory of the time. These similarities include the notion that human relations supersede individual rights, the theory that knowledge is context specific, her sensitivity to the role of power as an obstacle in the development of knowledge claims, and her method of conflict resolution through the integration of opposing interests. Her writings provide important insights into modern organization and management principles.[18]

While Follett's writings did not go unnoticed, they failed to score the impact that similar ideas would later achieve. This was perhaps due partly to the fact that she was a woman writing in a society not yet willing to take women thinkers seriously. Another serious obstacle, however, may have been that she was an iconoclast, challenging the sacred credos of her time. She died during the same year Elton Mayo wrote on the Hawthorne Experiments. Mayo's work was the first systematic research to expose the "human factor" in work situations. Mayo's study, as we have seen, marked a major turning point in the history of administrative theory and practice.

## ESSENTIAL VIEWS:

### ACADEMICS/PRACTITIONERS AT THE STREET LEVEL

**The Genius of Mary Parker Follett**
By Patrick S. Malone

Scholars of public administration are quite familiar with the more enduring conceptual frameworks of the field. Woodrow Wilson, of course, heralded the politics administration dichotomy. A host of writers followed suggesting a multitude of approaches to aid leaders in the challenging work of delivering civilization to our communities. Simon, Goodnow, Brownlow, Gulick. But it was a social worker and philosopher, an intellectual by every measure, who made one of the most significant and lasting contributions to leadership in the public service.

Mary Parker Follett was born in 1868 in Quincy, Massachusetts. At the age of 24, she was accepted into the Society for the Collegiate Instruction of Women in Cambridge, Massachusetts (later renamed Radcliffe College). She graduated in 1898 with specialties in the fields of economics, government, law and philosophy. And if you're still wondering who Mary Parker Follett was, you are definitely not alone. There were sadly few female voices in the early days of public administration and management, making Follett's impact even more extraordinary.

Follett emerged at a time when many in the field of public management were focused on mechanization and a strong inclination on the industrial and formal organizational aspects of work. Bureaucracy, process, and hierarchy were the order of the day. This perspective fueled much of the growth of a young administrative state and to its credit, formed a strong institutional framework from which our nation's civil service infrastructure grew.
But it wasn't enough. Governments don't succeed because of their formal bureaucratic structure. They succeed because of the people within them, and Follett tapped into that need. In fact, she made lasting contributions in the areas of:

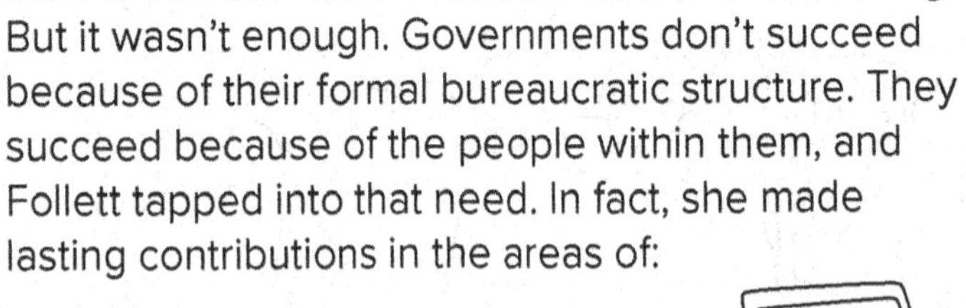

- *Diversity* – Follett understood well the impact of diversity on organizational productivity and mission accomplishment. At a time when hierarchical rule was the practice of the day, she called for dissimilar thought in group processes to ensure a variety of ideas were heard and considered.

- *Life-long Learning* – An educator at heart, she considered education to be the lifeblood of advancement and improvement, both at the organizational and individual levels. Not a popular line of thinking in her era, but Follett's vision laid the foundation for the approaches we see in adult learning today.

- *Engagement* – Follett considered discourse regarding shared experiences, humble inquiry, and a search for meaning to be the pathways to learning and improvement. Follett knew that getting a diverse group of people engaged with one another was a powerful force.

- *The Human Element* – Follett viewed humans, not processes, as the most valuable part of an organization. She was one of the earliest voices to argue for the value of positive organizational culture and the importance of placing people first.

These concepts were unheard of in Follett's time, yet many are presented today as "new" or "innovative." But the truth is that it was Follett who introduced these notions and the thoughts she espoused almost 100 years ago guide our leadership practices today. Her voice remains one of the most powerful in the field of public administration.

**Maslow, McGregor, and Likert**

Like Follett, organizational psychologists Abraham Maslow, Douglas McGregor, and Rensis Likert wrote from a progressive, humanistic viewpoint. They have profoundly influenced the teaching and practice of public administration concerning the role of democracy in bureaucracy, advocating an expanded scope and encouragement of individual initiative by allowing employees to make many of their own decisions on the job. These authors call for less hierarchy and more humanity in organizational life and emphasize the integration of individuals in organization.

Writing in *Motivation and Personality* (1954), Maslow identifies a hierarchy of personal needs that the organization must contend with to successfully integrate the individual. He writes that food and shelter are the first needs humans seek to meet. Once these needs are met, people seek freedom from physical harm and deprivation. Next, the desire for affectionate and supportive relationships with family, friends, and associates becomes a priority. Then people seek to gain the recognition of worth from their peers. Finally, when all these needs have been met, humans can seek to actualize their inner potential, to release their creative abilities, to achieve everything they hope for in life.[19]

Like Maslow's, McGregor's thinking is essentially optimistic concerning individuals' capacity for self-actualization. McGregor examines the possibilities for merging individual and organizational demands in ways that would prove satisfactory to both. In *The Human Side of Enterprise* (1960), McGregor outlines management's conventional view of harnessing human energy to meet organizational requirements. McGregor calls this Theory X, and then boldly steps forward with a new theory of administration he calls Theory Y.

Theory X is based on these assumptions:

- The average person is by nature lazy. They will work as little as possible. Such an individual lacks ambition, dislikes responsibility, and prefers to be led.
- By nature, resistant to change, such a person is gullible, not very bright, and the ready dupe of the charlatan and the demagogue. This person is furthermore inherently self-centered and indifferent to organizational needs.

Theory Y, or McGregor's new way of merging individual and organizational demands, takes a more humanistic approach:

- People are not naturally passive, lazy, and dumb. They are, on the contrary, eager for opportunities to show initiative and to bear responsibility.
- Work is a natural activity, and people by nature want to perform it.
- People work best in an environment that treats them with respect and encourages them to develop and use their abilities.
- There is no inherent and intrinsic conflict between the goals of the organization and the goals of the individual member. Meeting the goals of the individual will only result in a more productive organization.[20]

Rensis Likert, writing in *The Human Organization* (1967), develops four systems that positively or negatively influence the integration of individuals into organizations:

- System 1 is punitive authoritarian and closely resembles McGregor's Theory X. System 1 administrative leaders have no confidence or trust in their subordinates.
- System 2 is benevolent authoritarian and is more generous and humanitarian toward the employee. While System 1 takes everything from the individual and gives little in return, System 2 rewards employee behavior only if prescribed directives are followed. If the employee does his or her tasks as prescribed, he or she is dutifully rewarded. System 2 leaders are condescending in bestowing their confidence and trust, engaging in something resembling a master-servant relationship with subordinates.
- System 3 is consultative and allows still more participation by employees. Administrative leaders in such an organization may be democratic, allowing free discussion regarding policy making, but still assume final responsibility for all decisions. System 3 illustrates substantial but not complete confidence and trust in subordinates.
- System 4 is a participative group model and closely resembles McGregor's Theory Y. Senior bureaucrats promote complete confidence and trust in employees in all matters. Employees provide guidance and participate in coordinated problem solving. Employees are not treated punitively.

According to Likert, administrative leaders adopting the participative style achieve from 10 to 40 percent greater productivity, experience much higher levels of employee satisfaction and much better employee health, enjoy better labor relations, suffer less absence and less turnover, obtain better product quality, and, finally, record better customer satisfaction as a result of better products and services than managers operating with System 1, 2, or 3 styles.[21]

"In learning these diverse theories it is important to realize that your "philosophy" of human nature will affect the methods or practices you use in leading others—"authoritarian versus participative (democratic) leadership." In bringing knowledge to action, whether we are talking about motivation theory, leadership styles, or decision making techniques, remember the admonition that, "Theory without practice or theory without action leaves us 'high and dry' in the world of application and reality."

## THINK ABOUT IT!

**5 Key Elements of Employee Fulfillment**

A study by Glassdoor found the following as key factors in employee happiness.

| | | |
|---|---|---|
| • Meaningful Roles | • Work-life Balance | • Growth Opportunities |
| • Team Atmosphere | • Being Appreciated | |

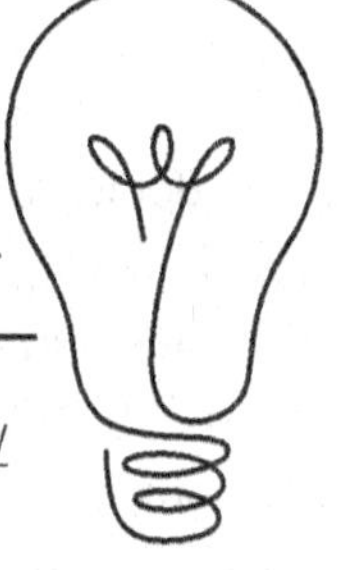

*Source:* https://www.organizationalpsychologydegrees.com/lists/5-surprising-factors-workplace-happiness/

## Summary

- Individualism is a priority in American life, with consumerism and the market following close behind. Satisfying short-term, private consumer wants is not a priority for public organizations. Meeting the needs of people and the community is.
- In efforts to redefine, reevaluate, and restate the parameters of public and private life, citizens determine what they owe the state (society)—and what the state owes them.
- Bureaucracy and democracy are not esoteric. They are at the center of what occurs in the public and private organizations of American society.
- Physiology is the study of life processes, activities, and functions.
- In a classical sense, our system of political economy, or politics and economics, is not a democracy, but a republic. We have a democratic type of government, but a republican form of government.
- Democracy implies equality, while bureaucracy implies hierarchy. Bureaucracy exists to accomplish tasks ranging from fighting dictators to fighting poverty.
- While democracy has a leveling, or horizontal, quality in its application, bureaucracy is vertical.
- The popular view of bureaucracy tends to be pejorative. The descriptive-analytical approach promotes our understanding of behavior, policies, processes, and institutions. Bureaucracy is neither good nor bad; it exists for accomplishing tasks.
- The norms or values of public administration entail concerns about efficiency and effectiveness, the adequacy of governmental processes, and representation and the exercise of discretion.
- Max Weber's ideal-type of bureaucratic organization emphasizes form, hierarchy, specialization of tasks, specified spheres of competence, established norms of conduct, and record keeping.
- The advent of large-scale bureaucracy has seen the shift of power from both the bourgeoisie, or economic elite, and the proletariat, or the masses, to the experts, those who possess valued skills and knowledge.
- The Hawthorne Experiments of the 1930s encourage managers to conceptualize organizations as social institutions.
- The functions of the executive are to maintain organizational communication, secure essential services from individuals, and formulate the purposes and objectives of the organization.
- The acronym POSDCORB outlines the work of the chief executive in terms of planning, organizing, staffing, directing, coordinating, reporting, and budgeting.
- Formal organization is only part of the study of bureaucracy. Every organization has its informal counterpart—the unconscious group feelings, passions, and activities that exist in any group of people. Informal organization is essential to the maintenance of formal structures and relationships.
- Systems theory originates from structural-functional sociology and promotes an understanding of the social system as a whole. Closed systems experience little or no vulnerability from external forces. Open systems emerge as social and technological changes bring uncertainty and interdependence.
- Weber stresses bureaucratic terms, Taylor productivity terms, Barnard organizational terms, and Simon decisional terms. Weber, Taylor, Barnard, and Simon all emphasize efficiency.
- Human relations thinkers—Follett, Maslow, McGregor, and Likert—emphasize principles of equality. They call for less hierarchy and more humanity in organizational life.
- Organization ideologies relate to power, role, task, or people.

## Videos, Films and Talks

Please visit *The Craft of Public Administration* at www.millenniumhrmpress.com for up-to-date videos, films, talks, readings, and additional class resources.

Elton Mayo Human Relations School of Thought I Theory of Motivation }
https://www.youtube.com/watch?v=Tlx5xovXDyc

Human Relations Approach & Hawthorne Experiments
https://www.youtube.com/watch?v=JPlgh7feCpM

Max Weber Bureaucracy
https://www.youtube.com/watch?v=zp554tcdWO8

## Suggested Readings

**Creating Leadership for the Twenty First Century**
https://govleaders.org/behn.htm

**Human Relations Management Theory: Summary, Examples**
https://nanoglobals.com/glossary/human-relations-management-theory/

**Good Ideas Get Government Employees Extra Cash**
https://www.governing.com/archive/gov-employee-suggestion-programs-interview-california.html

**What is the Human Relations Theory (and why you should care)?**
https://www.fingerprintforsuccess.com/blog/human-relations-theory

## Notes

1. Dwight Waldo, *The Enterprise of Public Administration* (Novato, CA: Chandler & Sharp, 1980), pp. 33–47.

2. H. H. Gerth and C. Wright Mills, eds., *From Max Weber: Essays in Sociology* (New York: Oxford University Press, 1946), p. 197.

3. Michael M. Harmon and Richard T. Mayer outline the most important contributions to conceptual theories of public organizations. They describe six perspectives that bridge the theoretical with actual practice in public organizations. These perspectives, as analyzed by various authors, focus on three organizational themes—system, hierarchy, and structure. See Harmon and Mayer, *Organization Theory for Public Administration* (Boston: Little, Brown, 1986).

4. John M. Pfiffner and Frank P. Sherwood, *Administrative Organization* (Englewood Cliffs, NJ: Prentice- Hall, 1960), pp. 56–57.

5. Ibid., p. 217.

6. Wellford W. Wilms, "Father Time: The One Best Way," *Los Angeles Times*, June 1, 1997, p. 6.

7. Frederick Winslow Taylor, *The Principles of Scientific Management* (New York: W. W. Norton, 1947), p. 9.

8. Elton Mayo, *The Human Problems of an Industrial Civilization* (New York: Macmillan, 1933). Also see F. J. Roethsberger and William J. Dickson, *Management and the Worker* (Cambridge, MA: Harvard University Press, 1946).

9. Stephen R. G. Jones, Was There a Hawthorne Effect? *American Journal of Sociology*, Vol. 98, No. 3, November, 1991, 451-468.

10. Tom Peters and Robert H. Waterman, Jr., *In Search of Excellence* (New York, NY: Harper Business, 1982), p. 6.

11. Chester Barnard, *Functions of the Executive*, (Cambridge, MA: Harvard University Press, 1938).

12. Ibid., p. 217.

13. Luther Gulick and Lyndall Urwick, eds., *Papers on the Science of Administration*, (New York: Institute of Public Administration, 1937).

14. Gulick, "Notes on the Theory of Organization," in Gulick and Urwick, *Science of Administration*, p. 13.

15. Herbert A. Simon, "The Proverbs of Administration," *Public Administration Review* 6 (Winter 1946): 53–67.

16. Herbert A. Simon, *Administrative Behavior: A Study of Decision-Making Processes in Administrative Organization*, 3rd ed. (New York: The Free Press, 1976).

17. Mary Parker Follett, *The New State: Group Organization—The Solution to Popular Government* (New York: Longmans, Green, 1918); *Creative Experience* (New York: Longmans, Green, 1924); and *Dynamic Administration: The Collected Papers of Mary Parker Follet*, Henry C. Metcalf and L. Urwick, eds. (London: Sir Isaac Pitman, 1960).

18. Noel O'R. Morton and Stefanie A. Lindquist, "Revealing the Feminist in Mary Parker Follett," *Administration & Society* 29, no. 3 (July 1997): 348–372.

19. Abraham Maslow, *Motivation and Personality* (New York: Harper and Brothers, 1954).

20. Douglas McGregor, *The Human Side of Enterprise* (New York: McGraw-Hill, 1960).

21. Rensis Likert, *The Human Organization: Its Management and Value* (New York: McGraw-Hill, 1967).

# Making the Essential Organization Effective

- **Unit 1:** Managing Employees as People and Assets
- **Unit 2:** Communications and Leadership

# UNIT 1: Managing Employees as People and Assets

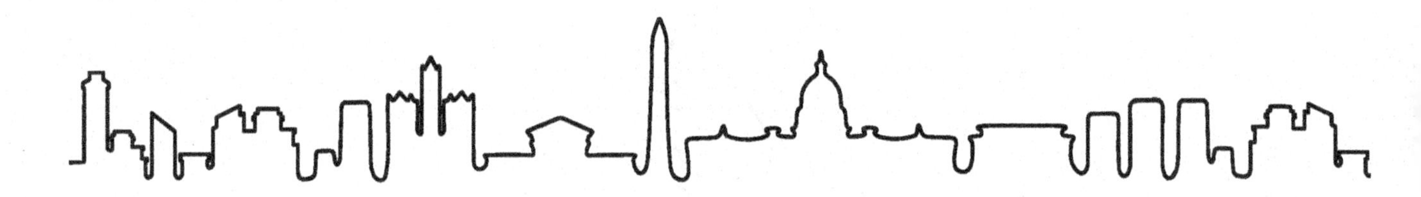

## Recruitment, Selection, Training, Retention and Compensation of Employees

The modern content and context of public human resources management are conveniently summarized by the following dozen or so important concepts that pertain to the world of work and how these notions are interconnected: changing, dynamic, global, diverse, flexible, customer driven, legalistic, fair, entrepreneurial, de-bureaucratized, uncertain, performance based, quality driven, teamwork, constant innovation and improvement, and people as assets rather than costs or liabilities.

"Let me control personnel," George Kennan, political realist and cold war era American diplomat and historian said, "and I will ultimately control policy. For the part of the machine that recruits and hires and fires and promotes people can soon control the entire shape of the institution."[1]

Few administrative theorists or practitioners would dispute this statement, and in the course of history, few able administrators have thought or acted otherwise. Their attitudes and approaches to the subject, however, have often differed.

This book emphasizes learning in a contemporary and global orientation. In a recent study entitled "College Learning for the New Global Century," the American Association of Colleges and Universities (AAC&U) present their belief in the value of liberal education in preparing learners for the third millennium. AAC&U is not only adamant that the quality of higher education be enhanced, but that the education provided enables the "...full development of human talent."[2] In this regard, they recommend "...an education that intentionally fosters, across multiple fields of study, wide-ranging knowledge of science, cultures, and society; high-level intellectual and practical skills; an active commitment to personal and social responsibility; and the demonstrated ability to apply learning to complex problems and challenges."[3] To this end, four "essential learning outcomes" are proposed: 1) Knowledge of human cultures and the physical and natural world (sciences, mathematics, social sciences, humanities, histories, languages, and the arts); 2) Intellectual and practical skills (inquiry and analysis, critical and creative thinking, written and oral communication, quantitative and information literacy, and teamwork and problem solving); 3) Personal and social responsibility (civic knowledge and engagement at the local and global levels, intercultural knowledge and competence, ethical reasoning and action, and lifelong learning skills); and 4) Integrative and synthesis learning.[4]

# THINK ABOUT IT!

**Trends in Public Personnel Administration**

The workplace of tomorrow will become more heterogeneous, especially in terms of its aging and immigration characteristics. Workplace diversity will grow, especially in areas of race and ethnicity, gender, age, disability, veteran status, national origin, religion, language and sexual orientation.

Increasingly, transactional HR activities will become a part of electronic Human Resource Management (eHRM) in areas such as pay and compensation, benefits (vacation time, personal time-off, health and insurance payments, pensions, 401(k) and retirement, direct payroll deposits, recruitment), and other administrative and record keeping areas.

Also, more and more of these transactional activities are being outsourced to organizations that specialize in HR management and development—or Professional Employer Organizations (PEOs). Most modern organizations have moved toward web-based HR systems and employees are encouraged to self-inform and manage their employment portfolio on a system that is always accessible 24 hours a day, seven days per week.

There is a cache of managerial and human resource issues that are of enduring importance, yet the efficacy in which line manager's deal with them remains problematic. A sample listing of these concerns include these salient topics: retention, pluralistic workforce, working mothers (nearly 70 percent of mothers with children under 18 are employed), paternity-maternity leave programs, dual career families, glass and bamboo ceilings, limited or low skilled educated employees, gender pay inequities, work/family issues, child and elder care, sequencing mothers (drop out and then reenter employment market), age and disability discrimination, and immigration and work policies. Also, team or group evaluation methods remain unresolved, along with individual performance evaluation, succession planning, bench-marking, broad banding, e-learning, team building and career planning, and the uses of technology. All of these issues, unresolved as they might be, are part of the staple diet of managers today; they also beg for solutions which blend the theory of our multidisciplinary field with known best practices

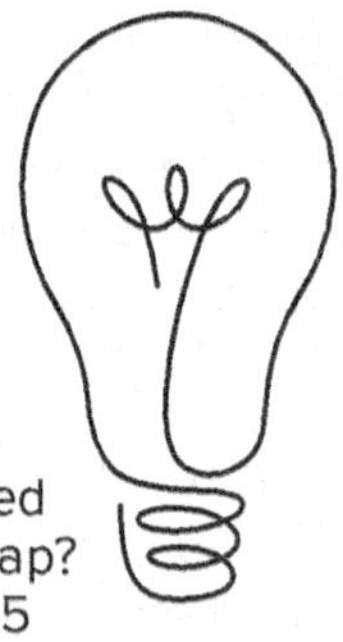

In the midst of a worldwide pandemic, the United States is faced with a unique problem: Nearly 10 million job openings and about 8 million unemployed persons. Why is there such a large gap? The answer is multifaceted. About 2.5 million women remain unemployed largely because of a lack of affordable day care provisions. Many previously employed persons have had time to reflect about their former jobs and desire to upgrade their job status, especially with jobs that telecommute from home. Some remain fearful of the contagion and choose personal health and security over employment, especially in the areas of production, retail sales, and service sectors of the economy. This period is also referred to as the Great Resignation.

The Bureau of Labor Statistics (BLS) shows that U.S. employment is projected to grow from 153.5 million to 165.4 million during 2020-2030—an increase of 11.9 million employed persons or 7.7 percent growth rate. Healthcare and computer mathematical occupations are expected to have the most rapid employment growth. For instance, nurse practitioners, a 68.2 percent change; physical therapist assistants, 35.4 percent; home health and personal care aides, 32.6 percent; medical and health service managers, 32.5 percent; physician assistants, 31.0 percent; epidemiologists, 29.6 percent and speech language pathologists, 28.1 percent. The fastest growth is expected for wind turbine service technicians, 68.2 percent; solar photovoltaic installers, 52.1 percent and Information security analysts, 44.3 percent.

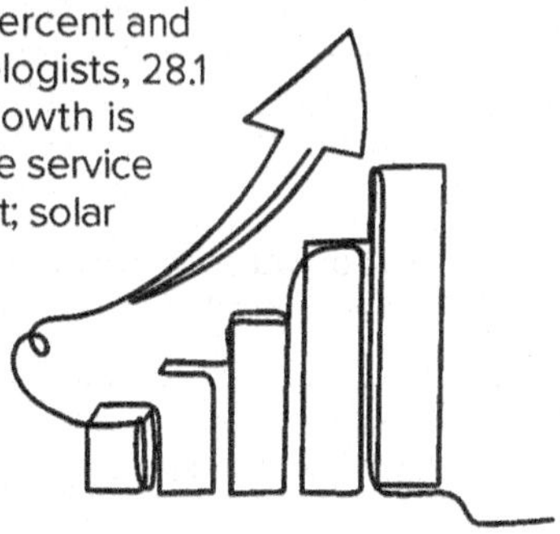

Embedded in these notions is the idea that these outcomes are connected to living and working in a contemporary free society and world that is global, collaborative and interdependent in nature. Yet, unfortunately, as AAC&U summarized, "...college students are underperforming in virtually every area of academic endeavor, from essential intellectual skills such as critical thinking, writing, and quantitative reasoning to public purposes such as civic engagement and ethical learning."[5] This underachievement does not bode well for the future workforce in America—not to mention our ability to compete globally. It is particularly distressing, that the United States continues to rank well below other industrialized democracies worldwide, such as Finland, France, Taiwan, South Korea, United Kingdom, Ireland, Spain, Japan, Canada, Iceland, and Germany.[6]

As stated earlier in this book, the authors believe in the necessity of integrating the notions of work, citizenship, and living in a world that is undergoing change at warp speeds and, therefore, producing added complexity, anxiety, and uncertainty in our lives. This is one of the core reasons why the case study method is increasingly being used in college and university curriculums. The goal is to help learners acquire multidisciplinary, scholarly scientific research, and couple it with experiential learning, and apply it effectively to a wide spectrum of settings, issues, and problems—incidents, cases, and "...issues of organizational living."

## Conflicting Doctrines in American Public Administration

Herbert Kaufman provided a foundation for describing conflicts in the doctrines of public administration—a foundation that remains solid today. He notes that different values are reflected in different periods in American history. The quests for representativeness, for neutral competence, and for executive leadership reflect succeeding norms of public personnel administration.[7]

The quest for representativeness has its roots in the colonial period. In our republican system, government bureaucrats are accountable to policies initiated by representatives of the voters. The quest for neutral competence originated in the 1880s with abuses of legislative supremacy, the long ballot, and the spoils system.

# THINK ABOUT IT!

**What Does the Losing of an Employee Cost?**

Josh Bersin, founder of Bersin of Deloitte, suggests the following costs must be considered when considering the true cost of employee turnover.

| | |
|---|---|
| • Cost of hiring a new person (advertising, interviewing, screening, hiring); • Cost of onboarding a new person (training, management time); | • Customer service and errors (new employees take longer and are often less adept at solving problems). In health-care this may result in much higher error rates, illness, and other very expensive costs (which are not seen by HR); |
| • Lost productivity (new hire may take 1-2 years to reach productivity existing person); | • Training cost (over 2-3 years you likely invest 10-20% of an employee's salary or more in training, that is gone); and |
| • Lost engagement (employees who see high turnover disengage and lose productivity); | • Cultural impact (whenever someone leaves others take time to ask "why?"). |

*Source: Josh Bersin, "Employee Retention Now a Big Issue: Why the Tide has Turned," August 16, 2013,* https://www.linkedin.com/pulse/20130816200159-131079-employee-retention-now-a-big-issue-why-the-tide-has-turned.

The goal of this quest was "taking administration out of politics." The quest for executive leadership was an effort to deal with such governmental issues as budgeting, reorganization, fragmentation, and the size of the bureaucracy. The personnel function is an essential part of these issues.

In addition to these "quests," it is helpful to examine Donald E. Klingner's and John Nalbandian's description of factors affecting public personnel practices that may contribute to the conflicting values in public administration. These factors are:

- **Value influences.** These considerations especially concern the rights of the individual, administrative efficiency, responsiveness, and social equity.
- **Mediating activities.** These interventions include affirmative action, human resource planning, productivity, and labor relations.
- **Core functions.** These essentials focus on the procurement, allocation, development, and sanction of human resources.[8]

## Procedures and Policies

Public organizations use essentially one of two different methods of establishing and operating personnel systems. One method stresses political appointment and election; the other emphasizes an objective determination of merit.

The selection of civil servants by merit and by political patronage are not mutually exclusive, argues James E. Leidlein. Fears that any relaxation of a merit-based system will lead to the returned dominance of political patronage are not warranted.[9]

Units of the Revolutionary army frequently elected their own officers, and once the hostilities ended, states and communities elected most of the administrators they would need. Many cities and towns, particularly older ones, continue to follow this practice. Some New England communities elect as many as fifty officials. Newer areas of the country, such as the Far West, disdain such practices, but even they maintain county organizations with many elective posts. No other major country in the world elects so many of its administrators as does the United States. Most state governments elect some officials whose tasks would be regarded in Europe or Canada as purely administrative.

Although election, dating back to the foundations of U.S. government, is supposed to give the people a deciding voice in determining who will administer their government, it can lead to abuses such as misleading promises and a reliance on campaign funding from special interests. Most of the electorate finds it impossible to know all the candidates for whom they must vote.

Political appointment also has a long history in the United States, dating back to colonial times. Even John Adams, who considered himself something of a paragon of political propriety, felt constrained to provide his ne'er-do-well son-in-law with a government job. Such practices gained increased favor with the arrival of Andrew Jackson at the White House. Jackson strongly adhered to Jefferson's views on rotating public servants in office. At the same time, Jackson did not believe that this would entail any loss of public confidence. As he put it, "The duties of all public servants are, or at least admit of being made, so plain and simple that men of intelligence may readily qualify themselves for their performance."[10] Jackson's espousal of this philosophy was fortified in that he had a virtual army of job seekers at his back clamoring loudly for the plums of patronage.

From Jackson's time on, U.S. presidents frequently found themselves besieged by persons seeking positions on the public payroll. One aggressive appointment seeker jumped into Abraham Lincoln's carriage to ask for a job while the president was riding through Washington. Lincoln started to listen to him but then drove him away, saying, more in despair than in anger, "No, I will not do business in the street."

NOTABLE QUOTES

A pile of rocks ceases to be a rock pile when somebody comtemplates it with the idea of a cathedral in mind.

— *Antoine Saint--Exupery*

When a disappointed job seeker assassinated President James Garfield in 1881, the nation's appetite for such administrative practices began to dampen. Political appointment continues to play a prominent role in U.S. administrative life, however. Our presidents, for example, fill nearly one hundred times more appointments than do British prime ministers.

The assassination of President Garfield did have its effect. It gave rise to an alternative method of recruitment, namely the merit system. Two years after the president's violent death, with the unanticipated backing of former spoils system supporter and now President, Chester A. Arthur, Congress passed the Pendleton Act, setting up a systematized procedure for hiring and employing vast numbers of federal civil servants in nearly every category. The merit system principle has continued to grow. It not only encompasses more than 90 percent of positions in the federal government but includes increasing numbers of employees in state and local governments. About two-thirds of our states have comprehensive merit systems that cover the vast majority of their job holders. Even those states without comprehensive merit systems make some provision for merit-style appointments. The federal government has helped prod states and municipalities to move in this direction, for federal grants-in-aid frequently require the recipient agency to operate a merit system of some sort.

***The Pendleton Act, passed in 1883, provided the substance of modern merit principles:***

- First, administrative reform focused on nonpolitical appointments in attempting to neutralize the civil service. Such nonpartisanship in selecting, promoting, and regulating public bureaucrats was a reaction against the evils of the spoils system.
- Second, the Pendleton Act embraced egalitarianism, the most important legacy of Jacksonian democracy. Congress, in adopting civil service reform, refused to pattern the U.S. career system after the British. The American merit system would be open to all applicants of appropriate aptitude and skills. Theoretically, at least, all classes of citizens may contest for government employment.
- Third, competence, as determined by competitive examinations, was instituted in the Pendleton Act's provisions. The requirement was that exams be practical, related to the duties to be performed, and not grounded in theoretical or scholarly essays based on academic achievement.[11]

By the late 1970s, the Civic Service Reform Act of 1978 established the key merit system principles that the government employs today: recruiting, selecting, and advancing employees on the basis of their abilities, knowledge, and skills; providing equitable and adequate

# THINK ABOUT IT!

**The Plum Book**

College learners may aspire to become Washington policy makers. The Plum book provides guidelines, facts, and positions for postgraduate students seeking jobs in the upper ranks of the federal government .

The Plum Book, released every four years alternately by the Senate Committee on Governmental Affairs or the House Committee on Government Reform, carries the formal title of United States Government Policy and Supporting Positions.

The Plum Book catalogs more than seven thousand jobs at the prerogative of the president. They usually are appointed positions—including agency heads, immediate subordinates, policy executives, and advisors.

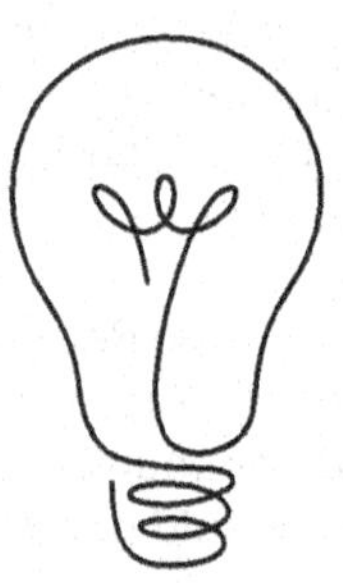

The Plum Book is designed to facilitate presidential transitions every four years. It combines interests of partisan, policy, and system politics.

compensation; training employees to assure high-quality performance; guaranteeing fairness for applicants and employees; and protecting against coercion for political purposes.

***The Act states, in addition to many other merit principles:***
Recruitment should be from qualified individuals from appropriate sources in an endeavor to achieve a workforce from all segments of society, and selection and advancement should be determined solely on the basis of relative ability, knowledge, and skills, after fair and open competition which assures that all receive equal opportunity.

***Another key part of the 1978 law states:***
Employees should be retained on the basis of the adequacy of their performance, inadequate performance should be corrected, and employees should be separated who cannot or will not improve their performance to meet required standards.

Despite the law, the merit system has its detractors, who say that such a system eventually leads to a triumph of mediocrity, with initiative and enterprise sacrificed to the pressures of security and the forces of stagnation. Even when a merit system encourages merit, the argument continues, it may lead only to a meritocracy that shuts out otherwise capable people who cannot pass the tests or meet formal and sometimes fatuous requirements of the system.

Supporters argue that even if it leads to a "meritocracy," it is still likely to be more egalitarian and democratic than a system built on political contacts and allegiances.

In a 1990 decision, the United States Supreme Court ruled that the U.S. Constitution prohibits partisan political considerations in hiring, promoting, or transferring most public employees. The ruling clearly prevents a mayor or local chief executive from reserving non-policy-making jobs such as road equipment operations, prison security, highway repair, or parks department positions for the party faithful. Although the practical impact of the ruling is difficult to assess, the Supreme Court dealt a sharp blow to political patronage at all levels.

## Dynamics of Federal Government Employment

In 2021, the federal government, excluding the U.S. Postal Service, employed early two million civilian workers, or about 1.3 percent of the nation's workforce. The federal government is the nation's single largest employer. Because data on employment in certain agencies cannot be released to the public for national security reasons, this total does not include employment at the Central Intelligence Agency, National Security Agency, Defense Intelligence Agency, and National Imagery and Mapping Agency.

The federal government makes an effort to have a workforce as diverse as the nation's civilian labor force. The federal government serves as a model for all employers in abiding by equal employment opportunity legislation, which protects current and potential employees from discrimination based on race, color, religion, sex, national origin, disability, or age. The federal government also makes an effort to recruit and accommodate persons with disabilities.

Even though the headquarters of most federal departments and agencies are in the Washington, D.C. area, approximately 16 percent of federal employees worked in the vicinity of the nation's capital. In addition to federal employees working throughout the United States, nearly 95,000-100,000, which includes foreign nationals, are assigned overseas, mostly in embassies or defense installations.

### Occupations in the Federal Service

The federal government employs workers in every major occupational group. Workers are not employed in the same proportions in which they are employed throughout the economy as a whole, however. The analytical and technical nature of many government duties translates into a much higher proportion of professional, management, business, and financial occupations in the federal government, compared with the economy as a whole. Conversely, the government sells very little, so it employs relatively few sales workers.

Professional and related occupations account for about of one-third of federal employment. The largest group of professional workers worked in life, physical, and social science occupations, such as biological scientists, conservation scientists and foresters, environmental scientists and geoscientists, and forest and conservation technicians. They do work such as determining the effects of drugs on living organisms, preventing fires in the national forests, and predicting earthquakes and hurricanes. Many health professionals, such as licensed practical and licensed vocational nurses, registered nurses, physicians, and surgeons, are employed by the Veterans Administration (VA) in VA hospitals.

Large numbers of federal workers also hold jobs as engineers, including aerospace, civil, computer hardware, electrical and electronics, environmental, industrial, mechanical, and nuclear. Engineers are found in many departments of the executive branch, but the vast majority work in the Department of Defense. Some work in the National Aeronautics and Space Administration as well as other agencies. In general, they solve problems and provide advice on technical programs, such as building highway bridges or implementing agency wide computer systems.

The federal government hires many lawyers, judges, and related workers, as well as law clerks to write, administer, and enforce many of the country's laws and regulations.

Computer specialists—primary computer software engineers, computer systems analysts, and network and computer systems administrators—are employed throughout the federal government. They write computer programs, analyze problems related to data processing, and keep computer systems running smoothly. This along with other computer related occupations total 17 percent of federal occupations.

Business and Financial Operation Occupations plus Operations Specialists make up another 45 percent of federal employment and are primarily responsible for overseeing operations. This category of workers includes a broad range of officials who, at the highest levels, may head federal agencies and programs. Middle managers, on the other hand, usually oversee one activity or aspect of a program. One management occupation—legislators—is responsible for passing and amending laws and overseeing the executive branch of government. Within the federal government, legislators are entirely found in Congress.

Other occupations in this category are accountants and auditors, who prepare and analyze financial reports, review and record revenues and expenditures, and investigate operations for fraud and inefficiency. Management analysts study government operations and systems and suggest improvements. Purchasing agents handle federal purchases of supplies, and tax examiners, collectors, and revenue agents determine and collect taxes.

About 11 percent of federal workers are in office and administrative support occupations. These employees aid management staff with administrative duties. Administrative support workers in the federal government include information and record clerks, general office clerks, and administrative assistants.

Compared with the economy as a whole, workers in service occupations are relatively scarce in the federal government. About seven out of ten federal workers in service occupations are protective service workers, such as correctional officers and jailers, detectives and criminal investigators, and police officers. These workers protect the public from crime and oversee federal prisons.

Federally employed workers in installation, maintenance, and repair occupations include aircraft mechanics and service technicians, who fix and maintain all types of aircraft, and electrical and electronic equipment mechanics, installers, and repairers, who inspect, adjust, and repair electronic equipment such as industrial controls, transmitters, antennas, radar, radio, and navigation systems.

The federal government employs a relatively small number of workers in transportation; production; construction; sales and related; and farming, fishing, and forestry occupations. However, it employs almost all the air traffic controllers in the country and a significant number of agricultural inspectors and bridge and lock tenders.

## Earnings

In efforts to provide agencies more flexibility in how they pay their workers, several pay systems are in effect. The two largest departments with updated pay systems are the Departments of Defense and Homeland Security. The new systems incorporate fewer, wider pay "bands" instead of grade levels. Pay increases under these new systems are based almost entirely on performance, as opposed to length of service. On the other hand, as in **Table 3.1.1,** the General Schedule incorporates GS-1 through GS-15 grades and pay ranges.

The majority of professional and administrative federal workers are still paid under the General Schedule (GS). The General Schedule, shown in **Table 3.1.1**, has fifteen grades of pay for civilian white-collar and service workers, and smaller within-grade step increases that occur based on length of service and quality of performance.

New employees usually start at the first step of a grade. However, if the position in question is difficult to fill, entrants may receive somewhat higher pay or special rates. Almost all physician and engineer positions, for example, fall into this category.

In an effort to make federal pay more responsive to local labor market conditions, federal employees working within the United States receive locality pay. The specific amount of locality pay is determined by survey comparisons of private-sector wage rates and federal wage rates in the relevant geographic area. At its highest level, locality pay can lead to an increase can approach 30 percent above the base salary. Every January, a pay adjustment tied to changes in private-sector pay levels is divided between an across-the-board pay increase in the General Schedule and locality pay increases.

Federal employees in craft, repair, operator, and laborer jobs are paid under the Federal Wage System (FWS). This schedule sets federal wages so that they are compatible with prevailing wage rates for similar types of jobs in the private sector. As a result, wage rates paid under the FWS can vary significantly from one locality to another.

**Table 3.1.1 Federal Government General Schedule (GS) Salary Table: 2022**

| GS LEVEL | ENTRANCE LEVEL | STEP INCREASE | MAXIMUM LEVEL |
|---|---|---|---|
| 1 | $20,172 | varies | $25,234 |
| 2 | $22,682 | varies | $28,546 |
| 3 | $24,749 | $825 | $32,174 |
| 4 | $27,782 | $926 | $36,116 |
| 5 | $31,083 | $1,036 | $40,407 |
| 6 | $34,649 | $1,155 | $45,044 |
| 7 | $38,503 | $1,283 | $50,050 |
| 8 | $42,641 | $1,421 | $55,430 |
| 9 | $47,097 | $1,570 | $61,227 |
| 10 | $51,864 | $1,729 | $67,425 |
| 11 | $56,983 | $1,899 | $74,074 |
| 12 | $68,299 | $2,277 | $88,792 |
| 13 | $81,216 | $2,707 | $105,579 |
| 14 | $95,973 | $3,199 | $124,764 |
| 15 | $112,890 | $3,763 | $146,757 |

*Source: www.generalschedule.org*

## ESSENTIAL VIEWS:

### ACADEMICS/PRACTITIONERS AT THE STREET LEVEL

**Room for Improvement: The Government Employee Experience**

By Bill Brantley

According to GQR, global talent acquisition and advisory firm, a good employee experience is valuable for four reasons:

1. A good employee experience helps attract top talent.
2. Candidates are spending more time researching organizations. Many online sources exist to learn about an organization's employee experience. 
3. Millennials and Generation Z want a good employee experience. According to a LinkedIn Workplace Culture report, 86% of millennials would take a pay cut if it meant they could work for a company with a mission and values they can identify with.
4. Research by the WorkHuman Analytics and Research Institute® and the IBM Smarter Workforce Institute established that "organizations that score in the top 25 percent for employee experience to have nearly three times the return on assets and more than double the return on sales compared to companies in the bottom quartile."

**Does Employee Experience Matter for Government Agencies?**

"Twenty-five percent of graduating college students rank government as one of the top three industries in which they would want to work, yet a much smaller percentage decided to actually launch a career in the public sector." As Federal, state, and local government agencies know, today's graduates have many career options to serve, such as numerous nonprofits and socially aligned business enterprises. Why join a public agency and fight the internal bureaucracy to have a small impact on society?

Improving employee experience for government workers doesn't require considerable investment. As Chris Cruz, the former deputy CIO for California, found, "engaging an organization's people is ultimately about removing pain points and distractions at work to create a better experience." For example, when Cruz adopted an aggressive telecommuting policy and an agile training program, the California Health

Care Services' IT department's vacancies dropped to 5% from 34%. As Howard Risher wrote in an April 26, 2018, Government Executive article, "Everyone wants recognition for their accomplishments. Employees want and need feedback to help them improve; they want challenges and opportunities to test their abilities. They also want respect from leaders, and they want to be treated fairly."

**Best Places to Work in the Federal Government**

For over a decade, the Partnership for Public Service has released its report on the best places to work in the Federal government. Improving the Federal government employee experience is especially vital because 33% of the federal workforce is eligible to retire in the next five years. With only six percent of Federal employees under 30, there are not enough young employees to replace retiring employees.

According to the Partnership's 2019 report, the private sector has a 77% employee engagement score while the Federal government scores only 61.7%. Eleven Federal agencies score higher than 77% in employee engagement because employees are recognized for good performance, and employees trust their agency leadership.

**Purpose-Driven Government**

President-elect Biden has stated that "Dedicated public servants are the lifeblood of democracy." Improving the government employee experience is the bold action needed to reinvigorate government service.

## Merit-Based Recruitment

Although the merit principle has become the most widely accepted basis for personnel operation in U.S. public administration, it nevertheless continues to arouse controversy and pose problems. In terms of recruitment, there is first the task of making sure that the system truly rewards merit. Most civil service systems make extensive use of comparative examinations to bring this about. Though such exams may weigh the merits of the various candidates more impartially than a system built on favoritism would, they present difficulties of their own.

To be valid measures, the exams must be predictive. In other words, high scores on the examinations should correlate with high performance on the job, and vice versa. This is not necessarily the case. The issue of validity (whether test results are accurate or appropriate) and other recruitment criteria have come to the fore because of the increased effort to recruit members of minority groups into government service. Civil rights supporters claim that many of these criteria serve to exclude historically discriminated groups. Specifically, they charge that these tests fail to measure the true capability of a job applicant.

The federal government encourages test validation as a means of ensuring and expanding equal opportunity. The move to include more members of minority groups in public administration is part of a larger movement aimed at making government agencies more representative of the public they serve. This brings us to another issue in administration. Government agencies have at times become "captive" to one or more sectors of society. The captive agency, a term used by public administration scholar Brian Chapman, tends to recruit heavily from one particular ethnic, religious, social, or geographical group.

## Limitations to Merit

A pure merit system for all public service appointments would be grounded in competition based on merit rules. However, no administration functions on a pure merit system. Exceptions always exist, including:

- Elected officials. Some officials are elected, not appointed. No civil service gauge is employed in an election.
- Political appointments. Elected officials may choose friends, neighbors, or college roommates as political advisers. No civil service gauge is employed for these appointments.
- Affirmative action. To hasten the advancement of members of a disadvantaged group such as women or certain ethnic minorities, that group receives hiring preference. No civil service gauge is employed for such hiring.
- Internal appointments and transfers. Sometimes promotion is restricted to existing staff. The search is conducted inside the organization, not externally, to minimize transaction costs. In such cases, opportunities are provided for insider career development.[12]

## Recruitment Procedures

Merit-based recruitment arrangements include these elements:

- A job analysis leading to a written statement describing duties, or a job description, and the knowledge and skills required of the job holder (the person specification)
- A standard application form
- Personnel specification based soring scheme
- A short-listing procedure to reduce applications, if pertinent, to a manageable number
- Final selection procedure based on personnel specification and panel interview
- Appointment procedure based on scoring scheme
- Notification of results to all candidates[13]

## Qualifications

The government hires people with nearly every level of education and experience—from high school students with no experience to Ph.D.'s with established careers. Jobs in some occupations, such as engineer, ecologist, and lawyer, require that workers have a bachelor's or graduate degree and credit for specific college classes. Other occupations require experience, education, or a combination of both. A few, such as office clerk, do not require education beyond secondary or experience to start.

The qualifications needed for each job are described in detail in the vacancy announcements that advertise job openings. Each job also has a code that corresponds to its minimum requirements. Understanding these codes will speed your search.

The coding systems used to classify jobs vary by agency, but the most common system is the General Schedule (GS). The GS assigns every job a grade level from 1 to 15, according to the minimum level of education and experience its workers need. Jobs that require no experience or education are graded a GS-1, for example. Jobs that require a bachelor's degree and no experience are graded a GS-5 or GS-7, depending on an applicant's academic credentials and an agency's policies.

**Table 3.1.2** shows the GS levels for entry-level workers with different amounts of education and little or no work experience.

College degrees only qualify you for a particular grade level if they are related to the job. For occupations requiring general college-level skills, a bachelor's degree in any subject can qualify you. But other occupations require a specific major.

After gaining work experience, people often qualify for higher GS levels. In general, one year of experience related to the job could raise your grade by one GS level in most clerical and technician positions. In administrative, professional, and scientific positions, GS level increases in increments of two until you reach a GS-12. After that, GS level increases one level at a time. With each additional year of experience at a higher level of responsibility, your GS level could continue to increase until it reaches the maximum for your occupation.

**Table 3.1.2 GS Levels by Education**

| GS LEVEL | EDUCATION |
|---|---|
| GS-1: | No high school diploma |
| GS-2 (GS-3 for clerk-steno positions): | High school diploma |
| GS-3: | High school graduation or 1 year of full-time study after high school |
| GS-4: | Associate degree or 2 years of full-time study after high school |
| GS-5 or GS-7 (Depending on agency policy and applicant's academic credentials) | Bachelor's degree or 4 years of full-time study after high school |
| GS 7: | Bachelor's degree plus 1 year of full-time graduate study |
| GS 9 (GS-11 for some research positions): | Master's degree or 2 years of full-time graduate study |
| GS-9: | Law degree (J.D. or LLB.) |
| GS-11 (GS-12 for some research positions): | Ph.D. or equivalent doctorate or advanced law degree (LL.M.) |

*Source:* http://www.federal-resume.org/gs-levels-explained.aspx

## The Post-Recruitment Phase

After a recruit qualifies for and receives an employment appointment, they still have obstacles to overcome before claiming full-fledged membership in the agency or organization. During the probationary period, agency personnel measure the skills, knowledge, expertise, and responsiveness of every employee. During this time, the recruit can be dismissed without the safeguards that protect those who have successfully completed such a phase. Probationary periods vary in length from six months to as long as seven years. Shorter terms are common in state and local governments, while the federal government and some other subnational jurisdictions require longer probations. The time frames may also vary depending on the nature of the position. While a fledgling sanitation person may acquire permanent status in six months, a police officer may have to wait a full year, and a teacher may not be awarded tenure until three years have passed. The longest probation periods are usually found at colleges and universities, where new faculty members may be scrutinized for seven years before achieving tenure. Some positions, such as high-level political appointments confer no privileges or permanency.

Training is also an aspect of the post-recruitment phase. Some agencies do nearly all their own recruit training; these include police departments, fire departments, and the like. Other public bodies, such as school systems and public health agencies, expect the newcomer to have the needed basic skills. Usually, the higher the professional level of the position, the more likely it is that the recruit will have obtained the essential training prior to appointment.

Training of all types is receiving increasing attention in public administration. A fast-moving and fast-changing society exhibits a strong need for, and must place increasing emphasis on, wide-ranging and high-level skills. Not so long ago, a police officer's training consisted of some on-the-job supervision. Today an officer is likely to receive many weeks or months of schooling at a police academy. The same holds true for many other public positions. Street cleaners are now apt to operate fairly complicated equipment where previously they may have pushed brooms, and so they, too, must receive a certain level of instruction to cope with once-simple tasks.

The fastest growing area of attention in recent years may be in-service training. The upsurge of interest in this training method arises from the growing realization that in a modern society scarcely anyone is ever fully trained for the rest of his or her career. Not only must skills be continually upgraded, but new skills must be acquired if the employee and the organization are to meet changing demands and work patterns. Administrators are progressively accepting the notion that education is a lifelong process and that the organizations they manage must provide training on a nearly nonstop basis throughout an employee's career.

## Promotion

Once an employee achieves tenure as a member of the organization, promotion possibilities may emerge. Advancement may come in the form of a pay increase; an increase in grade at the present level; or a move up to a new level, usually with at least some new duties and responsibilities.

*Not only must skills be continually upgraded, but new skills must be acquired if the employee and the organization are to meet changing demands and work patterns.*

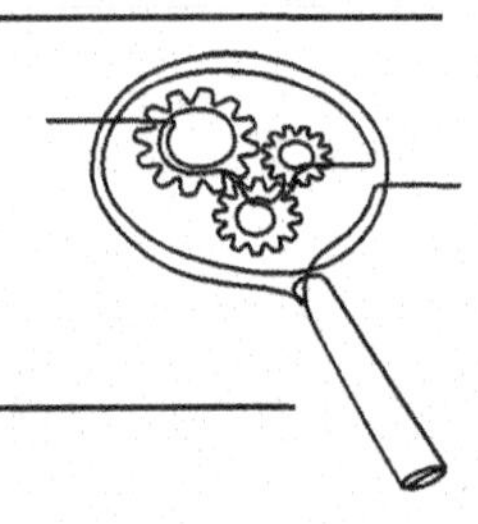

Merit systems customarily provide two basic criteria for promotion: seniority and merit. In the majority of instances, both factors enter into consideration. The question in evaluating this system is, "Which of these, seniority or merit, is more conducive to effective administration?"

The answer at first seems obvious: Merit is usually deemed the most effective method for determining who shall rise. But who determines what is meritorious? Seniority presents obvious drawbacks. It rewards the incompetent along with the competent. James E. Brennan argues that it is far better to raise the salaries of low- paid employees who have proved worthy to competitive averages while decelerating salary increases among the more highly paid. Once inequities are resolved, Brennan emphasizes, merit increases should be based on job values rather than human values.[14]

Organization sponsored training is an important amenity since it is associated with employee job satisfaction and employee retention. Also, one of the main benefits of offering employee fitness and wellness programs is that of increased morale and more positive employee attitudes. With fitness programs there are accompanying lower health care costs, fewer work-related accidents, and lower absenteeism and reduced employee turnover (separation) rates.

A promotion is a change to a position at a higher grade level within the same job classification system and pay schedule, or to a position with a higher rate of pay in a different job classification system and pay schedule. A promotion is always a change to a higher grade and should not be confused with periodic within-grade increases, quality step increases, or merit salary increases, which provide salary increases within the scheduled step rates of a particular grade.

Promotions may occur through several processes. Employees compete for promotion when they apply for higher-graded positions. Applicants are evaluated and ranked for the position based on their experience, education, skills, and performance record. Selections from among the best qualified applicants are based upon management's needs and the overall objectives of the organization. This type of promotion is characterized as a promotion through competitive procedures. A promotion may result from position reclassification to a higher grade due to a gradual accretion of responsibilities. The position to which an employee is promoted is clearly either an outgrowth of their present position or a successor to their present position.

## The Rationale for Job Tenure

Remuneration for government employment is based on position rather than performance. Good performance originates from an employee's sense of duty, not from incentive pay. A tenure system can be wholesale or piecemeal. Tenure may be provided for all existing civil servants who have held a particular position for a certain number of years or awarded to any public employee who holds a position for a certain amount of time.

Government employees enjoy greater protection from dismissal than do private-sector employees. Tenured employment in the civil services is grounded in three elements:

## THINK ABOUT IT!

**Perks Are Another Type of Employee Benefits**

Benefits offered by many organizations today: telecommuting, flexible schedules, compressed work weeks, day and eldercare (sandwiched care), stock options, tutoring for children, free tax planning seminars, tuition reimbursement, flexi-time, flexi-benefit, flexi-place, concierge services, healthcare insurance, paid time off, more liberal vacation plan, sick leave and sick child leave.

- Civil servants serve the state. They must be responsive to the government, but they have longer-term concerns than elected government officials.
- Long-term career paths encourage discipline within work. The risk of losing secure future employment is a serious threat.
- Long-term career paths publicly associate a civil servant with his or her job. This job identity make civil servants want to safeguard their reputations. More generally, long-term career paths encourage discipline and good community.[15]

## Public Personnel Administration Challenges

Federal, state, and local governments employ millions of workers. Almost all government employees are paid with tax dollars. Given the costs, the public has a real interest in keeping governments efficient, effective, and economical. To serve that interest, local, state, and federal governments must:

- Attract high-quality job applicants
- Hire a reasonable share of the high-quality applicants
- Train and develop employees
- Motivate employees to perform at their best
- Retain good performers and remove poor ones

Any employing organization's ability to achieve these goals is closely linked to its personnel policies, systems, and procedures. For the federal civil service, those policies, systems, and procedures are inextricably bound to the concept of merit as defined through various laws and regulations. Today the U.S. civil service is experiencing a "quiet crisis" in its inability to meet government goals. Evidence suggests that "the government is not perceived as an 'employer of choice' by many graduates of the country's most highly rated academic institutions."[16] Ironically, "since the federal government employs relatively more managers, professionals, and technicians than other U.S. employers, the skills required of federal workers are greater, on average, than those employees in the nation as a whole."[17] This negative attitude toward federal employment is therefore damaging. Results of one survey said that less than half of senior-level federal managers and executives would work for the government again if they had a choice.[18]

## Changing Federal Workforce Demographics

First, a quick snapshot of the distribution of government workers nationally. Approximately 24 million people make up the workforce for the national, state and local governments in the United States. Approximately 9.1 million are employed as federal workers, 2.1 million as civilian employees, 4.1 contract and 1.2million as grant employees; an additional 2.3 million active duty military and about 600,000 postal workers comprise the national workface. The total federal workforce makes up about 1 percent of the total U.S. workforce and approximately 70 percent of these workers have jobs in defense, security, the intelligence community and NASA. In contrast, roughly 40 percent of the Russian total workforce is employed in public service. The U.S. also ranks much lower than its European counterparts in terms of the number of public employees per 1,000 inhabitants. The remaining 16 million public employees, working in over 100,000 different jurisdictions, make up the rest of the public workforce in the U.S.

Those who are first introduced to the formal study of public administration often carry with them a false narrative of who makes up the federal workforce in terms of their basic demographic and occupational characteristics. Some of their ideas are mistaken about where federal civilian employees work, what they get paid, and other profile elements such as age, race/ethnicity, gender, level of education, veteran/non-veteran status, tenure and occupational status (white or blue collar). Typically, in mapping out these personnel traits, the standard definition of Federal Non-Seasonal Full-time Permanent Employees is used. In building the comprehensive profile as shown in **Table 3.1.3** on page 114, several different sets of national data are used that are not completely compatible with one another, thereby producing different total numbers and their corresponding percentages. The first misconception pertains to the size of civilian federal workforce and its percent change overtime.

Contrary to public opinion, federal agencies have not been growing at an alarming rate. If we go back to 1970, we find that 2,997,000 civilians worked for the federal government at that time. By 2009, that figure had actually gone down to 2,804,000. Today, the federal workforce hovers around 2.1 million. Historically, when John F. Kennedy was elected president in 1960, the federal executive branch of government employed about 1.8 million civilian employees (not counting military or postal workers). Then, 40 years later, George W. Bush was elected, and we had the same number of federal civilians as we now have under President Biden. Under President Reagan, we had 2.2 million and when Obama was reelected in 2012, about 2 million. Yet, during the past half-century, we added five federal cabinet agencies, many new sub-cabinet agencies and the pages in the Federal Register (congressionally mandated rules and regulations) went up seven-fold, and the nation's population doubled. In summation, the federal workforce has actually shrunk in size in relation to total U.S. population.[19]

An analysis of the federal civilian profile of non-postal employees has remained similar during the last decade (**Table 3.1.3** on the following page). By age, 47.5 years; length of service (tenure) 13.5 years; and level of educational attainment, approximately 52 percent have a bachelor's degree or above, and about 26 percent have veteran preference status due to previous military service, and 8.4 percent are retired military members. Some added, albeit nuanced characteristics, include the following: Nearly 95 percent of federal civilian employees work in the United States and about 15 percent are employed in the DC-MD-PA-WV CBSA (Core-Based Statistical Area); over 12 percent are employed in supervisory/management positions and about 91 percent are employed in white collar positions (27.2 percent professional, 37.5 percent administrative, 26.0 percent clerical or other), and, only 9.2 percent are blue collar civil servants.

The average annual base salary of federal employees is around $86,000 worldwide and the average General Schedule (GS) grade is 10.4, but somewhat higher in the D.C. CBSA with an average grade of 12.5. The cabinet departments with the largest number of federal civilian employees are the Department of Defense (35.0 percent), Department of Veteran Affairs (18.3 percent) and Department of Homeland Security (9.5 percent).

The important role that the federal governmental departments and agencies play in the provision of goods and services is especially realized when non-essential services of the national government are closed, accompanied by the non-payment of the salaries of government workers, for short or extended periods as occurred on October 6-8, 1990, November 14-18, 1995, December 16, 1995-January 5, 1996, October 1-16, 2013, and January 20-22, 2018.

Overall, since 1980, the federal government shutdown 16 different times for periods ranging from 2 days to a high of 38 days.[20] Under the Trump administration, the federal government was closed for business for a grand total of 38 days; under Bill Clinton, 26 days; under George H. W. Bush, three days; and under Ronald Reagan, eight times for a total of 14 days. Generally, a cessation takes place over unresolved conflicts between the legislative and executive branches. That is, unresolved disagreements when Congress fails to pass, or the president refuses to sign or vetoes legislation funding some or all-governmental agencies.

The varied reasons for shutdowns include such things as cuts in the spending bill, budget deficits, repeal of Affordable Care Act (ACA), Medicare premiums, funding of "Contra" militants, military spending (MX missiles), immigration dealing with DACA, and many other issues. Some of the departments and agencies considered non-essential include NASA, EPA, FDA, DOE, HHS, DOL, DOC, HUD and DOI. The costs for a government halt is considerable when the administrative costs and back pay for furloughed workers are taken into consideration. The estimated costs for stoppage in FY 2014, FY 2018, and FY 2019 was approximately $4 billion, and lost productivity of furloughed workers totaled 57,000 years.

One issue that continues to be debated in public administration circles is the size and role of government. According to Michael Hodges, government spends about half what the nation "earns" each year. Is this amount excessive? The percentage of gross domestic product (GDP) spent by the U.S. government is, in proportion to its economy, smaller than that of nearly any other industrialized nation.[21] Government spending is more precisely evaluated in the context of population demographics, economic consumption, citizen production, and environmental consequences, all considered over time.

**Table 3.1.3 Federal Civilian Workforce:**

**Non-Seasonal Full-Time Permanent Employees Comparison 2010-2018**

| CHARACTERISTIC | 2010 # | 2018 # | % CHANGE (+/-) |
|---|---|---|---|
| **Total Employed** | **1,831,719** | **1,872,141** | **2.2** |
| **Female** | **791,124 (43.2%)** | **798,766 (42.7%)** | **1.0** |
| Male | 1,040,594 (56.8%) | 1,072,698 (57.3%) | 3.1 |

**Employment for Selected Jurisdictions**

| STATE | 2010 # | 2018 # | % CHANGE (+/-) |
|---|---|---|---|
| California | 149,865 | 152,857 | 2.0 |
| Colorado | 35,420 | 36,559 | 3.2 |
| Florida | 81,048 | 90,166 | 11.3 |
| Illinois | 46,774 | 44,638 | -4.6 |
| Iowa | 7,736 | 8,124 | 5.0 |
| Kentucky | 23,240 | 21,546 | -7.3 |
| Maryland | 111,410 | 120,222 | 7.9 |
| District of Columbia | 144,598 | 138,621 | -4.1 |
| New Jersey | 28,638 | 24,658 | -13.9 |
| Texas | 128,229 | 133,457 | 4.1 |
| Vermont | 3,946 | 4,895 | 24.0 |
| Outside the U.S. | 33,864 | 33,634 | -0.7 |
| Washington D.C. CBSA | 283,333 | 279,082 | -1.5 |

**Ethnicity/Race Employees and Median Salary**

| | 2010 # | 2018 # | % CHANGE (+/-) | MEDIAN SALARY |
|---|---|---|---|---|
| American Indian / Alaskan | 32,348 | 29,395 | -9.1 | $61,218 |
| Native Asian | 95,064 | 113,167 | 19.6 | $95,617 |
| Black / African American | 327,832 | 351,313 | 7.2 | $70,304 |
| Hispanic Latino | 136,767 | 169,929 | 15.8 | $75,553 |
| More than one Race | 12,803 | 31,670 | 147.4 | $75,299 |
| Native Hawaiian / Pacific Islander | 6,396 | 9,653 | 56.9 | $67,031 |
| White | 1,208,899 | 1,166,246 | -3.5 | $84,522 |
| Unspecified | 1,610 | 768 | -52.3 | $68,636 |
| **Total** | **1,831,719** | **1,869,986** | **2.2** | |
| **Average Age** | **46.8 years** | **47.5 years** | **1 year** | |

**Educational Level**

| | 2010 # | 2018 # | % CHANGE (+/-) |
|---|---|---|---|
| Bachelors | 482,917 | 516,437 | 6.9 |
| H.S. or Equivalent | 491,855 | 447,397 | -9.0 |
| Below H.S. | 12,338 | 10,187 | -17.4 |
| Masters | 219,786 | 300,949 | 36.9 |
| Doctorate | 39,647 | 55,608 | 40.3 |
| Post Doctorate | 5,872 | 7,089 | 20.7 |

**Average Salary by Gender**

| | 2018 | MEDIAN SALARY | 75TH PERCENTILE |
|---|---|---|---|
| Female | $83,178 | $78,762 | $105,769 |
| Male | $88,206 | $83,159 | $110,706 |

*Sources: Adapted and compiled from Federal-executive-branch-characteristics-fy-2010-to-fy-2018%20(1).pdf and Profile%20of%20Federal%20Civilian%20Non-Seasonal%20Full-Time%20Employees.html; and /FedFigures_FY18-Workforce.pdf.*

To promote standards of a civil society, economic and political systems must proactively respond to population changes. The U.S. population increased from 151 million in 1950 to more than 330 million in 2021. Since the early 1800s, immigration has been a crucial component of America's growth and a periodic source of conflict. In recent years, immigration has surfaced as one of the most contentious issues on the nation's political agenda. According to Steven Camarota, about 1.25 million legal and illegal immigrants settle in the country each year. Net immigration into the United States has been increasing for five decades. The projected population increase comes mostly from legal immigration. The United States Census Bureau estimates that by 2045 the minority population will have clearly become the majority population by size with whites making up 49.7 percent of the population.

To summarize some of items presented above, these employment characteristics standout along with their percent change, increase or decrease:

1. The size of the federal civilian workforce in relation to the total pulsation size in the United Sates, continue to shrink;
2. The vast majority of the federal civilian employees work outside of the D.C. CBSA area;
3. A sizeable pay gap continues to exist between what women and men earn as federal employees;
4. The percentage of racial/ethnic identified employees at the federal level continues to increase, especially for those who identify as having multiple racial backgrounds, while the associated percentage of white employees decreases;
5. The percentage of women versus men employed in the federal workforce continues to close during the last decade, but only slightly;
6. The percentage of federal employees who hold bachelors and advanced degrees continues to increase, and the parentage of those with lower level of education, shows a sharp decline;
7. The percent increase in federal workforce numbers at the state level varies substantially and its percent change varies greatly between different jurisdictions;
8. As the occupational categories of the federal workforce become more white collar and professionalized, so does the average General Schedule (GS) grade increase as a whole, and especially so in the District of Columbia.
9. The bulk of the federal workforce is employed in defense, security and intelligence related activities
10. The federal government shutdowns are connected to Congress and the presidency unable to resolve budgetary and policy related disputes and are costly administratively and in terms of back pay for workers who have been furloughed.

## ESSENTIAL VIEWS:

### ACADEMICS/PRACTITIONERS AT THE STREET LEVEL

**What Will the Government Workforce of 2030 Look Like?**
By Bill Brantley

The Deloitte Center for Government Insights report, "Creating the Government of the Future," focuses on five domains of government activity. The domains are service delivery, operations, policy and decision making, talent/workforce, and regulation and enforcement. This article will focus on the five innovations to the talent/workforce domain. The report authors claim that cloud computing and digital identities will drive talent/workforce innovations.

#### Talent Cloud

You may use cloud computing to compose documents in Google Docs or Office 365. Like cloud computing, the talent cloud gives you access to talent from all around the world. For example, if you need help with Microsoft applications, you can hire a Microsoft expert to work on a quick project using Microsoft applications. Many government agencies such as NASA or the EPA have created talent marketplaces in the cloud. The talent clouds let agencies search for people with specific skills that can work on a short-term basis.

#### Human-Machine Collaboration

The second talent/workforce innovation is the use of artificial intelligence to augment people's everyday work. For example, when using Microsoft Teams, I can have the application record the meeting in Microsoft OneNote and create a task list with the corresponding snippet of the recording. Another AI innovation, robotic process automation, is rapidly being adopted in national, state, and local governments.

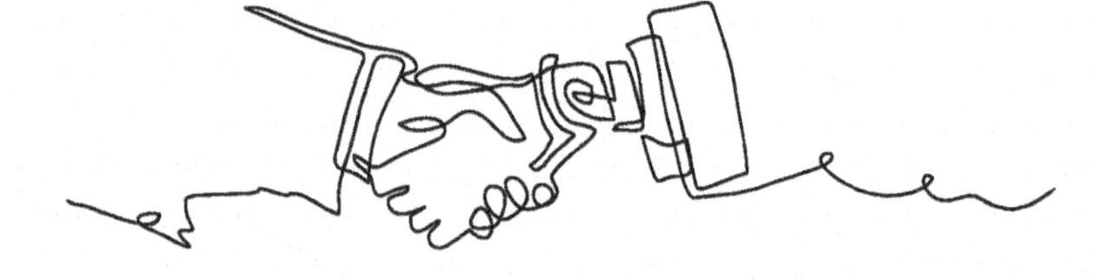

#### Just-In-Time Civil Service

Instead of a long career in government service and often in the same agency, just-in-time civil servants can come from inside or outside of government and serve short periods in government. Just-in-time civil servants could hop back-and-forth from serving in government, then in the private sector, and then back to public service.

### Open Talent Spectrum

The open talent spectrum includes:

- Partnership talent - “employees who are part of joint ventures,”
- Borrowed talent - “employees of contractors,”
- Freelance talent - “independent, individual contractors,”
- Open-source talent - “people who don’t work for the government at all but are part of a value chain of services.”

### Adaptive Workplace

The fifth innovation, adaptive workplace, advocates redesigning systems and processes for an in-office model to reflect the new realities of working from home. Of the five talent/workforce innovations, we see this now thanks to the largest (and unplanned) shift to teleworking for all national, state, and local government employees.

### The Elemental Building Blocks and Drivers of Change for Government Innovation

It is well worth reading the entire report to see how the other four domains of government activity (service delivery, operations, policy and decision making, and regulation and enforcement) have been influenced by COVID-19 quarantine. For example, think of how two drivers of change, “eroding trust” and “privacy,” can be affected by the three building blocks of “artificial intelligence,” “digital identity,” and “blockchain.” How would governments use these two change drivers and three building blocks to create regulation and enforcement innovations?

## Human Resource Management Issues at State and Local Levels

In the 2021 survey of state and local government human resources managers by MissionSquare Research Institute (formerly Center for State and Local Government Excellence), an environmental scan of trends taking place at these levels of government were assessed. The survey revealed that 32 percent of HR managers hired more full-time or part-time people than they did in 2019 and 30 percent said the number of retirements was higher than in 2019. The survey also revealed the skill sets most needed in new hires as shown in **Figure 3.1.1** below.

In addition, the HR managers indicated they continued to have a "hard time filling" these positions: accountants, building officials, corrections officers, dispatchers, engineers; finance (all types); information technology professionals; management (middle and upper levels); nurses, mental health professionals, police officers, and social workers. Also, all types of skilled trades were listed as positions that would be difficult to fill given the current economic climate in the United States.

**Figure 3.1.1 Skills Most Needed for New Hires**

Overall, the workforce issues deemed most important by 50 percent or more of HR managers to their organizations were ranked in the following order ranging from highest to lowest: employee morale; competitive compensation package; employee engagement; recruiting and retaining qualified personnel with needed skills to public service; employee development: leadership; equity: workforce diversity, equity, inclusion; mental health in the workplace; retaining staff needed for core services; equity: racial and social justice (in service delivery and society); workforce succession planning; and how to manage workload when current staff is at their limit and new staff cannot be hired. Interestingly, reducing employee health care costs, creating a more flexible workplace; and impact of technology both on training staff and modifying or eliminating jobs; and managing contract personnel, were ranked lower.

The Center's survey also revealed some pandemic induced workforce changes and issues in the last couple of years. During the survey administration period of February 25 to April 6, 2021, 28 percent of responding HR managers indicated a decrease in full-time workforce. Seventy-five percent of HR managers responding to the survey indicated an increase in the number of employees eligible to participate in flexible work practices. Only 16 percent of HR managers indicated no flexible work practices. Mental health in the workplace was a new answer option for important issues for the organization and was selected by 61 percent of HR managers as an important issue. Likewise, 31 percent of respondents indicated that managing long-term/ permanent telework (via policy and technology) is an important issue.

While previous surveys in 2015 saw 43 percent of HR managers indicating that their governmental agency shifted more health care costs from the employer to the employee in terms of higher premiums, co-payments, and deductibles, only 12 percent of respondents in 2021 indicated shifting more health care costs to employees. Meanwhile the percent indicating they had implemented wellness programs increased from 24 to 27 percent. In 2021 only three percent of HR managers indicated shifting more health care costs from the employer to retirees versus 11 percent in 2015. A small percentage of organizations have increased the requirements to qualify for retiree health benefits (age of eligibility, number of years to become vested, etc.) or eliminated retiree health care.[22]

## Equal Opportunity and Affirmative Action

Equal employment opportunity refers to the idea that "no person should be denied the opportunity for employment because of discrimination based on race, color, religion, sex, national origin, age, or disability or genetic information."[23] While equal opportunity is essentially a passive concept, affirmative action is an active one. Affirmative action implements equal opportunity for minorities and women.

In some ways, equal employment opportunity redefines the merit system to emphasize that the merit philosophy not only recruits, selects, and advances employees on the basis of their relative abilities, but also calls for a workforce representative of all people. Honest people often agree on the lofty goals of equal opportunity but disagree on the manner in which such a sometimes-vague philosophy is carried out.

As a passive strategy, equal opportunity implies non-discrimination. Equal opportunity and nondiscrimination are passive instruments of public policy because they rely on families, schools, and pertinent forces in U.S. society to abolish stereotypes and prejudices that prohibit the creation of a balanced workforce. Affirmative action is an active strategy, intended to ensure equal opportunity.

With the possible exception of trade unionism, which we shall examine in a subsequent chapter, no issue in the post–World War II era has engaged public personnel administration as has the quest for equal opportunity. Public administration is an integral part of modern society and, as such, is not impervious to society's pressures and concerns. As the campaigns for the rights of women and minorities emerged and accumulated legitimacy and recognition, they shook and buffeted public personnel administration along with the rest of American life. There is no question that personnel administration needed the shake-up. The federal government has a somewhat questionable record in equal opportunity.

The controversy over affirmative action arises from the noble aspiration of providing equal employment opportunity for all Americans. As noted earlier, in private administration the law tells administrators only what they cannot do, and in public administration the law tells administrators what they can do. The implementation of equal employment opportunity and affirmative action is, therefore, grounded upon a host of federal, state, and local laws.

Certain pieces of legislation have been crucial in the attempt to achieve social equity through proportional representation in the nation's workforce: Civil Rights Act of 1964, Executive Order 11246 of 1965, and the 1972 Equal Employment Opportunity Act.

The development of the affirmative action concept began in the mid-1960s with the passage of the most far-reaching civil rights law since Reconstruction following the Civil War. The Civil Rights Act of 1964 prohibits job discrimination on the basis of race, sex, religion, national origin, age, or physical disability, and the Equal Employment Opportunity commission was simultaneously created for the purpose of administering the law. The law gives operational meaning to the 1954 Supreme Court desegregation case of Brown v. Board of Education, which holds that the previous doctrine of "separate but equal" facilities for the races will no longer satisfy constitutional requirements and specifically that blacks everywhere are permitted to attend the same public schools as whites.

# THINK ABOUT IT!

**Affirmative Action: Settled Case Law?**

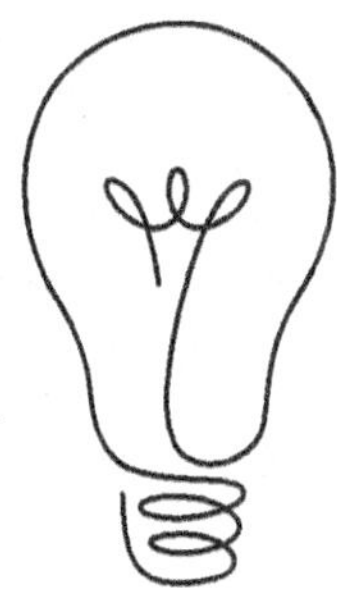

In December 2015, during oral arguments for the Fisher v. University of Texas case dealing with affirmative action and college admissions, Supreme Court Justice Antonin Scalia commented,

"There are—there are those who contend that it does not benefit African Americans to—to get them into the University of Texas where they do not do well, as opposed to having them go to a less advanced school, a less—a slower track school where they do well. One of—one of the briefs pointed out that—that most of the—most of the black scientists in this country don't come from schools like the University of Texas.

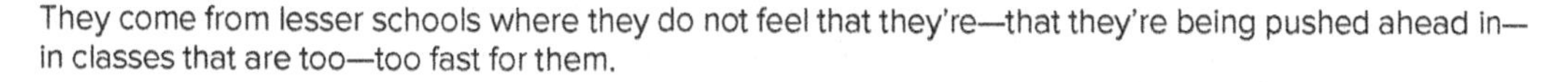

They come from lesser schools where they do not feel that they're—that they're being pushed ahead in—in classes that are too—too fast for them.

I'm just not impressed by the fact that—that the University of Texas may have fewer. Maybe it ought to have fewer. And maybe some—you know, when you take more, the number of blacks, really competent blacks admitted to lesser schools, turns out to be less. And—and I—I don't think it—it—it stands to reason that it's a good thing for the University of Texas to admit as many blacks as possible."

President Lyndon Johnson signed Executive Order 11246 in 1965. It repeated nondiscrimination and affirmative action language used earlier, requiring government contracts to prohibit discrimination by the contractor and to use affirmative action to ensure that workers are employed without regard to race, creed, or color. The 1972 legislation also requires state and local governments to develop affirmative action plans.

Other pieces of legislation with an impact on affirmative action include the Equal Pay Act of 1963; amendments to the Fair Labor Standards Act of 1938; the Age Discrimination in Employment Act of 1967, amended in 1978; Title VI of the Vocational Rehabilitation Act of 1973; and the Vietnam Veteran's Readjustment Assistance Act of 1974.[24]

# THINK ABOUT IT!

**Americans with Disabilities Act**

The purpose of the Americans with Disabilities Act (ADA) is to provide a clear and comprehensive national mandate for the elimination of discrimination against individuals with disabilities. The ADA gives people with disabilities access to employment, housing, public accommodations, education, transportation, communication, recreation, institutionalization, health services, voting, and public services. This affects approximately 50 million Americans with one or more physical or mental disabilities. The ADA defines "qualified individual with a disability" as a person with a disability who, with or without reasonable accommodation, can perform the essential functions of the job that such individual holds or desires.

The ADA prohibits discrimination on the basis of disability in employment, public services, and public accommodations. The Equal Employment Opportunity Commission (EEOC) issues regulations to carry out the requirements of the Act. New buses and trains must be accessible to the disabled. If not handicapped accessible, existing transportation facilities must be altered and rendered accessible. This regulation includes access to rapid and light rail systems. Telecommunications companies now operate relay systems that allow hearing- and speech-impaired Americans to use telephone service.

Employers with fifteen or more employees are prohibited from discriminating against qualified individuals with a disability in job application procedures; hiring, advancement, or discharge of employees; employee compensation; job training; and conditions or privileges of employment. Absence of persons with disabilities in the decision-making process impairs tenets of democratic values and deprives society of talents that contribute to economic and social developments. The United States Census Bureau reports that about one in every five Americans experience some level of disability.

Both de jure and de facto discrimination against the disabled occurs. Social and cultural norms, institutionalized by laws, may be a catalyst to discriminatory practices against persons with disabilities. Legislation is recognized as a mechanism for social change. Although costly and entangled in government regulations, the ADA enjoys support from partisan, policy, and system politics.

*Sources: United States Office of Personnel Management, Federal Civilian Workforce Statistic: Demographic Profile of the Federal Workforce as of September 30, 1996 (Washington, DC: U.S. Government Printing Office, 1997), 6. "Census: 1 in 5 Americans Has Disability: 53 million reported some level of disability in 1997, Census reports," March 17, 2001, "Nearly 1 in 5 People Have a Disability in the U.S., Census Bureau reports," July 25, 2012, https://www.census.gov/newsroom/releases/archives/miscellaneous/cb12-134.html; "Understanding The Americans with Disabilities Act," "The Consumer Law Page," Understanding The Americans with Disabilities Act," July 18, 2019, https://alexanderlaw.com/?s=understanding+the+americans+with+disabilities+act*

# THINK ABOUT IT!

**"A disability does not define who you are!"**

The recommendation often given by speech pathologists to persons who stutter (PWS) in contrast to their counterpart, person who does not stutter (PWNS)) has been thoroughly tested with the election of President Joseph Biden, 46th President of the United States. Stuttering is a type of speech fluency or impairment that is manifested in many ways, such as stammering, word reputation, prolongation vowels, syllables, words, blocks, slow speech, and speech disruptions, etc., and is often accompanied by other personal and employment related difficulties such as fear or extreme anxiety of speaking, social rejection, social isolation, etc., and a large number of stereotypes (less intelligent), and unfavorable perceptions.

President Biden, during an oft quoted CNN interview, discussed his history of stuttering from early childhood to becoming the 46th President of the United States. He said "[stuttering] It has nothing to do with your intelligence quotient. It has nothing to do with your intellectual makeup," and then he added, "you know, stuttering...is the only handicap that people still laugh about. That still humiliate people about. And they don't even mean to." Biden has frequently discussed his speech fluency problem from childhood on, and how he was bullied in the boy's prep school he attended. In his Latin class, because he stuttered, he was given the nickname of "Joey Impedimenta," and that caused him much frustration and anxiety. Fortunately, with the help of his devoted mother, his self-confidence stood the test of development and maturation, and he did not permit a speech problem from defining who he was. He stated that he learned to recite Emerson and Yeats and that in overcoming the stammering, it made him more empathetic, indeed his new moniker is "Empathy in Chief." He also talks about the fact that about 3 million people in the United States and 70 million people worldwide have this neurological disease. Biden joins a host of other household names who stuttered: Winston Churchill, James Earl Jones, Carly Simon and British King George VI—who was showcased in a popular movie that shared his impairment story.

Today, stuttering is recognized as a disability under the Americans with Disabilities Act, 1990 (as amended). In Stuttering and Labor Market Outcomes in the United States, Hope Gerlach, et.al., present interesting findings on stuttering and employment outcomes by comparing the differences between those who have those speech fluency issues, with those who do not. Based on 13,564 respondents in the National Longitudinal Study of Adolescent to Adult Health, 261 people indicated that they stutter. Their study showed a deficit of $7,000 for those who stuttered. Controlling for a wide number of demographic characteristics, they found fluency problems accounted for most of the earning gap for males, but little for their female counterparts. However, females who stutter were 23 percent more likely than their counterparts to be underemployed.

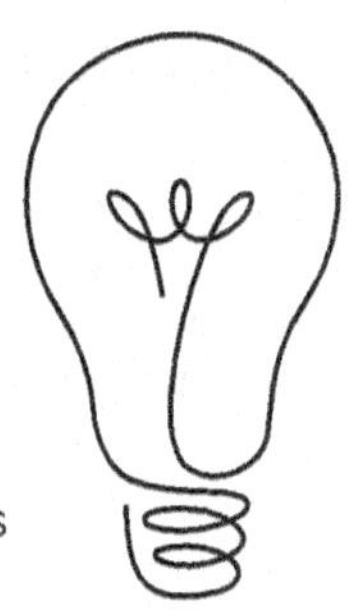

Although we are all only "temporarily abled," It takes courage, self-awareness and confidence to discuss one's disability, especially in a transparent and open environment among colleagues. But in a recent online course, the following Master of Public Administration graduate student, (quoted with his permission) shared his speech fluency and how it has impacted his career and life. What follows is a remarkable story of a resilient, compassionate, intelligent young academic and what he had to say about workplace discrimination in writing to his classmates who he only knew through writing and reading requirements in the discussion modules. It is noteworthy, how Zachary discusses how he communicated with his supervisors and how at least one gave him a chance to succeed. Although he did not mention it in his post, he could have shown how stuttering negatively affects promotion opportunities, pay level, and occupational and career status.

***I am a person who stutters: Zachary Rilling***

For those of you who have never met me in person, I have a slight stutter. However, its severity varies day to day, or even hour to hour. There are days where I can fluently recite Oberon's monologue from A Midsummer Night's Dream by William Shakespeare (for reference: https://www.youturbe.com/watch?y=3Ug98n-ydfs). Other days, I can barely get two words out without stuttering. Most of the time, I am much closer to the Shakespearean end of the spectrum. While I cannot control it, heightened stress and anxiety do make it worse. So, the two perfect scenarios for it to show are job interviews and first dates.

I try to control it [stuttering] but inevitably it comes out in the interview. Most of the time, at least one of the people interviewing me immediately stops listening. You can tell this by the body language. At best, it signals to the employer that there will be times where I just cannot get my words out. At worst, employers hear that I "lack sufficient intelligence to anything more than flipping burgers." (That is an actual quote from a supervisor at

*continued next page*

## THINK ABOUT IT! *(continued)*

**"A disability does not define who you are!"** *(continued)*

a previous job after I was promoted to lead.) While the Americans with Disabilities Act does prevent many employers from discriminating on this basis, that does not stop personal biases from rearing their ugly heads.

Now there is a discussion about bona fide occupational qualifications (BFOQ)...along with the requirements around being able to clearly communicate. However, few potential employers are willing to venture into that area due to the risk of it getting them into trouble. However, I have had potential employers attempt that conversation. One place that was willing to have this discussion ended up being the best place I ever worked. But once again, that is rare. Most of the time, it is just easier to write it off as an inability to clearly communicate and move on.

So...organizations need to take a serious look at what they actually define as "communicate clearly and professionally" when writing job descriptions and evaluating candidates. If the job communicates mostly through written means or regular meetings and conversations with the same few coworkers, does the stutter really matter?

If you have any questions about my stutter, how it affects me in my work, how to work with someone who has one, or anything else, let me know. I will be more than happy to answer any questions you may have. If you don't want to post it in the discussion for everyone to see, or a question pops up in the future, my email is .... The Stuttering Foundation also has some good resources.

***Back to President Joseph Biden...***
President Biden's stuttering is hardly noticeable when he is delivering a prepared speech; sometime present in gaffes he makes in informal conversations or when he is being interviewed. For those who are conversant with the medical and psychological science underlying this neurological disorder, of course, they often see him using circumlocution in word choice. This speech mechanism has led many political pundits to ridicule him as having the unset of dementia and the most insensitive, callous, and cruel pundits are content in merely mocking him.

*Source: Gerlach, Hope, et.al., "Stuttering and Labor market Outcomes in the United States," Journal of Speech, Language, and Hearing Research, Vol. 61, Issue 7, July, 2018. https://pubs.asha.org/doi/abs/10.1044/2018_JSLHR-S-17-0353*

### Reverse Discrimination

The problem of reverse discrimination emerged in the Supreme Court cases of Regents of the University of California v. Allan Bakke (1978) and Weber v. Kaiser Aluminum and Steel Corporation and United Steelworkers Union (1979). The Bakke case was a public-sector concern; the Weber case was a private-sector matter. The distinction is crucial, because legalism in general and laws in particular circumscribe and influence the operation of a public institution more than a private one.

Bakke was a white male suing the medical school of the University of California at Davis for admission, claiming that the medical school rejected his application in favor of less qualified minority students. In a voluntary attempt to correct years of minority discrimination, the medical school established a quota for minority students for each entering class. The Supreme Court's ruling agreed that Bakke had been unfairly denied admission, but the scope of the decision was carefully narrowed.

First, the medical school is a public institution, supported by taxpayers. Second, the case was one of admission to a public university, not a public-sector employment matter. Third, although the court outlawed the quota system, it played a different kind of judicial politics. If public-sector bureaucracies avoided an inflexible quota system, affirmative action programs would remain constitutional. In this way, the court allowed public organizations to consider racial and sexual differences in accepting students. In other words, quotas were made illegal for the public sector; but race and sex remain acceptable for consideration in entrance requirements. The Bakke decision confused employers, bureaucrats, lawyers, and court watchers.

If the Bakke case left the constitutionality of affirmative action in doubt, the Weber decision made at least some headway in settling the issue. Because the Weber case was a private concern, no public-sector monies were involved. As free agents in a democratic society, the Kaiser Aluminum Company and United Steelworkers Union cooperated in establishing an affirmative action program for minority employees.

Brian, a white lab technician with more seniority than two black applicants, filed suit, claiming reverse discrimination against him by the company and the union. By placing minorities in 50 percent of the openings in a training program, thereby establishing a quota system, management and labor created a voluntary program that gave special preference to blacks. The Louisiana plant was located in a region where 39 percent of the local workforce was black. Fifteen percent of the employees of the plant were black, but only two percent of the skilled craft workers were black. Therefore, the Weber case raised not only the issue of equal employment opportunity, but also concerns about a representative workforce.

The Supreme Court decided in favor of the affirmative action program sponsored jointly by management and labor, concluding that Title VII of the Civil Rights Act of 1964 was passed for the particular purpose of improving the economic plight of black Americans. In other words, private-sector employers could voluntarily establish a hiring and promotion program grounded upon improving the employment skills of blacks. To repeat an earlier distinction, the law tells managers in the private sector only what they cannot do, as in the Weber case; however, the law tells administrators in the public sector what they can do.

Technically, courts address only the particular set of facts of any case brought before them. To a large degree, the courts in the United States are passive units of fragmented and decentralized federal and state judicial bureaucracies. Courts consider only cases that merit jurisdiction before particular tribunals. Plaintiffs must take their particular set of grievances into court. To do so, plaintiffs need the skills of talented lawyers, money to finance such actions, and the patience and ego strength to see things through, win or lose.

Affirmative action issues concern quotas, layoffs, work environments, and compensation. The most controversial issue affirmative action raises is whether an employer can establish quotas for making employment decisions. Quotas, of course, specify that a precise percentage of appointments have to be minorities, women, and/or persons with disabilities.

**The Declining Importance of Affirmative Action**

David H. Rosenbloom maintains that the importance of affirmative action began declining in the 1980s for at least three reasons:

1. There is no strong consensus favoring affirmative action, which reduces the organizational coherence and political integrity of affirmative action programs.
2. There is a continuing constitutional stalemate concerning affirmative action, as shown by the nonlinear direction of various Supreme Court cases.
3. There are priority internal demands such as executive leadership, retrenchment, and productivity that affect the commitment to affirmative action.[25]

What is the significance of affirmative action in our society? Affirmative action challenges public-sector managers and some employees, but it also promotes representativeness in government bureaucracies. Affirmative action raises issues of potential and real discrimination that confront women, minorities, and disabled employees. The visibility of affirmative action issues heightens our awareness of discrimination in the workplace.

Perceptions about affirmative action produce a great deal of political and administrative rhetoric. However, the impact, in terms of concrete results, for the purported beneficiaries is questionable. Until the affected groups attain more education and experience, changes will come slowly, and progress will likely be incremental. To its credit, however, affirmative action forces government departments and agencies to broaden and intensify their recruiting efforts, to examine the validity of their examinations, and to question the value of recruitment and promotion criteria. It stimulates innovation and makes governmental organizations more open. The administrative branch becomes, as a result, more representative of the population it serves.

# THINK ABOUT IT!

**The Origins of Affirmative Action**

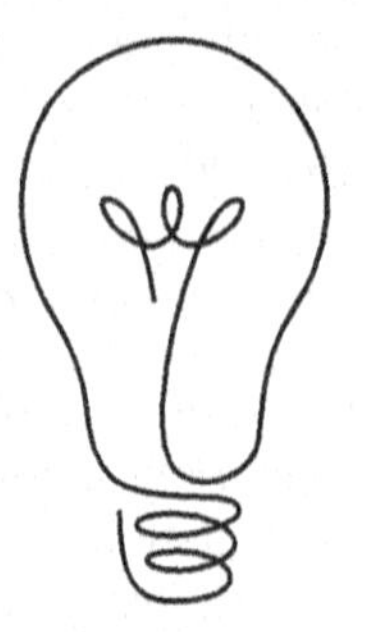

Affirmative action, the set of public policies and initiatives designed to help eliminate past and present discrimination based on race, color, religion, sex, or national origin, is under attack.

Originally, civil rights programs were enacted to help African Americans become full citizens of the United States. The Thirteenth Amendment to the Constitution made slavery illegal; the Fourteenth Amendment guarantees equal protection under the law; the Fifteenth Amendment forbids racial discrimination in access to voting. The 1866 Civil Rights Act guarantees every citizen "the same right to make and enforce contracts as is enjoyed by white citizens."

In 1896, the Supreme Court's decision in Plessy v. Ferguson upheld a "separate, but equal" doctrine that proved to be anything but equal for African Americans. The decision marked the end of the post–Civil War Reconstruction era as Jim Crow laws spread across the South.

In 1941, President Franklin D. Roosevelt signed Executive Order 8802, which outlawed segregationist hiring policies by defense-related industries which held federal contracts. Roosevelt's signing of this order was a direct result of the efforts of black trade union leader A. Philip Randolph.

During 1953, President Harry S. Truman's Committee on Government Contract Compliance urged the Bureau of Employment Security "to act positively and affirmatively to implement the policy of nondiscrimination."

The 1954 Supreme Court decision in Brown v. Board of Education overturned Plessy v. Ferguson.

The actual phrase affirmative action was first used in President Lyndon Johnson's 1965 Executive Order 11246, which requires federal contractors to "take affirmative action to ensure that applicants are employed, and that employees are treated during employment, without regard to their race, creed, color, or national origin."

In 1967, Johnson expanded the Executive Order to include affirmative action requirements to benefit women.

Other equal protection laws passed to make discrimination illegal were the 1964 Civil Rights Act, Titles II and VII of which forbid racial discrimination in "public accommodations" and racial and sex discrimination in employment, respectively; and the 1965 Voting Rights Act adopted after Congress found "that racial discrimination in voting was an insidious and pervasive evil which had been perpetuated in certain parts of the country through unremitting and ingenious defiance of the Constitution."

*Source: "The Origins of Affirmative Action" by Marquita Sykes, as it appeared on the website www.now.org, April 2, 2002. Reprinted by permission of the National Organization for Women, Inc.*

Affirmative action, referred to as equal opportunity under the Civil Rights Act of 1964, means to many Americans today the use of practices such as setting quotas and giving preferential treatment. Many argue that affirmative action should be based on criteria of class instead of considerations of race or sex.[26]

To others, affirmative action is a policy aimed at eliminating discrimination in employment. It does not encourage the hiring or promotion of unqualified people just because they are minorities or women, nor does it impose quotas. It is not reverse discrimination, because it promotes equal opportunity.[27]

Bill Clinton argued that affirmative action must be reformed rather than eliminated. Despite its flaws, affirmative action has been effective in providing equal opportunity to women and minorities. It must be eliminated only when discrimination is finally abolished.[28] Critics of affirmative action are often silent about the veterans' preference program, which benefits mostly males. Since 1944, federal agencies have provided preferential hiring consideration to veterans as a means of rewarding them for service to their country. Many argue that women are especially disadvantaged by veterans' preferences.[29] Opponents of affirmative action may have an easier time removing affirmative action from government offices and institutions than from American culture. In the following instance, even conservatives accepted the merits of an affirmative action candidate:

The curtailment of affirmative action may mean less than is generally expected. Affirmative action is now a firmly established institutional practice, indeed virtually a reflex of many university, corporate, and political decision makers. Just as discrimination did not end with formal rulings against it, neither will affirmative action end with formal rulings.[30]

The bottom line is that affirmative action has contributed to the process of public administration, if not to its substantive content. Affirmative action forces governments to hire, promote, and fire employees under the auspices of legal procedures and administrative due process.

Much of the opposition to affirmative action is framed on the grounds of so-called "reverse discrimination and unwarranted preferences." In fact, fewer than two percent of the employment discrimination cases pending before the Equal Employment Opportunities Commission

## THINK ABOUT IT!

**Sexual Harassment as Violent Behavior**

The following personal story was recently told to one of the co-authors of The Craft of Public Administration and reprinted with permission from the victim. In summation, her story illustrates the impact of harassing behavior and how it affected a young woman in her first job.

I can still remember the first time I was sexually harassed at work—I was 17 (for reference, I am 48 now). I was still in high school, and my manager was a young college student. He asked me out and when I declined, things changed. He would keep me at work longer, he would deny my requests for time off, he would schedule me in departments that he knew were my least favorite, and he would tell me all of these would end if—I just go out with him. I remember feeling almost claustrophobic. Like I was stuck and couldn't escape. I enjoyed my job and had worked there for some time—I didn't want to leave—but I also didn't know what my options were. I didn't understand sexual harassment and I certainly didn't even think about telling someone else about it—I didn't know it was wrong. I thought I had bad luck! I ended up leaving the job after some time and of course, would handle things differently now.

Sexual harassment includes many things in addition to physical assault, sexual assault, and even murder, and of course, unwanted pressure for sexual favors. The following list includes a sample of some behaviors and actions which may constitute sexual harassment as defined by the victim:

- Unwanted deliberate touching, leaning over, cornering, or pinching
- Unwanted sexual looks or gesture
- Unwanted letters, telephone calls, or materials of a sexual nature
- Unwanted pressure for dates
- Unwanted sexual teasing, jokes, remarks, or questions
- Referring to an adult as a girl, hunk, doll, babe, or honey
- Whistling at someone or making "Cat" calls
- Sexual comments, innuendos, or stories
- Turning work discussions to sexual topics
- Asking about sexual fantasies, preferences, or history
- Personal questions about social or sexual life
- Sexual comments about a person's clothing, anatomy, or looks
- Kissing sounds, howling, and smacking lips
- Telling lies or spreading rumors about a person's personal sex life
- Neck or back massage
- Touching an employee's clothing, hair, or body
- Hugging, kissing, patting, or stroking
- Touching or rubbing oneself sexually around another person
- Standing close or brushing up against a person
- Looking a person up and down (elevator eyes) or staring at someone (leering)
- Sexually suggestive signals
- Facial expressions, winking, throwing kisses, or licking lips
- Making sexual gestures with hands or through body movements

*Source: Adapted from https://www.un.org/womenwatch/osagi/pdf/whatissh.pdf*

are reverse discrimination cases. Under the law as written in Executive Orders and interpreted by the courts, anyone benefiting from affirmative action must have relevant and valid job or educational qualifications.

## Performance Rating and Measurement

If an organization is going to use merit rather than seniority as a standard for promotion or demotion, how does one determine job performance? The most common method is for a superior to give a subordinate a performance rating. The system seems simple, but in practice it generates complications and controversies.

The essence of the performance rating problem lies in the absence of objective data and procedures for making these systems work effectively. Even when a supervisor attempts to be fair and impartial, neutral criteria are often scarce. Administrative decision makers too often give into personal whims and capricious actions. However difficult these ratings systems are to administer; they are universally part of the government workplace and culture.

Workforce morale and government performance are closely related. The ability of a government to function effectively and efficiently is related directly to the quality, competency, and motivation of its workforce. Despite positive attitudes toward their jobs and the work they do, only about half the respondents in a survey of federal workers would recommend the federal government as an employer, and more than one-fourth say they definitely would not. Several factors traditionally viewed as reasons to remain in federal employment lost strength as retention factors in one three-year period, according to surveys conducted for the Merit Systems Protection Board. These included the intrinsic value of the work; salary; current health insurance benefits; and the opportunity to have an impact on public affairs.

Many employees argue that the federal government's performance management program does not create an atmosphere that strongly encourages quality performance. Large percentages of employees believe their work units can increase the quantity and quality of the work they perform with the same people.[31]

All public organizations find it necessary to measure employee performance. As the demands of governments have changed, the meaning of the term performance management has changed as well. Rating employees once involved using a trait-based form. Factors such as neatness, punctuality, politeness, and sociability were important indicators of performance satisfaction. Public-sector managers were less focused on work outputs. The evaluation process, even in the public sector, was often secretive. The employee did not participate. In some cases, he or she never knew the rating received.

This format is no longer considered good practice for the organization, the employees, or the citizen-consumers of public service. Instead, public-sector performance management should be:

- **Task-oriented.** The evaluation must be grounded in results—not in personal traits. Results are measured against predefined goals and targets.
- **Participative.** The employee participates in the evaluation alone with his or her supervisor. Both engage in setting goals at the start of the rating period. Employee and supervisor appraise results together at the end.
- **Developmental.** Evaluation processes do more than rate employees; they help employees to improve performance, identifying resources for training and support required to achieve this end.

Performance appraisals may define expectations, make clear when job performance is successful, specify when improvement is needed, and be used to set future goals. Taking responsibility for performance appraisals in local governments, developing performance standards, evaluating the appraisal system, distributing bonuses and cash awards and implementing incentive plans all make significant differences in creating productive governments.

## NOTABLE QUOTES

> Hard work creates results. Results enhance motivation. And, all around, when you're motivated, working is more enjoyable and fun. The more you work, the more results you have.
>
> I got into this very nice circle of success, motivation, work.
>
> — *Susan Polgar*

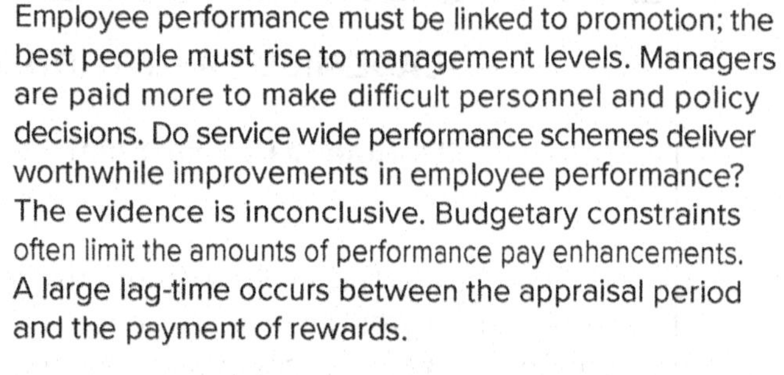

Employee performance must be linked to promotion; the best people must rise to management levels. Managers are paid more to make difficult personnel and policy decisions. Do service wide performance schemes deliver worthwhile improvements in employee performance? The evidence is inconclusive. Budgetary constraints often limit the amounts of performance pay enhancements. A large lag-time occurs between the appraisal period and the payment of rewards.

Performance-pay schemes permit managers to make variable payments. However, most employees receive similar ratings; managers are often unwilling to make distinctions regarding subordinate skills. Employees often perceive their pay as inadequate. Small performance-pay bonuses are thus unlikely to motivate employees, especially since more employees are left out than included in pay enhancements and the majority may resent any process that gives the minority more compensation. Finally, management's performance-pay decision-making methods may be skewed. Overall, employee morale may suffer under such programs.

## ESSENTIAL VIEWS:

### ACADEMICS/PRACTITIONERS AT THE STREET LEVEL

**It's Time to Rethink Employee Performance Management**
By Howard Rusher

The proposal to link layoffs to performance ratings was unexpected. If the ratings were valid, it would make sense, but ratings have little credibility. Jacque Simon, speaking for the American Federation of Government Employees, was correct in saying, "There's nothing objective about performance ratings." Simon's opposition is understandable; the proposal appears to be intentionally antagonistic. In the absence of badly needed changes in the way performance is managed, the proposal is not tenable.

The proposed rule does serve to highlight what is possibly government's weakest talent management practice. In other sectors policies focus on the high performers. That's true as well in sports and entertainment. Its common in other endeavors as well. Individuals aspire to be recognized. In contrast, government's management philosophy makes it more important to admonish poor performers.

The Trump administration is correct in emphasizing policies intended to make agencies more results-oriented and to hold employees accountable. It's hard to argue with the goal. However, the proposed policy would have triggered a different reaction if agencies had invested earlier in best practices and training for managing employee performance.

The proposal has been effectively nullified by the pandemic. The reason is reflected in a 2019 memo from OPM's Acting Director Weichert to 'Heads of Executive Departments and Agencies'. An early statement reads, ". . .let employees know what they need to accomplish and the standards that will be used to evaluate their performance." The message is clear – employees are to be told what standards they will have to meet. That's contrary to best practice thinking in high performance organizations. It's also contrary to what's needed to manage remote workers effectively.

**The Pandemic Made Change Essential**

One of the few positives to come out of the pandemic is that it triggered a need for agencies to rethink the way employee performance is managed. Working miles apart changes supervisor/subordinate working relationships and prompts both to adopt new behaviors. It should be seen as an opportunity for agencies to shift to proven practices. As the pandemic comes to an end, agencies should invest in defining a work management strategy for the new normal.

Through history, year-end ratings have been problematic. They are badly inflated. A number of laws and frequent directives have tried to address problems without real success. In the incoming Administration, well planned changes with adequate training could trigger significant performance gains.

The problems are not unique to government. Employers in every sector recognize the need for better answers. Articles have appeared in surprising publications like *Vanity Fair* ("Microsoft's Lost Decade"). In management journals, the new practices have been a frequent topic for more than two decades.

**It's Not a Simple Problem**

Completing performance appraisals has been time consuming but painless for supervisors – as long as the ratings are consistent with employee expectations. It's the old Lake Wobegon phenomenon "where . . . all the children are above average." The annual Federal Employee Viewpoint Survey confirms employees believe their personal rating is accurate—it's the others that are inflated! It's a problem that can be solved.

A largely unrecognized aspect of the problem in government is that "performance" has been addressed by two distinct groups of practitioners with minimal overlap. At the highest levels, there are experts who focus on agency mission and vision statements, strategic planning and goals, evidence-based decision making, and reporting systems. There is also a separate group of experts who focus on employee performance. Each group has its own technology concerns, laws and regulations, academic researchers, and consulting firms. The future needs to integrate the best thinking of both groups.

Government has also changed in a subtle but important way. The pandemic has given new emphasis to front line knowledge and capabilities. The nation's problems and threats are becoming more complex, require deeper expertise, and responsive local decision making. That is incompatible with top down, dictated performance standards.

An essential change is redefining how employee performance is evaluated. The most common practice has been to rely on a set of common performance dimensions or generic competencies. It makes ratings perfunctory for managers, but it ignores a core consideration—as employees gain experience and benefit from training and coaching, expectations should change. It also ignores the differences in jobs and professional fields. A far better approach focuses on each employee's strengths and weaknesses. It takes an investment of time to define criteria relevant to the job and career stage, but it pays off.

Here the past truly is prologue. The highest hurdle will be changing learned behaviors and habits. Training is essential but building commitment to a new way of managing will require leadership and the help of change management facilitators.

Gallup's research shows the daily interactions between managers and staff are key to employee engagement and to high performance. Their $Q^{12}$ survey results confirm the importance of managers. However, in government, the role of managers has been virtually ignored. Redefining and emphasizing supervisory practices proven to be effective in remote work settings is now essential.

**Government's Purpose Should Be an Advantage**

A thread prominent in discussions of high performance is the importance of creating a purpose-driven organization. Organizations that emphasize service, address difficult societal problems and/or build productive relationships with other organizations—that's government—should be exemplars. Purpose is the reason many employees opted for government careers. Emphasizing an agency's purpose gives employees a sense of meaning and value; its motivational.

Purpose-driven organizations benefit when the societal value of accomplishments is emphasized in recruiting, onboarding, training and in organization/team meetings. Accomplishments should be featured in internal and external communications. It has to be convincing but that should not be a problem in government organizations.

This new focus on purpose reflects what is important to Millennials and new Gen Z workers entering the workforce. They look for something more than the pay and benefits. Looking back, its consistent with statements like the Jack Kennedy inaugural line, ". . .ask what you can do for your country".

A practical example is the importance of serving customers. Too often government agencies are close to the bottom of lists comparing customer satisfaction measures with industry. That should be an easy problem to address. It would be straightforward to highlight stories of how federal agencies like Veterans Affairs benefited their 'customers'. Hospitals, for example, routinely monitor patient satisfaction. A simple but powerful practice would be to videotape customers discussing how a federal agency helped them.

Recognizing accomplishments would help to overcome that compliance culture. Internal communications highlighting how an employee or team solved difficult problems would influence others to do the same. Employees naturally want to be valued and recognized. It would benefit everyone.

**Current Best Practice Thinking**

If there is one overriding answer in the understanding of high performance, it's the importance of gaining employee commitment to what needs to be accomplished. In the right work environment, employees will work hard, go home exhausted but look forward to returning the next day. They enjoy the challenge and the chance to contribute to their organization's success. They may complain to co-workers, but their job satisfaction is high. There are many situations where that's proven to be true across government.

The goal in managing and evaluating performance should be to support and encourage a performance culture. A fundamental change gaining broad acceptance is emphasizing ongoing feedback and coaching by managers. That of course requires newly important coaching skills. It assumes employees are empowered to address problems. It's a radical change from the old, control-oriented approach to supervision.

A related argument gaining acceptance is that in this era of change its natural for performance plans and goals to need adjustment as the year unfolds. Its consistent with the argument for making organizations more agile and responsive. High expectations are fine; where there is trust, employees will accept the challenge, but they need to expect to be treated fairly.

A third trend is to solicit feedback on performance from customers, co-workers and subordinates. The buzzword is crowdsourcing. In a collaborative environment, relevant others are in the best position to observe an individual's strengths and weaknesses.

Metrics of course play a central role, but the data need to be available when needed to guide local decision making. Simply reporting performance data to senior management adds little value.

In combination, the new thinking shifts the focus from mandated, top-down performance standards to local managers. They need the training and support to transition to a new way of managing.

The final trend is eliminating those five and seven level rating scales, along with pass/fail ratings.

Organizations need to identify and recognize their best performers—the stars—and the few unsatisfactory performers. The majority of employees—70 to 80 percent or more—are performing as expected. That's three levels. A simple reward strategy is supplementing step increases with cash awards for the star performers. (That avoids replacing the General Schedule.)

As an added step to confirm the ratings, managers can be required to explain and justify the high and low ratings to a committee of peers. It assures the ratings are warranted and reinforces the recognition.

## Position Classifications

Public-sector personnel organizations have systems of position classifications. The premise for adopting position classification schemes is that different positions require varying degrees of ability and amounts of responsibility. The adoption of a classification plan has long been considered essential for the effective operation of a merit system, for it places the emphasis on what rather than who a person knows. An effective position classification program provides a basis for a fair and workable personnel operation that may reward good performance and penalize poor performance without fear or favor. In principle, such a position classification framework is open and objective.

One crucial question is, "How many classifications should there be?" Should the various jobs be distributed throughout a large number of separate grades and levels, or should they be compressed into a comparatively few broad categories? If the federal government's personnel system features fifteen grades with ten steps each, is this too many, too few, or about right?

The problem has no precise answer. There are no specific criteria defining narrow and broad classifications. To some, the federal government's fifteen grade levels may seem too numerous. To others, they may seem too few. We do know, however, that moving in either direction will yield both advantages and disadvantages.

A personnel system employing numerous narrow classifications organizes its job structures more precisely at each level. If there are two classifications for data entry specialists rather than one, better data entry specialists can be placed in the upper class and less capable data entry specialists can be put in the lower one. In principle, if data entry specialist A does better work than data entry specialist B, then A can be given a higher rating than B. It is further assumed that A will be given not only more money and more status, but also more difficult and more responsible assignments. In this sense, using many relatively narrow categories can be fairer to all concerned. Narrower categories also permit more extensive use of promotion as an incentive. More levels mean more possibilities for promotion, and at the same time, such promotional opportunities can be used as a sanction against those who fail to perform adequately.

Many public organizations have relatively few classification levels, particularly in the lower range of jobs. Postal workers, police officers, fire fighters, and others can usually move up only to a position of command. There are relatively few such positions in most organizations, so opportunities for promotion are limited.

Narrow and numerous job classifications also present distinct difficulties, however. The more classifications there are, the more personnel work the organization must do. Each classification must be carefully described and demarcated, and each job must be carefully plugged into the right classification. This results in a system that is not only costly but that can be cumbersome and complicated.

Use of numerous and narrow classifications may alleviate problems because those performing somewhat more demanding tasks can more easily receive recognition. This pattern can, for the same reasons, create tensions and prompt questions such as "Why should he be classified higher than I am when my job requires as much or more responsibility as his?"

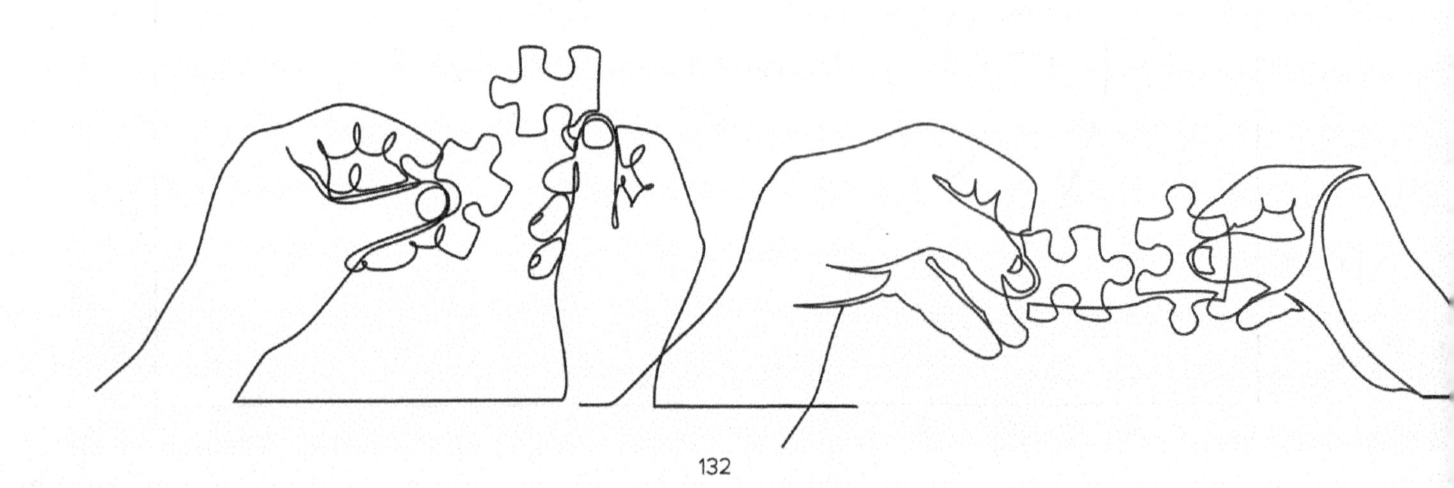

The application of state and federal position classification plans is documented in the appropriate codes of laws. For example, in Texas, the position classification plan, the salary rates, and provisions in the General Appropriations Act apply to hourly, part-time, temporary, and full-time salaried employments in the state departments, agencies, or judicial entities specified.

The position classification system in the federal government is based on two fundamental principles:

- There should be substantially equal pay for substantially equal work.
- Variations in pay should be proportionate to substantial differences in the difficulty or responsibility of the job and in the qualifications required.

The classification of a civilian position consists of the position title, pay plan, series, and grade. Classification decisions, whether made by managers or by human resources specialists, are based on the following:

- Nature and variety of the work
- Difficulty of the work
- Authority and responsibility exercised
- Extent of supervisory controls over the work
- Qualifications required to do the work

# THINK ABOUT IT!

**Equal Pay is a Major Family "Pay" Issue**

Despite the passage of the Equal Pay Act in 1963, women still make about 82 cents for every dollar that their male counterparts receive for doing the same job (Payscale.com, 2021). Note that a lifetime of unequal pay translates into women savings and pensions being less than a man's. With women occupying lower status and lower paying positions overall, the lower pay equates into a loss of approximately $500,000 over the span of a female's career. This is especially prominent fact given the issue of women and children living in poverty and women in retirement living in conditions of poverty.

Also, women are still filling, disproportionately, traditional positions in the workplace, such as secretarial, clerical, cashier, home health care, and teaching positions. In short, there are more implications to discrimination that legal ones. The rhyme of "glass ceilings, glass walls, sticky floors, and trap doors" still resonates for women in the workplace. Last, if women are not fully represented in the highest echelons of government or business, how do their interests get articulated in the shaping public or corporate policy?

"If present trends continue, by the next generation, more Iowa families will be supported by women than by men."

"Pay equity is not a woman's issue – it is a family issue as well as a nation's economic issue."

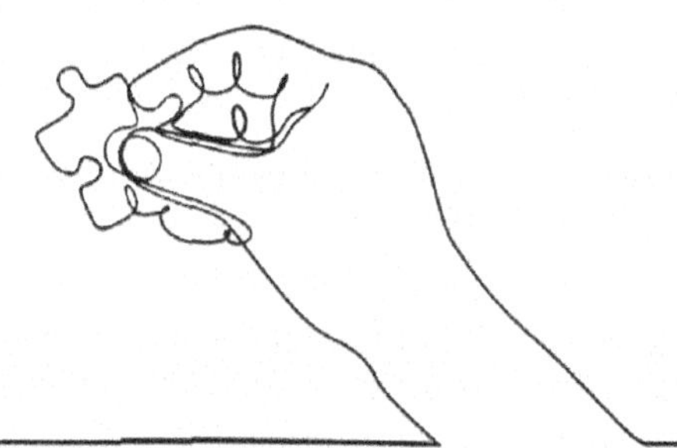

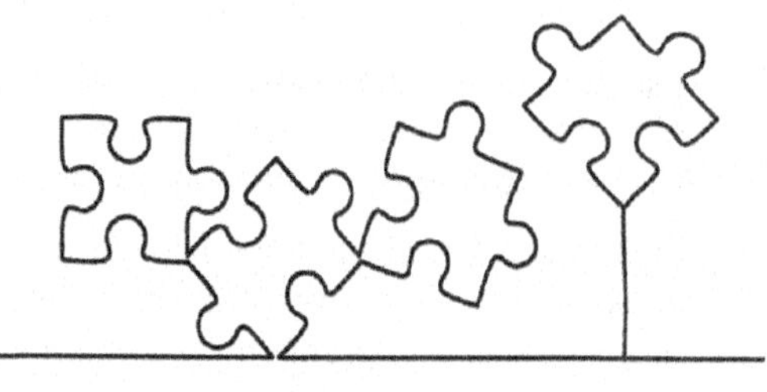

## Summary

- The quests for representativeness, neutral competence, and executive leadership are norms of public personnel administration. Value, mediation, and core functions are factors affecting public personnel practices.
- Public organizations in the United States use two methods of establishing and operating personnel systems: (1) political appointment and election and (2) an objective determination of merit.
- The Pendleton Act of 1883 questioned the practice of nonpolitical appointments, embraced egalitarianism, and recognized competence, as determined by competitive examinations related to duties performed.
- The expansion of the merit system and development of public service are closely associated with the passage of legislation and presidential leadership.
- Key merit system principles are recruiting, selecting, and advancing employees on the basis of their abilities, knowledge, and skills; providing equitable and adequate compensation; training employees to assure high-quality performance; guaranteeing fairness for applicants and employees; and protecting against coercion for political purposes.
- Equality provides no guarantees; it only provides access. Affirmative action—without ways to achieve— is limited.
- The Plum Book and the Prune Book are designed to facilitate presidential transitions every four years. They combine the interests of partisan, policy, and system politics.
- Test validity for predicting on-the-job performance and other selection criteria pose problems for public agencies grounded in merit principles.
- A pure merit system for all public service appointments would be grounded in competition based on merit rules. However, no administration functions on a pure merit system.
- Two basic criteria for promotion are seniority and merit.
- Training is receiving increasing attention. A fast-moving and fast-changing society exhibits a high need for wide-ranging and high-level skills.
- Federal, state, and local governments employ 20,392,000 wage and salary workers. Of this national distribution, local government units employ 53.5 percent, or 10,908,000, workers. State governments employ 6,102,000, or 30.0 percent. The federal, or national, government hires 3,381,000, or 16.5 percent, of America's government employees.
- A promotion is the change of an employee to a position of a higher-grade level within the same job classification system and pay schedule, or a position with a higher rate of basic pay in a different job classification system and pay schedule.
- Remuneration for government employment is based on position rather than performance. Good performance originates from an employee's sense of duty, not from pay.
- The average salary for all occupations in the federal government in 2007 was $65,463.
- The federal government hires people with nearly every level of education and experience—from high school students with no experience to PhD's with established careers. The qualifications needed for each job are described in detail in the vacancy announcements that advertise job openings.
- Private contractors provide public services for a price. Civil servants labor for a wage. Drawing lines between public and private may be especially difficult in such cases.
- Representative bureaucracy is a basic policy goal that public personnel managers pursue. A separate but related policy choice is whether to pursue that goal passively or actively. A passive strategy is equal opportunity. An active strategy is affirmative action.
- The importance of affirmative action is declining because: (1) no strong consensus exists favoring affirmative action; (2) U.S. Supreme Court decisions regarding affirmative action are nonlinear; and (3) executive leadership, retrenchment, and productivity take priority over affirmative action programs in government agencies.

- Public-sector performance management must be task-oriented, participative, and developmental.
- The demographics of the federal, state, and local workforces are changing.
- The average ages of federal and private-sector workers were 46 and 42, respectively. Among all federal workers, 43 percent held bachelor's degrees compared with 28 percent for all private- sector workers, and 46 percent of federal workers versus 42 percent of private-sector workers in management, professional, and related occupations were college graduates.
- The premise underlying position classification schemes is that different positions require varying degrees of ability and impose varying amounts of responsibility.
- The position description is a record of duties assigned to an individual position in a class. It compares positions to ensure uniformity of classification and describes assigned duties and responsibilities.
- Public personnel administration, more than anything else, is a process encompassing procedures, rules, and regulations.
- The recruitment, selection, and promotion phases are grounded in legislation and law, reflecting the values of accountability and responsiveness to the public.

## Videos, Films and Talks

Please visit *The Craft of Public Administration* at www.millenniumhrmpress.com for up-to-date videos, films, talks, readings, and additional class resources.

The Human Skills we Need in an Unpredictable World [15 min]
Margaret Heffernan, TED Talk
https://www.ted.com/talks/margaret_heffernan_the_human_skills_we_need_in_an_unpredictable_world

## Suggested Readings

**Hiring Challenges Confront Public-Sector Employers**
https://www.shrm.org/hr-today/news/all-things-work/pages/hiring-challenges-confront-public-sector-employers.aspx

**HR Holds the Keys to Revitalizing Public Service**
https://www.govexec.com/management/2020/06/hr-holds-keys-revitalizing-public-service/166324/

**Inspired to Serve: Steps to advance public service and build a stronger federal workforce**
https://ourpublicservice.org/blog/inspired-to-serve-steps-to-advance-public-service-and-build-a-stronger-federal-workforce/

**Serving the Future: Building a next-gen public-sector workforce**
https://media.erepublic.com/document/GD-NA-EN-NP-114840-101-Public-Sector_HR.pdf

**An Essential Building Block for the Public Workforce**
https://gettingbetterallthetime.com/wp-content/uploads/2016/03/an-essential-building-block-for-the-public-workforce_by_patrick-ibarra1.pdf

**Here's What Government Will Look Like in 2030**
https://www.govtech.com/magazines/gt-special-issue-nov-2020-heres-what-government-will-look-like-in-2030.html

**What Will Government Look Like in 2037**
https://www.governing.com/archive/gov-government-in-25-years.html

## Notes


1. Quoted in John Franklin Campbell, *The Foreign Affairs Fudge Factory* (New York: Basic Books, 1971), pp. 139–140.
2. The National Leadership Council for Liberal Education & America's Promise, "College Learning for the New Global Century," (2007), p. 3.
3. Ibid. p. 4
4. Ibid. p. 3
5. Ibid. p. 8
6. Ibid. p. 9
7. Herbert Kaufman, "Emerging Conflicts in the Doctrines of Public Administration," *American Political Science Review* 50 (December 1956): 1057–1073.
8. Donald E. Klingner and John Nalbandian, *Public Personnel Management: Contexts and Strategies* (Englewood Cliffs, NJ: Prentice-Hall, 1985).
9. James E. Leidlein, "In Search of Merit: A Practitioner's Comments on 'The Staffing Function in Illinois State Government after Rutan' and 'Curbing Patronage Without Paperasserie,'" *Public Administration Review* 53, no. 4 (July–August 1993): 391–392.
10. Quoted in Paul Van Riper, *History of the United States Civil Service* (New York: Harper & Row, 1958), p. 36.S
11. Steven W. Hays and T. Zane Reeves, *Personnel Management in the Public Sector* (Boston: Allyn and Bacon, 1984), p. 16.
12. The World Bank Group, "Administrative & Civil Service Reform," http://www1.worldbank.org/ publicsector/ civilservice/recruitment.htm.
13. Ibid.
14. James E. Brennan, "Merit Pay: Balance the Old Rich and the New Poor," *Personnel Journal* 64, no. 5 (May 1985): 82–85.
15. The World Bank Group, "Administrative & Civil Service Reform."
16. U.S. Merit Systems Protection Board, Attracting Quality Graduates to the Federal Government: A View of College Recruiting (June 1988), p. vii.
17. The Hudson Institute, Civil Service 2000, A Report Prepared for the U.S. Office of Personnel Management (June 1988), p. 10.
18. The Washington Times, May 25, 1989, p. B5.
19. John J. Dilulio, "Against Federal 'Leviathan by Proxy' and for a Bigger, Better Full-Time Federal Workforce," *Public Administration Review*, 2016-07, Vol.76 (4), p.535-537.

20. Robert Longley, "Why would much of the U.S. federal government shut down and what happens when it does?" *ThoughtCo.*, January 29, 2020, https://www.thoughtco.com/history-and-effects-of-government-shutdowns-3321444#:~:text=The%20most%20serious%20government%20shutdowns%20in%20the%20nation%27s,for%20Medicare%2C%20education%2C%20the%20environment%2C%20and%20public%20health.

21. Michael Hodges, "Grandfather Economic Report," https://grandfather-economic-report.com/fed_budget.htm.

22. Center for State and Local Government Excellence (2021), "State and Local Government Workforce: 2021," https://www.slge.org/wp-content/uploads/2021/05/statelocalworkforce2021.pdf.

23. Ralph C. Chandler and Jack C. Plano, *The Public Administration Dictionary* (New York: John Wiley & Sons, 1982), p. 246.

24. Klingner and Nalbandian, *Public Personnel Management*, pp. 62–69.

25. David H. Rosenbloom, "The Declining Salience of Affirmative Action in Federal Personnel Management," *Review of Public Personnel Administration* 4 (Summer 1984): 202–205, 248–249.

26. Raymond W. Mack, "Whose Affirmative Action?" *Society* 33, no. 3 (March–April 1996): 41–44.

27. Nancy Stein, "Questions and Answers about Affirmative Action," *Social Justice* 22, no. 3 (Fall 1995): 45–53.

28. "The Future of Affirmative Action: President Clinton's Remarks," *Congressional Digest* 75, nos. 6–7 (June–July 1996): 166–169.

29. Ann Crittenden, "Quotas for Good Old Boys," *Wall Street Journal*, June 14, 1995, p. A18.

30. Paul Starr, "Civil Reconstruction: What to Do Without Affirmative Action," *The American Prospect*, no. 8 (Winter 1992): 7–14.

31. Working for America: A Federal Employee Survey (Washington, DC: U.S. Merit Systems Protection Board, 1990).

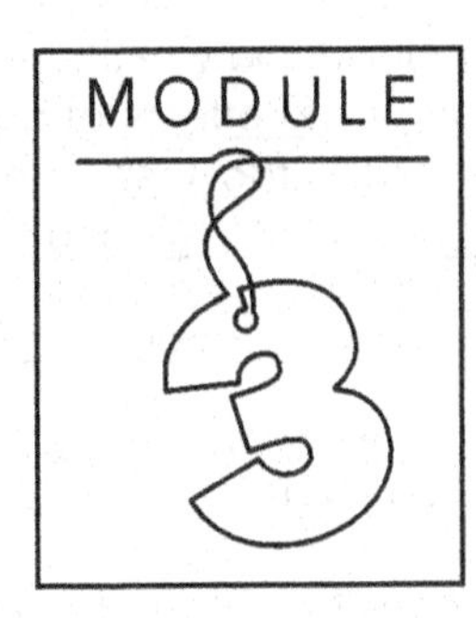


# UNIT 2: Communication and Leadership

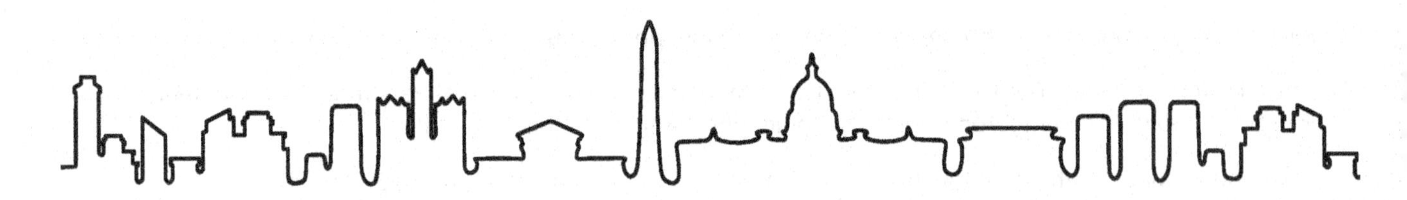

## Communication and Public Administration

Communication and public administration, or organizational structure, are crucial factors for achieving the integration and coordination of agency goals, rules, and human resources. Structures, processes, and cultures of government bureaus must be defined and communicated. Organizational structure sways communication direction and substance. Formal communication and the formal authority structure merge. Vertical communication is transmitted between government executives and agency employees. Horizontal communication probes the roles of tasks, work units, and divisions.

The Greek philosopher Heraclitus observed that "a man [or woman] can never step into the same river twice. The man [or woman] is different and so is the river."[1] Change and continuity are intertwined in a process of actions that flow through the ages. Communication is a process that flows like a stream through time.

Communication presents as many problems as any other aspect of administration, if not more. There are, first, the *technical* problems. Communication problems arise not only from information that is too slow, incomplete, or distorted, but also from information that is overabundant. This is the problem of *communication overload.* Occasionally, this communication problem arises by intent. For example, school superintendents sometimes purposely flood their school board members with reports and other documents, which although completely accurate, are so voluminous it is impossible for the board members to know what is happening. As the board members struggle in vain to keep abreast of the swelling tide of information, the superintendent calmly proceeds to do pretty much whatever they want to do.

Most overload problems, however, arise from sheer force of circumstance, and the circumstances that make for too much communication are increasing all the time. The growing complexity, specialization, and interdependence of today's organizational world are adding to the rising flood of information—a process being aided and abetted by the exponential growth of *communications technology.* An organization may take great care and achieve great success in developing excellent lines and flows of communication, only to sink under the profusion of information that may develop as a result.

## ESSENTIAL VIEWS:

### ACADEMICS/PRACTITIONERS AT THE STREET LEVEL

**From City Hall to Civic Hall: Government's Role in Civic Tech**
By Lisa Saye

Civic technology, or civic tech, is a movement that uses new and existing networks of technology to interpret open data in order to improve government services through public engagement. Civic tech applications (apps) enable citizens to renew licenses, file complaints, upload photos of dangerous potholes or check on the status of road or highway repairs and maintenance. Civic tech also allows governments to communicate with citizens using *chatbots* while simultaneously providing information on available housing, water quality or power outages.

In her 1904 article titled, "Problems of Municipal Administration," Jane Addams warned us against hesitating to use newer elements and strategies to improve government reach and capacity. Governments around the world have co-opted the skills of civic tech volunteers, designers, analysts and software engineers. In his 1949 book titled, *TVA and the Grass Roots,* Philip Selznick noted how in 1940, The Tennessee Valley Authority (TVA) and local governments used volunteer associations totaling almost 900,000 citizens in the planning and operation of its nine rural programs. By absorbing civic tech as part of program design and implementation, governments are employing all sectors in addressing and resolving society's problems, as suggested by David Osborne and Ted Gaebler in their 1992 classic book, *Reinventing Government.*

To say that the marriage of civic tech with government needs to have a political dimension would be oversimplifying an understatement. Public services—its legal structure and its enforcement apparatus—are defined by its enabling statute or the legislation that created the service. In this case, politics is the distribution system. So, that should settle any debate about the political parameters.

There has been an increasing dependence of governments on civic technology in capturing unused resources, in informing the planning process and in providing emergency information. *Vision Zero,* a 1997 civic tech approach, originally launched in Sweden and aimed at reducing traffic fatalities, has since been implemented in numerous cities in the U.S. including San Francisco, Los Angeles, San Jose, Chicago, Houston, New York City, Washington, D.C. and Fort Lauderdale. The 2014

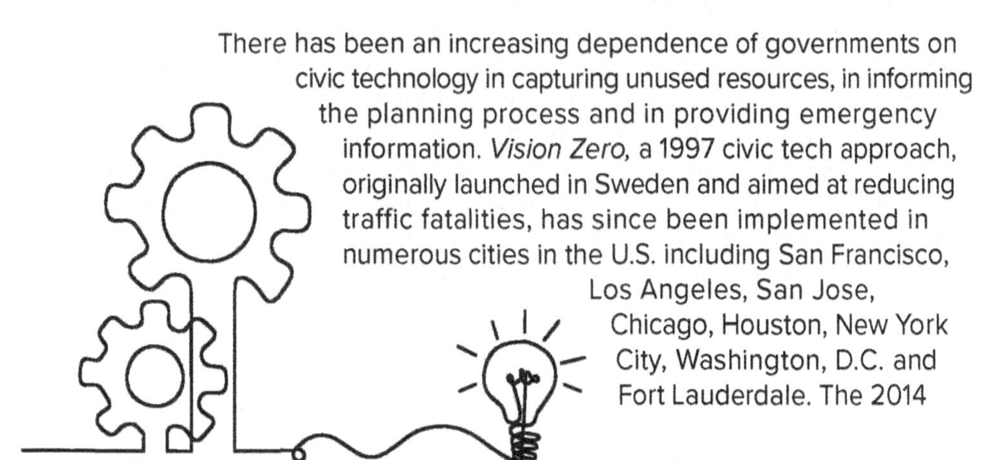

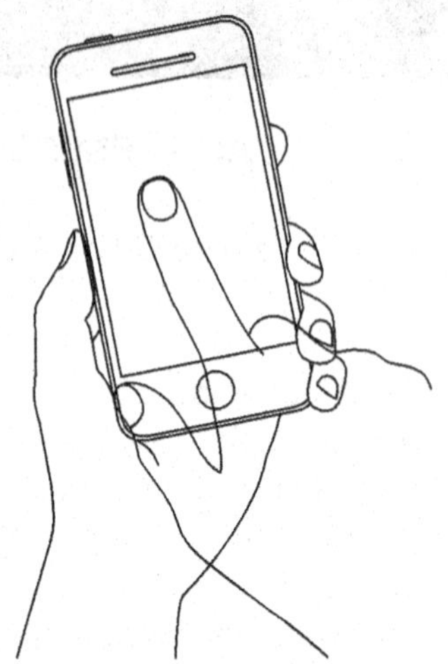

creation of the United States Digital Services (USDS) and 18F represent U.S. efforts to institutionalize civic tech at the federal level. Cities and states have co-opted civic tech, too. Before, during and after landfall of recent hurricanes, civic tech volunteers posted and tweeted out evacuation routes, shelter information, damage and road issues and rescue maps for citizens and city officials.

The collaboration of civic tech and government is not surprising. Governments are clever enough to know when they need help. Governments are also skilled at recognizing the transformation happening in the way the public uses technology to communicate. Advances in communication technologies have changed the built-environments of governments. Its buildings have changed, the furniture is different, and its lobbies are designed for short-term stays. Emergencies, disasters and pandemics, like COVID-19, have altered the built environment by making those environments more virtual, wherever the citizens happen to be or where injury or disease is less likely to affect public personnel and citizens.

As a result of the changes in the built environment, governments will have to expand the kind and type of public servant that it recruits and trains. This may mean that governments will create more positions specific to civic tech for individuals who are steeped in the knowledge of public policy and digital networks. The number of analysts and technicians skilled in creating *apps* that assist in gathering data and measuring outcomes in real time will need to increase in order to interpret the results that civic tech apps produce.

Who might these civic tech practitioners be? If Warren Bennis were advising us, he would say as he did in his 1967 article, "Organizations of the Future," that these practitioners should be a diverse population of highly-skilled specialists.

In her 2017 article in *Microsoft on the Issues* titled, "A Street-Level Look at an Innovative Data-Driven Partnership," Elizabeth Grossman explains that a diverse population of technicians is necessary in order to fully understand the issues and to identify possible and relevant solutions to address those issues. We know that government is listening. If you scan the civic tech employee profiles published on government websites in the U.S., France, Germany or Sierra Leone, you'll notice how consistently diverse the teams are in education, experience, age and background. In co-opting civic tech, governments are purposely *disrupting* old and inefficient ways to serve their communities while finding new ways to engage the public as partners.

## Formal and Informal Communication

Communication falls into two basic and easily defined categories, formal and informal. *Formal communication is written communication; informal is oral.* Of course, not all informal communication is verbal. Attitudes and even ideas can be transmitted by means of inflection, gesture, and body language, but although nonverbal communication has a place in organizational life, its role is usually not great and, in any case, it is hard to analyze and define with precision and reliability. Consequently, our discussion of informal communication will be directed toward verbal communication. What factors govern the use of one form of communication over the other? Under what conditions does formal communication take precedence over informal, and vice versa?

Usually, two factors foster the use of formal communication. One of these is *organizational size.* As organizations grow, they tend to make increasing use of formal communication and, correspondingly, diminishing use of informal. The other factor is *public character.* Public organizations tend to rely more heavily on formal communication than do private ones.

Formal communication fosters *accountability.* By facilitating accountability, formal communication places natural restraints on arbitrariness, capriciousness, favoritism, and discrimination. By proceeding on formal instructions and keeping records of their transactions, public officials find it much more difficult, although certainly not impossible, to depart from acceptable standards of impartiality and fairness. Of course, the rules and standards may be unfair, but if so, this is at least a matter of public record and can be easily determined. An administrator with integrity will welcome the opportunity to document his or her actions.

Proponents of formal communication argue that it is:

- Official, more binding, and more likely to be obeyed
- Written, more precise, and less likely to be misunderstood
- Inscribed, so that it can be traced at any time and preserved for numerous distributions
- Official, establishing responsibility of the sender and receiver beyond any doubt
- Routinized, saving time and effort otherwise consumed in informal talks, discussions, and even arguments
- More definite, avoiding the embarrassment of the face-to-face contact between persons if the communication is sensitive or painful[2]

The use of the written word tends to encourage its further use, and many governmental and private organizations have found themselves swamped in a sea of documentation. Detractors argue that formal communication is:

- Too rigidly defined, limiting information within the department to that sanctioned by the chief executive or supervisor
- Codified by language, obscuring the real meaning of communication, permitting more than one interpretation, or using cautious phraseology and "bureaucratic jargon," "bureaucratese," or "babble- fab"
- Substantively superficial, failing to identify the reasons for the message and causing the recipient consternation and frustration
- Costly in terms of secretarial efforts, reproduction costs, and delivery time
- Top-down, reflecting authoritarianism, as the formal arrangement is based on the descent of executive information and not on the ascent of employee concerns
- Impersonal and final, failing to motivate employees
- Elementary and trivial, devaluing the intelligence of recipients
- Divisive, separating personnel into "recipients" and "nonrecipients"[3]

## Internet of Things

Technology impacts modes of communication, formal and informal. Technological advances seemingly at the speed of light, are contributing to the narrowing of the gulf between formal and informal communication distinctions. The internet of things presents many opportunities for improving service delivery and infrastructure while reducing overall costs as systems such as infrastructure, traffic, public safety, environment, etc., achieve network connectivity allowing them to communicate to one another and for governments to analyze data for opportunities for streamlining efficiencies. Challenging these opportunities are concerns over diminishing privacy rights and the use of data collected, maintained and stored. While concerns continue about the impact of a digital divide, those with internet access and those without, **Figure 3.2.1** to the right shows that perhaps the divide is shrinking and that internet use if truly becoming universal.

With the global use of the internet, many security related and personal privacy issues have emerged. Samples of public and private computer security violations include the "hacking" of Target Corporation, the Office of Personnel Management, the Department of Defense and too many other public, private, and nonprofit organizations to list here, resulting in the compromising of hundreds of millions of personal employment and financial records and financial damages into the millions of dollars.

Technology is crucial in the development of the information highway that would link every home to a fiber-optic network over which voice, data, television, and other services would be transmitted. The internet's architecture is determined by an informal group of U.S.-based software and computer engineers. The internet's global scope and electronic commerce's growth make its management an international policy issue. Analysts and government believe a hands-off approach is best.[4]

**Figure 3.2.1**
**Income Levels and Technology Adoption**

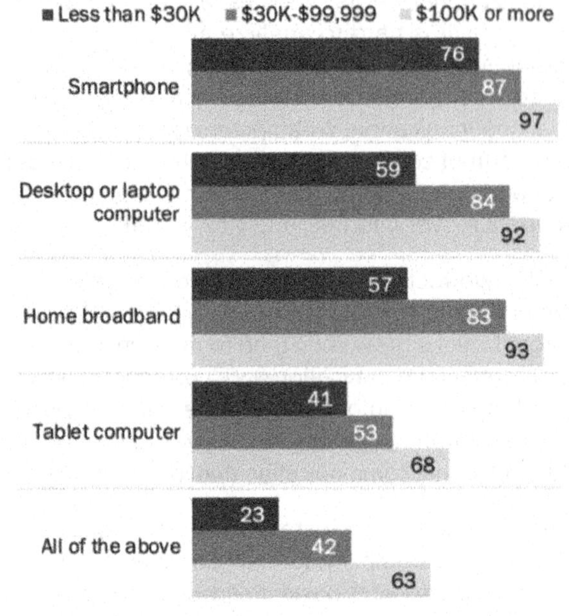


*Source: "Americans with lower incomes have lower levels of technology adoption." Pew Research Center, Washington, D.C. (June 22, 2021)* https://www.pewresearch.org/fact-tank/2021/06/22/digital-divide-persists-even-as-americans-with-lower-incomes-make-gains-in-tech-adoption/.

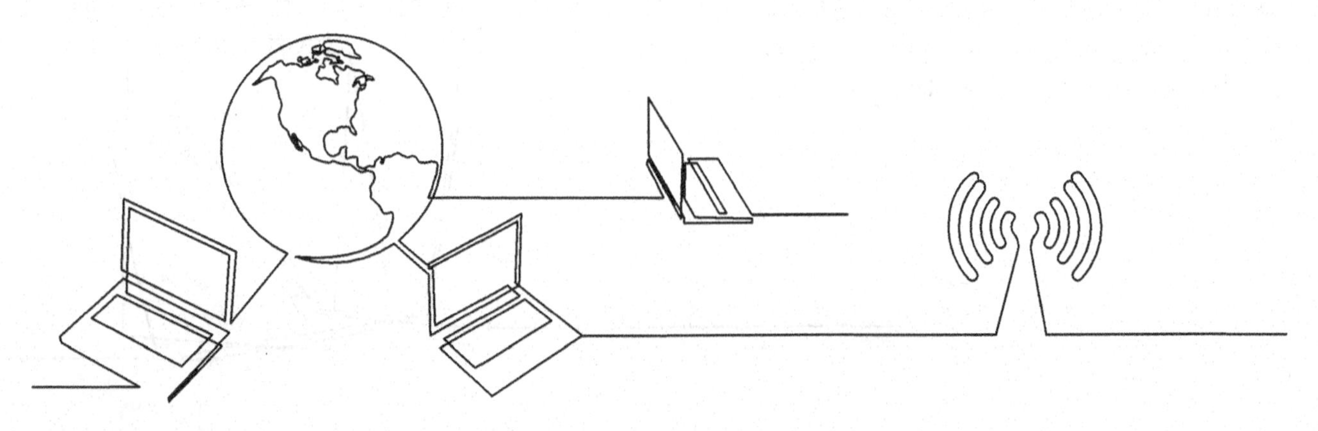

# THINK ABOUT IT!

**Net Neutrality: 2015**

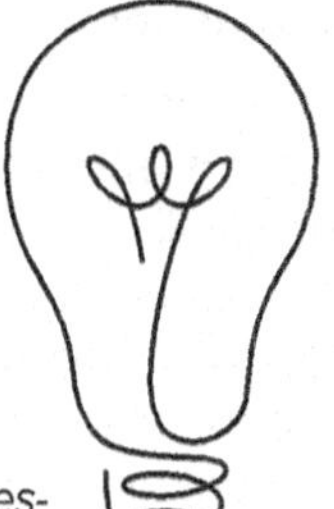

In February 2015 the Federal Communications Commission, under an interpretation of Title II of the 1996 Telecommunications Act, positioned the commission to regulate internet service providers. The issue is often discussed as "net neutrality," a term coined by Columbia University media law professor Tim Wu in 2003. The idea of net neutrality is that internet service providers should treat all data and users on the internet equally.

*Source: http://www.usatoday.com/story/money/2015/02/26/fcc-approves-net-neutrality-rules/24053057/, accessed October 17, 2015*

People and organizations, not computers, determine the course of the future. As a form of communication, the internet can be used by individuals, private corporations, and government agencies for good or bad, but it cannot influence the direction our society chooses to take. It has been argued, the internet only reflects the society in which it was created and operates, just like the telegraph and telephone. The development and use of the telegraph and telephone provide a definitive pattern for how the newest form of networked communication, the internet, will be used in the future.[5] Others disagree.

For the telephone to be widely used in the United States it took approximately 35 years respectively whereas the internet was used by one fourth of the United States population within four years of its development. Of course, it is so widely used today worldwide that it is often references as the "democratization" of communication and the media.

The lack of accountability and civility has increased as the anonymity in U.S. society has increased, states newspaper columnist Ellen Goodman. She cites the anonymous zones of talk radio and cyberspace among the foxholes for people who want to say anything and everything with impunity.[6]

Despite the downside of the information highway, internet access, boosted by the proliferation of smart phone use in every segment of the population, has made communication between local government and citizens much easier nationwide. Public records access, personnel postings, permit applications, legislative updates, and accessibility to many other services and venues, are available online in many cities and counties.[7]

The technology of the internet may afford the masses access to much more information and many more options. Internet technology is neither evil nor good. "Thanks to the internet and satellite TV, the world is being wired together technologically, but not socially, politically, or culturally," concludes *New York Times* columnist Thomas L. Friedman. "We are now seeing and hearing one another faster and better, but with no corresponding improvement in our ability to learn from, or understand, one another. So integration, at this stage, is producing more anger than anything else."[8]

The internet educates people faster than any previous technology the world has known. However, the internet can just as easily infiltrate the minds of millions with lies, half-truths, and hatreds. "The internet," says Friedman, "at its ugliest, is just an open sewer: an electronic conduit for untreated, unfiltered information." The internet and satellite TV may inflame emotions and cultural biases, resulting in less understanding and tolerance.

Also, religious and sectarian groups sometimes use this powerful medium for propagandization, misinformation, and for the recruit of those that are sympathetic to either radical or mainstream ideologies (cyber-terrorism to legitimate civic engagement). Government programs are built on political consensus. Legislation is enacted for the long term. Compromises are based on education, exchanges, diplomacy, and human interaction.

Advances in the use of information technology (IT) and the internet continue to change the way that federal agencies communicate, use, and disseminate information, deliver services, and do business. Electronic government (e-government) refers to the use of technology, particularly web-based internet and mobile applications.

### Informal Communication

Oral communication offers a solution to many of the problems encountered in written communication. It does not flood the office worker's desk or clog the files. It can evoke immediate feedback, which, in turn, can lead to a resolution of issues or clarification of misunderstood points. In the process, the one communicating can be assured that his or her information has been received. Speaking and listening permit shading, emphasis, and gesture. Conversation is also significantly more intimate, personal, human and often more humane. People are dealing together directly.

Efforts have long been underway to substitute oral for written communication. In the 1960s, President Johnson's task force on cutting red tape, for example, urged federal officials to make more extensive use of the telephone and less use of "time-consuming written communications."[9] It is possible that the use of oral communication will grow apace in governmental agencies, although it will most likely never replace formal communication. For reasons noted earlier, the written word and the printed document (red tape) will probably continue to serve as the mainstay of the communications process in any developed democracy, if for no other reason than that it records, in written or digital form, the historical legacy of organizations and society.

### Grapevines

Any agency that has an informal organization will also have an informal communications system, often referred to as the "grapevine." Informal organizations are found in almost all organizations; therefore, grapevines are ubiquitous.

The grapevine, or informal communication network in government organizations, can have negative effects such as resentment, embarrassment for upper-level administrators, distorted messages, rumor diffusion, and subversion of administrative decision making. Grapevines develop when employees share common hobbies, lunch schedules, family ties, hometowns, and social relationships. These informal networks operate quickly, often accurately, and with resilience. It is suggested that management should use the network for its own purposes to complement formal networks. Administrators should also be candid about information if possible.[10]

Grapevines can also be terribly efficient. "With the rapidity of a burning powder train," says Keith Davis, a professor of management who has studied grapevines for years, "information flows out of the woodwork, past the manager's door and the janitor's mop closet, through steel walls or construction-glass partitions."[11] What is more, Davis claims, more than three-fourths of this information is accurate.

Even when it is not accurate, says Davis, the grapevine may convey a psychological truth, for many rumors that run rampant through an organization are "symbolic expressions of feelings." If the rumor is that a certain employee is planning to quit, it may reflect the wish on the part of fellow employees that he or she would quit. Or it may reflect the employee's own desire to leave.

Proponents of informal communication argue that it is:

- Less official and less intimidating, enhancing the new flow of ideas and solicits plans without fear of punishment
- Personal, embracing enthusiasm, reflecting the zeal of the participants, and playing down the relevance of dry, bureaucratic logic
- Usually verbal, allowing informal communication, permitting exploration of hidden dimensions of government organization, and facilitating two-way communication
- Revealing of underlying motives and pressures, promoting an atmosphere of free yet discreet discussion, and explaining to employees why the department works the way it does
- Better at refuting rumors and putting an end to office gossip filtering through the formal environment, complete with unanswered questions
- Reflective of a spirit of comradery that unites workers by the discovery of shared concerns and interests
- Able to sustain a harmonious relationship between officers and their superiors, promoting cooperation based on mutual understanding and concern
- Detractors argue that informal communication is:
- Difficult to define or apply in systematic ways
- Inaccurate, spreading half-truths and sometimes resulting in second- and third-hand information being represented as original, factual, and trustworthy
- Indiscriminate, possibly leading to disclosure of classified information

- Emotional, distorting or changing meaning to fit the personal sentiments of the messenger
- Verbal and difficult to trace, making further inquiry problematic
- Of questionable social advantage, as it is only as constructive as participants deem it to be[12]

Formal communication—certainly historic and more traditional—functions as a means of controlling agency activities. Authoritative policies and procedures circulate among personnel. Formal specifications state what is to be done when, where, how, and by whom. Formal communication allows the organization to "track" issues through organization "channels."

Organizations are groupings of social beings, however. A certain amount of informal and personal communication occurs within the ranks. Participants seek the "right" mixture of informal and formal communications. No magic formula exists for arriving at this mixture. A proper blend of formal and informal communications depends upon participants and organization leaders.

The organization's environment and the needs of personnel—along with the maturity and intelligence of leaders—determine the appropriateness of a given mixture of informal and formal communications. Informal communications—in a trustworthy language—may supplement the formal structure. In this fashion, workers are reassured, improve their attitudes, and deepen their commitments to the department.[13]

## Implications and Effects of E-Government

E-government seeks to improve relationships between the private citizen and public-sector services. E-government is not exclusively an internet-driven activity. Cost-effective and efficient, e-government enhances citizens' access to government information, services, and expertise. Five guiding principles ensure citizen participation in—and satisfaction with—the governing process.

- Building services around citizens' choices
- Making government and its services more accessible
- Promoting inclusive social relations
- Providing information in responsible fashion
- Using human resources effectively and efficiently[14]

E-government, then, is not "just putting government online. It is changing the way agencies interact with citizens, businesses and federal employees as they perform the government's business."[15] The demands for more effective government services increase as the days pass. E-government initiatives keep pace as government leaders and employees search for innovations to meet the demands.

Effective communications are vital to the well-being of American democracy and bureaucracy. Commitments to government online systems lead to:

- *Connected governments*, or improved communications and information management between federal, state, and local governments—and private and nonprofit organizations
- *Connected communities*, or online integrated services readily available and conveniently accessed twenty-four hours a day, seven days a week, delivered to homes, businesses, and other locations by the internet and other media
- *Connected people*, or effective and efficient electronic communication used by elected leaders, government officials, agencies, and the community at large[16]

What do citizens say they want from electronic government services? Peter D. Hart and Robert M. Teeter surveyed 1,003 citizens; 150 government officials in federal, state, and local governments; and 155 institutional customers of government in the business and nonprofit sectors about the potential uses of e-government services, the benefits of e-government, how quickly e-government develops, and what concerns them about the digital divide. Issues of mobility, voting, and recreation were at the top of their lists, which included:

- Driver's license renewal
- Voter registration
- State park information and reservations
- Internet voting
- Access to one-stop shopping (one portal for all government services)
- Birth, death, and marriage certificate retrieval
- State tax filing
- Hunting and fishing licenses
- Accessing medical information from the National Institute of Health[17]

Citizens are now using e-government services for everything from applying for employment, renewing car registrations or helping design their city of the future. A survey of 5,000 citizens in Australia, Germany, Singapore, United Kingdom and the United States reported by SmartCitiesWorld in June 2019 found, "51 percent of respondents would increase their use of digital government services if they could access multiple government services from an online portal. Additionally, almost three-fifths (56 percent) said their trust in government would increase if the government better communicated how the technology innovations they were deploying would improve the lives of citizens."[18]

First Amendment advocates claim that e-mails have replaced public meetings and other public information forums. The reasons for these reforms range from expediency to a desire for secrecy. The e-mail technology makes holding public officials accountable more challenging, difficult, and problematic. Discussions and decision making are conducted outside the public view when they should be taking place in public.[19]

Media reporters and freedom of information advocates argue that millions of e-mails coming and going in government circles of partisan, policy, and systems politics entail a "double-edged sword." Texts of e-mails provide access to more information. However, retaining, storing, and maintaining government cyberspace communications in e-mail archives occur within emerging versions of technological political cultures. As Dwight Waldo explained, public and private are not categories of nature. They are categories of history and culture, of law and custom. They are contextual and subject to change and redefinition.[20]

What came about as reforms and communication access evolves into developing human rigidities, technological breakdowns, increased expenses, and new interpretations of bureaucracy and democracy. Government agencies' obligations to maintain electronic records are either expanding or in some cases yet unresolved as governments at all levels struggle with keeping up with these massive types of new records that many deem public information that should be archived and publicly available. They are matters of public— and private.

**The Other Organization**

The study of human relations involves an interdisciplinary curriculum that enables learners at all levels, practitioners, and those in the allied fields of sociology, social work, psychology, management and a host of other disciplines, to learn those skills required in many traditional employment areas. For example, for those who direct and manage organizations in the three economic sectors (public, private and nonprofit), it is necessary to understand a diverse array of topics, such as minority-majority relations, human resource development, creative problem-solving skills, intervention and alternative dispute resolution strategies, as well as basic organization and group leadership skills. In positions where interpersonal and intergroup coordination skills intersect with the skills used in resolving conflict and reducing or alleviating tension, such as employee relations, organizational development and crisis intervention, human relation theory is indispensable. And for those employed in training, affirmative action, employee assistance programs, and the many areas of counseling, social work, chemical dependency, etc., effective human relations is required if the individual and organization seeks successful results.

Not only is the study and understanding of human relations important for those who work in the traditional areas of employment where human relations graduates have been drawn, but it will become nearly obligatory for the newest knowledge and biotechnological occupations that are quickly coming on board. The world and changing nature of work is not becoming simpler. Indeed, it is becoming more dynamic as we are expected to address the impact of technology, diversity, knowledge, globalization or internationalism, entrepreneurialism, innovation, creativity, changing demographics and quality management, etc., and at the same time recognize basic civil and human rights and fight against the insidiousness of discrimination (gender, age, ability, appearance, religion, lifestyle, and so on), when and where it rears its ugly head.

Organizational charts and manuals of procedure rarely provide us with an accurate picture of an organization. What is not official or even readily visible may often be the most important. Even the most formal organizations, which pride themselves on going strictly "by the book," rarely do so. An informal system of authority, which supersedes, at least to some extent, the formal one, may arise. In the army, for example, the lieutenant clearly outranks the sergeant. But when the sergeant has had twenty years of army service and the lieutenant is fresh from a college Reserve Officers Training Program (ROTC), the sergeant, rather than the lieutenant, may end up running the platoon.

Communication also frequently flows through informal channels. The office grapevine is usually faster and more complete than the office memo. Aboard a ship, the real communications center is often not the captain's office, but the kitchen or galley, and navy cooks are usually better sources of news than commanding officers. This is how the term "scuttlebutt" came to have its current meaning. The informal organization may spawn a network of relationships for which the organization chart and the manual of procedure provide few clues.

One of the most extreme examples of how the informal organization can overwhelm the formal organization is the U.S. prison system. Ostensibly, prisons are run by wardens and corrections officers according to prescribed rules and regulations. In practice, this has rarely been the case. Sociologists and criminologists who have studied prisons have found that most prisons have traditionally been run by the prisoners.[21]

In most cases, the informal organization does not loom so large on the administrative scene, and its role should not be overstressed. It usually colors the formal organization but does not radically alter it. No matter how expert and experienced a sergeant may be, and no matter how naive and nervous the lieutenant may be, it is the lieutenant and not the sergeant who bears the final responsibility for the platoon. There is a limit to how much authority the sergeant can acquire and how much the lieutenant can abdicate. Nevertheless, informal elements influence the operation of nearly all organizations, and the administrator must be alert as to what these elements are and what they do.

The informal group is the workhorse of the modern organization. Two aspects of informal organization merit special attention. One concerns the role of *informal rules;* the other concerns the role of *small groups.*

**Whose Rules?**

Employees of organizations, like citizens of nations, tend to obey only those rules in which they believe. Workers will accept a rule only if they regard it as legitimate in terms of their values. They will not accept it just because those who issued it had a legal right to do so.

Employees have also become adept at evading rules or bending them to suit their needs and desires, and the more rules the organization tends to set down, the more dexterity its members may show. The informal organization not only achieves frequent and sometimes spectacular success in sabotaging the formal organization's rules, but it also manages to establish and enforce rules of its own. Many of these rules concern work output. Those who exceed the informal quota may be branded as "rate-busters," while those who fail to carry their fair share of the load may earn the title of "slacker" or "chiseler." Seniority is another rule that governs many procedures of many informal organizations. Those with job seniority get the better assignments and more congenial conditions. The most junior members may not only get the less desirable assignments, but may also experience various petty harassments, like being sent to fetch the "left-handed monkey wrench." Sometimes the harassment is not so petty. College fraternities' hazing rituals have resulted in injuries and occasional deaths.

Probably no informal rule is more widespread than the ban on "whistle blowing," (mismanagement, waste, fraud, abuse). This prohibition is instilled in most Americans during their school years and tends to stay with them the rest of their lives. The taboo against "whistle blowing" is so widely and deeply ingrained that even those who would stand to benefit from it tend to dislike it. The "informer" or "whistle blower," no matter how useful he or she may be, rarely wins esteem in the eyes of management, and though the informer may increase his or her earnings, "whistle blowing" seldom enhances one's chances for promotion.

While the formal organization often encounters difficulty in enforcing its rules, the informal organization usually succeeds in securing support and adherence to its own codes of behavior. Sanctions against offenders can take many forms, not excluding violence.

Many informal rules are benign. While the *golden rule* remains an unattainable goal, it has become a nearly universal governing principle and, as such, governs a good deal of organizational behavior. If people do not naturally love their neighbors as themselves, they do tend to help others who have helped them, or at least try to refrain from injuring them.

### The Small Group

The basic unit for the formal organization may be the division, the department, the section, or all three, plus others. The primary basis for the informal organization is usually the small group. Although many informal norms and rules apply organization wide, many others are promulgated and enforced by small work groups. The small group consists of no set number of individuals. Rather, it designates any group whose members are in continual, face-to-face contact with each other. Such groups often follow the structural lines of the formal organization. The small group in the army infantry is typically the squad. In the university, it is usually the department. Whether it conforms to any formally recognized structure, forces from within customarily dictate a good deal of its behavior.

The importance of the small group springs chiefly from the importance of primary relationships over secondary relationships in human behavior. Those people we work with every day invariably become more important to us than those whom we see infrequently or with whom we conduct relations at a distance. Out of such primary relationships come norms, codes, procedures, and the means for their enforcement. The famed "silent treatment" is most powerfully exercised on those with whom we are in daily contact. Such are the workings of small groups and informal organizations.

## Upward, Downward, and Lateral Communications

Information and feedback in government agencies moves in three basic directions:

- Upward from staff to management
- Downward from management to staff
- Horizontally from one organizational unit to another No matter which way it flows, it runs into problems.

### Communicating Upward

According to Daniel Katz and Robert I. Kahn, communication up the line may occur in many forms, but such information can be reduced to what the person says:

1. About themself, their performance, and their problems
2. About others and their problems
3. About organizational practices and policies
4. About what needs to be done and how it can be done[22]

The basic problem of upward communication is the nature of the hierarchical administrative structure, because the first role requirement of executives and supervisors is to direct, coordinate, and control the activities of persons below them. Therefore, employees fear that information passed along the hierarchical chain of command may be used for control purposes. The employees are unlikely to pass along information that may affect them adversely. This concern makes the upward route the most difficult.

### Communicating Downward

According to Katz and Kahn, there are five varieties of communications down the line, from management ("superior") to staff ("subordinate"):

1. Specific task directives: job instructions
2. Information designed to produce understanding of the task and its relationship to other organizational tasks: job rationale
3. Information about organizational procedures a nd practices
4. Feedback to the junior staff person about his or her performance
5. Information of an ideological character to inculcate a sense of mission: indoctrination of goals[23]

While downward communication is less problematic than upward, communication down the line; nevertheless, encounters numerous obstacles and impediments. When it is oral, downward communication is subject to almost all the alterations that can creep in when communication moves upward.

When downward communication is written, other difficulties may develop. The message may not be complete, or the recipient may not be willing to accept it. The biggest problem, however, is probably the inability or the refusal of the recipient to absorb the information that seems to be cascading downward. Memorandum senders encounter persistent problems in this respect.

**Communicating Laterally**

According to Katz and Kahn, communication among peers, in addition to providing task coordination, also furnishes emotional and social support to the individual. The mutual understanding of colleagues is one reason for the power of the peer group. Psychological forces always push people toward communication with peers; people in the same boat share the same problems.

On the other hand, if no problems of task coordination are left to a group of peers, the content of their communication can take forms irrelevant or destructive to the organization's functioning.[24] The communication channels become dysfunctional if line officials in the organizational hierarchy are charged with initiating all communications. The agency softball team or annual picnic, for example, should be informal arrangements for which someone other than the line officials communicates directions.

Staff meetings can be particularly helpful in stimulating lateral communication.

Physical arrangements can also play an important role in either helping or hampering lateral communication. Organizational practices designed to resolve other problems may foster lateral communication as well. In-service training, for example, may bring people from various parts of the organization together and result in a good deal of lateral communication. Organization wide activities, such as bowling teams or hobby clubs, and an organizationally run cafeteria or dining room will also bring employees together and may lead to an interchange of information. Rotation of employees is also useful in improving lateral communication.

## Leadership and Needs of the Situation

Anyone who hopes to spell out the qualities of a leader is engaged in a perilous and problematic mission. One helpful observation, however, can be made at the outset. *Leadership is, to a great extent, determined by the needs of the situation.* "It is more fruitful to consider leadership as a relationship between the leader and the situation than as a universal pattern of characteristics possessed by certain people," Douglas McGregor notes.[25] In a similar vein, William J. Reddin, after surveying the research on management style, concludes that "no single style is naturally more effective than others. Effectiveness depends on a style's appropriateness to the situation in which it is used."[26] There is, in short, no ideal leadership style and most probably no ideal leader if we accept the major thesis embedded in situational leadership.

We can conclude from the Hawthorne studies and the writings of Elton Mayo the following ideas that will help us better understand the organizations in which we work and the people who comprise them.

- Organizations are social systems and small group behavior is important;
- Informal organizations develop with their own informal leaders, establish and enforce their own work norms through group sanctions;
- There are a variety of incentives, other than money, which motivate workers to produce, such as recognition by superiors; and
- Worker participation in setting goals impacts production in a positive manner and if workers are involved in making decisions that affect them, they treat the task as more important.

Different types of organizations may demand different types of leaders. Many a successful business executive has failed miserably after attempting to transfer with all his or her administrative prowess to the public sector. Few public-sector executives test their leadership skills directing a business firm. If so, they would probably frequently fail. Furthermore, an organization may need different leaders at different stages of its existence.

The relationship of leadership ability to the particular situation that calls the leader into being makes the task of defining and detailing a list of general leadership qualities elusive and difficult. Certain qualities do, however, seem to characterize most leaders in most situations. Although this list does not constitute a formula, since one could possess all the qualities on the list and still be unable to lead, it does provide a basis from which the learner may gain a perspective on one of the most intriguing and enigmatic aspects of the administrative craft.

## Leadership Qualities

Probably no quality is more pertinent and pervasive among successful leaders than the quality of *optimism*. To lead successfully, one must believe that his or her leadership will make a difference. No matter how dismal a journey, the leader must be able to see positive results.

That *energy* and *enterprise* must accompany such optimism should be reasonably obvious. This does not mean that every luminary in the ranks of leadership has been a whirlwind of activity, but one cannot hope to meet leadership's obligations without some deliberate and diligent application of one's talents. Leaders often do not seem to be working hard at their jobs, but such appearances can be deceptive. A leader may be relaxed and easygoing, but laziness and indolence will usually lead to failure.

What about *intelligence*? Certainly, it is rare to find a leader who is not intelligent yet successful, and some have been extraordinarily brilliant. Take Napoleon and William Pitt, those young titans who confronted each other across the English Channel at the beginning of the nineteenth century. Each was at home in a variety of disciplines, including mathematics, languages, and the law. In this country, and during the same period, a president (Thomas Jefferson) had come to power that was accomplished in architecture, science, agriculture, law, political theory, and many other fields of study. Nevertheless, when it comes to correlating intellectual ability with leadership, some qualities seem more crucial than others.

According to Albert C. Yates, good leaders must be virtuous people who can be trusted to make the right choices to restore optimism and spirit to the society. Intelligent leaders without virtue can lead society toward selfishness and cynicism. *Virtue* embodies all that is good and right in human life and is a combination of values such as commitment, integrity, compassion, truth, and competence. A dynamic relationship between leadership and values sustains a good democratic society.[27]

One vital intellectual skill is *verbal ability*. Communication skills usually accompany leadership ability, no matter what the situation. A ditch digger who becomes the foreman of the work gang will probably be able to communicate better than all, or at least most, of the other members of the gang.

Much more complex is the question of *creativity* and *judgment*. The problem is that these two qualities are not always compatible. Good idea people, as Daniel Katz and Robert L. Kahn point out, tend to be enthusiastic and somewhat impulsive and may fail to subject their ideas to searching criticism. They frequently have a hard time translating ideas into action, and when they do, they may fail to follow through because they soon sprout another idea that they want to work on.

Katz and Kahn maintain that leadership puts more of a priority on reasoned judgment than creativity, and if a leader can have only one of these qualities, they are better off with the former. One can always make up for lack of creativity by surrounding oneself with

# THINK ABOUT IT!

**Peter Drucker's Five Questions for Successful Leadership**

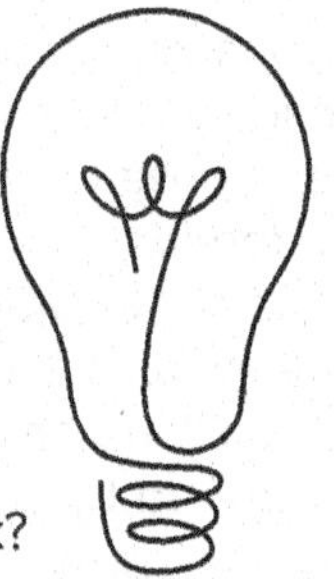

Peter Drucker is known for having transformed the discipline and field of management through the forty books that he penned over 90 years of living, researching, and teaching. He is the father of such basic management concepts as management by objectives, the knowledge worker, and rules for successful leadership in any of the three economic sectors. Drucker admonishes us to ask these five questions which affect leadership:

1. What is your mission?
2. Who is your customer?
3. What does your customer value?
4. What results do you seek?
5. What is your plan?

These questions do not submit to a casual analysis. They will take careful reflection and analysis and do not respond easily to poorly planned and thought out decision-making.

people who are creative.[28] Realistically, it is essential that successful leaders have a clear sense of vision—where they want the organization to be directed or go—and the ability to effectively communicate that overarching vision with clarity, meaning, passion, integrity, and congruity—matching words with action.

## Leadership and Charisma

The relationship between leadership and charisma is important in understanding both. Katz and Kahn argue that charisma originates from people's needs and from dramatic events in association with leadership. Most persons are in no position to evaluate suggestions for organizational change; therefore, charismatic leadership is most appropriate for formulating policies and altering organizational structures. Since followers are often not knowledgeable concerning specific programs for attaining organizational goals, subordinates allow leaders much flexibility for such decisions.

However, as Katz and Kahn emphasize, charisma is not the objective assessment by followers of the leader's ability to meet their specific needs. It is a means by which people abdicate responsibility for any consistent, tough-minded evaluation of the outcome of specific policies. They put their trust in their leader, who will somehow take care of things. Charisma requires some psychological distance between leader and follower. Immediate superiors exist in the work-a-day world of constant objective feedback and evaluation. They are very human and very fallible, and immediate subordinates cannot build an aura of magic about them. Day- to-day intimacy destroys illusion. But the leader in the top echelons of an organization is sufficiently distant from the membership to make a simplified and magical image possible.[29]

To put charisma into operation, Katz and Kahn emphasize the use of two particular measures. The degree of emotional arousal among followers and the global character of the leader's power as perceived by followers are crucial for charismatic success. Both adherents and opponents react emotionally to charismatic personalities; the leader's portrait is global and not discriminating. Specific weaknesses are overlooked in the great leader.

Katz delineates three types of interpersonal relations between charismatic personalities and followers:

- One type of charismatic leader may symbolize the followers' *wishful solutions to internal conflicts.* Instead of searching for deeper meanings and motives, followers seek release from their internal conflicts. They project their fears, aggression, and aspirations upon social measures that facilitate symbolic solution. In his or her personality and program, the charismatic leader offers symbolic solution.
- A second type of charismatic leader entails an *aggressor,* or father figure, who possesses overwhelming power; the follower is unable to escape the exercise of such power. In this type of interpersonal relation between leader and followers, there is no new ideology; but the followers identify with the aggressor, or father figure.
- A third type of charismatic leader maintains an interpersonal relationship void of internal conflict with followers. In assuming that their charismatic leader may advance their interests, followers magnify the power of their leader.[30]

The concepts of power and leadership enjoy common properties; however, they are not the same. Leaders exercise power. A leadership act involves choosing power instruments. Leadership is the point at which power is activated. Leadership entails attempts on the part of a leader, or influencer, to affect, or influence, the behavior of a follower or followers.

A charismatic leader may fail to fully develop the abilities of subordinates, as they become overly dependent upon the leader. When the leader is absent, the organization tends to flounder, and when he or she departs for good, it may fall to pieces.

Charismatic leadership also may inhibit communication. Subordinates become reluctant to give the leader unpleasant information or advise against policies that may be unwise. Often, they lose the ability to discriminate between wise and unwise policies because they have surrendered much of their capacity for independent judgment. This can be crucial because a charismatic leader may be not only forceful but also foolish.

While charisma is positive in many ways, its main danger in public administration is the possibility that a charismatic leader's personality may negate important advice and challenges from subordinates and citizens.

### Max Weber and Charisma Power Centers

Max Weber, the founder of modern organizational theory, was a renaissance scholar and eloquently and persuasively wrote in the areas of sociology, economics, and religion in such enduring standards as *The Protestant Ethic* and the *Spirit of Capitalism*. In his writings, Weber identified three "pure types" of authority—*rational, traditional,* and *charismatic.* In his rational emphasis, Weber believed in the "legality" of patterns of normative rules. He insisted upon the right of those elevated to authority under these rules to issue commands. This focus constituted legal or *rational* authority. In his traditional emphasis, Weber believed in the sanctity of immemorial traditions. He recognized the legitimacy of the status of those exercising authority under such traditions. This focus constituted *traditional* authority. In Weber's charismatic emphasis, the German scholar espoused devotion to the specific and exceptional sanctity, heroism, or exemplary character of an individual person. This focus constituted *charismatic authority*.[31]

Weber focused on the function and exercise of power in society. He concluded that there are three major points of influence for examining charismatic leaders and their impacts.

- The law and the traditional taboos of the particular culture or society. These might include laws, rules, regulations, customs, mores, taboos, routines, and certain ascribed standards. These properties are thought to be rational, grounded in prescribed ways of acting and behaving.
- Individual leadership, largely emotional, which Weber labeled charisma. This is also referred to as the cult of personality. These personalities might include the president, governor, mayor, coach, pastor, priest, rabbi, or other community leaders. This property is thought to be often irrational, as it goes against the grain of how issues confronting the organization have been handled, dealt with, brokered, and accepted.
- The mass of administrators who carry out the laws and policies of the organization, or government; in short, the bureaucracy, also referred to as the followers. In a governmental office, it's the employees. In U.S. society, it's the citizens. In a religious organization, it's the parishioners. On the state university's athletic teams, it's the players. These properties emphasize a rational response, grounded in prescribed ways of responding to the dictates of leaders, manager, and other authorities.

Charisma, then, is not merely the appearance of a dynamic, excited, motivated, committed, passion-filled person. Charismatic persons persuade followers to change their old ways of responding to the organization's challenges and problems and act in creative, determined, and new ways to accomplish the tasks assigned to the government bureaucracy. In the history of organizations, there are occasions when a great man or woman arrives on the scene or comes from the ranks of the organization.

The immense personal magnetism of the charismatic leader causes followers to rid themself of their old, dysfunctional ways and become more productive than ever for the new leader and the organization. The charismatic leader dominates decision making regardless of the logic of his or her positions. The followers abandon rational thinking and follow the new leader, into the unknown future of the organization. Charismatic leaders encounter challenges in democratic societies. Their followers are often educated and not easily seduced, for long periods of time, by leaders turned Pied Pipers.[32]

# THINK ABOUT IT!

**Major Concepts in Leadership**

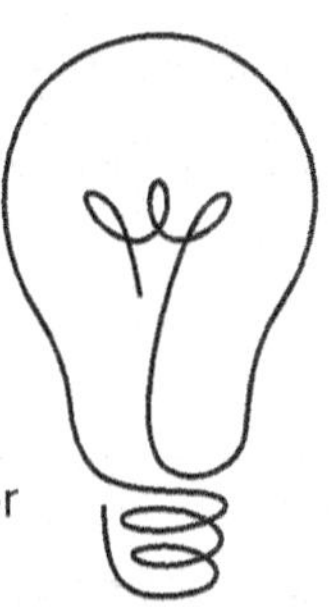

"Managers are people that do things right. Leaders are people that do the right things." – Warren Bennis

A leader is a person who has the authority to decide, direct, and represent the objectives and functions of an organization.

A manager is a person who has the authority to direct specific organizational resources in order to accomplish objectives.

Authority is the license an organization grants that gives an individual the right to use its powers and resources.

Credibility is the recognition by an organization that one is competent to use its powers.

### Charismatic Leader Behaviors

Perspectives on charismatic leadership in times of cultural and technological change are pertinent to understanding the dynamics of charisma. What common behaviors do charismatic leaders exhibit?

Robert J. House offers six categories of charismatic leader behaviors:

1. *Role modeling.* The role model espouses a set of values and beliefs in which followers should believe. The model's emotional responses to rewards or punishments elicit similar emotional reactions from followers.
2. *Image building.* In the cult of personality, charismatic leaders portray an image or images to followers. In the institutionalization of charisma, perceptions are as important as realities. Therefore, the creation and maintenance of an image or images are crucial considerations.
3. *Goal articulation.* In organizational leadership, the development of an institutional mission and goals is an ongoing process. The creation and maintenance of an institutional mission and goals require leadership skills whereby the leader merges his personality characteristics with the organization's social structure. The leader provides the organization with a special identity. In pointing out organizational goals, the leader articulates goals that transcend the movement or cause. Such goals are ideological rather than pragmatic. Moral overtones abound.
4. *Exhibiting high expectations and showing confidence.* Charismatic leaders communicate high performance expectations for followers. Such leadership enhances subordinates' self-esteem and affects the goals followers accept for themselves. As the charismatic leader spells out to his followers that they are competent and personally responsible, subordinates perceive themselves as competent. Leaders seek to enhance motivation, performance, and satisfaction in followers.
5. *Effect on followers' goals.* Followers may evaluate their performance according to standards the leader has articulated in terms of specific and high expectations. The leader's expectations allow followers to derive feedback on their personal behaviors.
6. *Emotional arousal.* Adherents and opponents react emotionally to charismatic leaders. The enthusiasm of one group's responses is matched by the mistrust of the other group. The organizational maintenance of emotional arousal is pertinent to the long-term success of the charismatic leader.[33]

House describes four personal characteristics of charismatic leaders. Charismatic leaders exercise *dominance*, personify *self-confidence*, exhibit *influence*, and maintain *strong convictions* in the moral righteousness of their beliefs.[34]

Why does charismatic leadership emerge in the environment of movements for change? What historical circumstances explain such emotional arousals among followers? Weber indicates that charisma and personality blend most readily "in times of psychic, physical, economic, ethical, religious, political distress."[35]

NOTABLE QUOTES

Travel is the only thing you buy that makes you richer.

— *Unknown*

### Historical Conditions Favoring Charisma

Erik H. Erikson suggests that large numbers of people become "charisma hungry" under historical conditions in which religion wanes. Charismatic leaders minister well during three kinds of distress:

- One distress condition is *fear.*
- A second, and related, condition is *anxiety.* The condition of people not knowing who they are creates an "identity vacuum" and "anxiety."
- A third historical condition, in Erikson's terms, is *existential dread.* In this type of distress, people experience circumstances in which the rituals of their human existence become dysfunctional. The leader, under such conditions, may offer meaning and provide followers with a greater sense of community, emerging as a charismatic leader. In offering salvation from fear, anxiety, and existential dread, the charismatic leader creates new forms of safety, identity, or rituals.[36]

Crisis, therefore, is important to the emergence of charismatic leadership. Crises foster the emergence of charismatic leaders judged as more effective than the group leaders who emerge in non-crisis situations.[37]

Thus, charismatic movements develop and multiply during times of widespread distress in society. The charismatic leader, by virtue of unusual personal qualities, promises the hope of salvation. Perceived by followers as specifically salvationist or messianic in nature, the charismatic leader offers himself or herself to those persons in distress as peculiarly qualified to lead them from their distressful predicament.

## THINK ABOUT IT!

**The Functions of Institutional Leadership**

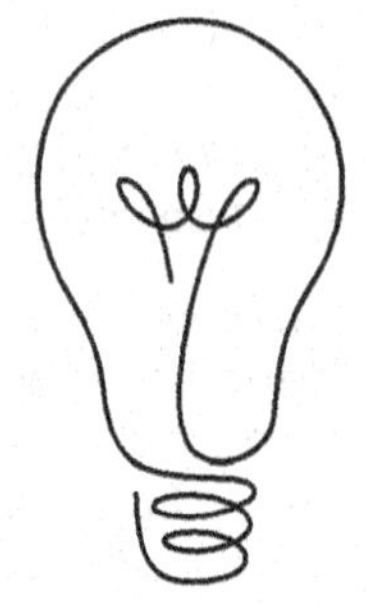

The relationship between leadership and organizational character is more transparent when examined in the context of the leader's key tasks.

The definition of institutional mission and role. The setting of goals is a creative task that entails self- assessment and discovery of the true commitments of the organization as determined by effective internal and external demands. The failure to set aims in the light of these commitments is a major source of irresponsibility in leadership.

The institutional embodiment of purpose. The task of leadership is not only to make policy but to build policy decisions into the organization's social structure. This too is a creative task. It means shaping the "character" of the organization, sensitizing the organization to the complex dynamic of thinking and responding, so that the execution and elaboration of policies, according to their spirit as well as their letter, will be achieved more reliably.

The defense of institutional integrity. The leadership of any policy fails when it concentrates on sheer survival; institutional survival, properly understood, is a matter of maintaining values and distinctive identity.

The ordering of internal conflict. Internal interest groups form naturally in large-scale organizations because the total enterprise is, in one sense, a polity composed of a number of sub-organizations. The struggle between competing interests always has a high claim on the attention of leadership. This is so because the direction of the enterprise as a whole may be seriously influenced by changes in the internal balance of power.

*Source: Phillip Selznick, Leadership in Administration (University of California Press, 1984), pp. 61–63.*

## Summary

- Administrators and administrative theorists place increasing emphasis on communication.
- Communication problems arise not only from information that is too slow, incomplete, or distorted, but also from information that is too abundant. This is a problem of communication overload.
- Communication falls into two basic categories—formal and informal. Formal communication is written. Informal communication is oral. Formal communication fosters accountability, while informal communication does not produce mounds of paperwork.
- Formal communication restrains arbitrariness, capriciousness, favoritism, and discrimination.
- Organizational size and public character are factors affecting the use of formal communication.
- The informal communications system is often referred to as the "grapevine."
- Organizations are groupings of social beings.
- A certain amount of informal and personal communication occurs within the ranks. Participants seek the "right" mixture of informal and formal communications.
- The internet educates and connects people faster than any previous technology that the world has known.
- Upward communication focuses on the employee, his or her performance, and problems; others and their problems; organizational practices and policies; and what needs to be done and how it can be done.
- Information moves in three basic directions: upward from subordinate to superior, downward from superior to subordinate, and horizontally from one organizational unit to another.
- Downward communication includes job instructions, job rationale, information about organizational procedures and practices, feedback to the subordinate about his or her performance, and indoctrination of goals.
- The informal group is the workhorse of the modern organization.
- The growth of specialization and interdependency is making it increasingly vital for information to flow through the organization as well as to move up and down its ranks.
- Informal organization is more important in determining worker cooperation than formal organization. In this "other organization," the output is set by social norms, not individual abilities, and the group greatly influences the behavior of individual workers.
- Employees of organizations, like citizens of nations, tend to obey those rules in which they believe.
- The importance of the small group is based upon the centrality of primary relationships over secondary relationships in human behavior.
- Leadership is, to a great extent, determined by the needs of the situation.
- Leadership qualities include optimism, conviction, humor, civility, energy, enterprise, virtue, intelligence, verbal ability, creativity, and judgment.
- Max Weber's "pure types" of authority are *rational, traditional,* and *charismatic.* Weber believed in the "legality" or rationality of patterns of normative rules and in the sanctity of immemorial traditions. He also espoused devotion to the specific and exceptional sanctity, heroism, or exemplary character of an individual person, or charisma.
- Weber focused on the function and exercise of power in society. He proposed three major points of influence for examining charismatic leaders and their impacts: (1) the law and the traditional taboos of the particular culture or society; (2) individual leadership, largely emotional, which Weber labeled *charisma;* and (3) the bureaucrats, or mass of administrators, who carry out the laws and policies of the organization or government.

- Charisma is not the objective assessment of a leader's ability to meet followers' specific needs. It is a means by which people abdicate responsibility for any consistent, tough-minded evaluation of the outcome of specific policies. They trust their leader, who will somehow take care of things.
- As an organization achieves stability and value, it becomes an institution. In processes of organizational institutionalization, stability and values merge. The longer the organization exists, the greater the prospects for developing distinguishing structures, capabilities, and liabilities.
- The functions of institutional leadership are (1) definition of the institutional mission and role, (2) institutional embodiment of purpose, (3) the defense of institutional integrity, and (4) the ordering of internal conflict.

## Videos, Films and Talks

Please visit *The Craft of Public Administration* at www.millenniumhrmpress.com for up-to-date videos, films, talks, readings, and additional class resources.

Demand a More Open-source Government [17 min]
Beth Noveck, TED Talk
https://www.ted.com/talks/beth_noveck_demand_a_more_open_source_government?language=en

What a Digital Government Looks Like [13 min]
Anna Piperal, TED Talk
https://www.ted.com/talks/anna_piperal_what_a_digital_government_looks_like

The Crisis of Leadership—and a Whole New Way Forward [14 min]
Halla Tómasdóttir and Bryn Freedman, TED Talk
https://www.ted.com/talks/halla_tomasdottir_and_bryn_freedman_the_crisis_of_leadership_and_a_new_way_forward

How Great Leaders Inspire Action [17 min]
Simon Sinek, TED Talk
https://www.ted.com/talks/simon_sinek_how_great_leaders_inspire_action/transcript#t-9852

How to have construction conversations [10 min]
Julia Dhar, TED Talk
https://www.ted.com/talks/julia_dhar_how_to_have_constructive_conversations/transcript

Ethical Leadership and Communication [6 min]
Alex Lyon, communication coach
https://www.youtube.com/watch?v=CHzL4PJIKLw

## Suggested Readings

**Citizen-centric Approach for e-Governance, by Devendra Nath Gupta**
https://docplayer.net/64514335-Citizen-centric-approach-for-e-governance.html

**Three tips government leaders can use to communicate effectively**
https://ourpublicservice.org/blog/three-tips-government-leaders-can-use-to-communicate-effectively/

**Acceleration and Evolution: Emerging Trends from the Digital Stats Survey**
https://media.erepublic.com/document/CDG21_DSPI_Best_Practices_Guide_V_Updated.pdf

**The New Digital Workplace**
https://papers.govtech.com/The-New-Digital-Workplace-138354.html?promo_code=channel

**Keys to Government's Digital Transformation**
https://www.governing.com/archive/col-5-keys-government-digital-transformation.html

**The Temperament of a Great Leader**
https://www.governing.com/archive/col-temperament-great-civic-leader.html

## Notes

1. David K. Berlo, *The Process of Communication: An Introduction to Theory and Practice* (New York: Holt, Rinehart, & Winston, 1960), pp. 23–24; Harold F. Gortner, Julianne Mahler, and Jeanne Bell Nicholson, *Organization Theory: A Public Perspective,* 2d ed. (Fort Worth, TX: Harcourt Brace, 1997), pp. 135–141.
2. See http://www.ualr.edu/dllauferswei/cj3306/ formalcomm.html.
3. Ibid.
4. Kenneth Cukier, "Who Runs the Internet?" *World Press Review* 45, no. 5 (May 1998): 39–41
5. David E. Nye, "Shaping Communication Networks: Telegraph, Telephone, Computer," *Social Research* 64, no. 3 (Fall 1997): 1067–1092.
6. Ellen Goodman, "Anonymity Breeds Incivility," *Boston Globe,* September 5, 1996, p. 17A.
7. Brandi Bowser, "Opening the Window to Online Democracy: www.localgovernment.com," *American City & County* 113, no. 1 (January 1998): 36–38.
8. Thomas L. Friedman, "Global Village Idiocy," *New York Times,* May 12, 2002.
9. *Detroit Free Press,* September 28, 1967.
10. Alan Zaremba, "Working with the Organizational Grapevine," *Personnel Journal* 67, no. 7 (July 1988): 38–41.
11. *Time,* June 18, 1973, p. 67.
12. See http://www.ualr.edu/dllauferswei/cj3306/ formalcomm.html.
13. Ibid.
14. UNPAN, "Global Survey of E-Government; What Is E-Government?" See https://publicadministration.un.org/egovkb/en-us/.

15. "Tech Watch: Give Federal Employees Tools to Exploit E-Government," *Federal Times*, December 17, 2001.

16. See http://www.jerseyisc.org/e-government/ e-government-introduction.html.

17. Meghan E. Cook, "What Citizens Want from E-Government," Center for Technology in Government, State University of New York, Albany. See http://www.ctg.albany.edu/egov/ what_want.html.

18. SmartCitiesWorld News Team, "A third of citizens unaware of digital government services, SmartCitiesWorld. See https://www.smartcitiesworld.net/news/news/a-third-of-citizens-unaware-of-digital-government-services-4359.

19. Henry C. Jackson, "Government's Move to E-mail Eases Access but Worries Some," *Chicagotribune. com*, March 15, 2008.

20. Dwight Waldo, *The Enterprise of Public Administration* (Novato, CA: Chandler & Sharp, 1980), p. 164.

21. Vincent O'Leary and David Duffy, "Managerial Behavior and Correctional Policy," *Public Administration Review* (November–December 1971).

22. Daniel Katz and Robert L. Kahn, *The Social Psychology of Organizations* (New York: John Wiley, 1966), p. 245.

23. Ibid., pp. 245–246.

24. Ibid.

25. Douglas McGregor, *Leadership and Motivation* (Cambridge, MA: MIT Press, 1966), p. 73.

26. William J. Reddin, *Managerial Effectiveness* (New York: McGraw-Hill, 1970), p. 35.

27. "Good Leaders Must First Be Good People," *Black Issues in Higher Education* 13, no. 9 (June 27, 1996): 64.

28. Katz and Kahn, *The Social Psychology of Organizations*, pp. 293–294. 28. Ibid., pp. 545–546.

29. Daniel Katz, "Patterns of Leadership," *Handbook of Political Psychology* (San Francisco: Jossey-Bass, 1973), pp. 216–217.

30. A. M. Henderson and Talcott Parsons, eds., *Max Weber: The Theory of Social and Economic Organization* (New York: Oxford University Press, 1947), p. 328.

31. Rom. 12, New English Bible with Apocrypha.

32. John M. Pfiffner and Frank P. Sherwood, *Administrative Organization* (Englewood Cliffs, NJ: Prentice- Hall, 1960), pp. 55–56.

33. Robert J. House, "A 1976 Theory of Charismatic Leadership," in *Leadership: The Cutting Edge*, eds. James G. Hunt and Lars L. Larson (Carbondale, IL: Southern Illinois University Press, 1977), pp. 193–204.

34. Ibid., p. 204.

35. Reinhard Bendix, *Max Weber: An Intellectual Portrait* (Garden City, NY: Doubleday, 1947), p. 245.

36. Robert C. Tucker, "The Theory of Charismatic Leadership," *Daedalus* 97, no. 3 (Summer 1968): 745.

37. Rajnandini Pillai, "Crisis and the Emergence of Charismatic Leadership in Groups: An Experimental Investigation," *Journal of Applied Social Psychology* 26, no. 6, (March 16, 1996): 543–563.

## Purse, Performance and Policy

- **Unit 1:** Taxing, Budgeting and Spending
- **Unit 2:** The Productivity Challenge
- **Unit 3:** Administrative Law—the Legal Foundation of Public Administration

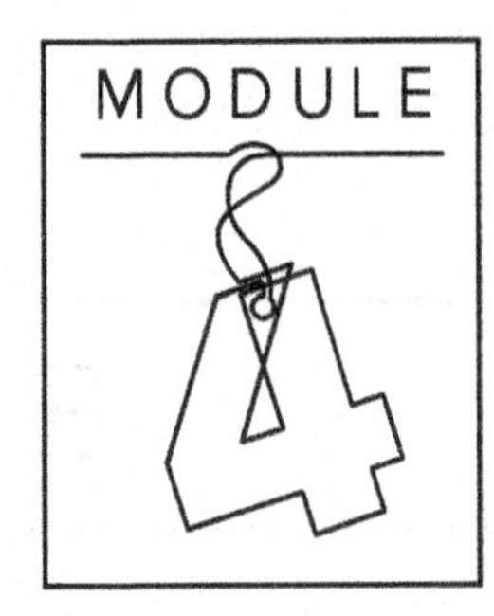


# UNIT 1: Taxing, Budgeting and Spending

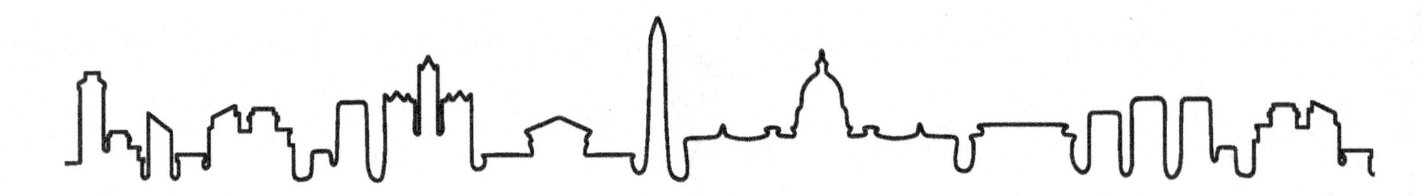

If politics is sometimes defined as the process of deciding who gets what, administrative politics often becomes the process of deciding *who gets what amount of money, when and where*, or "who gets the cookies." Consequently, whether one department or individual is favored over another or whether one program or policy is supported over another usually translates into a budgetary decision. In this sense, budgets are fragmented, incremental, and political documents.

It is not enough, however, to call attention to the political aspects of budgeting to define what budgeting is. Budgets are also instruments of *coordination, control, planning, distribution and redistribution of resources.* They govern nearly all aspects of administration and confer a great deal of power on those who prepare them.

## Who Gets What Amount of Money

Budgeting practices in the United States are the result of American ideology, federalism, and decision- making models. The political environment of budgeting is defined by our democratic ideology, which involves varying concepts of representative government. Democratic ideology is, in turn, defined by the idea of capitalism, a system that assumes that a growth-directed economy supports government's ability to appropriate sufficient funds for public services.

Public-sector monies are raised from taxes on *individuals* and *businesses.* It's tough to maintain viable public services, especially as population grows and citizen demands for governmental services and goods increase, if revenues supporting such activities are low or nonexistent. Whether citizen taxpayers are providing education, unemployment compensation, health care, infrastructure, or national defense, they need a growth economy to finance these citizen benefits. From a capitalistic economy we are, therefore, able to afford programs that benefit all citizens. The appropriate mix of capitalism and socialism affects the size and scope of government and budgeting policies.

Deciding which level of government should provide a certain service is a matter of *federalism,* with its ever-changing division of power. The American system of federalism helps determine the scope, size, and nature of national, state, and local budget priorities. If state law conflicts with federal law, state law gives way. If local legislation conflicts with state or federal provisions, local ordinances are overruled.

State boundaries, overlapping jurisdictions, the economic decline of certain states and cities, and suburban growth patterns contribute to the dilemmas of budgeting in a highly political and fragmented federal system.

# THINK ABOUT IT!

**What Is the Budget?**

The federal budget is:

- *A plan for how the government spends your money.* What activities are funded? How much does it spend for defense, national parks, the FBI, Medicare, and meat and fish inspection?
- *A plan for how the government pays for its activities.* How much revenue does it raise through different kinds of taxes—income taxes, excise taxes, and social insurance payroll taxes?
- *A plan for government borrowing or repayment of borrowing.* If revenues are greater than spending, the government runs a surplus. When there is a surplus, the government can reduce the national debt.
- *A plan that affects the nation's economy.* Some types of spending—such as improvements in education and support for science and technology—increase productivity and raise incomes in the future. Taxes, on the other hand, reduce incomes, leaving people with less money to spend.
- *A plan that is affected by the nation's economy.* When the economy is doing well, people earn more, and unemployment drops. In this atmosphere, revenues increase, and the deficit shrinks.
- *A historical record.* The budget reports on how the government has spent money in the past and how that spending was financed.

*Source: Tax Foundation, "How Does Uncle Sam Plan to Spend Your Federal Tax Dollar in FY 2003," http://www.taxfoundation.org/taxdollar.html, 2002.*

## The Federal Budget Process

Many landmark pieces of legislation have impacted and resulted in the federal budget process we know today. Federal budget process landmarks include the following.

- **1921:** Bureau of Budget created within the Treasury Department.
- **1939:** Bureau of Budget placed in the newly created Executive Office of President. This gives the President greater authority over budget by providing the president the responsibility for developing a comprehensive budget to be presented to the Congress.
- **1970:** Bureau of Budget's functions expanded to oversee management of federal agencies and renamed as Office of Management and Budget.
- **1974:** Congressional Budget Act passed. Congress creates Congressional Budget Office (CBO) to provide an independent source of economic and fiscal analysis. Thus, CBO is on the legislative side, while OMB is on the executive side. CBO and OMB projections and estimates do not necessarily match (this is a good example of the checks and balances). Start of fiscal year moved from July 1 to October 1.
- **1990:** The Budget Enforcement Act (BEA) passed, which essentially limits discretionary spending and ensures that new entitlement programs and/or tax cuts do not worsen tax deficit. BEA provisions expired in 2002.
- **1997**: The Balanced Budget Act passed.
- **2010:** Pay-As-You-Go Act

The annual budget process, or appropriations process, involves only one-third of the federal government budget. This one-third, called the discretionary budget, is what Congress debates and sets the levels for on an annual basis. Military and education programs are examples of discretionary spending. For details of this process, see www.nationalpriorities.org on which the next few sections are based.

The other two-thirds of the federal budget consists of mandatory spending, primarily federal entitlement programs such as Supplemental Nutrition Assistance Program (SNAP), Medicare, Medicaid, interest on the national debt, and Social Security. Congress sets controls by establishing eligibility rules and other payment guidelines, but the appropriations process is basically automatic. The numbers given in the annual budget are simply estimates based on the eligibility and/or payment rules. The annual budget process comprises a series of steps visible to the public:

| | |
|---|---|
| **Step 1.** | The president submits a budget proposal. |
| **Step 2.** | Congress passes a budget resolution. |
| **Step 3.** | Congressional subcommittees "mark-up" appropriation bills. |
| **Step 4.** | The House and Senate vote on appropriation bills and reconcile differences. |
| **Step 5.** | The president signs each appropriation bill, and the budget is enacted. |

Within these steps are a number of activities not readily visible to the citizenry. We outline them here in chronological order.

**First Monday in February:** The president submits a "budget request." The President's Budget is a proposal for the coming fiscal year, which starts on October 1 and continues through September 30 of the following year. For example, FY2023 begins on October 1, 2022, and ends September 30, 2023.

A lengthy preparation process, largely invisible to the public, determines the shape of the budget. Initially, the president and the cabinet decide on their policy priorities. Based on these priorities, the Office of Management and Budget (OMB) offers guidelines to federal departments and agencies for preparing their strategic plans and budgets. These administrative units then submit their budget requests.

OMB then evaluates these documents and prepares the President's Budget, which is published in four comprehensive volumes:

- Budget of the United States Government
- Analytical Perspectives
- Historical Tables
- Appendix

**February to mid-April:** After the president submits the budget, the House and Senate traditionally prepare budget resolutions. A "budget resolution" is a framework for making budget decisions about spending and taxes. It does not set binding spending amounts for particular programs. After the two chambers pass budget resolutions, a joint conference is formed to reconcile differences. Each chamber must approve conference compromises.

**Late Spring to Early Fall:** The 12 House and Senate subcommittees "mark-up" appropriations bills. Based on the budget resolution, the Appropriations Committee of each chamber sets allocations for each of its subcommittees. Each committee takes budget requests and justifications submitted by agencies. Hearings are conducted.

Committee staffs follow up with agencies to obtain answers to questions about agency requests. Having sought comprehensive information, each committee writes a first draft of its appropriation bill. This effort is known as the "chairman's mark." The committee then votes on its bill. After passage, the bill moves back to the Appropriations Committee, which reviews it and sends it to the floor for a vote. Special riders may also be attached. This process of appropriations may include one or more pieces of tax or other legislation affecting federal revenues.

**Summer to Early Fall (in practice, through December):** The individual appropriation bills are debated and voted on by their respective chambers. After both House and Senate versions of a particular appropriation bill have been passed, a conference committee is set up to resolve differences between them. The House and Senate then vote on a conference report for each bill and send it to the president.

**October 1: The budget is enacted.** The president must sign each appropriation bill after it has passed Congress. When all the bills have been signed, the budget is enacted. However, the process is not normally complete by October 1. In recent years, this budget process has not been finished until December. If the budget is not enacted by October 1, Congress must pass "continuing resolutions" in order for the government to continue its functions. These resolutions simply continue funding for agencies and programs at current levels until the budget for the fiscal year is enacted.

## Federal Spending

The federal budget for fiscal year 2022 is estimated to be $5.3 trillion accounting for nearly 22 percent of the U.S. gross domestic product (GDP) or more than $16,000 for every person in the United States of America.

In the 1920s, the federal government spent less than $40 billion in today's dollars. This was approximately 3 percent of the GDP. Direct government spending did not have a significant impact on the economy. However, the federal government did allocate land to railroad companies, and to encourage mining, it set low mining fees on public lands.

Federal spending increased significantly during the New Deal and especially during World War II. In 1954, government spending peaked at just under 52 percent of GDP.

During the 1990s, federal spending did not keep pace with the expansion of the economy or population growth. Federal spending declined, and by the end of the decade, federal spending was at a low not seen for almost thirty-five years. More recently, federal spending has increased as a result of significant increases in military spending, rising health costs, and a growing number of citizens retiring and collecting Social Security.

Following the recession that began in 2008, the subsequent federal bailouts of the finance and automotive industries and establishment of the American Recovery and Reinvestment Act (ARRA), federal government spending reached 41 percent of GDP. A graphical representation of fiscal year 2019 federal spending is seen in **Figure 4.1.1**.

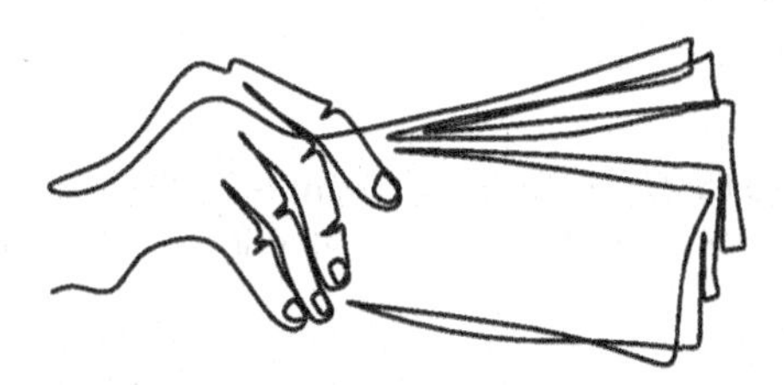

NOTABLE QUOTES

You can have wealth concentrated in the hands of the few, or democracy. But you cannot have both.

*— Louis Brandeis*

In FY 2019 the total spending was $4.4 trillion. Of this amount, mandatory spending consumed 61 percent of the total spending or $2.7 trillion of which Social Security and Medicare accounted for $1.7 trillion (**Figure 4.1.1**). The Congressional Budget Office predicts interest on the national debt as the fastest growing component of the national budget. The remaining 31 percent of the budget is for discretionary spending for all the other functions and activities that the federal level of government provides.

Of this total discretionary spending, $1.375 trillion, $730 billion will go towards military spending, such as veterans' benefits, war and defense related functions. Thus, only $645 billion remains to pay for all the domestic programs and the lion's share of this will be spent on housing and community development ($88 billion), veterans ($87 billion), health and human services ($79 billion), and education ($74 billion).

**Figure 4.1.1 Total Federal Fiscal Year 2019 Budget by Percentage**

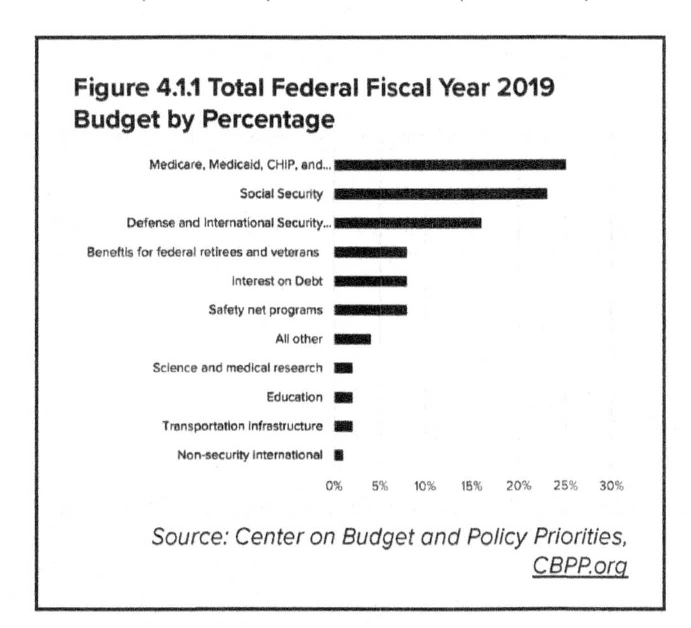


*Source: Center on Budget and Policy Priorities, CBPP.org*

# THINK ABOUT IT!

**The Infrastructure Investment and Jobs Act (IIJA)**

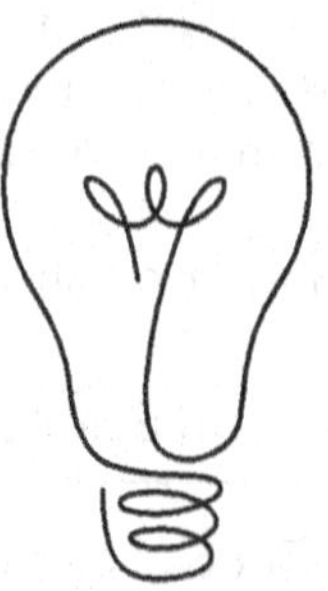

Upon passing and signing into law the Infrastructure Investment and Jobs Act, the Whitehouse stated that it would "...build America's roads, bridges and rails, expand access to clean drinking water, ensure every American has access to high-speed internet, tackle the climate crisis, advance environmental justice, and invest in communities that have too often been left behind." Additionally, it would create 1.5 million jobs each year for the next decade. The total cost of the IIJA is $1.2 trillion although the American Society of Civil Engineers estimated that $4.59 trillion was needed to make the following improvements.

- Deliver clean water to all American families and eliminate the nation's lead service lines.
- Ensure every American has access to reliable high-speed internet.
- Improve transportation options for millions of Americans and reduce greenhouse emissions through the largest investment in public transit in U.S. history.
- Upgrade our nation's airports and ports to strengthen our supply chains and prevent disruptions that have caused inflation. This will improve U.S. competitiveness, create more and better jobs at these hubs, and reduce emissions.
- Make the largest investment in passenger rail since the creation of Amtrak.
- Build a national network of electric vehicle (EV) chargers.
- Upgrade our power infrastructure to deliver clean, reliable energy across the country and deploy cutting-edge energy technology to achieve a zero-emissions future.
- Repair and rebuild our roads and bridges with a focus on climate change mitigation, resilience, equity, and safety for all users.
- Make our infrastructure resilient against the impacts of climate change, cyber-attacks, and extreme weather events.
- Deliver the largest investment in tackling legacy pollution in American history by cleaning up Superfund and brownfield sites, reclaiming abandoned mines, and capping orphaned oil and gas wells.
- *A historical record.* The budget reports on how the government has spent money in the past and how that spending was financed.

*Source: Tax Foundation, "How Does Uncle Sam Plan to Spend Your Federal Tax Dollar in FY 2003," http://www.taxfoundation.org/taxdollar.html, 2002.*

---

**What the Infrastructure Investment and Jobs Act (IIJA) gives to Minnesota**

Former speaker of the U.S. House of Representatives Tip O'Neill coined the phrase that "All politics is local." Whether this is empirically true has been debated over the years, with some suggesting that national trends and tendencies politics influence what is thought about the issues at the local level. For example, based on Whitehouse estimates, the following federal grants are projected to benefit the state of Minnesota in these areas:

- Highways: $4.5 billion
- Bridges: $302 million
- Public transit: $818 million
- Electric vehicles: $68 million for charging stations
- Internet access: $100 million for broadband access
- Airports: $297 million
- Water infrastructure: $680 million
- Wildlife protection: $20 million
- Cybersecurity: $17 million

The American Society of Civil Engineers (ASCE) issues a report card for the U.S. infrastructure every four years. The report estimates the amount of money that needs to be invested in order to make improvements in the overall infrastructure. See **Table 4.1.1** on the following page.

**Table 4.1.1 American Society of Civil Engineers Infrastructure Report Card 2021**

| CATEGORY | 1988* | 1998 | 2001 | 2005 | 2009 | 2013 | 2017 | 2021 |
|---|---|---|---|---|---|---|---|---|
| Aviation | B- | C- | D | D+ | D | D | D | D- |
| Bridges | – | C- | C | C | C | C+ | C+ | C |
| Dams | – | D | D | D+ | D | D | D | D |
| Drinking Water | B- | D | D | D- | D- | D | D | C- |
| Energy | – | – | D+ | D | D+ | D+ | D+ | C- |
| Hazardous Waste | D | D- | D+ | D | D | D | D+ | D- |
| Inland Waterways | B- | – | D+ | D- | D- | D- | D | D- |
| Levees | – | – | – | – | D- | D- | D | D |
| Ports | – | – | – | – | – | C | C+ | B- |
| Public Parks & Recreation | – | – | – | C- | C- | C- | D+ | D- |
| Rail | – | – | – | C- | C- | C+ | B | B |
| Roads | C+ | D- | D+ | D | D- | D | D | D |
| Schools | D | F | D- | D | D | D | D+ | D- |
| Solid Waste | C- | C- | C+ | C+ | C+ | B- | C+ | C- |
| Transit | C- | C- | C- | D+ | D | D | D- | D- |
| Wastewater | C | D+ | D | D- | D- | D | D+ | D- |
| **GPA** | **C** | **D** | **D+** | **D** | **D** | **D+** | **D+** | **C-** |
| **Cost to Improve**** | **–** | **–** | **$1.3T** | **$1.6T** | **$2.2T** | **$3.6T** | **$4.59T** | **$5.93T** |

*The first infrastructure grades were given by the National Council on Public Works Improvements in its report "Fragile Foundations: A Report on America's Public Works," released in February 1988. ASCE's first "Report Card for America's Infrastructure" was issued a decade later.

**The 2017 and 2021 Report Cards' investment needs are over 10 years. The 2013 Report is over eight years. In the 2001, 2005, and 2009 Report Cards the time period was five years.

*Source: infrastructurereportcard.org/wp-content/uploads/2020/12/National_IRC_2021-report.pdf*

## Federal Revenue

Total federal revenues for fiscal year 2019 were approximately $3.46 trillion (see **Figure 4.1.2**). The largest portion, almost 50 percent, is from individual income taxes. The next largest share is payroll taxes at nearly 35 percent.

Corporate income taxes contribute less and less to total tax collections. The burden of taxation has increasingly shifted from corporations to individuals. Over the last half century, corporate taxes have declined from 27 percent of federal revenues to 7 percent (see **Figure 4.1.3** on the following page). Individual income taxes, meanwhile, have remained relatively stable.

**Figure 4.1.2 Federal Fiscal Year 2019 Revenue Sources (in trillions)**

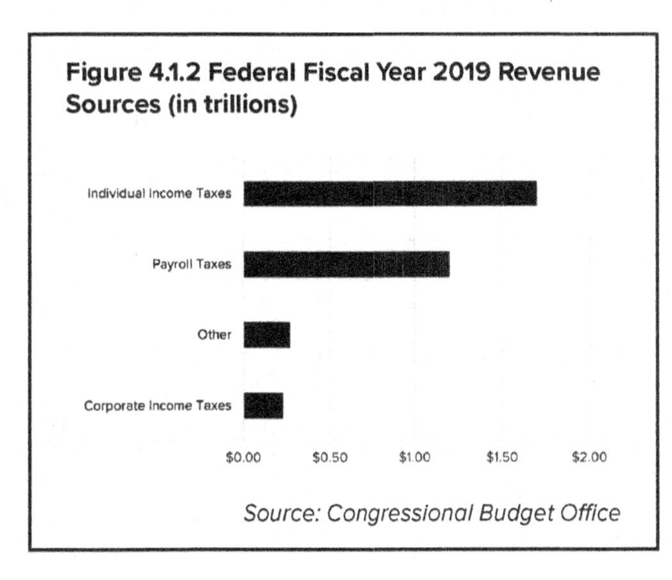


*Source: Congressional Budget Office*

**Figure 4.1.3 Federal Fiscal Year 2019 Revenue (percentage)**

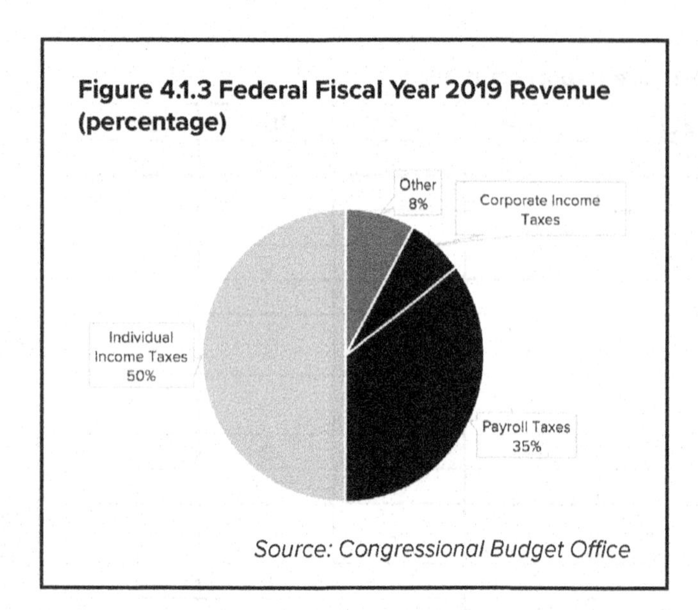


*Source: Congressional Budget Office*

The U.S. Constitution grants Congress power to "collect taxes, duties, imposts and excises." Early federal government taxation was mostly in the form of excises on goods such as alcohol and tobacco. Although a tax on personal income existed briefly during the Civil War, not until 1913, when the 16th amendment to the Constitution was passed was the income tax firmly established. At that historical juncture, less than one percent of the citizenry paid income taxes. While an income tax was firmly established on the citizenry more than one hundred years ago in 1913, in 2021 the Institute on Taxation and Economic Policy reported at least 55 publicly traded companies avoided paying U.S. federal taxes in 2020. Examples of companies reporting a zero percent effective tax rate for 2020 include Archer Daniels Midland, Seaboard, Ecolab and FedEX. **Table 4.1.2** provides the names of some large corporations effectively paying zero federal taxes in 2020.

**Table 4.1.2 Examples of Profitable Companies Avoiding Taxes in 2020**

| COMPANY NAME | U.S. PRE-TAX INCOME | CURRENT FEDERAL INCOME TAX | EFFECTIVE TAX RATE | INDUSTRY |
|---|---|---|---|---|
| Treehouse Foods | $8.00 | $-96.00 | -1,167.1% | Food, beverages, tobacco |
| Westlake Chemical | $227.00 | $-208.00 | -91.6% | Chemicals |
| Telephone & Data Systems | $284.00 | $-175.00 | -61.6% | Telecommunications |
| Ecolab | $95.00 | $-50.00 | -52.6% | Chemicals |
| Mohawk Industries | $87.00 | $-34.00 | -38.9% | Miscellaneous manufacturing |
| Tutor Perini | $96.00 | $-36.00 | -37.7% | Engineering & construction |
| Archer Daniels Midland | $438.00 | $-164.00 | -37.4% | Food, beverages, tobacco |
| Seaboard | $136.00 | $-50.00 | -36.8% | Food, beverages, tobacco |
| Duke Energy | $826.00 | $-281.00 | -34.0% | Utilities, gas and electric |
| Verisign | $447.00 | $-124.00 | -27.7% | Computers, office equip., software, data |
| Danaher | $1,583.00 | $-321.00 | -20.3% | Miscellaneous manufacturing |
| UGI | $420.00 | $-85.00 | -20.2% | Utilities, gas and electric |
| FedEX | $1,218.00 | $-230.00 | -18.9% | Miscellaneous services |
| Interpublic Group | $284.00 | $-53.00 | -18.5% | Miscellaneous services |
| Jacobs Engineering Group | $213.00 | $-37.00 | -17.4% | Engineering & construction |
| Ball | $193.00 | $-33.00 | -17.1% | Miscellaneous manufacturing |
| DTE Energy | $1,531.00 | $-247.00 | -16.1% | Utilities, gas and electric |
| Penske Automotive Group | $505.00 | $-78.00 | -15.5% | Motor vehicles and parts |
| Nucor | $1,220.00 | $-177.00 | -14.5% | Metals & metal products |
| Lincoln National | $423.00 | $61.00 | -14.4% | Financial |

*Source: Institute on Taxation and Economic Policy analysis of Securities and Exchange Commission filings of publicly traded corporations*

NOTABLE QUOTES

An imbalance between rich and poor is the oldest and most fatal ailment of all republics.

— *Plutarch*

During World War I, a need for more revenues dominated tax policy making. The top income tax rate rose from seven percent to 77 percent. Changes occur continuously in the tax code regarding exemptions, deductions, and rates of taxation. During World War II, the number of people subject to the income tax increased tenfold. In the first decade of the twenty-first century, more than 100 million tax returns were filed annually. The federal income tax is progressive, meaning that the rich pay a larger percentage of their income than middle- or low-income taxpayers, although this may vary depending on applicable tax credit expenditures.

Taxes to finance Social Security were established by the Social Security Act of 1935. More benefits have been added over time, including Medicare, which provides health care coverage for senior citizens. Taxes to fund Medicare are increased as needs demand. Social Security taxes now stand at 12.4 percent of income, of which half is paid by the employer.

The employee pays 6.2 percent for Social Security and 1.45 percent for Medicare. However, as of 2022, Social Security taxes apply only to the first $147,000 of personal income. This formula causes the Social Security tax to be regressive, in that high-income taxpayers pay a lower percentage of their income than do lower-income taxpayers. About 75 percent of taxpayers actually pay more in payroll taxes (Social Security and Medicare) than they do in individual income taxes.

## Discretionary and Mandatory Spending

Congress appropriates the federal budget into two types of spending: *discretionary* and *mandatory*. Discretionary spending is subject to the annual appropriations process. Congress directly sets levels of spending on discretionary programs; it may choose to increase or decrease spending on any program in a given year. The discretionary budget of $1.375 trillion is about one-third of total federal spending. **Figure 4.1.4** indicates how discretionary spending was allocated in fiscal year 2019.

**Figure 4.1.4 Total Discretionary Fiscal Year 2019 (in billions)**

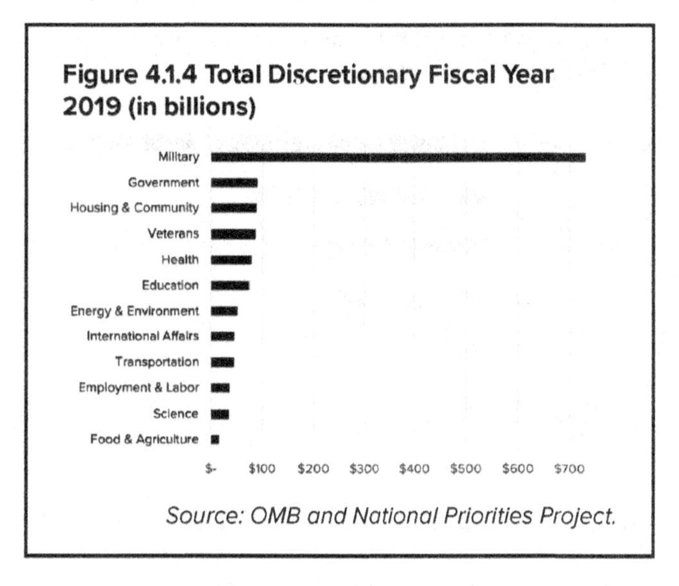


*Source: OMB and National Priorities Project.*

More than half of the discretionary budget is "national defense." This government-defined category is roughly equivalent to the term, "military." Discretionary spending also includes education, health, and housing programs amongst others.

Mandatory spending consists mostly of entitlement programs, whose funding is determined by eligibility or payment rules. Congress decides to create a program, such as SNAP, and determines who is eligible. It also establishes other criteria for SNAP administration. How much money is appropriated for SNAP each year is then determined by estimates of how many Americans will be eligible and apply for SNAP.

Unlike discretionary spending, Congress does not increase or decrease the SNAP budget each year. It periodically reviews eligibility rules and may alter them in order to include or exclude more recipients. Mandatory spending accounts for two-thirds of the total federal budget. Social Security is by far the largest mandatory federal program. Social Security comprises one-third of mandatory spending and continues to increase as U.S. demographics shift toward an older population. **Figure 4.1.5** shows the breakdown of different types of mandatory spending in fiscal year 2019.

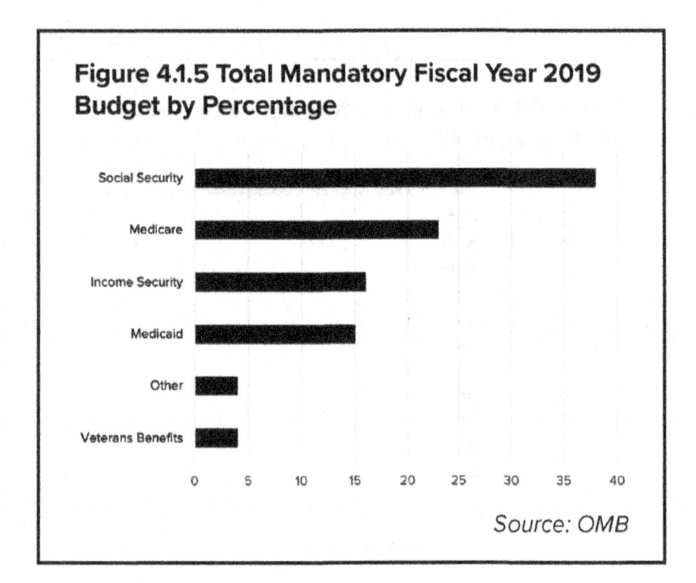


**Figure 4.1.5 Total Mandatory Fiscal Year 2019 Budget by Percentage**

*Source: OMB*

## Deficit, Surplus, and National Debt

In January 2022, the U.S. Treasury placed the national debt at $29.5 trillion. The national debt has assumed political, economic, and even cultural, significance—with both short- and long-range effects. *Debt* is sometimes confused with *deficit*. A deficit occurs when spending exceeds revenues in any given year; a surplus is the opposite—revenues exceed spending. The gross federal debt is the total of all federal net borrowing over the course of years.

The gross federal debt is held by federal entities and by the public. Government trust funds, such as Social Security, are typically required by law to put any surpluses into Treasury securities, which represent shares of debt. Some of the government's debt is actually owned by government trust funds. Intra-governmental holdings include revolving funds, special funds, Federal Financing Bank securities, and other government accounts.

The gross federal debt is also held by the public—individuals, corporations, local, state, and foreign governments, any entity that is not the U.S. federal government. The Federal Reserve System, a federal entity, is an exception. It holds debt that is classified as public. In order to conduct monetary policy, the Fed buys and sells federal securities. If the debt is ever completely eliminated, the Fed may buy securities to conduct policy making.

**Figure 4.1.6** indicates the amount of national debt from 2016-2021. Similar to the large spikes in national debt during the onset of war in the early 21st century and recovery from the national recession in 2008-2009, note that the national debt increased noticeably during the efforts to combat the Coronavirus Disease 2019 pandemic 2020-2021.

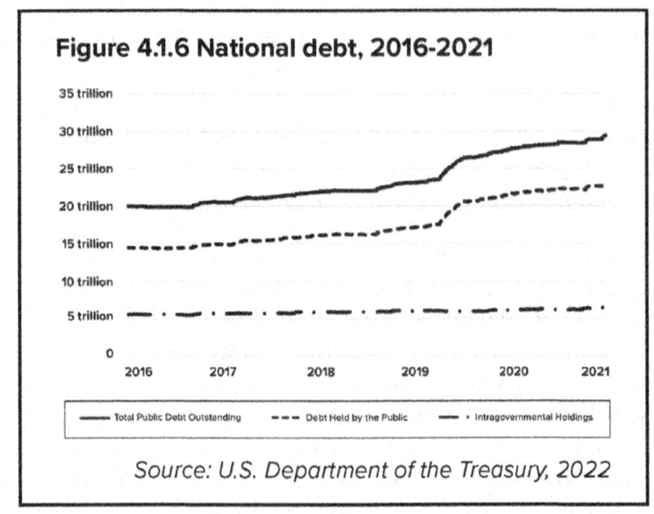


**Figure 4.1.6 National debt, 2016-2021**

*Source: U.S. Department of the Treasury, 2022*

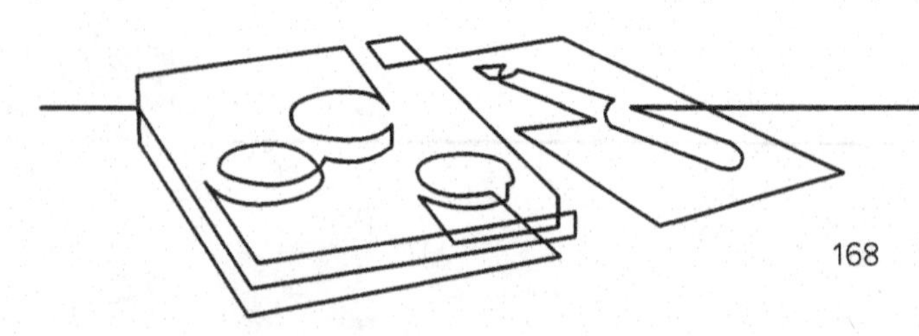

Absolute numbers do not give the whole story, however; the size of the economy also matters. If the economy grows more quickly than the debt, more resources are available to pay back the debt. As a percentage of the economy, the federal debt declined significantly after World War II. Policy making in the Ronald Reagan era—boosting military spending and promoting tax cuts—resulted in huge federal deficits. As seen in **Figure 4.1.7**, in the economic boom of the Clinton years, debt as a percentage of GDP declined.

The huge deficits of the 1980s and budget surpluses of the 1990s are also evident in **Figure 4.1.7**. In 1998, the federal budget was in surplus for the first time since 1969. The last surplus was in 2001. Surpluses that in 2000 amounted to $265 billion turned into a nearly $2.8 trillion deficit by fiscal year 2021 as the government reacted to terrorism, the great recession and COVID-19. and coronavirus 2019. The federal budget is unlikely to yield a surplus again unless significant new tax and/or spending policies are enacted.

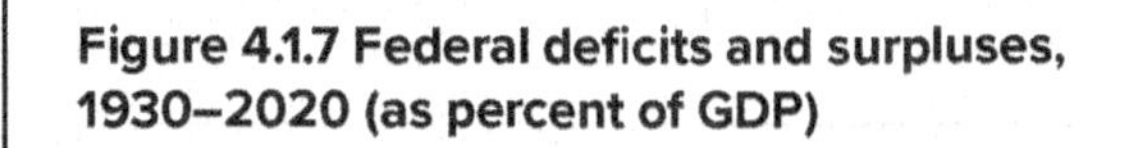

**Figure 4.1.7 Federal deficits and surpluses, 1930–2020 (as percent of GDP)**

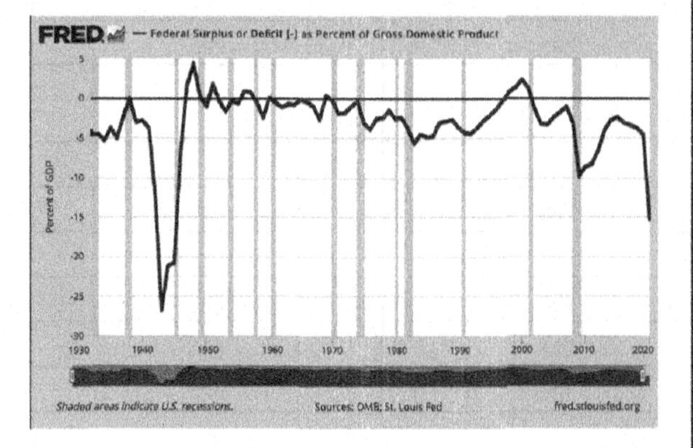


*Source: U.S. Department of the Treasury, 2022*

## Federal Funds, Trust Funds, and Off-Budget Spending

Federal budgeting consists of *federal funds* and *trust funds,* which earmark revenues for particular purposes. Social Security, Medicare, unemployment compensation, federal employment retirement, veterans' retirement, highway construction, and airport development all have their own trust funds. The designation is largely arbitrary, as trust funds and federal funds may finance very similar activities. See **Table 4.1.3** on the following page for examples of the more than 200 federal trust funds.

Federal fund revenues come from a variety of sources including individual, corporate, excise, estate, and gift taxes, special collections, and borrowing.

An *off-budget* program is not considered part of the federal budget and it is not included in the budget totals. In fiscal year 2019, off-budget spending alone on Social Security and U.S. Postal Service operations was nearly $1.1 trillion.

A program is typically placed off-budget for political reasons. Instead of raising revenues and/or cutting spending, placement of programs off-budget gives the appearance of a smaller budget deficit and has been used to circumvent congressional balanced budget legislation.

The Social Security trust fund is financed through dedicated payroll taxes. It is positioned off-budget in order to support a decent quality of life for the elderly. Payroll taxes were raised in the late 1980s to anticipate retirement of the baby boomer generation. Government, however, returned to on-budget deficit spending in 2001. The federal government borrows from Social Security surpluses in order to pay for current program demands—rather than taxing and cutting spending now to prepare for future necessities.

**Table 4.1.3 Selected Trust and Other Dedicated Funds and Budget Authority in Fiscal Year 2018**

| ACCOUNT NAME | MANDATORY BUDGET AUTHORITY? | ENTITLEMENT AUTHORITY? |
|---|---|---|
| **Non-resolving Trust Funds** | | |
| Federal Old-Age and Survivors Insurance Trust Fund | Yes | Yes |
| Federal Disability Insurance Trust Fund | Yes | Yes |
| Federal Supplementary Medical Insurance Trust Fund | Yes | Yes |
| Federal Hospital Insurance Trust Fund | Yes | Yes |
| Federal-Aid Highways | Yes | No |
| Trust Fund Share of Federal Aviation Administration Activities (Airport and Airway Trust Fund) | No | No |
| Civil Service Retirement and Disability Fund | Yes | Yes |
| Military Retirement Fund | Yes | Yes |
| Unemployment Trust Fund | Yes | Yes |
| Foreign Military Sales Trust Fund | Yes | No |
| Social Security Administration Limitation on Administrative Expenses | Yes | No |
| Railroad Social Security Equivalent Benefit Account | Yes | Yes |
| **Special Funds** | | |
| Universal Service Fund | Yes | No |
| National Flood Insurance Reserve Fund | Yes | No |
| Department of Defense Medicare-Eligible Retiree Health Care Fund | Yes | Yes |
| Revolving Trust Fund | | |
| Employees and Retired Employees Health Benefits Funds | Yes | Yes |
| **Public Enterprise Funds** | | |
| National Flood Insurance Fund | Yes | No |
| Postal Service Fund | Yes | No |
| Tennessee Valley Authority Fund | Yes | No |
| Commodity Credit Corporation Fund | Yes | Yes |
| Federal Crop Insurance Corporation Fund | Yes | Yes |
| Federal Student Loan Reserve Fund | Yes | No |
| Pension Benefit Guaranty | Yes | Yes |

*Source: GAO analysis of OMB data and applicable laws*

## Phases of the Budget Cycle

Federal budgeting can be understood in four phases: executive preparation, legislative consideration, implementation and control of the enacted budget, and audit and evaluation. According to Douglas Lee, a "budget, after all, is only an accounting of the financial cost of many political and social decisions.[1] The term *budget* originates from the Middle English word for pouch or purse.[2] Federal budgeting is a continuous and overlapping process, with stages of the budget cycle linked. The findings of audit/evaluation are important data for preparation of future budgets. The federal fiscal year begins in October. Many local governments start their fiscal years in January. A majority of states begin their fiscal year on July 1. New York begins its fiscal year on April 1, Texas on September 1, and Alabama and Michigan begin their fiscal year on October 1. Sixteen of the 50 states typically enact a bi-annual budget, meaning they approve a budget every two years.

*Executive preparation.* The president (or governor, mayor, or chief executive on the state and local levels) transmits general directions for department and agency request preparation. The department or agency reviews current operations, program objectives, issues, and future plans as they relate to the upcoming annual budget. Cabinet secretaries and agency heads submit projections for requirements reflecting current operations and future plans. Supporting memoranda and related analytic studies identify major issues, alternatives for resolving issues, and comparisons of costs and effectiveness.

The Office of Management and Budget (OMB) develops economic assumptions, obtains forecasts of international and domestic situations, and prepares fiscal projections. The OMB compiles total outlay estimates for comparison with revenue estimates. It develops recommendations for the president on fiscal policy, program issues, and budget levels.

As appropriate, the president discusses budgetary outlook and policies with the director of the OMB and with cabinet secretaries and agency heads. The president reviews budget recommendations and decides on department and agency budget estimates, grounding decisions on overall budget assumptions and policies. He/she may often revise their budget message and transmit recommended budget estimates to Congress.[3]

*Legislative consideration.* The predominant legislative power in the Western world is the power of the purse.[4] Congress acts on requests for budget authority and does not vote directly on outlays of taxpayer dollars. Instead, Congress grants budget authority to departments and agencies. Budget authority permits the agencies to incur obligations and to spend federal monies. This is accomplished through passage of appropriation bills.

The budget committees hold hearings as they prepare for the drafting of the first concurrent resolution on the budget. The appropriations committees hold special hearings on the budget overview with the director of the OMB, Secretary of the Treasury, and Chair of the Council of Economic Advisors. Subcommittees of the appropriation committees also hold hearings and review justifications from each department and agency. The House appropriations subcommittees draft appropriation bills and reports. The budget committees receive the views and budget estimates of all committees and draft the first concurrent resolution.

Congress receives the president's budget within fifteen days after Congress convenes. It adopts the first concurrent resolution on the budget by April 15. The House of Representatives debates and passes appropriation bills, with or without amendments. The Senate receives the House-passed versions of appropriation bills and refers them to the Senate Appropriations Committee. The Senate debates and passes appropriation bills with or without amendments. If Senate bills differ from House versions, bills are sent to conference. Conference committees consider items of disagreement between the two houses and make recommendations for resolving differences in conference reports. These reports are submitted to each body for action. Congress adopts the second concurrent resolution of the budget on August 15.

Authorizing legislation is substantive legislation enacted by Congress that sets up or continues the legal operation of a federal program or agency either indefinitely or for a specific period or sanctions a particular type of obligation or expenditure within a program. Authorizing legislation is usually a prerequisite for appropriations. An appropriation act is a statute, under the jurisdiction of the House and Senate Committees on Appropriations that provides authorization for federal agencies to incur obligations and to make payments out of the treasury for specified purposes. There are twelve regular appropriation acts enacted annually.

# THINK ABOUT IT!

**Ten Principles of Sound Tax Policy**

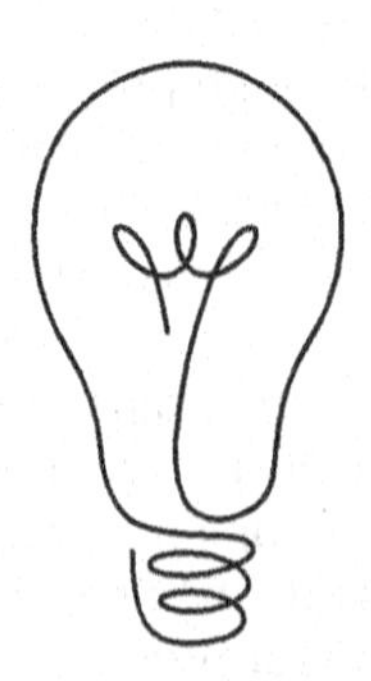

**Transparency is a must.** A good tax system requires informed taxpayers who understand how taxes are assessed, collected, and complied with. It should be clear to taxpayers who and what is being taxed, and how tax burdens affect them and the economy.

**Be neutral.** The fundamental purpose of taxes is to raise necessary revenue for programs, not micromanage a complex market economy with subsidies and penalties. The tax system's central aim should be to minimize distortions in the economy, and to interfere as little as possible with the decisions of free people in the marketplace.

**Maintain a broad base.** Taxes should be broadly based, allowing tax rates to be as low as possible at all points.

**Keep it simple.** The tax system should be as simple as possible and should minimize gratuitous complexity. The cost of tax compliance is a real cost to society, and complex taxes create perverse incentives to shelter and disguise legitimately earned income.

**Stability matters.** Tax law should not change continuously, and tax changes should be permanent and not temporary. Instability in the tax system makes long-term planning difficult and increases uncertainty in the economy.

**No retroactivity.** Changes in tax law should not be retroactive. As a matter of fairness, taxpayers should rely with confidence on the law as it exists when contracts are signed and transactions are made.

**Keep tax burdens low.** It makes a difference how large a share of national income is taken by government in taxes. The private sector is the source of all wealth, and is what drives increases in the standard of living in a market-based economy. Taxes should consume as small a portion of national income as possible and should not interfere with economic growth and investment.

**Don't inhibit trade.** In our increasingly global marketplace, the U.S. tax system must be competitive with those of other developed countries. Our tax system should not penalize or subsidize imports, exports, U.S. investment abroad or foreign investment in the U.S. Taxes on corporations, individuals, and goods and services should be competitive with other nations.

**Ensure an open process.** Tax legislation should be based on careful economic analysis and transparent legislative procedures. Tax legislation should be subject to open hearings with full opportunity to comment on legislation and regulatory proposals.

**State and local taxes matter.** The same general principles that apply to federal taxes also apply at the state and local level. Local, state and federal tax systems should be harmonized to the extent possible, including consistent definitions, procedures and rules.

*Source: Andrew Chamberlain, Tax Foundation, October 7, 2005, https://taxfoundation.org/ten-principles-sound-tax-policy/*

*Implementation and control of the enacted budget.* Spending of federal taxpayer dollars must proceed in a manner consistent with appropriation laws. Once the appropriation bill is approved, the Treasury Department draws an appropriation warrant, countersigned by the General Accountability Office (GAO) and forwarded to the department or agency. The departments and agencies revise operating budgets in view of approved appropriations and program developments.

The director of the OMB distributes budget authority to each department and agency by time periods, usually every three months, or by activities over the duration of the appropriation. The departments and agencies allot apportioned funds to various programs or activities. The budgetary term for allotments is *apportionment.* Central budget office discretion to curtail allotments is often limited. The term for the president's withholding of federal appropriations is *impounding.* Since 1974, presidents have been able to continue to impound funds. Congress, however, can veto these impoundments.

## THINK ABOUT IT!

**Congressional Budget Timetable**

The Congressional budget process begins nine months prior to the beginning of the budget year, which begins on October 1.

**5 days before** — *Five days prior to the transmittal of the President's budget to Congress:* The Congressional Budget Office (CBO) issues its sequestration preview report for the year beginning October 1 (the budget year).

**1ST Monday in Jan.** — *On or after the first Monday in January,* but no later than the first Monday in February: The President's budget is transmitted to Congress.

**by Feb. 15** — *On or before February 15:* The CBO issues its Budget and Economic Outlook for the budget year.

**on Feb. 25** — *February 25:* Deadline for Congressional committees to submit their budget estimate to Budget Committees.

**on April 15** — *April 15:* Congress completes action on budget resolution. June 15: Congress completes action on reconciliation bills. June 30: House completes action on appropriation bills.

**on July 15** — *July 15:* The OMB (Office of Management and Budget) mid-session budget estimate report is due.

**on Aug. 15** — *August 15:* The CBO issues its updated sequestration report. August 20: The OMB issues its updated sequestration report. October 1: The new fiscal year begins.

**10 days after** — *Ten days after the end of the congressional session:* The CBO issues its final sequestration report for the year that began on October 1.

**15 days after** — *Fifteen days after the end of the congressional session:* The OMB issues its final sequestration report.

**45 days after** — *Forty-five days after the end of the congressional session:* GAO (General Accounting Office) issues its sequestration compliance report.

*Sources: Tax Policy Center, Congressional Research Service, and Congressional Budget Act of 1974, https://www.govinfo.gov/content/pkg/CPRT-112HPRT75001/pdf.*

*Audit and evaluation.* An audit is an "examination of records, facilities, systems, and other evidence to discover or verify desired information. Internal audits are those performed by professionals employed by the entity being audited; external audits are performed by outside professionals who are independent of the entity."[5] Different forms of audits include:

- Financial audit, or a review of financial records to determine whether the funds were spent legally, if receipts were properly recorded and controlled, and if financial records and statements are complete and reliable.
- Management or operations audit, or a focus on the efficiency of operations, on waste of government resources, and on use and control of resources.
- Program audit, or an examination of the extent to which desired results are being achieved, objectives of the program being met, and whether there might be lower-cost alternatives to reach the desired results.
- Performance audit, a part of sunset legislation, which establishes "a set schedule for legislative review of programs and agencies unless affirmative legislative action is taken to reauthorize them. Thus, the 'sun sets' on agencies and programs,"[6] causing an assessment of the total operations of a department or agency, including compliance, management, and program audits.

To illustrate the focus of each audit, consider a state highway department appropriation to purchase road salt or brine solution for snow and ice removal. A financial audit considers whether the department purchased the salt, if the salt was actually delivered, if competitive practices were used in selecting a supplier, and if the department spent the correct amount on salt. A management audit considers whether the salt inventory is adequately protected from the environment, if the inventory is adequate or excessive, and if other methods of selecting a supplier would result in lower costs. A program audit considers whether the prevailing level of winter highway clearing is an appropriate use of community resources and if alternatives to deployment of salt would be less costly to the community. Finally, a performance audit examines all operations of the highway department.[7]

The GAO conducts an independent audit of financial records, transactions, and financial management and makes reports to Congress. The departments and agencies review compliance with established policies, procedures, and requirements. They evaluate the accomplishments of program plans and the effectiveness of management and operations. The OMB reviews department and agency operations and evaluates programs and performance. The OMB conducts and guides departments and agencies in organization and management studies and assists the president in improving management and organization of the executive branch.

The Budget and Accounting Act of 1921 set July as the start of the fiscal year. It created the Bureau of the Budget (changed in 1970 to the Office of Management and Budget) and the General Accounting Office (changed in 2004 to the General Accountability Office) This legislation authorizes the president's budget message to Congress. The Congressional Budget and Impoundment Control Act of 1974 set the start of the fiscal year as October 1. It created the Congressional Budget Office and House and Senate Budget Committees. It requires the current services budget and congressional budget resolutions.

# THINK ABOUT IT!

**Worth the Lost? Fewer IRS staff, fewer taxes collected.**

IRS Commissioner Charles Rettig estimated in April 2021 that the gap in taxes legally owed and revenue collected has increased from $441 billion in 2011 to approximately $1 trillion in 2021. In that same time period, new sources of income such as cryptocurrencies have escaped taxation and those owing taxes have become increasingly sophisticated at avoiding taxes. Meanwhile in the last ten years federal budgets have trimmed the IRS enforcement staff by 17,000.

*Source: Lawder, David. IRS chief says $1 trillion in taxes goes uncollected every year. Reuters.* https://www.reuters.com/article/us-usa-treasury-irs/irs-chief-says-1-trillion-in-taxes-goes-uncollected-every-year-idUSKBN2C0255.

## The Incrementalism Budgeting Perspective

The incrementalism perspective of budgeting states that budgeting is primarily, if not exclusively, a process of political strategy.[8] Budgeting is incremental, says Aaron Wildavsky. "The largest determining factor of the size and content of this year's budget is last year's budget. Most of the budget is a product of previous decisions. The budget may be conceived of as an iceberg with by far the largest part below the surface, outside the control of anyone. Many items in the budget are standard and are simply reenacted every year unless there is a special reason to challenge them."[9]

*Incremental budgeting* demands little inquiry because the increment, not the base, is considered. Incremental decision-making entails routine, requires negotiations and accommodation grounded on mutual respect, is delegated to specialists, and is almost invisible. Most definitive, the budget is distributive, historical, annual, repetitive, predictable, automatic, political, and fragmented. It is rewarding and can create stable coalitions.

Incremental budgeting distributes only the increment, but takes nothing away from anyone; decremental budgeting, meanwhile, redistributes resources from people who absorb cuts in appropriations. Incremental budgeting rewards increments to everyone, as credit for such enhancement is to be shared; decremental budgeting engenders blame for the pain of losing accustomed funding.

The incremental model minimizes the intellectual task of creating a new budget every year, facilitates the political task of adopting a budget, and appears ethical. Such a model, accepting the base as a given, eliminates the necessity for rethinking the entire budget. The political task of building a coalition to support this year's new budget allows a majority of political interests with economic stakes to form and take hold. No one appears hurt; everyone gains a little in incremental budgeting.

*Decremental budgeting* is chaotic and conflict laden. It may result in coercion, involve confrontation, generate mistrust, and increase interdepartmental and program competition. It is clearly redistributive, breaks precedents, is multiyear, erratic, unpredictable, painful, can foster unstable coalitions, and requires active leadership for overcoming such obstacles.

Decrementalism suggests a centralized political system dominated by top-down budgeting. Incrementalism treats budgeting as a bottom-up process. What's the difference? The budgeting process includes the countervailing forces of centralization and decentralization, autonomy and interdependence, micropolitics and macropolitics. The president and his key advisors dominate the top-down process. A limited number of people are involved in such an approach; the developments are less visible to the public. Top-down strategy confronts the mixture of defense and domestic components of the budget, the budget's size, the impact of the budget on fiscal policies, and the executive's policy initiatives to force cutbacks. As suggested in our discussion of decrementalism, routine is not a common feature of the top-down process.

There have been top-down characteristics of the budgetary process since the passage of the Budget and Accounting Act of 1921. Top-down elements are more difficult to document as the process is less routine, involves fewer people, and receives less publicity, and as such have garnered less attention than the bottom- up developments. Researchers find it difficult to observe, conceptualize, and explain the top-down process. According to budget theorists Barry Bozeman and Jeffrey D. Straussman, such features are often ignored or relegated to historical "disturbances."[10]

Incrementalism reflects the bottom-up budgeting process. The late budget theorist Aaron Wildavsky reported that incrementalism focuses on the significance of adjusting the margins from last year's budgetary base with little, if any, examination of the assumed baseline.

Why the emphasis upon the bottom-up process? First, incrementalism is explainable. Budget variations may be explained by using simple projections. Second, incrementalism gives an adequate account of the bottom-up process. Third, incrementalism is emphasized extensively in the administration and budgeting literature. Finally, incrementalism dominates policy makers' perceptions of how budgeting actually occurs and portrays the actual experience of policy makers themselves.

Top-down and bottom-up processes are operative in every budget cycle. As the demands of the budget cycle change with developments in fiscal policy, presidential leadership, mercurial characteristics of economic growth and stagnation, foreign conflict, congressional assertiveness, and other political factors, the use of the respective processes changes. Although the top-down process of federal budgeting grew more important in the Ford and Carter administrations, the Reagan administration implemented perhaps the most important shift in budget policy, determining that the "controllable" portion of the budget includes entitlements offering social services to the middle class.

The baseline federal outlay projections for entitlements consist of social insurance programs such as Social Security, Medicare, unemployment insurance, and railroad retirement; means-tested programs such as Medicaid, SNAP, assistance payments, supplemental security income, veterans' pensions, guaranteed student loans, and child nutrition; civilian and military employee retirement and disability; and programs offering veterans' benefits, farm price supports, general revenue sharing, and other social services.[11]

The desire to curb the development of middle-class entitlement spending, promote economic changes, and alter public perception of economic issues and economic thinking encouraged Reagan administration policy makers to adopt top-down strategies. Bozeman and Straussman state that conventional budgeting wisdom did not keep pace with events. Concluding that budget theory should be reformulated, these theorists argue that the political and economic environments changed and led to a perceived demand for reductions in the rate and level of spending. Such cutback management, they argue, can be achieved only through coordinated fiscal management with top-down strategies. Under such conditions, incrementalism becomes a less satisfactory explanation of federal budgeting.[12]

## THINK ABOUT IT!

### Budget Components and Reform Techniques

**The Capital Budget.** A budget that deals with large expenditures for capital items normally financed by borrowing. Capital projects calls for long-range returns and life spans, are relatively expensive, have physical presence, and involve investments in community facilities. Examples include buildings, roads, and sewage systems.[1]

**The Operating or Expense Budget.** This is an annual projection of revenues and expenditures for regular and recurring operations of governments that serves as a primary instrument of planning and financial control. Examples of expenditures include wages, salaries, personnel costs, supplies, materials, and travel costs.

**Performance Budgets.** Performance budgets focus on departmental objectives and accomplishments. They do not emphasize the purchase of resources utilized by the department. This technique accounts for the cost of performing measured accomplishments during the fiscal year. A performance budget includes sections on demand, workload, productivity, and effectiveness.[2]

**Program Budgets.** In a program budget, the focus is on output. The concept rests not on what governments purchase, nor on the tasks in which government is involved, but on the outputs of government, as nearly as they can be defined. This technique delineates the goals of a department and categorizes tasks contributing to each goal. The focus is on product, not input. Planning Programming Budgeting Systems or PPBS, focuses on accountability.[3]

**Zero-Based Budgets (ZBB).** ZBB requires its practitioners to adopt two basic terms and three procedures for implementation. The ZBB terms are decision units and decision packages. The ZBB steps are identification, formation, and ranking.[4]

**New Performance Budgeting or Budgeting for Results.** Over the years, nearly all attempts to make federal budgeting a rational decision-making process have failed. The failure is largely due to the fact that budgeting is a political process which is also fragmented. In the Government Performance & Results Act, 1993 (GPRA) efforts were made by Congress to tie performance to budget decisions. As such, agencies established five-year strategic plans, including performance goals and measurable accomplishments. Although it is based on rational criteria and theoretically makes an improvement over earlier budgeting attempts, it too has some major shortcoming, such as the failure to connect the budgeting process across a myriad of programs and agencies. With the 2004 budget, OMB added a new method to assess federal agency performance—Program Assessment Rating Tool (PART). In short, PART is a technique intended to achieve budgeting results and enable OMB to assess the overall performance of departments, agencies and progress at the federal level of government.[5]

[1] *Jonathan Rauch, "A Capital Idea for the Budget," National Journal 18, no. 49 (6 December 1986): 2948–2949.*

[2] *John L. Mikesell, Fiscal Administration, 135–155.*

[3] *Samuel M. Greenhouse, "The Planning-Programming-Budgeting System: Rationale, Language, and Idea-Relationships," Public Administration Review 26, no. 6 (December 1966): 271–277.*

[4] *See Peter A. Pyhrr, "The Zero-Base Approach to Government Budgeting," Public Administration Review 37, no. 1 (January– February 1977): 1–8; see also Allen Schick, "The Road from ZBB," Public Administration Review 38, no. 2 (March–April 1978): 177–180.*

[5] *Smith, Kevin B., and Michael J. Licari. Public Administration: Power and Politics in the Fourth Branch of Government. Los Angeles, CA: Roxbury Pub., 2006. 204.*

Budgets are grounded in percentage increments to the historic budget base according to some notion of fairness for continuing the funding of each department and agency. The annual focus is on determining percentage monetary adjustments to existing programs.

*Operating departments and agencies* are units of government bureaucracies that spend taxpayer monies for the delivery of services. They focus on the clientele they serve. Their purpose is to expand service opportunities.

*The office of the chief executive* (president, governor, mayor) employs budget specialists to argue on behalf of government departments and agencies and their programs. At the federal level, the budget specialists are located in the OMB. In the states, various titles designate the units of executive office budget specialists such as Budget Office, Finance Division, Department of Management or Office of Planning and Fiscal Management.

Budget analysts are guided by the priorities of the chief executive. The chief executive must balance the priorities and interests of the population. Departments and agencies have a clientele orientation. Not all programs have equal weight. Those with the strongest support in the legislature will do better in the budgeting process than others.

Elected members of the national, state, and municipal legislatures champion the priorities of their constituencies. They advocate programs and projects that benefit the people who elect them.

But legislators often cannot compete with the expertise of chief executives, departments, and agencies. Most state legislators are part-time legislators. The role and institutional history of the national legislature are more developed than those at the state, local government, and special district levels.

Executives, department and agency heads, legislators, and numerous clientele use budgetary strategies for maintaining or increasing the monies available to them.[13] These strategies emphasize *cultivating clientele* and *developing confidence.*

Departments and agencies cultivate active clientele for lobbying the legislature and chief executive. Most departments and agencies experience little difficulty in locating clientele. Interest groups find ways to petition government decision making and spend funds. Departments and agencies accessing and servicing large and strategically placed clientele are less likely to have their budgets reduced. They not only concentrate on individual constituencies but seek to expand their clientele. They proactively secure feedback on their programs and their effectiveness. They want constituents to offer suggestions for improving services.

The development of confidence or deploying actions of personnel and programs to fit in with the expectations of others playing the power game, is a vital part of group strategies. Budget officials are guardians of the department or agency treasury. Presentations are geared to that end. As guardians, budgeteers espouse the effectiveness of programs and promise efficiency in spending taxpayer dollars. Preparation is important as administrative leaders develop and maintain confidence. Public hearings afford officials opportunities to exude confidence in their department or agency missions and programs. Requests for information must be met promptly and in appropriate detail.

*Contingent strategies* depend on budget circumstances. In defending its base for budget cuts, officials might suggest that a politically popular program be eliminated. In Indiana, for example, where the political culture nurtures high school basketball programs, budget officials call for reduction of athletic budgets when school districts confront fiscal problems. Officials argue that the community's high school basketball program faces an all-or-nothing choice. Any budgetary reduction would make the program impossible. It might as well be eliminated. In the Hoosier state, high school basketball has a jurisdictional, or statewide, clientele base. Strong clientele may prevent across-the-board reductions. Therefore, Indiana school districts and their elected school boards may decide to cut art, music, or history programs, rather than basketball appropriations. This is only one of the many strategies often used by experienced budgeteers.

Departments and agencies prepare their budgets incrementally. The most rational guide for next year's budget is based on the full development, implementation, and evaluation of this year's appropriations. Departments and agencies must not strive to be "too successful," for they may "win" their "program war," making next year's budget unnecessary.[14]

# THINK ABOUT IT!

**Budget Terms**

**Authorizations:** Involves the determination of maximum spending levels for each program approved by the legislative branch; the responsibility of standing committees of the U.S. House of Representatives and U.S. Senate.

**Appropriations:** One of the most crucial aspects of budget making; entails the power to spend or to incur financial obligations; "spending" committees in the U.S. House of Representatives and U.S. Senate exercise major roles in this stage of the budgetary process.

**Authorizing Legislation:** Legislation enacted by Congress to permit the establishment or continuation of a federal program or agency. Authorizing legislation is normally required before the enactment of budget authority, and such authority is usually provided in separate legislation.

**Budget Authority (BA):** Authority provided by law to enter into obligations that will result in immediate or future outlays. It may be classified by the period of availability, by the timing of congressional action, or by the manner of determining the amount available.

**Budget:** The president's request to Congress for new programs, allocation of resources to serve national objectives, embodiment of fiscal policy for programs, and information about the national economy essential for the private sector.

**Budget Cycle:** Executive formulation and transmittal, legislative authorization and appropriation, budget execution and control, review and audit.

**Budget Enforcement Act (or Pay-As-You-Go (PAYGO):** Budget rule requiring that any tax cuts or mandatory spending be balanced by a cut in other spending or a tax increase.

**Continuing Resolution:** Legislation that provides budget authority for specific ongoing activities when a regular appropriation for those activities has not been enacted by the beginning of the fiscal year. Some continuing resolutions provide interim funding for part of the fiscal year until the regular appropriations bill is enacted. Others provide funding for the full fiscal year.

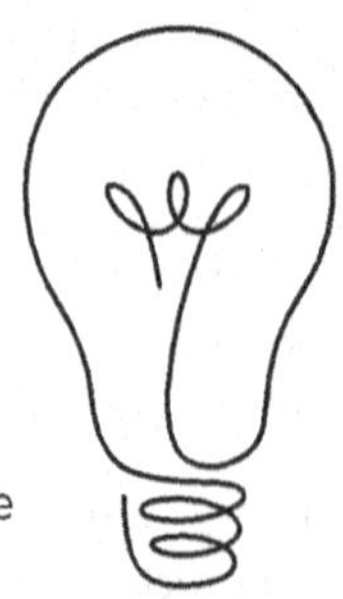

**Debt:** Total amount of money the federal government owes its debtors.

**Deficit:** The amount each year federal budget expenditures exceed federal revenue.

**Entitlement Programs:** A government program where benefits of a certain kind have been guaranteed to a certain segment of the population.

**Fiscal Year:** The federal government's yearly accounting period, which begins on October 1 and ends on the following September 30.

**Mandatory Spending:** Spending on certain government programs required by law.

**Outlays:** Government spending. Outlays are payments, normally in the form of checks issued, cash disbursed, and electronic fund transfers, net of refunds, reimbursements, and offsetting collections. Outlays include interest accrued on public issues of the public debt.

**Receipts:** Government income. All income collected from the public by the federal government in its sovereign capacity, primarily through the exercise of its power to tax.

**Sequestration:** Reduction of new budget authority or other budgetary resources, as defined in the Balanced Budget and Emergency Deficit Control Act of 1985, as amended.

## Roots of the Deficit Problem

The budget deficit was not of major concern to policy makers from the end of World War II through the mid-1970s. From 1947 until 1974, deficits averaged less than 1 percent of the gross domestic product (GDP). As a result of World War II and the Great Depression, the public debt reached 114 percent of the GDP in 1946. But the budget situation became significantly worse after the mid-1970s.

Deficits averaged 2.9 percent of GDP during the last half of the 1970s, 4.0 percent during the 1980s 4.4 percent during the 1990s and nearly 4.4 percent from 2002-2014. In 2014, the federal government had revenues of $3.821 trillion and a deficit of $483 billion, the lowest deficit since 2008. The budget deficit equaled $3.13 trillion in 2020 and $2.77 trillion in 2021 or 91.5 percent of revenues and 15 percent of GDP. The U.S. experienced budget deficits all but 12 years out of the 80-year period from 1940-2020.

The deterioration of the country's fiscal circumstances was caused by the interaction of several factors. There were systemic policy mistakes. Unanticipated and unpredictable changes occurred in the fiscal environment. The policy makers had little or no direct control over these changes.

First, an unexpected economic slowdown began in the mid-1970s. The slowdown baffled economists. The rate of economic growth slowed by approximately one percent after 1973. From the late 1940s through 1973, real per capita GDP expanded at an average annual rate of 2.5 percent, and real output per hour of labor expanded at an average rate of 2.1 percent. From 1973 through 1995, real per capita GDP expanded at only 1.5 percent a year, and output per hour of labor expanded at only 0.8 percent a year. Federal revenues expand as the economy increases. This economic slowdown had a significant impact on federal budgets.[15]

Second, the domestic entitlements the federal government committed to during the 1962–1972 period contributed significantly to growing deficits. Congress and three presidents enacted laws establishing Medicare, Medicaid, SNAP, guaranteed student loans, Title XX social services, and supplemental security income programs. The slowdown in the economy resulted in a decline in income growth. Increasing numbers of people became eligible for means-tested domestic programs. Unexpected demographic developments made more persons eligible for domestic entitlements: The divorce rate doubled. The fraction of births to unwed mothers more than tripled. The poverty rate declined from 22.4 percent in 1959 to 11.1 percent in 1973. The poverty rate increased an average of more than 14 percent from 1980 through 1995 reaching 14.5 percent in 2013. Health care costs, new entitlement commitments, were unexpectedly expensive. With the enactment of Medicare and Medicaid in 1965, the federal government assumed more responsibility for the provision of health care.

Third, the Reagan administration began the 1980s with large increases in defense spending. The Republican president made an ambitious effort to increase defense capabilities. Defense outlays increased from 4.9 percent of GDP in 1980 to 6.3 percent in 1986. Reagan called for cutbacks on the domestic side of government. Wage increases had elevated many Americans into higher tax brackets. Reagan promoted reductions in tax burdens, an effort that made the deficit problems worse. The nondefense domestic discretionary budget declined from 5.2 percent of GDP in 1980 to 3.8 percent in 1986. However, the Reagan administration could not convince the Democratic congress to significantly slow the increase in domestic entitlement spending programs.

NOTABLE QUOTES

A leader, once convinced that a particular course of action is the right one, must have the determination to stick with it and be undaunted when the going gets rough.

*— Ronald Reagan*

Finally, the weak cyclical performance of the economy after 1974 contributed to growing deficits. Between fiscal years 1955 and 1974, the economy operated at or above its capacity in twelve of the twenty fiscal years. Between fiscal years 1964 and 1974, the economy operated at or above its capacity in nine of eleven fiscal years. Between fiscal years 1975 and 1996, the economy operated at or above capacity in only four fiscal years. The 1964–1974 period economic indicators were misleading.

The economic practice of sustaining increasing domestic entitlements without corresponding tax increases was sliding into deficit spending. Rising interest rates contributed to economic downturns. The growing size of the structural deficit caused federal expenditures on net interest to rise. Between 1951 and 1977, federal expenditures on net interest amounted to no more than 1.5 percent of GDP. After 1984, they expanded to 3 percent or more. Profound changes occurred in the composition of federal spending and taxes. Entitlements, other mandatory expenditures, and interest payments had lawmakers reconsidering benefit levels and eligibility criteria.[16]

In summary, factors contributing to growing federal deficits over the last fifty years were:

- The unexpected economic slowdown of the mid-1970s
- Domestic entitlement commitments the federal government enacted between 1962 and 1972
- Policies for increasing national defense capabilities and appropriations, decreasing nondefense discretionary budget spending, and reducing tax burdens
- A weak cyclical performance of the economy from mid-1970s to mid-1990s
- Expenditures to combat international terrorism and invest in an elaborate set of domestic security programs and departments (TSA and Department of Homeland Security)
- Investments to respond to the great recession of 2008-2009
- Spending to combat the expected and actual impacts of the coronavirus pandemic

President Clinton did achieve a balanced budget, but subsequent administrations reverted to the 1980s legacy of large budget deficits.

According to John Steele Gordon, five trends have increasingly affected government fiscal policies over the last sixty plus years.

First, a powerful but fundamentally flawed concept in the discipline of economics has completely changed the way both economists and politicians view the national economy and their responsibilities toward it.

Second, the responsibilities of government in general and the federal government in particular, as viewed by the public, have greatly increased.

## THINK ABOUT IT!

**Fiscal and Monetary Policies**

Fiscal policy encompasses federal government policy with respect to taxes, spending, and debt management, and is intended to promote the nation's macroeconomic goals, particularly with respect to employment, gross domestic product, price level stability, and equilibrium in balance of payments. The budget process is a major vehicle for determining and implementing federal fiscal policy.

The other major component of federal macroeconomic policy is monetary policy. Monetary policy entails policies that affect the money supply, interest rates, and credit availability, and is intended to promote maximum sustainable output and employment along with stable prices. Monetary policy is directed primarily by the Board of Governors of the Federal Reserve System and the Federal Open Market Committee. Monetary policy works by influencing the cost and availability of bank reserves.

Third, a shift in power from the Executive to Congress has balkanized the budget process by sharply limiting the influence of the one politician in Washington whose constituency is national in scope, the President.

Fourth, the decay of party discipline and the seniority system within Congress itself has further balkanized the budget process, dividing it among innumerable committees and subcommittees. This has made logrolling (you vote for my program, and I'll vote for yours) the order of the day on Capitol Hill.

Finally, the political-action-committee system of financing congressional elections has given greatly increased influence to spending constituencies (often called special interests, especially when they are funding someone else's campaign) while sharply reducing that of the electorate as a whole, which picks up the tab.[17]

## Economic Progress, Taxes, and Savings

Economic progress, central to many of the country's concerns as a society, requires investment, which, over the longer term, depends on savings. The nation's savings consist of the private saving of households and businesses and the savings or lack of savings of all levels of government. In general, government budget deficits represent the opposite of savings; they subtract national savings that could be used for investment. Conversely, government surpluses add to savings.

American hostilities toward taxes are well documented. However, the per capita tax level in the United States is not considered high; the people of the United States are not overtaxed. Taxation as a percentage of national income is lower in the United States than in any other major industrialized country (see **Figure 4.1.8**). The opposition to taxes clearly cannot be traced to a heavy tax burden. Citizens rebel against higher taxes because they believe that governments are inefficient—even wasteful—in spending assessed revenues for their various operations.[18]

**Figure 4.1.8 Total tax revenue as percent of gross domestic product, 2020**

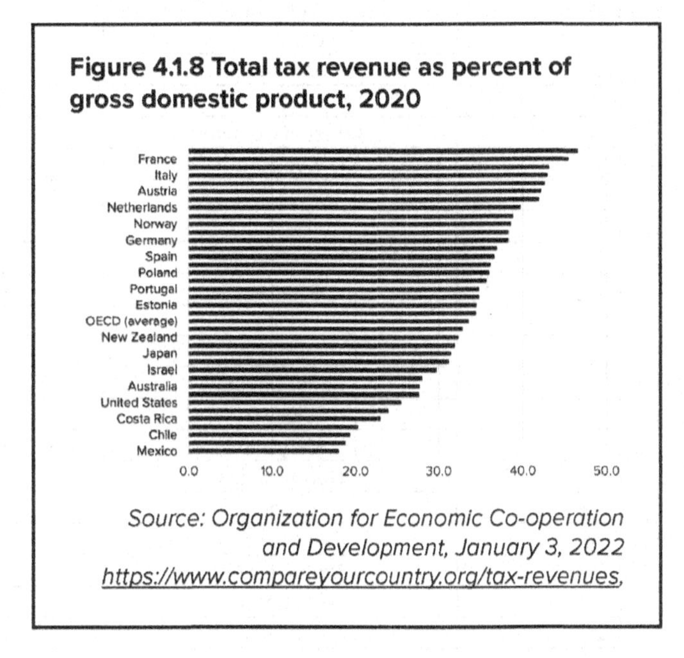


*Source: Organization for Economic Co-operation and Development, January 3, 2022 https://www.compareyourcountry.org/tax-revenues,*

Some states assume much larger federal spending than others. The federal tax burdens on states can be compared with their receipt of federal expenditures. **Table 4.1.4** on the following page shows federal spending by state per tax dollar sent to Washington.

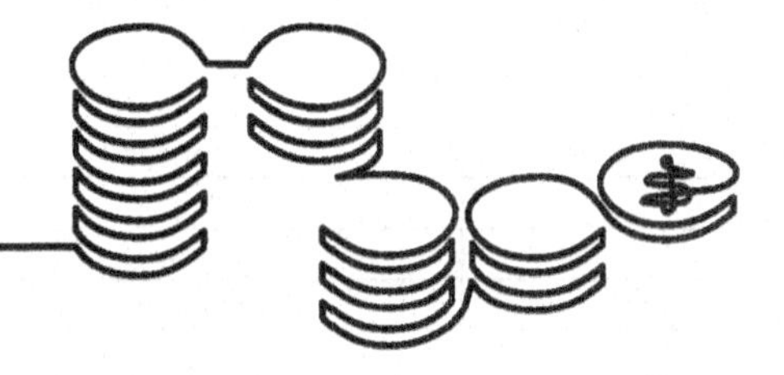

**Table 4.1.4 Federal Spending by State per Tax Dollar Sent to Washington**

| RANK | STATE | RETURN ON TAX DOLLARS | FED FUND % OF STATE REVENUES |
|---|---|---|---|
| 1 | New Mexico | $4.33 | 25.94% |
| 2 | West Virginia | $3.74 | 27.18% |
| 3 | Mississippi | $3.40 | 27.10% |
| 4 | Alaska | $3.19 | 28.64% |
| 5 | Montana | $2.25 | 29.23% |
| 6 | Kentucky | $2.05 | 27.77% |
| 7 | Alabama | $2.46 | 23.32% |
| 8 | Arizona | $2.30 | 24.35% |
| 9 | Louisiana | $1.81 | 29.07% |
| 10 | Vermont | $1.97 | 24.40% |
| 11 | Maine | $2.31 | 20.42% |
| 12 | District of Columbia | $1.78 | 23.78% |
| 13 | Wyoming | $1.58 | 25.32% |
| 14 | Oklahoma | $2.02 | 19.78% |
| 15 | Hawaii | $2.49 | 15.14% |
| 16 | South Carolina | $2.17 | 17.76% |
| 17 | Arkansas | $1.09 | 26.66% |
| 18 | Idaho | $1.75 | 19.73% |
| 19 | Michigan | $1.45 | 22.46% |
| 20 | South Dakota | $1.65 | 19.96% |
| 21 | Indiana | $1.23 | 22.99% |
| 22 | Maryland | $1.51 | 19.34% |
| 23 | North Dakota | $1.83 | 15.90% |
| 24 | Oregon | $1.51 | 19.11% |
| 25 | Pennsylvania | $1.15 | 21.91% |
| 26 | Rhode Island | $1.13 | 21.65% |
| 27 | North Carolina | $1.27 | 19.97% |
| 28 | Virginia | $1.91 | 13.50% |
| 29 | Wisconsin | $1.23 | 19.55% |
| 30 | Missouri | $1.14 | 20.40% |
| 31 | Nevada | $1.45 | 17.00% |
| 32 | New Hampshire | $1.34 | 17.65% |
| 33 | Connecticut | $1.30 | 17.81% |
| 34 | Tennessee | $1.17 | 18.67% |
| 35 | Ohio | $0.90 | 20.71% |
| 36 | Georgia | $1.23 | 17.46% |
| 37 | Iowa | $1.43 | 15.37% |
| 38 | Texas | $1.20 | 17.47% |
| 39 | Florida | $1.15 | 16.60% |
| 40 | New York | $0.93 | 18.65% |
| 41 | Massachusetts | $0.88 | 19.10% |
| 42 | Colorado | $1.14 | 15.85% |
| 43 | Utah | $1.12 | 15.74% |
| 44 | California | $1.00 | 16.92% |
| 45 | Delaware | $0.63 | 20.39% |
| 46 | Kansas | $1.24 | 13.88% |
| 47 | Illinois | $0.94 | 16.54% |
| 48 | Minnesota | $0.85 | 16.17% |
| 49 | Washington | $0.94 | 14.54% |
| 50 | Nebraska | $0.93 | 14.33% |
| 51 | New Jersey | $0.78 | 15.43% |

The economic benefits of a sustainable budget policy include increased saving and investment levels and faster economic growth, which results in higher living standards. The future implications of current policy decisions are usually not captured in the budget process. The budget is a short-term, cash-based spending plan focusing on the short- to medium-term cash implications of government obligations and fiscal decisions. While the sustainability of the government's fiscal policy is driven primarily by future spending for Social Security and health care commitments, the federal government's commitments and responsibilities extend far beyond these programs.

The main influence of budget policy on long-term economic performance is through the effect of the federal deficit on national savings. Conversely, the rate of economic growth helps determine the overall deficit or surplus through its effect on revenues and spending. Federal deficits reduce national savings, while federal surpluses increase national savings. The level of savings affects investment and, in turn, GDP growth.[20]

Tax policy making combines elements of partisan, policy, and system politics. The citizenry welcomes lower taxes. But do legislators deliver on corresponding government spending cuts? Frequently not. Local, state, and federal tax policies determine the range of programs and services government offers.

The purpose of tax policy is to spur economic growth. Expanding economic growth means more revenues for government coffers and more profits and wage increases. Tax policy also includes prospects for balancing budgets, lowering the national debt, and recession spending.

The conventional wisdom is that the Republican Party favors lower taxes and the Democratic Party campaigns for higher taxes. This assertion is partly true, but it is misleading and incomplete. The economy cannot cope with excessively high taxes, but basic government services cannot be provided if taxes are excessively low. The crux of tax policy is to find some happy medium between too few and too many revenues—or between what the state owes the citizenry and what the citizenry owes the government or state.

Democrats favor tax cuts targeting certain segments of the population. Democrats usually do not favor tax cuts for the wealthiest Americans. Republicans promote tax breaks that favor people in all taxing categories. These tax cuts tend to be larger but require more reductions in government services in order to cover costs.[21]

Borrowing and selling assets are ways out of debt for citizens and countries. In the case of nations, creditors and buyers of assets are foreigners. Why should we be concerned about this development? If the debt is small and remains under control, the creditors are not worried. But if the debt is out of control and the debtor becomes less credible, the creditors may decide not to finance a country's growing debt. This scenario could bring very unpleasant consequences for Americans. Depreciation of the dollar would make imports very expensive and exports very cheap. They might be eliminated.[22]

America's persistent and growing trade deficit is rapidly deteriorating. A nation accumulating deeper debts is more and more dependent on its creditors, who are private investors and governments from Europe and Asia. The creditors have no advantage in disrupting their unfettered access to the largest consumer market in the world—producing trade surpluses and greater market shares for their countries. Creditor nations will eventually ask the United States to pay its debts. Creditors want their money. "You can't sustain an empire from a debtor's weakening position—sooner or later, the creditors pull the plug," emphasizes William Greider. Deficits at $400 billion a year will grow the trade debt to alarming levels.[23] Historically, however the record trade deficit (balance of trade deficit) was set in 2017 at $796 billion. Today, the annual trade deficit typically exceeds $600-$700 billion. The widening of the trade deficit causes citizens to question free trade policies, unfair trade competition, and American loss of manufacturing jobs.

Trade and budget deficits (or balances) appear to be simple, easy to measure and understand, and often raise this commonsense inquiry: "Your family has to keep a balanced budget—why not your government?" However, certain economists argue that the two balances are the least significant and most unreliable indicators of the economy's health and prospects.[24]

A trade deficit (or an import surplus) often reflects strong demands of a booming economy for investment, consumption, and intermediate goods. A trade surplus often reflects weak demands of a depressed, deflationary economy. Internal savings outstrip the availability of domestic opportunities for profitable investment.

These are some of the advantages associated with international trade and free trade agreements with other countries.

- Increased global competition
- Reduction of subsidization of local industries, thereby providing more funds for other uses
- Increase in foreign direct investment
- Increased technology transfer
- Increase in domestic jobs
- Whereas the legendary disadvantages cited by free trade opponents are as follows.
- Stimulates poor and unsafe working conditions, especially in developing countries
- Increasing job outsourcing
- Abuse and theft of intellectual property
- Increased deterioration and exploitation of natural resources
- Tendency to destroy native cultures

In the balanced budget debate, the proportion of any budget that is allocated for public investment in roads and productive infrastructure may go unnoticed. Tax revenues fall and transfer payments rise when the economy is doing poorly. When the economy prospers, as were the circumstances in the mid- to late 1990s, offers of all governments grow larger.

The budget deficit—or balance—is a certain indicator of what any community, society, or greater good values for that particular year of financial accounting. Budgets are instruments of coordination, control, and planning. They surely can tell us who gets what amount of money. *Washington Post* writer David Broder warns of a "fiscal train wreck that awaits this country unless it mends its ways."[25]

The trade deficit is the broadest measure of foreign trade. It covers not only trade in goods and services; it also follows investment flows between countries. The trade imbalance represents the amount the United States must borrow from foreigners to cover the shortfall between exports and imports.[26]

Foreign governments and investors hold about 30 percent of U.S. debt. The nations holding the largest amount of U.S. debt are Japan, China, United Kingdom, Ireland and Luxembourg.

The concern is what would occur should foreigners at some point decide they want to hold less in dollar-denominated assets.

# THINK ABOUT IT!

**Trends in Public Finance, Taxation, and Budgeting**

The looming gorilla in the "crystal boutique" of government is that of fiscal budgeting and financial austerity. Currently, with nearly 20 states facing financial shortfalls (2015) accompanied by a reduced but large annual federal deficit, huge annual balance of payment deficits, and a federal debt approaching $20 trillion, taxation and spending will remain central to all policy and administrative decision making. As extraordinary as it is, the unfunded federal obligation account looms large on the horizon with estimates well exceeding $120 trillion.

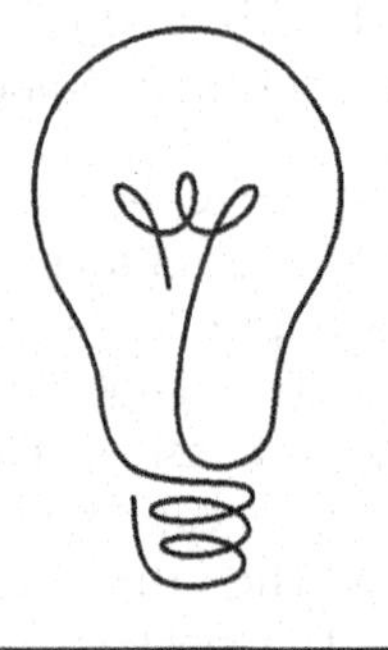

## Summary

- The federal budget is a plan for how the government spends your money, how the government pays for its activities, and for government borrowing or repayment of borrowing. It is also something that affects the nation's economy, something that is affected by the nation's economy, and a historical record.
- If politics is sometimes defined as the process of deciding who gets what, administrative politics often becomes the process of deciding *who gets what amount of money.* If budgets are essentially political documents, the politics involved are often veiled.
- It is not enough to call attention to the political aspects of budgeting to define budgeting. Budgets are also instruments of *coordination, control,* and *planning.* They govern nearly all aspects of administration and confer a great deal of power on those who prepare them.
- Public-sector budgets are raised from taxes on individuals and businesses. It's tough to maintain effective public services if revenues supporting such activities are low or nonexistent. Whether we are providing national defense or unemployment compensation, we need a *growth economy* to finance government benefits.
- Deciding which level of government should provide a certain service is a matter of federalism, with its ever-changing division of power.
- *Functions of budgeting* include allocating resources to achieve governmental priorities, goals, and policies; raising funds through taxes and loans to finance the budget; stabilizing the economy through fiscal and monetary policies; holding operating agencies accountable for the use of budgeted resources; controlling expenditures; transferring funds from one level of government to another; achieving planned social and economic development; and improving management in operating departments and agencies.
- Tax and spending changes affect incentives to work and save, distribution of disposable income, and the business cycle. President Bush called for making his tax cuts permanent. Revenue loss from the tax cuts resulted in policy changes that enlarged federal deficits. The safety net became more porous.
- Programs that make transfer payments from one age group to another, such as Social Security and Medicare, have profound effects on private savings and the fiscal burdens borne by different generations. The rising deficits come as the United States faces the challenge of fulfilling Social Security and Medicare promises to retiring baby boomers.
- The annual budget process, or appropriations process, mainly concerns only one-third of the budget. This one-third of the budget, called the discretionary budget, is what Congress debates and sets the levels for on an annual basis. Mandatory spending makes up the other two-thirds of the federal budget.
- Almost 40 percent of federal spending, $1.7 trillion in FY 2019, was devoted to Social Security and Medicare—programs aimed at senior citizens, the disabled, and children and spouses of deceased workers.
- About half of the discretionary budget is "national defense," a government-defined function area that roughly corresponds to the military. Discretionary spending also includes budgeting for education, health, and housing.
- Mandatory spending includes most entitlement programs, which are funded by eligibility rules or payment rules. Social Security is by far the largest mandatory spending program and accounts for one-third of the mandatory budget.
- The gross federal debt has grown to $29.5 trillion. A significant increase occurred during World War II. The debt increased most rapidly during the 1980s. The gross federal debt is the total of all federal borrowing. A deficit occurs when spending exceeds revenues for one year; a surplus is the opposite, revenues exceed spending. Debt represents the long-term accumulation of deficits.
- Government spending can expand the capacity of the economy. Governments are involved in building transport and communications infrastructures. These investments are necessary to develop a modern economy. Deficit spending may expand the capacity of the economy. Economic growth provides a larger resource, or tax, base to pay back incurred debts.
- The federal budget consists of two major groups of funds: trust funds and federal funds. Trust funds earmark revenues for particular purposes, including Social Security, Medicare, and unemployment compensation. Federal funds constitute all other government funds.

- Transparency, neutrality, broad base, simplicity, stability, no retroactivity, low tax burdens, free trade, openness, and relevance of state and local taxes are ten principles of sound tax policy.
- Main actors in the congressional budgetary process are the Congressional Budget Office (CBO), the House and Senate Committees on the Budget (Budget Committees), and Appropriations Committees in the House and Senate.
- *Stages of the budget cycle* are executive preparation, legislative consideration, implementation and control of the enacted budget, and audit and evaluation.
- Operating departments and agencies, chief executives, and legislatures play roles in the budget process and offer strategies for cultivating clientele and developing confidence in their ideas, priorities, and programs.
- Growing deficits and the resulting lower savings lead to dwindling investments, slower economic growth, and finally decline in real gross domestic product. Living standards, in turn, stagnate and fall.
- Major progress was made on deficit reduction in the 1990s, culminating in the passage of the *Balanced Budget Act of 1997.* Policy action accounted for about 25 percent of the improvement in the Congressional Budget Office's budget estimates. The remainder of the improvement was due primarily to economic factors.
- The roots of federal deficits are grounded in the unexpected economic slowdown in the mid-1970s, the domestic entitlements the federal government committed to during the 1962–1972 period, the Reagan administration's commitment to increased defense spending in the 1980s, and the weak cyclical performance of the American economy after 1974.
- *Fiscal policy* entails federal government policies with respect to taxes, spending, and debt management, and is intended to promote the nation's macroeconomic goals, particularly employment, gross domestic product, price level stability, and equilibrium in balance of payments.
- *Monetary policy* entails policies that affect the money supply, interest rates, and credit availability, and is intended to promote maximum sustainable output and employment along with stable prices.
- Incremental budgeting demands little inquiry because the increment, not the base, is considered.
- Decremental budgeting is chaotic and conflict-laden. It may result in coercion, involve confrontation, and generate mistrust.
- Some states assume much larger federal tax burdens than do others.
- The 1990s were boom times for government at all levels, including state and local governments.
- Most of America's governments divide their budgets into two sections, one for *capital* projects, the other for *expenses.*
- Line-item budgets usually include categories for personnel, equipment, and maintenance, among others.
- Performance budgets, program budgets, and zero-based budgets constitute budgetary reforms.
- The per capita tax level in the United States is not high compared with America's economic competitors. Taxation as a percentage of national income is lower in the United States than in any other major industrialized country.
- The American philosophy of taxation is: "Don't tax me. Don't tax thee. Tax the fellow behind the tree."
- Taxes are the price we pay some argue for civilization.

## Videos, Films and Talks

Please visit *The Craft of Public Administration* at www.millenniumhrmpress.com for up-to-date videos, films, talks, readings, and additional class resources.

What if You Could Help Decide How The Government Spends Public Funds? [10 min] Shari Davis, TED Talk
https://www.ted.com/talks/shari_davis_what_if_you_could_help_decide_how_the_government_spends_public_funds

## Suggested Readings

**How Government Procurement is Different Now**
https://media.erepublic.com/document/CDG21_PUB_REPORT_Ivalua_V.pdf

**Central Government and Frontline Performance Improvement: The Case of "Targets" In the United Kingdom**
https://ash.harvard.edu/files/central_government_and_frontline_performance.pdf

**Denver's Peak Academy Practices What it Preaches—and Pivots**
https://bloombergcities.medium.com/denvers-peak-academy-practices-what-it-preaches-and-pivots-97f4c8697a38

**Unleashing Breakthrough Innovation in Government**
https://ssir.org/articles/entry/unleashing_breakthrough_innovation_in_government

## Notes

1. L. Douglas Lee, "How Congress Handles the Budget," *Wharton Magazine* 4 (Winter 1980): 29.
2. Marshall E. Dimock, Gladys Ogden Dimock, and Douglas M. Fox, *Public Administration* (New York: Holt, Rinehart and Winston, 1983), p. 359.
3. John L. Mikesell, *Fiscal Administration: Analysis and Applications for the Public Sector,* 2nd ed. (Chicago: Dorsey Press, 1986), pp. 75–85.
4. Dimock, Dimock, and Fox, *Public Administration,* p. 367.
5. Peter F. Rousmaniere, *Local Governments Auditing—A Manual for Public Officials* (New York: Council on Municipal Performance, 1980), p. 83.
6. Advisory Commission on Intergovernmental Relations, "Sunset Legislation and Zero-Based Budgeting," *Information Bulletin* 76, no. 5 (December 1976): 1.
7. Mikesell, *Fiscal Administration,* p. 48.
8. Ibid. pp. 56–60.
9. Aaron Wildavsky, *The Politics of the Budgetary Process* (Boston: Little, Brown and Co., 1984), pp. 63–126.
10. Barry Bozeman and Jeffrey D. Straussman, "Shrinking Budgets and the Shrinkage of Budget Theory," *Public Administration Review* 42, no. 6 (November–December 1982): 509–515. See also Lance T. LeLoup, *Budgetary Politics* (Brunswick, OH: King's Court Communications, 1986), pp. 16–21.
11. Murray L. Weidenbaum, "Budget Dilemma and Its Solution," in *Control of Federal Spending,* ed. C. Lowell Harris (New York: Academy of Political Science, 1985), pp. 47–58.
12. Bozeman and Straussman, "Shrinking Budgets," p. 511.
13. Mikesell, *Fiscal Administration,* pp. 56–60.
14. Ibid.
15. Robert D. Reischauer, "The Budget: Crucible for the Policy Agenda," in *Setting National Priorities: Budget Choices for the Next Century,* ed. Robert D. Reischauer (Washington, DC: Brookings Institution Press, 1997), pp. 4–11.
16. Ibid.
17. John Steele Gordon, "The Federal Debt," *American Heritage* 47, no. 7 (November 1995): 82–92.
18. For more detailed explanations of the comparatively low U.S. tax burden, see Louis Ferleger and Jay R. Mantle, "America's Hostility Toward Taxes," *Challenge* 14, no. 4 (July–August 1991): 54; "No Pain, No Gain: Taxes, Productivity, and Economic Growth," *Challenge* 36, no. 3 (May–June 1993): 11–20; and *A New Mandate: Democratic Choices for a Prosperous Economy* (Columbia, MO: University of Missouri Press, 1994).

19. See *Federal Debt and Interest Costs* (Congressional Budget Office, May 1993), and *Federal Debt: Answers to Frequently Asked Questions* (November 27, 1996).

20. *Budget Issues: Analysis of Long-Term Fiscal Outlook* (Congressional Budget Office, October 1997; GAO/ AIMD/ OCE-98-19).

21. "Tax & Economic Policy," http://www.onlytheissues.com/politics.cgi?issue=4.

22. Franco Modigliani and Robert M. Solow, "America Is Borrowing Trouble," *New York Times,* April 9, 2001.

23. William Greider, "The End of Empire," *The Nation* 275, no. 9 (September 23, 2002): 13–15.

24. See Charles Wolf, Jr., and Walter Wriston, "Two Deficits That Just Don't Matter," *Hoover Digest,* no. 4 (1997); William A. Niskanen, "The Uneasy Relation Between the Budget and Trade Deficits," *Cato Journal* 8, no. 2 (Fall 1988): 507–532.

25. David S. Broder, "New Task for a Budget Straight-Talker," *Washington Post,* March 16, 2008, p. B7.

26. "Trade Deficit at 2nd Highest Level Ever," *New York Times,* September 8, 2006.

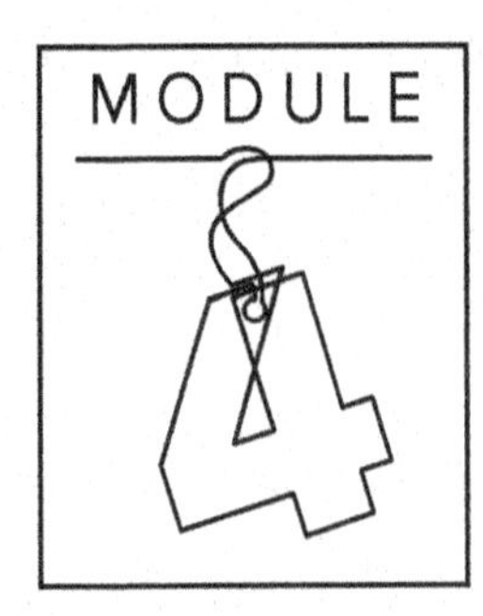


# UNIT 2: The Productivity Challenge

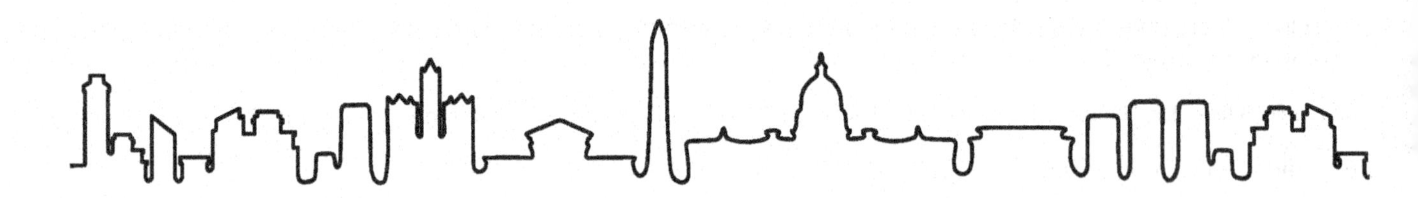

## What Is Excellence?

Productivity in the public sector refers to excellence in individual and collective performance—especially in times when public employees are expected to do more with less. The employees could be public school teachers, occupational safety inspectors, highway patrol officers, firefighters, air traffic controllers, maintenance crews removing snow from the streets, or sanitation workers removing waste and technological excess from communities.

Among these areas of worker expertise, there are widely divergent views as to what excellence is. *Excellence,* in its various forms, is based on the cultural context of a particular function. Therefore, measuring excellence and employee productivity in government-funded organizations is a problematic assignment. The public sector usually deals in services, which, because they are intangible and often widely variable, almost always present problems in productivity measurement. Many government experts concede that some public sector functions are not measurable with the mechanisms currently available and often used in the private sector.

Despite these difficulties, an organization should adapt excellence as its main component. The system should enable an organization to achieve high performance levels from their employees. Outstanding performance not only benefits the organization but also improves

## THINK ABOUT IT!

**Innovations in American Government Awards**

The Harvard Kennedy Schools' Ash Center for Democratic Governance and Innovation has highlighted hundreds of exemplary models of government innovation since 1985, "bringing creative and effective solutions to some of government's most urgent and seemingly intractable challenges." Case studies are developed for select award recipients including those with model examples of performance measurement.

In addition to the Innovations in American Government Awards, the Ash Center created an online community called Bright Ideas to propose, share and disseminate innovative ideas.

# THINK ABOUT IT!

**National Guard and NASCAR**

In 2012, the National Guard spent $26.5M to place its logo on NASCAR cars for 20 races. Sen Claire McCaskill, D-Mo., admonished the Guard for "...wasting a bunch of money on a very expensive sports sponsorship." Based on this marketing and recruitment strategy, no new soldiers were added to the Guard ranks—not one. In 2012, the Guard received 24,800 prospects for enlistment, but only 20 met the qualifications for joining the Guard and none joined! In 2013, the prospects associated with the advertisement fell to 7,500. USA Today, 1B, May 8, 2014.

the delivery of services to the citizens.[1] Most citizens care about the performance of their public institutions. Parents worry about the quality of their children's schools. City dwellers anxiously scan the latest crime statistics. Drivers wish for better roads, transit riders for dependable buses and subways, air travelers for effective and safe air traffic control.[2]

Posing particular difficulties for analyses are numerous staff operations, such as personnel work and social casework. One has only to think of the complexities involved in trying to measure the productivity of a caseworker in a public welfare office to realize some of the difficulty. Should the caseworker be rated on how many cases they clear from the government support system rolls, or on how many people they add? Using either standard can produce distortions.

## Efficiency and Effectiveness

Related to these problems is the central task of distinguishing between efficiency and effectiveness. Efficiency means *doing things well,* while effectiveness means *doing the right things well. Efficiency,* essentially, is the input of labor, capital, and other resources into an effort matched against the output of product, regardless of the mechanism selected to gauge output. *Effectiveness,* meanwhile, calls for a pre-established standard of comparison; a focus upon a certain quality of production; an ability to mobilize, organize, and direct resources for specified purposes, taken within a certain cultural context.

As one commentator noted, someone might be efficient in driving nails into a table. Effectiveness enters the picture when we question whether they should be driving nails into a table at all. Questions regarding quality make the public productivity measurer's task even more challenging. A fiddler isn't necessarily producing more by fiddling faster. Nor can a pianist be hailed as especially productive for playing Chopin's Minute Waltz faster than designed. On a more mundane and realistic level, a narcotics squad that made a lot of arrest quotas for their narcotic divisions had to change them when they realized that such productivity measures were not producing "quality" arrests—in other words, arrests of major dealers.[3]

## Privatization of the Public Sector

*Privatization* means that a service previously produced by a government agency is now produced by a nonprofit or private organization. The government may sell to private buyers, or a private concern may sell to government. *Contracting* out, as it is often called, is thought to be more efficient because:

- It harnesses competitive forces and brings the pressure of the marketplace to bear on inefficient workers.
- It permits better management, free of most of the distractions characteristic of overtly political organizations.
- It places the costs and benefits of managerial decisions more directly on the decision maker, whose own rewards are directly at stake.[4]

As government at all levels has come under attack, the conclusion that the private sector performs and produces more effectively has received considerable credibility. If privatization is the answer in general; however, no one seems to agree on the particulars, such as what products will be produced privately or what provisions for private entrepreneurship will follow.

Conflicting definitions of privatization center on provision, or providing, and production, or producing.[5] Executives, legislators, and judges make and interpret policies that provide services. Government functions as buyer and seller. A good example of services that are privatized to varying degrees are security services. One can lay out a four-part scheme of possible overlap of sectors, government and nongovernment, providing and producing security services. Of the four possibilities, there are two admixtures of responsibility and two possibilities where one sector or the other takes full responsibility for the provision and production of security.

***Case 1.*** Government does both. The legislature writes the law and provides the money; the Department of Corrections runs the prison. Neither function is private.

***Case 2.*** Production is private. The city of Bloomington decides to provide security when the high school hockey teams play at the city arena. The city contracts with Pinkertons for the guards.

***Case 3.*** Provision is private. Government sells to private buyers. The North Stars hockey team wants security at Metropolitan Sports Center, and it contracts with the Bloomington city police.

***Case 4.*** *Both activities* are private. A department store decides that it wants uniformed security and employs (or contracts privately for) its own guards. Government performs neither activity.[6]

The policy decision in Case 1, the pure-case public sector, shows government as a public bureau producing the service. Case 2 entails the controversial system of a government contracting out. Case 3 illustrates government selling services to a private buyer. Case 4 portrays a pure case of a private agency selling to a private buyer. Of the two words, *provision* is the more complicated to explain. The word *providing* can be confusing.

For example, society (or government) provides medical care to the elderly; however, medical doctors are the providers. To provide in this context means to make policy, to decide, to buy, to regulate, to franchise, to finance, to subsidize.

---

*A **publicly** provided service is described in this manner:*

1. The decision whether to have the service (and the decisions about who shall have it and how much of it) is a political decision.
2. Government arranges for the recipients not to have to pay directly for the service themselves.
3. Government selects the producer that will serve them.

..............................

*A **privately** provided service is described in this way:*

1. Individuals and nongovernmental organizations make their own decisions whether or not to have the service.
2. If they choose to have it, they pay for it in full out of their own resources, whatever these may be.
3. They select the producer themselves.[7]

---

There are mixed cases of public and private provisions as well. Government may provide a service and allow citizens to decide whether to use it. The financing of such provisions may be divided between public and private sectors as users finance part and the government pays part of the costs. Some citizens (the wealthy) may pay the full cost of provisions, while government picks up the complete tab for others (the poor). Government may finance the complete cost but permit the user to choose the vendor. The provision of schools is financed, publicly, via taxes.

Nontax devices, such as regulations and franchising, are used as well. Government regulations require restaurant owners to clean the premises themselves at their own expense; in franchising provision of water, gas, or electricity, government allows a monopoly to develop, which, in turn, permits an average price, overcharging some customers while subsidizing others. In privatizing the provision of services, government withdraws or reduces its role as buyer, regulator, standard setter, or decision maker.

Now let us examine the concept of *production* as it applies to activities of government. Government officials decide to produce the services they determine should be provided. In other words, government operates, delivers, runs, performs, sells, and administers services. As emphasized, service production is less complicated than service provision. Production may be divided into line services and support or staff services; production may be divided into labor-intensive functions, equipment and facilities; production may focus on the substance of the work or on the management or administration of work. For example, a municipality may divide refuse collection among several garbage collection companies, or the management of worker pension funds among several financial institutions.

In privatizing public-sector production, the question of competition is an important one. If the shift is merely from a public-sector provider to a single private sector one, a monopoly supplier still exists. The deregulation of railroads, aviation, trucking, banking, health care, and telecommunications has taken place in the private sphere to encourage competition. Despite such efforts, questions concerning competitiveness remain, especially when these areas are characterized by economic concentration.

The neat distinctions between government's primary policy decision providing a service and the secondary decision producing a service are not, in reality, easily discerned. The Federal Aviation Administration administers air safety for public and private good. The Department of Defense contracts with private providers for base support and maintenance at its nearly 6,500 installations. Pinkerton and Wells Fargo, private security firms, have a long history of public service. Public day-care centers allow parents economic opportunities in the private sphere.

Privatization of some government services, notably Social Security, turnpike authorities, military housing, and the Postal Service, have been considered to decrease costs and increase efficiency. Proponents think that the competition created by contracting out will improve federal government programs. So far, the federal government and many state and local governments are experimenting with privatization, but the federal government resists. Unions oppose the practice because they fear the adverse effects on employee salaries and benefits.[8]

In the early 2000's, the president did not need approval of Congress to place nearly half the federal civilian workforce, approximately 850,000 government jobs, in the private contractor competitive marketplace. The Bush privatization plan was a major expansion of trends taking place in government at all levels for the past two decades. According to OMB, 60 percent of the privatized jobs make their way to small businesses and companies owned by women and minorities.

The administration's goal was to "create a market-based government unafraid of competition, innovation and choice." Savings from privatization plans are targeted to be 20 to 30 percent. However, after taking over government jobs, contractors may perform poorly or encounter legal or financial trouble. Bobby L. Harnage, Sr., president of the American Federation of Government Employees (AFGE), a government union representing 600,000 federal workers, protested that the administration had "declared all-out war on federal employees." Harnage insisted that federal employees almost always offer more expertise and experience than outside contractors.[9]

Contract compliance programs help companies comply with numerous laws governing contracts and subcontracts with the federal government, avoid criminal prosecution, and reduce violation fines. Contract compliance programs include the following.

- Codes of ethics to be adhered to by private sector employees.
- Strategies for effective delegation of responsibilities.
- Procedures for reporting violations, corrective measures for noncompliance, and constant evaluation of the compliance program.
- A records management system for keeping records for the contract duration as specified by law.[10]

Privatization is an effective way of providing necessary services usually provided by the government while overcoming the problem of shrinking federal, state, and local government budgets and ailing infrastructure. The government plays the role of prudent purchaser and manager of services offered by private-sector contractors. Privatization aims at creating a market-driven partnership for the betterment of taxpayers, although it faces resistance from citizens who fear elimination of services.[11] Privatizing government functions, then, is seen as a way of increasing efficiency and producing significant savings.

The Cornell University College of Architecture, Art and Planning maintains online an extensive literature review on government privatization. Although empirical studies do not provide clear evidence on the costs and benefits of privatization, public perception and pressure for improved government efficiency will keep privatization on the government agenda.[12]

## Evaluating Government Programs

Taxing, budgeting, and government spending priorities place program evaluation *at the center, not at the periphery,* of policy making in the public sector. To improve the effectiveness of program evaluation, such priorities need to assume their rightful place at the center of the policy-making and budget-making processes. Program evaluation needs consideration alongside financial and political lines. When Planning Programming Budgeting Systems (PPBS) began to diminish in the federal bureaucracy, many found a replacement in another analytical device—program evaluation. Some state and municipal governments have warmly welcomed this technique and have set up offices to evaluate their program performance.

According to Ralph C. Chandler and Jack C. Plano, program evaluation is an assessment of the effectiveness of a program through the application of a research design aimed at obtaining valid and verifiable information on the structure, processes, outputs, and impacts of the program. Program evaluation is an effort to help decision makers determine whether to maintain, modify, or discontinue a specified program. Program evaluation is concerned with whether program activities have been successful in resolving the public problem identified, and the extent to which other factors may have contributed to the problem's resolution."[13]

There are three phases in program evaluation:

1. Selection and identification of goals and objectives of the program.
2. Execution of the evaluation according to scientific guidelines.
3. Feedback on results and recommendations.

The overall goals of program evaluation, or PE as it is sometimes called, can be simply stated. PE increases our understanding of government activities, leads to governmental improvements, and produces financial savings. The tools it uses seem familiar—for the most part, they greatly resemble the types of analytical devices developed for PPBS, zero-based budgets (ZBB), and management by objectives (MBO).

Legislative backing and buttressing have played a major role in the flourishing of program evaluation at all government levels.

The productivity challenge in the public sector is hampered by structural and environmental barriers; therefore, the need for evaluation of productivity is always present. In the private sphere, technology becomes an intervening factor between monetary rewards and corporate failures. However, productivity indices in the public sector are grounded in politics, with merit principles sometimes receiving less emphasis. As citizens, elected officials, and administrators consider the effectiveness of the bottom-line delivery of public services, there will be enhanced interest in pro-active, rather than reactive, program evaluations and employee performance evaluations.

Citizens and policy makers seek evidence regarding program results from taxpayer-supported programs. Program evaluation efforts may identify problems and demonstrate results. Findings may impact state policies. In California historically, program evaluation of government support system reforms, smoking prevention efforts, and state prison drug treatment programs resulted in definitive policy impacts.

Problems with program assessment and evaluation results may arise and indeed, should be anticipated. Policy makers, legislative staff, and state government evaluation specialists reveal that evaluation reports sometimes do not focus on key policy questions. Legislators seek analytical reports when reviews merely describe clients and activities. Certain key stakeholders may be omitted. Findings may be misunderstood and not utilized. The request for program evaluation may come too soon in the life of the government program. Earmarked funding may prove inadequate for the rigorous work demanded. If the evaluator is not independent of the program, evaluation findings may lack credibility. Local government programs may not be required or mandated to collect standardized data.[14]

The United States Department of Education shifted in 2002 to a new approach to program evaluation—the Performance-Based Data Management Initiative. This centralized, consolidated, electronic system replaces the department's myriad data collections. The reform dramatically reduced reporting burdens on elementary and secondary schools. The focus is to gather much better data about program effectiveness.[15]

The Centers for Disease Control (CDC) Office on Smoking and Health (OSH) assists state tobacco control program managers and staff in the planning, design, implementation, and use of comprehensive evaluations of tobacco control efforts. Tobacco use, both smoke and smokeless, is the leading preventable cause of death and disease in the United States—contributing to more than 480,000 deaths annually.

Tobacco control programs are designed to reduce disease, disability, and death related to tobacco use. To determine the effectiveness of prevention and control programs, evaluators document and measure program implementation and effects.

Program evaluation examines implementation protocols and operations, effectiveness, and accountability. CDC goals call for preventing the initiation of tobacco use among young people, promoting quitting among young people and adults, eliminating nonsmokers' exposure to environmental tobacco smoke, and identifying and eliminating disparities related to tobacco use and its effects among different population groups.

Accountability includes assessing and documenting the effectiveness of programs, measuring program outcomes, documenting implementation and cost effectiveness, and increasing the impact of programs. Strategies stress community mobilization, policy and regulatory action, and the strategic use of media. Program evaluation examines the effectiveness of these strategies for meeting program goals.[16]

## Citizen-Driven Government Performance

A market has developed for citizen-driven, results-oriented government performance. The emphasis is on assessing and improving how local governments serve their communities. Involvement of community stakeholders in assessing performance is a priority; citizen-driven influence is paramount. Elected leaders and government services respond to community needs and priorities—as stakeholders get involved, participate, and contribute.

How do citizens think impartial experts rate agency performance? What grades do these experts give your city bureaucracies—A, B, C, D, or worse? Is performance improving or deteriorating? How city services should be measured draws little political consensus. However, democratic institutions— cities, towns, counties, states, and even the country—function effectively only with satisfactory levels of trust in government and the long-term health of legally formalized communities.[17]

Improvements in the performance of governments is a widespread expectation for democratic capitalism. The principal idea of the Government Performance and Results Act of 1993 is that federal agencies will produce strategic policy-making plans for revitalizing government units.

# THINK ABOUT IT!

**Problems with Biased Research and Evaluations**

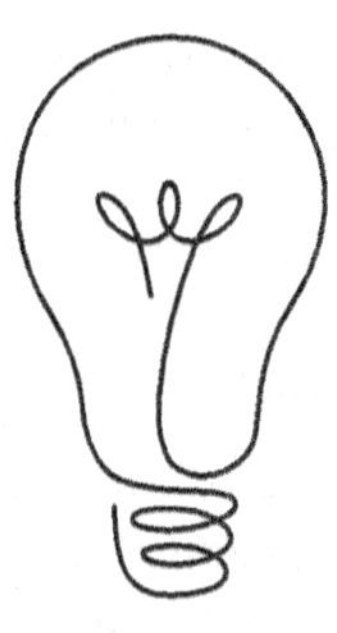

In the real world of organization behavior, evaluation may be biased when performed by agency or program personnel, especially personnel who have a stake in the continuation of a program or in the outcome of the evaluation. Edward Suchman calls politically oriented evaluations "pseudo evaluations" and he identifies five common types:

- **Eye-wash** — an attempt to justify a weak or bad program by deliberately selecting for evaluation only those aspects that "look good" on the surface. Appearance replaces reality.
- **White-wash** — an attempt to cover up program failure or error by avoiding any objective appraisal. Vindication replaces verification.
- **Submarine** — an attempt to "torpedo" or destroy a program regardless of its effectiveness. Politics replaces science.
- **Posture** — an attempt to use evaluation as a "gesture" of objectivity or professionalism. Ritual replaces research.
- **Postponement** — an attempt to delay needed action by pretending to seek the "facts." Research replaces service.

Although most veteran elected officials and public administrators are familiar with the use of the pseudo evaluations observed by Suchman, there is a sixth type, which requires some explication. Obfuscation, or an attempt by the researcher to camouflage what has been observed through the maximum utilization of a highly abstract and specialized vocabulary that is unintelligible to the average lay person. In this type of pseudo evaluation, pedantry replaces communication.

## Performance Measurement in Local Governments

Performance management contributes to better decision making, performance appraisal, accountability, service delivery, public participation, and civic discourse.[18]

Performance measurements, as shown in **Table 4.2.1**, include input, outputs or workload, outcome or effectiveness, cost-effectiveness, and productivity indicators. Explanatory information probes indicators for service efforts and accomplishments.

**Table 4.2.1 Types of Performance Measurement Indicators: An Example**

| MUNICIPAL FUNCTION | INPUT MEASURES | OUTPUT/ WORKLOAD MEASURES | EFFICIENCY MEASURES | EFFECTIVENESS MEASURES | PRODUCTIVITY MEASURES | EXPLANATORY INFORMATION |
|---|---|---|---|---|---|---|
| Sanitation | Amount of labor hours of the Sanitation Department | Tons of refuse collected | Employee-hours per ton of refuse collected | Percentage of clean streets (e.g., measured by periodical visual inspection) | Cost per mile of a clean street (i.e., total cost of all road cleaning divided by the total miles of clean streets) | Composition of solid waste; climatic conditions; terrain; crew size of vehicles; type of vehicles |
| | Budget of the Sanitation Department | Miles of road cleaned | Dollars spent for one mile of snow removal | Citizen surveys | | |
| | Number of vehicles | Number of customers served | | | | |

*From "Citizen-Driven Government Performance," www.newark.rutgers.edu. Reprinted by permission of Professor Marc Holzer. 2015. Also see National Center for Public Productivity at Rutgers University-Campus at Newark for additional indicators.*

Designing and implementing a performance measurement system requires a thorough understanding of what the program is attempting to accomplish and who the clientele are, as well as knowledge of the public services currently provided by the government unit. Steps in the process include the following.

***Step 1:*** *Identification of a program.* Government activities are identified by distinct programs. Street resurfacing, patching, seal coating, and repairing are part of street maintenance. Animal control, the clerk's office, code enforcement, corrections, courts, fire prevention, fire suppression, housing code enforcement, landfill operations, library, parks maintenance, police patrol, recreation services, senior services, waste collection, street cleaning, utility billing, wastewater collection, and water distribution are popular local government programs. These programs are included in the city's operating budget.

***Step 2:*** *Statement of purpose.* Preparation of a well-articulated statement of purpose for a program reflects a clearly understood mission. Programs are not self-serving. They provide services to the citizens of a certain government jurisdiction.

***Step 3:*** *Identification of program inputs, outputs, efficiency, and productivity indicators.* Operating budget, number of labor-hours, and full-time-equivalent employees are delineated. Outputs reflect workload measures—or the quantity of service delivered to users. Unit of output spells out the quantity of each service. Efficiency and productivity measures address how the service is provided, and efficiency measures focus on costs (dollars and/or employee hours).

***Step 4:*** *Setting targets for accomplishment.* Service effectiveness and quality measures are established. How do government officials determine if objectives are met? Goals, quantities, dates, and targets are closely adhered to. The goals of a program are set according to a specified period of time. Quantities include percentages for recognizing achievements; dates focus on a time frame. Targets include input and output factors.

***Step 5:*** *Monitoring.* Continuous monitoring of targets is a given. Monitoring is a way of keeping tabs on program operations. Monitoring gauges whether the target has been reached or not. Is everything going as a planned? Are there seasonal or cyclical patterns to clientele satisfaction? Data gathering should be reasonable—and not overwhelm the unit's fiscal and human capacities. Monitoring varies according to the service and the target.

***Step 6:*** *Performance reporting.* Indicators are summarized. Results are compared to set targets. Reports include comparisons with previous time frames, similar jurisdictions, technically developed standards or norms, geographic areas of clientele within the same jurisdiction, and public-sector/private-sector costs and results. Performance reporting includes the program name, unit jurisdiction, purpose statement, workloads/ outputs, inputs, productivity and/or efficiency ratios, and synopses of explanatory information.

***Step 7:*** *Analysis and action.* Well-developed performance measurement systems permit clientele to recognize weaknesses, strengths, threats, and opportunities. Relevant actions may be taken. Unit growth capabilities may be diagnosed.[19]

## Public-Private Partnerships

Public-private partnerships, sometimes referred to as P3, seek to share and maximize the various skills and expertise that both the public sector and private sector can bring to a project or service. In addition to sharing resources and expertise, the public and private sector also share in the risks and potential rewards from more effectively delivering a service or project.

While P3 has seen significant use in Europe for decades, use of P3 in the United States has only really become more mainstream in recent years as cities and states struggle to finance basic and large projects from highways to wastewater to schools. The National Council for Public-Private Partnerships has found that the average U.S. city works with private partners to perform 23 out of 65 basic municipal services.

The use of P3 to spread project risk and to access private financing expertise and expedited project delivery can be quite attractive, but these benefits are often complicated by citizen concerns about project oversight, appearance of selling government assets, and concerns about maximizing profit over quality service delivery.

## People Crisis and/or Opportunity?

People are the federal government's most valuable asset, as they are in all organizations. Studies of private and public-sector organizations show that high-performing organizations value and invest in their employees— their human capital—and align their "people policies" to support organizational performance goals. In the federal government, however, strategic human capital management is a pervasive challenge.[20]

The GAO includes human capital on its high-risk list. Critical skill shortages in federal departments and agencies cause difficulties in the implementation of the programs and agendas of the president and Congress.[21] Several reforms are in process.

First, an emphasis on workforce planning and restructuring requires federal agencies to flatten their organizational hierarchy and improve their work processes. To optimize the services provided to citizens, federal employees must understand the link between their daily work and the results their government employer seeks to achieve.

Second, administrative reforms must recast job descriptions. Job responsibilities need restructuring to make work more interesting and promote greater employee teamwork. The very way in which agencies design work for their employees needs rethinking. Narrow job descriptions are not attractive to employees who are likely to strive to make contributions in the public arena. In addition, the vast number of job classifications at the state and federal levels of government are excessive, unduly complex, and confusing, and can be reduced by moving to newly devised systems of pay and classification banding.

# THINK ABOUT IT!

**7 Keys to Success Public-Private Partnerships**

The National Council for Public-Private Partnerships identified these keys to successful P3 agreements.

1. **Public-Sector Champion:** Recognized public figures should serve as the spokespersons and advocates for the project and the use of a P3. Well-informed champions can play a critical role in minimizing misperceptions about the value to the public of an effectively developed P3.

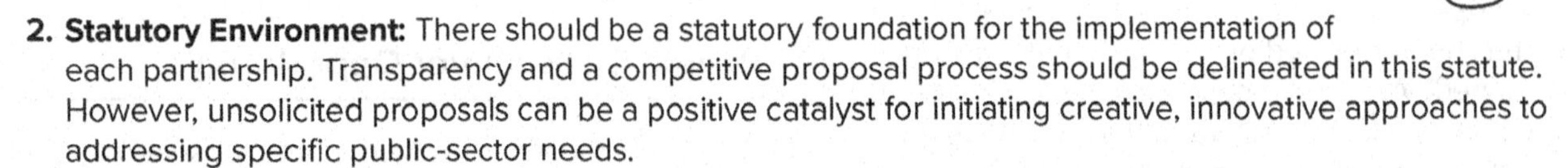

2. **Statutory Environment:** There should be a statutory foundation for the implementation of each partnership. Transparency and a competitive proposal process should be delineated in this statute. However, unsolicited proposals can be a positive catalyst for initiating creative, innovative approaches to addressing specific public-sector needs.
3. **Public Sector's Organized Structure:** The public sector should have a dedicated team for P3 projects or programs. This unit should be involved from conceptualization to negotiation, through final monitoring of the execution of the partnership. This unit should develop Requests for Proposals (RFPs) that include performance goals, not design specifications. Consideration of proposals should be based on best value, not lowest prices. Thorough, inclusive value for money (VFM) calculations provide a powerful tool for evaluating overall economic value.
4. **Detailed Contract (Business Plan):** A P3 is a contractual relationship between the public and private sectors for the execution of a project or service. This contract should include a detailed description of the responsibilities, risks and benefits of both the public and private partners. Such an agreement will increase the probability of success of the partnership. Realizing that all contingencies cannot be foreseen, a good contract will include a clearly defined method of dispute resolution.
5. **Clearly Defined Revenue Stream:** While the private partner may provide a portion or all of the funding for capital improvements, there must be an identifiable revenue stream sufficient to retire this investment and provide an acceptable rate of return over the term of the partnership. The income stream can be generated by a variety and combination of sources (fees, tolls, availability payments, shadow tolls, tax increment financing, commercial use of underutilized assets or a wide range of additional options) but must be reasonably assured for the length of the partnership's investment period.
6. **Stakeholder Support:** More people will be affected by a partnership than just the public officials and the private-sector partner. Affected employees, the portions of the public receiving the service, the press, appropriate labor unions and relevant interest groups will all have opinions, and may have misconceptions about a partnership and its value to all the public. It is important to communicate openly and candidly with these stakeholders to minimize potential resistance to establishing a partnership.
7. **Pick Your Partner Carefully:** The "best value" (not always lowest price) in a partnership is critical in maintaining the long-term relationship that is central to a successful partnership. A candidate's experience in the specific area of partnerships being considered is an important factor in identifying the right partner. Equally, the financial capacity of the private partner should be considered in the final selection process.

*Source: National Council for Public Private Partnerships, "7 Keys to Success," July 28, 2015, http://www.ncppp.org/ ppp-basics/7-keys/.*

Third, performance management measures are ineffective. The Government Performance and Results Act (GPRA) requires agencies to be performance-driven. But agencies must restructure their performance appraisal systems to measure individual performance against target outcomes.

Finally, hard-to-fill positions require organizations to reevaluate the recruitment process.

Agencies evaluated in this study include the Federal Aviation Administration, the Office of Personnel Management, the Veterans Benefits Administration, the Internal Revenue Service, and the Federal Emergency Management Agency. By studying the efforts of these five agencies, the GAO found that directly involving employees in performance planning and important agency decisions empowered the workforce. The provision of regular training to employees, proactive communication with unions on personnel changes, and serious efforts to make human resources a visibly high priority resulted in positive employee impacts.

For the initiatives GAO reviewed, agencies had to overcome organizational and cultural barriers—including lack of trust, resistance to change, lack of buy-in from front-line employees and managers, and workload demands. The agencies developed open communication with employees and reevaluated their systems for reassigning and hiring personnel.[22]

According to the GAO, granting employees decision-making authority not only improved morale, but also streamlined government processes. Once managers and employees perceived the benefits of improved communication and new personnel practices, they adapted to agency changes.

Personnel and motivation are better than ever. Most government employees join the public-sector workforce because they like what they do. If partisans cannot agree on what bottom-line policy principles should exist, the public administrative sector systems may become dysfunctional—at least in part. Public-sector productivity remains uniquely political.

Nevertheless, there are three admonitions that every manager regardless of the sector in which they are employed should heed:

1. "Qui numerare incipit, incipit numerare," Latin – when you begin to count you begin to err.
2. What gets measured gets done.
3. There is general agreement over the usefulness of the many evaluative tools that are now available; the conflict today however is over what constitutes the evidence in evaluation designs.

## Summary

- Program evaluations are context-dependent.
- Market values drive program functions, organization structures, standards, and emerging technologies.
- Most citizens care about the *performance* of their public institutions.
- Productivity in the public sector refers to excellence in individual and collective performance. There are widely divergent views as to what excellence is because excellence is based on the cultural context of a particular function.
- *Efficiency* means doing things well; *effectiveness* means doing the right things well.
- Efficiency is essentially the input or contribution of labor, capital, and other resources into an effort measured against the output produced, regardless of the mechanism selected to gauge output.
- Effectiveness calls for a pre-established standard of comparison; a focus on a certain quality of production; and an ability to mobilize, organize, and direct resources for specified purposes, all taken within a certain cultural context.
- The reasons for citizen complaints with government performance are: Democracy is messy. Government takes a bum rap. Government must shape up. The country must shape up.
- Democratic governments are designed to promote equity and fairness. Pluralism is central to the way American society is organized.
- Government has a role to play in restoring morality to public life.
- Privatization of public responsibilities center around *provision,* or providing, and *production,* or producing, of goods and services. *Privatization,* often called contracting out, means that a service previously produced by a government agency is now produced by a nongovernmental organization.
- Program evaluation increases our understanding of government activities, leads to governmental improvements, and produces financial savings.
- Accessibility, use, safety, attractiveness, and overall satisfaction constitute preset ways of measuring the effectiveness of public services.
- The purposes of program evaluation are to bring rigorous analytical perspective to influence agency budget requests, assess agency effectiveness for meeting program objectives established by elected leaders, and develop program performance measures for agency implementation.
- Empowering employees begins with vision— meaning purpose, values, image, and goals.
- Performance measurement includes indicators of productivity, effectiveness, quality, and timeliness.
- Information provided by performance measurement includes inputs, outputs, outcomes, and efficiency.
- The purpose for doing performance measurement focuses on setting goals and objectives, planning, allocating resources, monitoring and evaluating results, and modifying program plans to enhance performance.
- Performance measurement in local governments contributes to better decision making, performance appraisal, accountability, service delivery, participation, and civic discourse.
- Personal convictions of integrity vary widely from person to person.
- The mismatch between our convictions, or values, and talents, or personal skills, affects how we perceive factors both internal and external to us.
- Failure implies a high level of moral discomfort with the choices that define a person's life.
- People are government's most valuable asset.
- Most government employees join the public-sector workforce because they like what they do.
- Be mindful of what you measure as "What gets measured, gets done!"

## Videos, Films and Talks

Please visit *The Craft of Public Administration* at www.millenniumhrmpress.com for up-to-date videos, films, talks, readings, and additional class resources.

*A few ways to fix a government* [11 min]
Charity Wayua, TED Talk
https://www.ted.com/talks/charity_wayua_a_few_ways_to_fix_a_government

*The Puzzle of Motivation* [18 min]
Dan Pink, TED Talk
http://www.ted.com/talks/dan_pink_on_motivation.

*Why it's Time to Forget the Pecking Order at Work* [15 min]
Margaret Heffernan, TED Talk
https://www.ted.com/talks/margaret_heffernan_forget_the_pecking_order_at_work

## Suggested Readings

**The Opportunity in Government Productivity**
https://www.mckinsey.com/industries/public-and-social-sector/our-insights/the-opportunity-in-government-productivity

**Roles: How Nonprofits Work with Public Agencies**
https://www.pps.org/article/pppp-chapter2

**How Companies, Governments, and Nonprofits Can Create Social Change Together**
https://hbr.org/2018/05/how-companies-governments-and-nonprofits-can-create-social-change-together

**Program Evaluation and Performance Measurement at the EPA**
https://www.epa.gov/evaluate/program-evaluation-and-performance-measurement-epa

**Performance Measurement to Evaluation**
https://www.urban.org/sites/default/files/publication/78571/2000555-performance-measurement-to-evaluation-march-2016-update_1.pdf

**Capital Budgeting: Budget Better with 3 Key Steps**
https://media.erepublic.com/document/ClearGov_-_eBook_-_Capital_Budgeting.pdf

**How Government Procurement is Different Now**
https://media.erepublic.com/document/CDG21_PUB_REPORT_Ivalua_V.pdf

**Annual Privatization Report: Examining Privatization and Government Reform Efforts at all Levels of Government**
https://reason.org/privatization-report/annual-privatization-report-2019/

**How can we Measure Productivity in the Public Sector?**
https://blogs.worldbank.org/governance/how-can-we-measure-productivity-public-sector

**The Wrong Way to Measure Government Productivity**
https://www.forbes.com/sites/jeffreydorfman/2015/08/27/the-wrong-way-to-measure-government-productivity/?sh=43f15d454c52

## Notes


1. G. Chris Hartung, "Institutionalized Excellence: Not Just More Pop Government Jargon?" *Public Management* 78, no. 7 (July 1996): 25–29.
2. David Osborne, "Grading Governments, *Washington Post,* April 13, 1997, p. A8.
3. *New York Times,* April 20, 1971.
4. E. S. Savas, *Privatizing the Public Sector* (Chatham, NJ: Chatham House, 1982), p. 89.
5. Ted Kolderie, "The Two Different Concepts of Privatization," Public Administration Review 46, no. 4 (July–August 1986): 285–291.
6. Kolderie, "Two Different Concepts," p. 285.
7. Ibid., p. 286.
8. Richard L. Worsnop, "Privatizing Government Services: Can For-Profit Businesses Do a Better Job?" *CO Researcher* 6, no. 30 (August 9, 1996): 699–717.
9. Richard W. Stevenson, "Government Plan May Make Private Up to 850,000 Jobs," *New York Times,* November 15, 2002, http://www.nytimes.com/2002/11/15/politics/15PRIV. html?pagewanted=print=top.
10. Richard D. Lieberman, "The 'Criminalization' of Government Procurement," *Civil Engineering* 63, no. 3 (March 1993): 68–70.
11. Charles R. Rendall, "Privatization: A Cure for Our Ailing Infrastructure?" *Civil Engineering* 66, no. 12 (December 1996): 6.
12. Cornell University College of Architecture, Art and Planning, "Restructuring Local Government," July 26, 2015, http://www.mildredwarner.org/restructuring/privatization.
13. Ralph C. Chandler and Jack C. Plano, *The Public Administration Dictionary* (New York: John Wiley & Sons, 1982), p. 91.
14. David A. Dowell, "Guidelines for Legislative Language for State Program Evaluation," Long Beach, CA: California State University, 1998, http://www.csulb.edu/ddowell/guidelines.htm.
15. David Thomas, "Department of Education Announces New Approach to Program Evaluation," Department of Education, April 5, 2002.
16. Centers for Disease Control and Prevention, "Introduction to Program Evaluation for Comprehensive Tobacco Control Programs," February 6, 2002, http://www.cdc.gov/tobacco/ evaluation_manual/ executive_summary.html.
17. David Margolis, "Performance-Based Management in PENNDOT," *PA Times* 25, no. 6 (July 2002): 3.
18. "Editor's Notebook," *Government Executive Magazine,* January 1, 1997; http://www.govexec.com/news/ index/cfm.
19. David Osborne and Peter Plasrik, "Grading Governments," http://www.psgrp.com/ resources/ Publications/op4-13.html.
20. The National Center for Public Productivity, "A Brief Guide for Performance Measurement in Local Government," http://newark.rutgers/ncpp/Manual.htm.
21. Gail C. Christopher and Robert J. O'Neill, Jr., "The Federal Government's People Crisis," *Federal Times,* December 2000.
22. General Accounting Office, *Human Capital: Practices That Empowered and Involved Employees,* GAO- 01-1070, September 14, 2000.

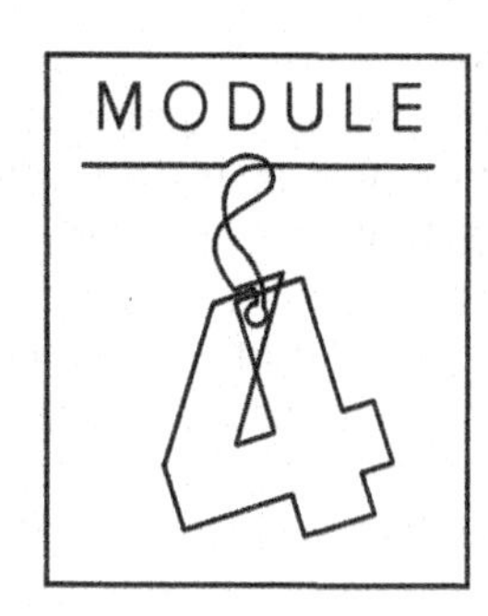


# UNIT 3: Administrative Law—the Legal Foundation of Public Administration

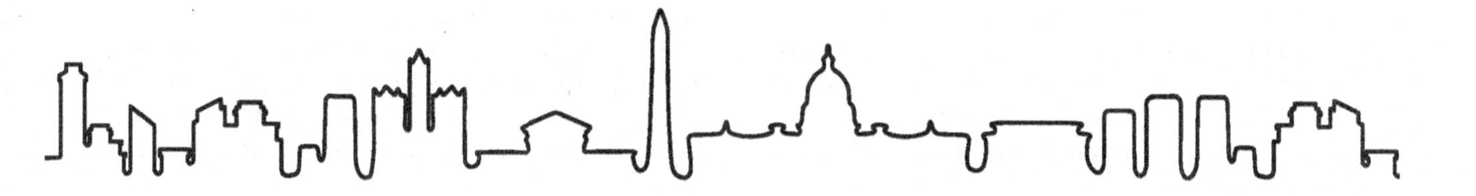

## The Impact of Administrative Growth on Democratic Ideals and Administrative Law

The United States, a country espousing democratic capitalism, exists in the era of the *administrative state*.

The administrative presidency, with corresponding implications for state governors, county executives, and municipal mayors, finds philosophical origins in George Washington's first cabinet. Thomas Jefferson, the original "outsider" advocating states' rights and decentralization of power, called for the pluralist model of presidential leadership. Alexander Hamilton—called our first accountant of the nation's purse—called for a strong chief administrator with direct, accountable lines of program authority.

Jefferson represented values of equality of uniform participation, or democratic ideals, while Hamilton called for efficient administration, articulated in hierarchy and bureaucracy. How has the emergence of the modern administrative state redefined the basic democratic principles of our 1787 U.S. Constitution? Tenets of administrative law are grounded in constitutionalism, shared governmental powers, popular government, Individualism, and political equality.[1]

Constitutionalism. A constitutional governmental system regards the people, not the government, as sovereign. The rule of law emphasizes supremacy of the law and the notion of limited government. A constitutional government is politically legitimate if it rests securely on popular consent.

Many Americans believe that the growth of administrative expertise challenges the primacy of democratic constitutionalism. According to this argument, administrative discretion permits public administrators to "govern" the United States, and governmental regulations are threats to democratic constitutionalism. The undemocratic character of administrative experts compromises constitutional democracy. The new cadre of governmental experts forms an administrative elite that evolves into a democratically irresponsible oligarchy.

Shared Powers. The division of powers among the chief executive, administrative, legislative, and judicial branches and among different levels of government permits each political entity a limited check over the powers of other authorities in the governmental system. Decision-making powers in this system are not monopolized by a single governmental branch. Presidents, legislators, and judges tend to delegate more of their prescribed powers to government bureaucrats as the weight of increasing governmental regulation increases.

The expansion of administrative policy-making powers is enhanced as other branches of government become increasingly bogged down with peripheral concerns. Public administrators, for example, absorb more power as constitutionally elected politicians agonize over the role of government in the resolution of moral dilemmas. Many citizens perceive the public administration system as a closed political system that circumvents the open decision-making structure authored by the constitutional framers. Political bureaucracy emerges with a less than well-defined philosophy of the public interest.

*Popular Government*. Democratic government implies that the ultimate determination of public policy resides with the people. Stressing majority will, individual rights, and liberty, popular government is the opposite of absolutism. The shift of power from political institutions to administrative agencies raises questions about the democratic functioning of popular government.[2]

If public policy making is "farmed out" to government bureaucrats, how "popular" can government be? The administrative state, grounded in structures, functions, and rationality, may not be suited to the flexibility required to meet the public's demands. A system based on knowledge, skills, and expertise conflicts with a system based on partisan politics and spoils. All government officials, elected and appointed, are servants of the people and should be held accountable for their performance in the public's interest. It can be difficult to ensure that a nonelected official can be that accountable.

Individualism. Freedom, personal well-being, and capabilities of individuals may conflict with the regulation of society by public bureaucracies. According to some, bureaucracy stymies the will of citizens, expressing the powers of the system and not the individual.

The tug of war between societal rights and individual rights challenges the political consensus of democratic governments. Regulatory agencies prescribe rules that may destroy the freedom of individuals, with new structures of apolitical power over individuals emerging in their place.

In balancing societal and individual rights, government regulators are called upon to implement guidelines of federal, state, and local laws in a "fair" manner. Issues of administrative law ultimately involve questions of due process of law. The question is, due process or fair treatment for whom? Liberty is sacrificed and our way of life is altered when an administrative agency or a court makes a decision that benefits a larger group at the expense of the individual. The rights of the individual— bolstered by the Fourth Amendment to the U.S. Constitution, which monitors unreasonable searches and seizures, and the Fifth Amendment, which guards against self-incrimination—can be undermined by the exercise of excessive regulatory control.

Political Equality. Grounded in democratic philosophies of equality under the law and equal opportunity for all persons, government is to treat and represent all persons equally. Laws forbid arbitrary treatment of citizens by government officials, but in practice U.S. administrative agencies do not afford complete equality to all persons or groups. The reality of U.S. political bureaucracy is that preferential treatment is given to special interests.

Sexual and racial discrimination are well known and publicized aspects of our society. Since the Great Society of the 1960s, citizen groups have been organized to represent the interests of women and minorities. Affirmative action programs call for special compensatory measures from government to rectify past discriminatory practices by society. In theory, at least, the rule-of-law principle demands that government bureaucrats treat all individuals equally. Public bureaucracy, as prescribed by Max Weber's "ideal type," rests upon knowledge, skills, and expertise, and not upon equality or political influence.

Constitutionalism, shared powers, popular government, individualism, and political equality are the political philosophies upon which administrative laws find implementation in modern American society. The individual needs the assurance of protection in law from the potential misuse of regulatory power. The conflicts between individual citizens and their governments and the resolution of these conflicts by the law allow understanding of how these philosophies are played out in American life.

Historically federal government growth has been categorized and described by James Q. Wilson and later supplemented by Kenneth F. Warren as depicted in **Table 4.3.1** on the following page.

**Table 4.3.1 James Q. Wilson's Periods of Bureaucratic Growth**

| PERIOD | FOCUS | KEY ACT PASSED |
|---|---|---|
| 1887-1890 | Control monopolies and rates | Interstate Commerce Act, Sherman Act |
| 1906-1915 | Regulate product quality | Pure Food and Drug Act, Meat Inspection Act, Federal Trade Commission, Clayton Act |
| 1930-1940 | Extend regulation to cover various socioeconomic areas, especially new technologies | Food, Drug, and Cosmetic Act, Public Utility Holding Company Act, National Labor Relations Act, Securities and Exchange Act, Natural Gas Act |
| 1960-1979 | Expand regulation to make America a cleaner, healthier, safer, and fairer place to live and work | Economic Opportunity Act, Civil Rights Acts of 1990, 1964, and 1968, National Environmental Policy Act, Clean Air Act, Occupational Safety and Health Act |
| 1878-1993 | Deregulation movement as a reaction to bureaucratic overexpansion | Paperwork Reduction Act, Air Deregulation Act, Radio and TV deregulation, Banking deregulation |

*Sources: James Q. Wilson, "The Rise of the Bureaucratic State," Policy Making, ed. Francis E. Rourke, 4th ed. (Boston: Little, Brown, 1986), pp. 125–148; and Kenneth F. Warren, Administrative Law in the Political System, 3d ed. (Upper Saddle River, N.J.: Prentice-Hall, 1997), p. 45.*

## Traditional and Contemporary Cornerstones of American Administrative Law

The traditional cornerstones of administrative law are the independent regulatory agency, a uniform administrative procedure law (Administrative Procedure Act, 1946, as amended), substantial evidence judicial review, and notice and comment ruling.[3]

The independent regulatory agency, as a descriptive concept, is a misnomer. All agencies are, in unique ways, dependent directly upon the executive and legislative branches of government and indirectly upon the judicial branch. The independent agencies, as they are called, emerged from the American constitutional provision of separation of powers.

There are three types of regulation. The best known is old-style economic regulation. The second type, the new social regulation, is a product of the 1970s. A third type of regulation is subsidiary regulation.[4] Economic regulation emerged from the social and economic challenges of the 1930s. From the devastating consequences of the Depression, the New Deal created the Federal Deposit Insurance Corporation (FDIC), Tennessee Valley Authority (TVA), Federal Communications Commission (FCC), Securities and Exchange Commission (SEC), National Labor Relations Board (NLRB), and Civil Aeronautics Board (CAB). These regulatory bodies were established from 1933 through 1938.

After World War II, other agencies were created to monitor and confront emerging national problems. The Atomic Energy Commission (AEC), Selective Service System (SSS), National Aeronautics and Space Administration (NASA), Federal Maritime Commission (FMC), Equal Employment Opportunity Commission (EEOC), Environmental Protection Agency (EPA), Occupational Safety and Health Administration (OSHA), and Consumer Product Safety Commission (CPSC) were created to administer and regulate.

*The development and enactment of a uniform administrative procedure law is the second traditional cornerstone of administrative law.*

These agencies were created to regulate, respectively, programs concerning atomic energy, military conscription, space exploration, shipping, employment discrimination, environmental protection, occupational safety, and consumer product safety. In addition, there is a need to regulate the activities of agencies implementing Social Security, medical care, welfare, SNAP, veterans' benefits, and internal revenue programs.

The development and enactment of a uniform administrative procedure law is the second traditional cornerstone of administrative law. The Administrative Procedure Act, enacted in 1946, brings a degree of standardization to administrative practices and procedures and public access to those procedures. Before the enactment of APA, administrative practice and procedure questions were decided on a constitutional basis. The APA brought order from chaos. Unless they can find a justifiable exception, agencies must follow the fundamental outlines of APA's broad and general statute. Such legislation was an advance of immeasurable proportions in administrative law and the protection of citizen rights.

Judicial review is the third traditional cornerstone of administrative law. Substantial evidence review is a dominant feature of administrative practice and procedure. The courts may rule on the merits of agency action if things go askew. Derived from statutory and non-statutory sources, judicial review permits judges to scrutinize allegedly illegal administrative actions. Judicial review, as a basic right, rests on the congressional grant of general jurisdiction under Article 3 of the U.S. Constitution.

The rule-making procedure (notice and comment ruling) constitutes the fourth and final traditional cornerstone of administrative law. Rulemaking guides the subsequent application of policy, and, it is argued, clear rules promote fairness. Rulemaking is also a forceful, efficient, yet democratic way for agencies to implement their mandates. Prior to the advent of rulemaking, agencies resorted to policy interpretation on a case-by-case, ad hoc basis. Rulemaking is a more rational means of policy making than adjudication because adjudication is reactive and potentially disjointed. Rulemaking is more comprehensive, facilitating planning and coordination.

Contemporary pressing demands call attention to new cornerstones of administrative law. These are public participation in the administrative process, administrative process in informal and discretionary governmental activity, and the evolving definition of the mission of administrative agencies and development of effective oversight of their activities.[5]

The courts have held that public participation is pertinent to sound and equitable decision making in administrative processes. Until the mid-1960s, the prevailing perspective was that the agency was representative of the public interest. The courts insisted upon citizen rights to participate in the administrative process; Congress and the agencies soon recognized the validity of public participation as well.

The administrative process in formal and discretionary governmental activity is a second contemporary cornerstone. The development of procedural law to cover persons in public institutions, aliens, and the governance of educational institutions emphasizes the broadening development for protecting the rights of citizens in previously neglected areas. Aspects of administration once thought purely discretionary are subject to regulation as well.

A third, and final, contemporary cornerstone of administrative law is the continuing definition of the mission of administrative agencies and development of effective oversight of their activities. Each new administration advocates regulatory reform, but each administration fails to redefine the mission with sweeping regulatory reform. Congress may strengthen its oversight functions by demanding better analyses of the potential effects of proposed legislation, stronger program evaluation requirements in legislation, greater oversight of program design and development of regulations, and more use of program evaluation information. The final cornerstone, then, is the continuing development and fulfillment of mission and likewise improvement in oversight.

## What Is Administrative Law?

There is no commonly agreed upon subject matter of administrative law. There are, however, certain parameters wherein the application of administrative law is appropriate.

Bernard Schwartz argues that administrative law does not relate to public administration in the same manner that commercial law relates to commerce and land law relates to land. Rather, the definition of administrative law centers around powers and remedies to answer the following questions: (1) What powers may be vested in administrative agencies? (2) What are the limits of those powers? (3) What are the ways in which agencies are kept within these limits? [6]

All law may be generally categorized as either procedural or substantive. For example, the Environmental Protection Agency establishes New Source Performance Standards that prohibit emissions from industrial, stoker-fired boilers in excess of 0.10 pound of fly ash per million BTU of heat input. The Administrative Procedure Act specifies that such a rule be published in the *Federal Register* so that interested persons may comment before the ruling becomes final. The requirement for publishing the rule in the *Federal Register* is procedural; the rule for limiting emissions from stoker-fired boilers is substantive.[7]

Administrative law originates primarily from interpretations of legal statements that describe procedures agencies follow. Such judicial interpretations emanate primarily but not exclusively from due process clauses as detailed in constitutions, from applicable administrative procedure statutes, and sometimes from clauses within statutes establishing an agency and also prescribing a procedure to follow.Administrative law is not regulatory law. The differences between regulatory and administrative law will be discussed later in the chapter. Numerous government agencies and departments, cooperating with legislatures, create regulatory laws that affect even the most trivial of activities. Several of the more recognizable regulatory agencies are the Federal Communications Commission (FCC), which regulates broadcasting and interstate telephone rates; the Occupational Safety and Health Administration (OSHA), which regulates the safety of the workplace; and the Food and Drug Administration (FDA), which tests drugs for marketing and monitors the contents of the food we eat. The laws, consent decrees, rules, and regulations made and enforced by these agencies are not administrative law. Instead, "regulatory law governs the citizenry; administrative law governs the government. We might say that administrative law governs the bureaucracy as other constitutional provisions govern the judicial, legislative, and presidential powers in government."[8] Administrative law applies legal principles originating from statutes, common law, constitutions, and regulatory laws to the government agencies affected.

In attempting to set up standards for administrative due process, the courts, basing their findings on the federal government's Administrative Procedure Act and similar state acts and on their new interpretations of the Constitution, have worked out a fairly strict set of rules that administrators must follow. These rules have developed to meet four basic due process requirements:

- Adequate notice
- Disclosure of reasons
- The right to a hearing
- The right to further appeal

## Administrative Law Judges and Federal Regulations

The Administrative Procedure Act of 1946 ruled out any evidence that would be "irrelevant, immaterial or unduly repetitious," but did not go so far as to outlaw hearsay evidence as such. In 1971, the Supreme Court held that uncorroborated hearsay evidence can constitute "substantial evidence," sufficient to support an administrative ruling.[9] This did not mean that all such evidence was to be indiscriminately accepted. It would have to be relevant and reliable and support the point for which it was being used. Material "without a basis in evidence having rationality and probative force" would not meet the Court's standard.

# THINK ABOUT IT!

**Defining Administrative Law**

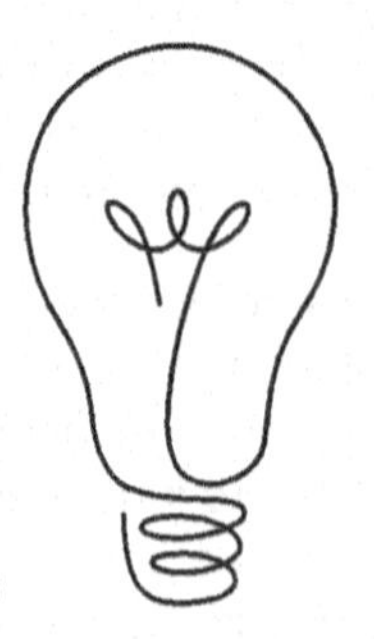

Administrative law is an amorphous body of law. Administrative law is created or affected by the activities of government agencies. The term administrative law is akin to many other conceptual terms and is hard to define. – *Joseph J. Simeone*

Administrative law controls a system: a system which, in the simplest terms, has only one goal: to deliver government services to its citizens. – *Charles Koch, Jr.*

That branch of law concerned with the procedures by which administrative agencies make rules and adjudicate cases; the conditions under which these actions can be reviewed by courts.

The legislation that creates administrative agencies. The rules and regulations promulgated by administrative agencies. The law governing judicial review of administrative actions. – *Jay M. Shafritz*

Broadly speaking, administrative law deals with the ways in which power is transferred from legislative bodies to administrative agencies; how administrative agencies use power; and how the actions taken by administrative agencies are reviewed by the courts.

More specifically, administrative law is concerned with the legal developments which have so dramatically increased the powers and scope of the administrative branch. – *Kenneth F. Warren*

---

*Sources: Joseph J. Simeone, "The Function, Flexibility, and Future of United States Judges of the Executive Branch," Administrative Law Review 44, no. 1 (Winter 1992): 159–161; Charles Koch Jr., Administrative Law and Practice (New York: West Publishing Co., 1985); Jay M. Shafritz, The Dorsey Dictionary of American Government and Politics (Chicago: The Dorsey Press, 1988); Kenneth F. Warren, Administrative Law in the Political System, 3d ed. (Upper Saddle River, N.J.: Prentice Hall, 1997), p. 23.*

Such a ruling does not close the door on the issue but only opens it wider. Hotly contested disputes can erupt at any time on whether a particular piece of hearsay evidence meets the criteria for relevance and probative value. Many, meanwhile, still question whether any hearsay evidence should be allowed to influence administrative action. The consequences of administrative decision making can frequently exceed those of a court trial, therefore it is only right and proper, so the argument goes, that those who would have to bear these consequences should benefit from the safeguards enjoyed by those subject to a court trial. Others contend, however, that there is nothing inherently evil about hearsay evidence. Such evidence is admissible in even criminal trials in most countries in the world, including most democratic countries. To bar it from the hearing room, they contend, would only hinder administrative tribunals from making informed and judicious decisions.

The dilemma of hearsay evidence is not the only controversy confronting administrative law judges. The prospect that the administrative law judges prosecute and adjudicate cases brought before him or her is a very serious concern. When an agency discharges or demotes an employee or deprives an individual or a group of some benefit or right, the agency first brings the charges and then, during the hearing, sits in judgment on these charges. In effect, it seems to be sitting in judgment on itself. To many lawyers, this is inherently unfair and contrary to both the spirit and intent of due process. They claim the affected party should possess the right to have the charges decided by a completely external body.

While most administrative agencies adjudicate their own charges and complaints, they usually use special employees to do so. These officials are customarily called hearing examiners in most local and some state bureaucracies, but in a few states as well as at the federal level they bear the more prestigious title of administrative law judges. Formerly referred to as "Washington's hybrids," "the hidden judiciary," "trial examiner," or a "hearing officer," they adjudicate cases for federal agencies.[10]

The administrative law judge exercises his or her prerogatives when a corporation or a private citizen disputes the decision of a federal department or agency. For example, if your grandfather is denied a disability pension from the Social Security Administration or if a state university is charged with unfair labor practices by the faculty union, the administrative law judge decides the case. Until 1978, the 1,100 administrative law judges were called "hearing officers." They, according to the United States Supreme Court, are "functionally comparable" to federal court judges. The Office of Personnel Management certifies the administrative law judge and maintains a central registry from which agencies select judges. Administrative law judges (ALJs) then interpret federal regulations enforced by a particular department or agency to which they are assigned.

Although federal ALJs are employees of the agency whose cases they adjudicate, their qualifications and civil service status have given them virtual immunity from normal agency pressures. They frequently counteract and contradict the policies of their agencies. When the Social Security Administration attempted to use the Reagan administration's stricter guidelines to pare nearly a quarter million people from the rolls of its recipients, it found itself on a collision course with its ALJs. The ALJs, using the more liberal standards of the Supreme Court, reinstated approximately three-fifths of those who appealed their loss of benefits. Their actions infuriated the heads of Social Security, who overruled many of the reinstatements. This, in turn, riled the ALJs, who felt they had acted as they should, as independent judicial officers and not as "mere bureaucrats."

Judicial review of agency action provides controls over administrative behavior. For the person who is harmed by a particular agency decision, judicial review operates to provide relief. Over a period of years, judicial review has evolved into a complex system of statutory, constitutional, and judicial doctrines. These doctrines define the proper boundaries of the oversight system.

The trend of judicial decisions and the APA is to make judicial review more widely and easily available.[11]

Despite the independence and integrity that ALJs have usually shown, some observers continue to express doubts as to whether an agency employee should preside over a case in which the agency itself is a party of interest. Suggestions have been made to divorce ALJs completely from any particular agency, setting up, in effect, a new administrative unit in the federal bureaucracy that would assign them to different agencies as cases arose. This would give them more independence but would reduce their expertise in the matters under dispute, for they would no longer be specialized in the work of one agency.

Critical examination of the formal agency adjudicative process and the role of the ALJ reveals two trends. First, there is growing dissatisfaction with formal trial procedures for resolving licensing, merger, and related economic regulation policy issues. Second, the number of benefits and enforcement cases has increased dramatically. Enforcement is another growth area. ALJs discipline license holders, revoke licenses, issue cease-and-desist orders, and impose civil money penalties.

ALJs deal with license and route certification of transportation by air, rail, motor vehicle, or ship; regulate radio and television broadcasting; establish rates for gas, electrical, communication, and transportation services; monitor compliance with federal standards relating to interstate trade, labor-management relations, advertising, communications, consumer products, food and drugs, corporate mergers, and antitrust; regulate health and safety in mining, transportation, and industry; regulate trading in securities, commodities, and futures; and adjudicate claims relating to Social Security benefits, workers' compensation, international trade, and mining. The brief history of ALJs reflects tension between the need for fact-finder independence and the need for policy and management control.

## Internal and External Administrative Controls

In the fifty-first of their famous *Federalist Papers*, James Madison and Alexander Hamilton pointed out,

If men were angels, no government would be necessary. If angels were to govern men, neither external nor internal controls on government would be necessary. In framing a government which is to be administered by men over men, the great difficulty lies in this: you must first enable the government to control the governed; and in the next place oblige it to control itself. A dependence on the people is, no doubt, the primary control of the government; but experience has taught mankind the necessity of auxiliary precaution.[12]

As the writers of *The Federalist Papers* perceptively noted, there are two aspects of administrative control, internal and external.

Internal control is the control that agencies exercise over their own constituent elements, be they subunits or individuals. Staff units and their personnel frequently perform a controlling function even when they have no authority or mandate to do so. This is what frequently makes them suspect to line employees. Staff services provide internal control, even when they are not expressly designed to do so. Many staff services are, however, expressly designed with a control function in mind.

Internal control mechanisms include the personnel department. If it enjoys appropriate authority, the personnel department influences how line departments and line officials confront personnel problems. The budget office of any agency or any government obviously exercises a high degree of control, for it may decide who gets what amount of money for what purpose. Another staff department that exercises financial control is the purchasing office. Perhaps the most important financial control unit is the auditing branch. Field inspections support internal controls.

External control over administration is exercised primarily by the legislative branch of government. Legislatures control expenditures and confirm appointments. The best-known power legislative bodies exercise over administrative ones is the power to investigate and expose.

A form of government employee control at times controversial, yet often effective, is that of whistle-blower. The term whistle-blower was originated by Ralph Nader to categorize those public employees who, in effect, blow the whistle on acts by their own agencies when they deem such acts to be improper.[13] Some of the more famous whistleblowers during the early 1970s were Gordon Rule, the Navy's director of procurement, who challenged extravagant cost overruns and claims for extra compensation by Navy suppliers; A. Ernest Fitzgerald, the Pentagon cost analyst who called attention to similar cost overruns in conjunction with the Air Force's C-5A transport jet; Frank Serpico, the New York City police officer whose reports on corruption in his department touched off a wide-ranging investigation that culminated in numerous indictments and shake- ups in the city's constabulary.

Many factors account for the growing prominence of whistleblowers as agents of administrative control. One of them is the development of administrative law and the safeguards it extends to public employees. When the Nixon administration attempted to discharge Fitzgerald, for example, by eliminating his job, he fought back through the courts and won.[14]

A second factor that has encouraged whistleblowing has been the development of the *news media.* In this connection, the press has long played an active and aggressive role in controlling administrative actions. "I fear three newspapers more than I fear three thousand bayonets," Napoleon once remarked, while an English contemporary, philosopher Jeremy Bentham, observed that "Without publicity, all checks are inefficient; in comparison to publicity, all checks are of small account."[15]

The development of broadcast journalism, particularly television news, and the growth of public awareness and interest in government have made the news media a form of control that rivals, if it does not exceed, that exerted by legislative bodies.

This is particularly true in the United States, which does not have a government-owned television and radio network and has a long muckraking tradition. The media are not only important for what they do on their own but for the help they provide other forms of control. The media have encouraged and strengthened whistleblowing by providing considerable publicity to the whistleblowers. The press also has stimulated legislative control by providing headlines and coverage for legislative exposés. Furthermore, many newspapers and radio and TV stations act as ombudspersons, soliciting citizen complaints against the bureaucracy and then checking them out.

A third instrument of control over an administrative agency is its clientele. For reasons that will be more fully discussed later in the chapter, administrators, particularly in the United States, need considerable cooperation from their clientele, and the clientele often seize upon this to exercise some countervailing influence over administrators. Sometimes this takes dramatic and violent forms, such as the client takeovers of welfare offices, the student rebellions of the 1960s, and the prison riots of the early 1970s. More often, however, clients exercise control by refusing to comply with policies they do not like.

Finally, a form of control that often receives little attention but that plays an important role in constraining many administrative agencies is the control exercised by *competing agencies.* Agencies are frequently locked in combat over jurisdiction, funding, and so on. In their continual jousting for power and position, agencies tend to control each other. James Madison saw this as one of the most effective forms of control. In a well-known passage in *The Federalist* he noted, "Ambition must be made to counteract ambition . . . the constant aim is to divide and arrange the several offices in such a manner that each may be a check on the other—that the private interest of every individual may be a sentinel over the public rights."[16]

## ESSENTIAL VIEWS:

### ACADEMICS/PRACTITIONERS AT THE STREET LEVEL

**It Isn't the Whistle that Pulls the Train**
By Anna Marie Schuh

Are whistleblowers heroes or rogues? More importantly, how does the workplace successfully deal with a whistleblower?

In my 36 years as a federal employee, I only had one experience with a whistleblower. It happened in 1978 when I chaired a Performance Rating Act appeal board for the Civil Service Commission. The employee considered himself a whistleblower while the three-member board (one member selected by the employee, one member selected by the agency, and me as the Civil Service Commission designated chair) unanimously decided the employee was just someone not doing his job. As a result, the employee sued the board members (including me) and the leadership of his agency. My agency counsel said he had never seen a more quickly dismissed suit. Still this same "whistleblower" was able to get his story on a popular prime time news program. Was this whistleblower a hero or rogue. In the appeal process I saw a rogue, but some whistleblowers are heroes and others may be both.

The question of hero or rogue makes the agency response difficult because whistleblowers can be an asset to an organization. Organizations require effective whistleblowers to surface problems that need quick resolution. Often, early and respectful problem resolution can avoid litigation. Court cases and appeals waste agency resources even when agencies prevail which they do 79 percent of the time. Healthy organizations provide employees who have criticisms with effective internal mechanisms to air their concerns because such systems give the organization internal credibility and assist in maintaining good morale.

Employees blow the whistle for various reasons. Some, particularly in the private sector, raise an issue for a monetary reward. Monetary reward is rarely the reason for public-sector employees. More often the concern, involves operational or ethical issues, e.g., waste, fraud, and abuse. In the Performance Rating Act appeal described earlier, the issue involved waste and mismanagement. The whistleblower in that case contended the government was mismanaging its human resources and wasting money by assigning him work beneath his grade level. As a result, that whistleblower refused to complete his assignments. However, his job was not unique and others with the same background and training were completing the same assignments. So, the question presented to the board involved whether the employee was properly performing, not whether the employee was raising legitimate whistleblower concerns.

Organizations need well-functioning whistleblower protection policies to sort through issues at the lowest level where the best problem resolution can occur. Although most organizations have such policies, it is important to make sure that all managers are trained on the policies and have a healthy respect for them. It is also important periodically to review the policies to ensure that they meet current standards.

The most important current standards include four key areas. The first area involves a clear process for employee disclosure. A clear policy provides both managers and employees a complaint roadmap and information about their rights and responsibilities. More importantly, a clear policy gives managers direction for handling employee concerns.

The second area consists of providing safety in the outlet that employees use to raise concerns. Such an outlet requires disclosure and investigation by an individual or unit outside the employee's supervisory chain. Safety is important for several reasons. It encourages employees to use the process rather than beginning with an external disclosure. Using the process is particularly important to an organization that wants to identify and resolve problems at the earliest stage. Safety also reinforces employee trust in the organization. The use of a safe disclosure outlet functions as a relief valve that allows the organization to address issues before the issues affect organization morale.

The third area relates to follow-up. Every policy should have a timetable for quick issue resolution. Resolving problems quickly limits workplace disruption. In addition, employees need to know what happens to the issues they raise both in terms of process and outcomes. Employees must have confidence that the organization wants input on problematic issues before disclosure occurs. A clearly documented complaint process provides necessary reassurance.

Finally, the entire effort requires credible top management support. That support includes identification in the policy and regular reinforcement. Management support is the area where organizations often fail. Typically, organizations develop strong policies, train managers and stop. However, top management needs to periodically provide public support for the policy so that employees recognize internal whistleblowing as a legitimate problem resolution process.

An old American proverb notes that "It isn't the whistle that pulls the train." However, it is the whistle that assists the train in avoiding accidents. Whistleblowers function in a similar way because they help organizations avoid serious problems. Viewing whistleblowers as heroes or rogues is not useful. Instead, managers need to view whistleblowers as alarms of potential organizational failure.

*Source: Adapted from Anna Marie Schuh, "It Isn't the Whistle that Pulls the Train " PA Times Online, August 9, 2016.*

## Government Regulation

Government regulations affect all Americans—through the food and beverages we consume, the medications our doctors prescribe, the way we invest our savings, how we develop private property, and the procedures by which we operate profit-making businesses. The direct costs of regulation are typically imposed on businesses and governments. These costs, however, are passed along to consumers.

Critics of regulation point out that federal agencies have not developed systems for making rational, well-informed decisions on ways to allocate human resources efficiently—to maximize health, safety, and environmental protection. Would citizens rather have local health boards not inspect restaurants, the Food and Drug Administration not regulate prescription drugs, the zoning commission not check the use of private property, the Securities and Exchange Commission not monitor financial investments, and government safety experts not probe the quality of our automobiles? As imperfect as they are, government regulations are here to stay.

The conflicts between public and private are never ending. Regulations typically do not require substantial burdens of taxation or government spending, but they act as hidden taxes. The indirect costs are passed along to consumers, employees, and employers. Regulatory impacts are more difficult to measure. From this perspective, regulations are politically convenient ways to implement public policies. This appeals especially in times of fiscal budget constraint.[17]

# THINK ABOUT IT!

**Sample of Federal Regulatory Offices Through the Years**

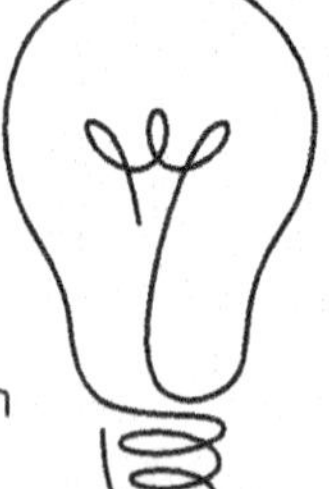

- Office of Information & Regulatory Affairs
- Office of Management & Budget
- Animal and Plant Health Inspection Service
- Bureau of Alcohol, Tobacco, Firearms & Explosives
- Commodity Futures Trading Commission
- Comptroller of the Currency
- Consumer Product Safety Commission
- Federal Aviation Administration
- Federal Communications Commission
- Federal Election Commission
- Federal Energy Regulatory Commission
- Federal Maritime Commission
- Federal Motor Carrier Safety Administration
- Federal Railroad Administration
- Federal Trade Commission
- Fish & Wildlife Service
- Food & Drug Administration
- Food Safety & Inspection Service
- International Trade Commission
- Mine Safety & Health Administration
- National Highway Traffic Safety Administration
- National Labor Relations Board
- Nuclear Regulatory Commission
- Occupational Safety & Health Administration
- Securities & Exchange Commission
- Small Business Administration
- Surface Transportation Board

## Market Failure and Regulations

Regulations take force because the market or markets fail or otherwise do not work effectively. U.S. regulations commenced with the establishment of the Interstate Commerce Commission in 1887. Information is a scarce commodity. Decision makers cannot collect all relevant information; they act in a state of partial ignorance and uncertainty. They use the best source of information available: what has just happened. Government oversight and information occur in this perspective. Public choice may be defined as "the economic study of nonmarket decision making, or simply as the application of economics to political science."[18] Public choice assumes that rational individuals pursue their own interests.

Market failure. The normal operations of the marketplace fail to protect the public from actual or potential abuses of power by business firms, leading to calls for regulation.

## Is the United States a Regulatory State?

In 1789, Congress granted the president the prerogative to select an administrator to "estimate the duties payable on imports." Since then, Congress continues to delegate rule-making power to administrative agencies. The full scope of regulatory power, in addition to the power to formulate rules, includes the authority for interpreting laws and regulations, enforcing rules and regulations, trying cases concerning violations of those rules, holding hearings investigating and adjudicating such circumstances, and imposing sanctions on violators. In a single agency, administrative regulatory power combines legislative, executive, and judicial powers.[19]

Administrative power expands as the power and responsibilities of government in our society expand. An industrialized, urbanized, interdependent society requires a more active role for government. The protection of individual rights, mediation of disputes, provision of benefits, and stabilization of the economy reflect accepted activities of modern U.S. government.

Federal departments and agencies such as the FDA, EPA, OSHA, and at least fifty others are called *regulatory agencies.* They are empowered to create and enforce rules— regulations—that carry the full force of law. According to the Office of the Federal Register, in 1970 the Code of Federal Regulations (CFR) contained 54,834 pages; today's volume contains more than 150,000 pages, filling more than 200 volumes and 25 feet of shelf space. The General Accounting Office (GAO) reported that between 1996 and 1999, a total of 15,286 new federal regulations went into effect, of which 222 were classified as "major" rules.[20]

The highest number of bills passed in Congress was in 1955-1956. Today a typical session of Congress enacts 300-400 laws.

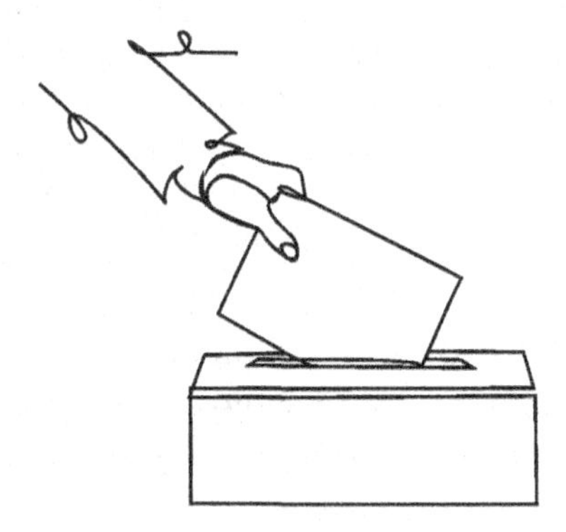

## Introduction to Laws and Regulations

Laws and regulations are a major tool in protecting the environment. Congress passes laws that govern the United States. To put those laws into effect, Congress authorizes certain government agencies, including the Environmental Protection Agency (EPA), to create and enforce regulations. The following is a basic description of how laws and regulations come to be, what they are, and where to find them, with an emphasis on environmental laws and regulations.

### 1. Creating a Law

*Step 1:* A member of Congress proposes a bill. A bill is a document that, if approved, will become a law.

*Step 2:* If both houses of Congress approve a bill, it goes to the president, who has the option to either approve it or veto it. If approved, the new law is called an Act, and the text of the Act is known as a public statute. Some of the better-known laws related to the environment are the Clean Air Act, the Clean Water Act, and the Safe Drinking Water Act.

*Step 3:* Once an Act is passed, the House of Representatives standardizes the text of the law and publishes it in the United States Code. The U.S. Code is the official record of federal laws.

### 2. Putting the Law to Work

Now that the law is official, how is it put into practice? Laws often do not include all the details. The *U.S. Code* would not tell you, for example, what the speed limit is in front of your house. To make the laws work on a day-to-day level, Congress authorizes certain government agencies, including the EPA, to create regulations. Regulations set specific rules about what is legal and what isn't. For example, a regulation issued by EPA to implement the Clean Air Act might state what levels of a pollutant—such as sulfur dioxide—are considered safe. It would tell industries how much sulfur dioxide they can legally emit into the air and what the penalty will be if they emit too much. Once the regulation is in effect, EPA then works to help Americans comply with and enforce the law.

**3. Creating a Regulation**

First, an authorized agency, such as the EPA, decides that a regulation may be needed. The agency researches it and, if necessary, proposes a regulation. The proposal is listed in the *Federal Register* so that members of the public can consider it and send their comments to the agency. The agency considers the comments, revises the regulation accordingly, and issues a final rule. At each stage in the process, the agency publishes a notice in the *Federal Register.* These notices include the original proposal, requests for public comment, notices about public meetings where the proposal will be discussed, and the text of the final regulation. A complete listing of *Federal Register* notices issued by the entire federal government is available from the Government Printing Office.

**4. Carrying Out the Law**

Select examples of the more than 50 major laws enacted by Congress and carried out by the EPA include:

- 1938 Federal Food, Drug and Cosmetic Act
- 1946 Atomic Energy Act
- 1970 National Environmental Policy Act
- 1971 Lead-Based Paint Poisoning Prevention Act
- 1973 Endangered Species Act
- 1974 Safe Drinking Water Act
- 1980 Asbestos Hazard Emergency Response Act
- 1988 Medical Waste Tracking Act
- 1990 Pollution Protection Act
- 2007 Energy Independences and Security Act

Administrative regulatory powers are vested in state and local government agencies as well. State regulatory powers and responsibilities include licensing of physicians, barbers, lawyers, architects, cosmeticians, liquor dealers, and funeral directors. States regulate commerce within their boundaries and supervise the governance of all public educational institutions. Local government agencies enforce building codes and fire, health, and safety regulations and standards. Agencies of state or local governments may also be charged with implementation of national programs via functional federalism.

The process of regulation is not widely understood. Regulation is the way in which a national priority or concern is translated into a specific rule. Regulation does not commence when a government department or agency issues a ruling. Regulation has its origins in Congress, when the national legislature passes a law establishing a regulatory agency, providing a mandate to issue rules governing a particular activity. The writing of a particular statute is usually the most important action of an extended rule-making process. The regulatory department or agency cannot cure basic defects in the enabling legislation.

First, Congress perceives a "market failure," or private sector inability to achieve a social goal. Departments or agencies promulgate regulations in response to laws passed by Congress to correct that market failure. Regulatory proceedings are not mere matters of procedure and conformance. Regulations originate from demands for clean air, safe drinking water, safe workplaces, reliable financial markets, improved medicines, and competitive industries. The regulatory process, however, is fundamentally bureaucratic—with all the powers and defects of government institutions—and at best is a blunt and imperfect mechanism for attempting to create a better society.[21]

As argued earlier in the chapter, the United States is a *regulatory state.* The vast majority of direct contacts for most citizens are likely to be with federal, state, or local administrative agencies. We are a society in which nearly every activity, whether of organizations or individuals, is included in the scope of administrative regulation and control. Overhead operations, independent regulatory commissions, cabinet departments, independent agencies, government corporations, the Executive Office of the President (EOP), and assorted other federal agencies of more and lesser consequence issue administrative regulations daily in the *Federal Register* and annually in the *Code of Federal Regulations.*

Overhead units carry out functions for the entire federal government. The General Accountability Office (GAO), Government Printing Office (GPO), Congressional Budget Office (CBO), Office of Management and Budget (OMB), General Services Administration (GSA), and Office of Personnel Management (OPM) issue regulations and administer support functions for most of the federal bureaucracy.

Since the creation of the Interstate Commerce Commission more than one hundred years ago, independent regulatory commissions have been prominent in the government regulation of business. Such commissions are multi-headed, bipartisan in composition, organizationally separated from other departments and agencies, and not directly in the president's chain of command. They provide nonpartisan flexibility, continuity, and expertise in the regulatory process; assign commissioners with terms longer than the president's; protect commissioners from presidential dismissal; and allow lengthy tenure for maximizing commissioner expertise and independence. These characteristics and aspirations may not be realized in each commission on every day of every year; however, these commissions possess widespread responsibilities for regulating specific industries and for protecting consumers and workers.

Examples of prominent, independent regulatory commissions are the Federal Communications Commission (FCC), Surface Transportation Board, Nuclear Regulatory Commission (NRC), Postal Rate Commission, Securities and Exchange Commission (SEC), Federal Maritime Commission (FMC), Federal Reserve System (FED), Consumer Product Safety Commission (CPSC), and Equal Employment Opportunity Commission (EEOC).

Cabinet departments enjoy regulatory power of a scope, type, and impact similar to that of independent regulatory commissions. Major distinctions between the two types of agencies include administrative form and operations within executive departments or agencies. Cabinet agencies are led by a single administrator; cabinet secretaries are directly responsible to the president for programming. For example, the Food and Drug Administration (FDA), within the Department of Health and Human Services (HHS), is responsible for ensuring the purity and safety of food, drugs, and cosmetics; the Internal Revenue Service (IRS), within the Treasury Department, implements tax laws; and the Occupational Safety and Health Administration (OSHA), within the Department of Labor, attempts to ensure that places of work are free from hazards affecting the health and safety of workers.

Independent agencies, such as the Federal Emergency Management Agency (FEMA), the National Foundation for the Arts and Humanities, and the Small Business Administration (SBA), share characteristics in common with independent regulatory commissions and cabinet departments. Independent agencies are accountable to the president for direction and control; they have a single administrative leader, and they are not positioned within a cabinet department.

Government corporations, such as Amtrak, a passenger railroad; the Federal Deposit Insurance Corporation (FDIC), an insurance company; the Tennessee Valley Authority (TVA), an electric power generating facility; and the U.S. Postal Service, issue regulations as well. Such public corporations are multi-headed (with a board of directors); however, the president may dismiss corporation board members.

Distrust and dislike of the chief executive may encourage the establishment of independent regulatory commissions. A powerful clientele group, such as the environmental lobby, may call for the promotion and protection of a particular concern or interest within a single-headed independent agency. An agency within a department may seek refuge there from hostile or corrupt influences.

The total administrative regulatory process includes ten procedures, or steps. Most regulatory activities do not touch all ten bases, either because the rule is obeyed without discussion or controversy, or the agency does not actively enforce the regulation. The procedures or steps of the administrative regulatory process are summarized in **Table 4.3.2**.

**Table 4.3.2 Steps of the Administrative Regulatory Process**

| | |
|---|---|
| *Step 1:* | Authorizing legislation |
| *Step 2:* | Agency interpretation-enforcement (rulemaking) |
| *Step 3:* | Complaint |
| *Step 4:* | Investigation |
| *Step 5:* | Informal proceedings |
| *Step 6:* | Prosecution |
| *Step 7:* | Formal hearing (adjudication) |
| *Step 8:* | Agency review |
| *Step 9:* | Judicial review |
| *Step 10:* | Agency enforcement |

*Source: Florence Heffron with Neil McFeeley, from The Administrative Regulatory Process, 1983. Reprinted by permission of Pearson Education, Inc.*

## Economic, Social, and Subsidiary Regulations

Social regulatory programs deal with health, safety, and environmental issues. Social regulatory agencies are limited to a specific policy area, but they have power to regulate across all industries. Social regulatory agencies include the Environmental Protection Agency (EPA), Drug Enforcement Administration (DEA), Food and Drug Administration (FDA), Occupational Safety and Health Administration (OSHA), National Transportation Safety Board (NTSB), and National Labor Relations Board (NLRB). The social regulatory functions are divided into (1) consumer safety and health, (2) transportation, (3) job safety and other working conditions, (4) environment, and (5) energy.

Economic regulatory agencies focus on specific industries. Economic controls include the use of price ceilings and service parameters. The Federal Communications Commission (FCC), Federal Deposit Insurance Corporation (FDIC), and Federal Trade Commission (FTC) are economic regulatory agencies. Economic regulatory tasks are divided into (1) finance and banking, (2) industry-specific regulation, and general business.[22]

The costs of compliance with federal requirements have shifted over the decades. Thomas Hopkins identifies three groups of federal regulation compliance requirements:

- *Environmental and risk reduction regulations* attempt to lessen pollution and other societal risks. These include air emission and water pollution, solid waste disposal regulation, handling and labeling of hazardous materials, noise regulations, superfund compliance, and nuclear power safety.
- *Price and entry control regulations* restrict rates on business entry and include government controls on labor markets and on product prices and availability.
- *Paperwork regulations* entail tax compliance procedures. Taxpayers spend time complying with the intricacies of the tax code.[23]

Public-sector expenditures are a small proportion of the total cost of regulation by society. Regulatory behaviors fall into three categories: economic, social, and subsidiary regulations.

### Economic Regulations

What we will call Regulation I, or economic regulation, focuses on market aspects of industrial behavior, including rates, quality, and quantity of service, and competitive practices within a specific industry or segment of the economy. Categories of economic regulation include finance and banking, industry-specific regulation, and general business regulation.

Economic regulation is usually industry-specific and focuses on market structure and firm conduct, regulating the entry, exit, merger, and rates within markets.[24]

For example, the ICC regulates railroads and trucking, and the FCC regulates communications. The ICC and FCC each concentrate on a specific industry, and each agency has no other responsibilities. Regulation I also concerns enforcement of congressionally mandated antitrust policies. The Justice Department and FTC regulate the frequency of mergers and combinations within particular industries. The goal of antitrust policies is maintaining and restoring competition within the market system. Competition and economic efficiency are objectives of Regulation I.

One of the most criticized forms of economic regulation is the effort of the FTC to demand that businesses tell consumers the truth, the whole truth, and nothing but the truth. The disclosure of full and accurate information by business, however, should prove compatible with desired outcomes of sellers and buyers in the market system.

### Social Regulations

Regulation II, or social regulation, controls the nature and types of goods and services and production processes. Social regulations involve consumer safety and health, job safety and working conditions, environment, and energy.

Social regulation usually cuts across industries, regulating issues such as employment opportunity, environmental protection, and occupational safety.[25] Social regulation seeks control or elimination of socially harmful impacts occurring as byproducts of the production process and protection of consumers and the public from unsafe or unhealthy products. If conservatives find Regulation I unpopular, they believe Regulation II an anathema. Regulation II focuses on the subtle regulation of clean air, occupational safety, poison prevention, boat safety, lead-based paint elimination, product safety, political campaigns, pesticide control, water pollution, noise control, flood disaster, energy, commodity futures trading, hazardous materials transportation, and similar potential abuses.

Regulation II covers more industries and directly affects more consumers than Regulation I. For example, OSHA's regulations govern the activities of every employer whose business affects commerce. In other words, government is involved with detailed, sometimes minute, facets of the production process.

Two concerns are raised by Regulation II. First, the apparatus of the presidency concentrates significant power and influence regulating health, safety, and environmental activities. Second, the accretion of new regulatory powers and controls could undermine citizens' faith in government, a negative reaction to the over strengthening of government and regulatory excesses of the mid-1970s.

Social regulation may be costly because certain regulatory decisions are grounded in grossly inadequate information. Even if information is forthcoming, regulatory decisions may reflect the most extreme and unrealistic assumptions about the problem's potential social interference. There could be strong resistance to alternative and innovative problem solutions.

**Subsidiary Regulations**

Regulation III, or subsidiary regulation, entails all regulatory activities accompanying Social Security, Medicare, Medicaid, Temporary Assistance to Needy Families (TANF), Supplemental Nutrition Assistance Program (SNAP), veterans' benefits programs, Internal Revenue Service regulatory concerns, and categorical grant program regulations. Subsidiary regulations impact individuals and state and local governments.

The general public has mixed feelings toward Regulation III. Americans would like to believe that there is no such thing as a free lunch. Freeloaders, government support system cheats, and supplemental nutrition assistance program chiselers invoke citizen suspicion, mistrust, and hostility. Most Americans do, however, consider Social Security, unemployment compensation, and veterans' benefits as legitimate.

Unless there are clear and specific regulations for such benefit programs, the opportunities for cheating are almost limitless, making the costs and benefits of Regulation III difficult to quantify. Programs range from deciding eligibility for benefit programs to providing equal sports opportunities for women in college and equal educational opportunities for the handicapped. Costs are largely intangible; the market value is not readily apparent.

Economic, social, and subsidiary regulations are diverse, contradictory, and value laden. The growth of administrative regulatory power changes responsibilities and relationships among branches and levels of government. Regulations control or restrict one's choices and/or behavior and are blamed for all sorts of societal ills, including inflation, recession, and the demise of the family, individual initiative, and the federal system. Despite criticisms, the societal conditions demanding counterbalance to the vast power that private corporations and industry exercise over the lives, health, safety, and happiness of Americans are still evident. In addition, nationwide polls indicate that the American public supports, generally, the concept of regulations.[26]

## Administrative Rules and Rule Making

Rulemaking and adjudication are not the same process. Rulemaking, in general, focuses on the future and is broad in scope. Adjudication is particular, focusing on an instance in the present or the past. Prior to the adjudication of a person's rights, the individual is entitled to a hearing under the due process clause of the Fifth Amendment for federal agencies and the Fourteenth Amendment for state agencies. The development of administrative rules follows the commercial development of the American West, tragedies of transportation accidents, development of the federal government as collector of revenues, government as benefit provider, and the populist rebuttal to the exploitation of the farmer by the rail trust.[27]

Regulatory law and administrative law, as stated earlier, work in tandem, but are not the same thing. Congress does not like controversy. Congress is a provincial political institution. In other words, members of Congress do not enjoy conflict-laden issues where they are likely to have constituents split over the solutions. Each member of Congress comes from a narrow, provincial political base. Each member of Congress looks out for their district's narrow economic interests and not those of the entire nation. Partly because Congress is composed of politicians representing 535 political jurisdictions, they pass laws that do not speak clearly. It is not difficult, therefore, to explain the presence of vague, ambiguous, and general laws that allow wide human discretion.

Administrative agencies serve to interpret the vagueness, ambiguity, and generality of these laws. For example, the FCC, by rule, restricts the number of commercial broadcasting stations a private corporation may operate. The IRS, by rule, determines which groups in society must pay or are exempted from paying taxes. The FCC creates communications law; the IRS makes tax law. Independent regulatory commissions, cabinet agencies, independent agencies, public corporations, and the EOP have similar functions.

## The Administrative Procedure Act

The Administrative Procedure Act (APA), although not a comprehensive code of administrative procedure, provides a general framework of fundamental importance. The APA, in the minds of some authorities, serves as the "Magna Carta of administrative law." Regulatory law regulates citizen behaviors; administrative law oversees the administrative discretion of bureaucrats.

Judges interpret legal statements and prescribe the procedures that agencies and their employees follow. Judicial interpretation originates from constitutions; the primary, but not exclusive, origin for interpretation comes from due process clauses. Judges also interpret administrative procedure statutes, if applicable; some clauses within a statute require agencies to follow certain procedures, including conducting a full hearing. Administrative law, meanwhile, applies legal principles originating from statutes, common law, constitutions, and regulatory law.[28] Public administrators, as implementers of regulatory law, implement rules. The terms rule and regulation are nearly synonymous. Unless rules are successfully undermined in a lawsuit unconstitutional, rules have the force of law. What is a rule? The APA defines a rule as

"The whole or a part of an agency statement of general or particular applicability and future effect designed to implement, interpret, or prescribe law or policy or describing the organization, procedure, or practice requirements of an agency and includes the approval or prescription of the future of rates, wages, corporate or financial structures or reorganizations thereof; prices, facilities, appliances, services, or allowances thereof; or of valuations, costs, or practices bearing on any of the foregoing."[29]

The first of the two types of rulemaking delineated by the APA is informal or "notice and comment" rule making. The characteristics of this procedure are advance notice and public participation. Notice of proposed rulemaking gives the time, place, and nature of the rule-making proceeding, refers to the authority, or statute, under which the rule is proposed, and includes the terms or substance of the proposed rule or a description of the subjects and issues therein.

**The Stages of Rulemaking:**

- *Stage 1:* Origin of rulemaking activity
- *Stage 2:* Origin of individual rule making
- *Stage 3:* Authorization to proceed with rule making
- *Stage 4:* Planning the rule making
- *Stage 5:* Developing the draft rule
- *Stage 6:* Internal review of the draft rule
- *Stage 7:* External review of the draft rule
- *Stage 8:* Revision and publication of a draft rule
- *Stage 9:* Public participation
- *Stage 10:* Action on the draft rule
- *Stage 11:* Post-rule-making activities

The second type of rulemaking, "on the record" formal rule making, occurs when a "trial-type" hearing precedes rules. The hearing is an adversarial process entailing production of evidence, testimony by witnesses, cross-examination, and representation by counsel. The more formal requirements apply when a statute determines that rules must be cited "on the record after opportunity for an agency hearing."

The *Federal Register* and the *Code of Federal Regulations* publish notices of proposed rulemaking. The Federal Register Act of 1935 established a system of federal rules publication. The Act designated the *Federal Register* as the official publication of federal rules, regulations, orders, and other documents of "general applicability and legal effect." On March 14, 1936, the *Federal Register* began publishing every day, Monday through Friday. The first issue was 16 pages; the seventieth anniversary edition came in at 256 pages. The first year, 1936, recorded 2,620 pages. In 1936, the *Register* published 2,620 pages of rules, orders, and other actions. The inaugural edition included rules for the new Social Security system. It published trade practices for buttons on clothes and ivory.[31]After each year, the issues of the Register are bound and indexed. The regulations published in the Federal Register for the preceding year are codified with regulations previously issued and still in effect. The Code of Federal Regulations, a collection of paperback books grouped together by agency, is divided into fifty titles, with each title more or less representing a particular agency or a broad subject area.

Bruce James, head of the U.S. Government Printing Office, stated that Congress passed legislation in 1935 authorizing the *Federal Register*'s existence after acknowledging that "no real place [existed] to capture the work of what the agencies were doing." The *Register* was sent gratis to 1,300 public and research libraries. The 1936 mail subscription was $10 annually.

The Register came to the internet in the 1990s and by 2010 the Federal Register 2.0 was live. In 2011 a new application programming interface was implemented to allow further access. Federal departments and agencies post proposed rules and regulations for publication in the Register. Time for public comment is offered. Final rules that carry the force of law are published.

The 6,653-page antitrust settlement between the Justice Department and Microsoft Corporation, published May 3, 2002, represents one of the largest single documents ever in the *Federal Register.*

## ESSENTIAL VIEWS:

### ACADEMICS/PRACTITIONERS AT THE STREET LEVEL

**The Public-Sector Accountability-Responsiveness Paradox**
By Thomas E. Poulin

Public administrators seek to provide optimal services, recognizing limitations imposed by legislation, community will, and available resources. Within this framework, public-sector leaders have been able to perform creatively and responsively. They have continually worked within a paradox of accountability and responsiveness. All public administrators would be well served pondering how to approach the challenges this paradox creates.

**Responsiveness to Community**
For decades, demands for public agencies to be more responsive to community expectations have grown. This message has emerged from all quarters at the local, state, and federal levels. Put simply, public agencies are here to fulfill community expectations, and this should be the focus of all their activities.

This requires the mindset one will do so, and a commitment to do so actively. This means reaching out to the public to determined desired levels of service quantity and quality, then attempting to provide such services effectively and efficiently. This requires the ability to be entrepreneurial and opportunistic. It involves recognizing community needs and expectations evolve, requiring public administrators at all levels to adapt. Within this mindset, the focus is on outcomes, not processes.

**Accountability for Activities**
The public sector grew exponentially at the federal level during the Civil War, with larger agencies created to meet evolving demands. This trend has since continued at all levels, as populations grew, as society grew more complex, and as more was demanded of public agencies. Concurrently, there was an emergent concern these public agencies might exceed their authorities or perform unethically, contributing to the accountability debate.

In 1887, Woodrow Wilson, in The Study of Public Administration, framed appropriate limits on the performance of public administrators—such debates continue today. The fundamental thrust of accountability revolves around the argument public servants are employed to perform specific functions in a prescribed manner under the oversight of senior appointed or elected officials. Within this mindset, the primary focus is on directed, controlled processes.

**The Paradox: The Challenge for Public Administrators**
As presented, there is a paradox. To be fully responsive to evolving service demands, we must be adaptive and entrepreneurial, working beyond existing practice. To hold ourselves fully accountable, we must perform within the limits of accepted practices, ensuring we work as directed. A paradox exists between these competing public expectations. We must consider the implications of this paradox, both for ourselves and our agencies.

Instead of viewing this as a paradox, we might consider it a continuum. Complete flexibility of public administrators is counter to community values—some level of control is desirable. Complete inflexibility is also negative in the public eye, interpreted as focusing on internal rules, not public service. There is no single response to this—no, "magic bullet," to resolve concerns with such issues.

Successful public administrators must work within this environment, finding means to adapt on an individual level in their own work, seeking higher-level support for adaptation without hesitation when necessary. They must imbue this mindset in subordinates, seeking to unleash the talent of employees working to provide the best services possible, permitting them, when possible, the flexibility to "work outside the box."

Approaching the paradox requires we recognize it and the potential implications on performance. Second, we must find means of working within this paradox in a manner comfortable for us, and which best serves the needs of the community and agency. Third, we must communicate this to our subordinates, enabling them to adapt effectively within such an environment. Last, we must create a culture embracing this paradox, enabling public agencies to adapt as necessary, working within the limitations on public agencies the community expects.

In the end, while some in public service might believe they should be free to act in an unfettered manner, the public will always expect some level of oversight and control over their employees, much as any employer might have on employees regardless of setting. All public servants must keep in mind the "servant," role they play professionally, taking pride in how they provide such services.

*Source: Abridged version of "Has the Administrative State Lost its Mandate," PA Times Online, February 14, 2020.*

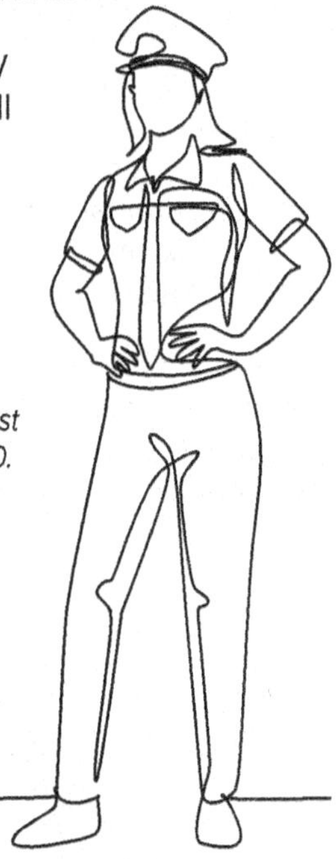

## What Is the Public Interest?

In casting about for answers to the question of responsibility, we are at the outset likely to come across the phrase "the public interest." Many see the entire solution to the question neatly encapsulated in this phrase, as though an administrator need only resolve to serve the public interest, and his or her problems concerning responsibility will vanish.

This solution, like so many other easy solutions to difficult problems, raises more questions than it answers. The most basic is this: *What is the public interest?* Walter Lippman once claimed that "The public interest may be what a person would choose if they saw clearly, thought rationally, and acted disinterestedly and benevolently."[32] This leaves us with the task of defining "clear" vision and "rational" thought, concepts that, in practice, seem susceptible to varying interpretations. Even deciding what course of action is "benevolent" and "disinterested" may produce more controversy than it settles. "It may be somewhat difficult for some readers to accept the conclusion that there is no public interest theory worthy of the name," concluded political scientist Glendon Shubert.[33]

Another maxim that often presents itself is "following one's conscience." This, too, fails to furnish a usable guideline. The enforcers of the Inquisition who burned thousands of heretics at the stake felt they were following the loftiest appeals to conscience. The same can be said for many other appalling actions that people have perpetrated on others. As Carl Friedrich noted, "Autocratic and arbitrary abuse of power has characterized the officialdom of a government service bound only by the dictates of conscience."[34]

While Friedrich rules out the use of conscience as a means of ensuring responsibility, he does have some positive ideas to offer in its place. "We have a right to call such a policy irresponsible if it can be shown that it was adopted without proper regard to the existing sum of human knowledge concerning the technical issues involved; we have also a right to call it irresponsible if it can be shown that it was adopted without proper regard for existing preference in the community and more particularly its prevailing majority."[35]

In keeping with this admonition, Friedrich sees the solution to the question of administrative responsibility as lying in two areas: professionalism and participation. Professionals usually have been conditioned to uphold certain standards, and they usually subscribe to a code of ethics that governs the practice of their profession. As Friedrich sees it, professionalism constitutes something of an "inner check" on administrative irresponsibility. Participation, meanwhile, means that administrators must consult more interests and listen to more points of view. Allowing divergent parties to share in decision making should make that process less arbitrary and subjective and more responsive and responsible.

To Friedrich's twin safeguards of professionalism and participation can be added a third protective device: publicity. Directing the public spotlight onto administrative decision making should make such decision making more responsible. Secrecy has rarely led to improved administrative decisions or better administrative behavior.

Professionalism, participation, and publicity do not in themselves guarantee responsible administration. Professionals can act irresponsibly, and shared decision making can produce irresponsible decisions. Publicity can, on occasion, distort an administrator's perspective, because what is immediate "good press" is not always most beneficial to the public. These caveats notwithstanding, these three "Ps"—professionalism, participation, and publicity—provide a basis for better public management. As they become more a part of bureaucratic behavior, such behavior may move closer toward meeting the desires and demands of the people.

# THINK ABOUT IT!

**American Society of Public Administration Code of Ethics**

Since 1984, ASPA has promoted a commitment to high standards of ethical practice by public servants. The Code of Ethics presents the key principles that public servants should advance, and its educational and review activities support the ethical behavior of members and hold them accountable for adhering to these principles.

**ASPA Code Of Ethics**

The American Society for Public Administration (ASPA) advances the science, art, and practice of public administration. The Society affirms its responsibility to develop the spirit of responsible professionalism within its membership and to increase awareness and commitment to ethical principles and standards among all those who work in public service in all sectors. To this end, we, the members of the Society, commit ourselves to uphold the following principles:

1. **Advance the Public Interest.** Promote the interests of the public and put service to the public above service to oneself.
2. **Uphold the Constitution and the Law.** Respect and support government constitutions and laws, while seeking to improve laws and policies to promote the public good.
3. **Promote democratic participation.** Inform the public and encourage active engagement in governance. Be open, transparent and responsive, and respect and assist all persons in their dealings with public organizations.
4. **Strengthen social equity.** Treat all persons with fairness, justice, and equality and respect individual differences, rights, and freedoms. Promote affirmative action and other initiatives to reduce unfairness, injustice, and inequality in society.

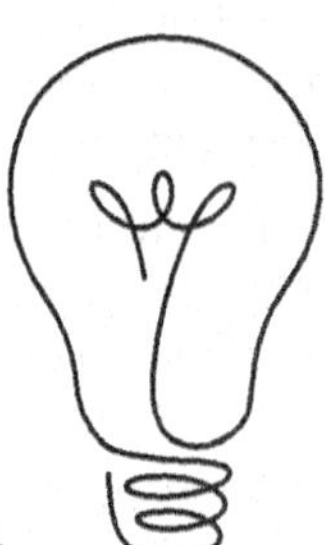

5. **Fully Inform and Advise.** Provide accurate, honest, comprehensive, and timely information and advice to elected and appointed officials and governing board members, and to staff members in your organization.
6. **Demonstrate personal integrity.** Adhere to the highest standards of conduct to inspire public confidence and trust in public service.
7. **Promote Ethical Organizations:** Strive to attain the highest standards of ethics, stewardship, and public service in organizations that serve the public.
8. **Advance Professional Excellence:** Strengthen personal capabilities to act competently and ethically and encourage the professional development of others.

*Members of ASPA commit themselves to support the Code of Ethics and may be sanctioned for their failure and refusal to uphold the Code.*

*Source:* http://www.aspanet.org/public/ASPA/About_ASPA/Code_of_Ethics/ASPA/Resources/Code_of_Ethics/Code_of_Ethics1.aspx?hkey=222cd7a5-3997-425a-8a12-5284f81046a8, 2015.

## Summary

- The principles of administrative law are grounded in constitutionalism, shared powers, popular government, individualism, and political equality.
- Independent regulatory agencies, uniform administrative procedure law, judicial review, and rulemaking are traditional cornerstones of administrative law. Public participation in the administrative process, the administrative process in formal and informal governmental activity, and the evolving definition of the mission of administrative agencies and development of oversight of their activities are contemporary cornerstones of U.S. administrative law.
- Honesty, fairness, and productivity are characteristics of American patriotism and must be practiced by every government employee. Even from the standpoint of effectiveness, it is smart for public administrators to be moral in carrying out government functions. The credibility of government is at stake. Laws, rules, and government regulations should be grounded in ethics, integrity, and organizational commitments.
- Administrative law and regulatory law act in tandem, but they are not the same. Agencies and departments, cooperating with legislatures, create regulatory law. Regulatory law governs the private activities of citizens; administrative law governs the regulators, applying principles originating from statutes, common law, constitutions, and regulatory laws. The provisions of adequate notice, disclosure of reasons, the right to a hearing, and right to further appeal entail a set of rules that administrators must follow to meet due process requirements.
- After a century of intense litigation and adjudication, the field of administrative law is still alive with issues. Hearsay evidence and the double role of judge and prosecutor are key controversies of administrative law, affecting public administrators and clientele.
- The major aspects of the administrative process include delegation of power, judicial review, the investigatory power, the rule-making process, the right to be heard, adjudicatory policy making, informal activity and the exercise of discretion, remedies against improper administrative acts, and opening up the government.
- Administrative agencies adjudicate individual claims or cases. The procedures are diverse. Administrative hearings focus on disputed questions of fact.
- An administrative hearing has no jury. The administrative law judge, or hearing examiner, is likely to be concerned about overall policies. The particular merits of one party's case have less consequence.
- Agencies accomplish most work with informal procedures. They exercise discretion granted to them by statute.
- Judicial review of agency action provides controls over administrative behavior. For the person who is harmed by a particular agency decision, judicial review operates to provide relief.
- The question of administrative control has two distinct aspects—internal and external controls.
- Democratic government rests on principles such as accountability and responsibility; the realization of such principles requires a comprehensive system of administrative control. The public has a right to demand, and administrators have a need to accept, a widespread network of restraints and restrictions on administrative activity. Democratic government is controlled government.
- Regulations take force because the market or markets fail or otherwise do not work effectively. U.S. regulatory activities began with the establishment of the Interstate Commerce Commission in 1887. Decision makers cannot collect all relevant information, so they use the best source of information available: what has just happened. Government oversight and information reflect this perspective.
- The full scope of regulatory power—in addition to the power to formulate rules—includes the authority for interpreting laws and regulations, enforcing rules and regulations, trying cases concerning violations of those rules, holding hearings for investigating and adjudicating such circumstances, and imposing sanctions on violators. Administrative regulatory power combines legislative, executive, and judicial powers.
- The United States is a regulatory state where nearly all activities of organizations and individuals are part of administrative regulations and controls. There are three types of regulatory behaviors: economic, social, and subsidiary.

- Economic regulation is the more traditional, industry-specific form of regulation. These regulators employ economic controls such as price ceilings and service parameters. These departments and agencies regulate a broad base of activities in particular industries. Examples of economic regulatory agencies are the Federal Communications Commission, the Federal Deposit Insurance Corporation, and the Federal Trade Commission.
- Social regulation focuses on achieving cleaner air, equal employment opportunity, safer work environments, and consumer safety. Social regulatory departments and agencies are limited to a specific issue, but their prerogatives include regulatory powers that penetrate and spread through industry boundaries. Examples are the Environmental Protection Agency, the Drug Enforcement Agency, and National Labor Relations Board.
- Subsidiary regulation includes regulatory activities related to Social Security, Medicare, Medicaid, SNAP, veterans' benefits, and other entitlement programs.
- The Federal Register provides a uniform system for making available to the public regulations and legal notices issued by federal departments and agencies. The Register includes presidential proclamations and Executive Orders and federal agency documents having general applicability and legal effect.
- The Code of Federal Regulations is a codification of the general and permanent rules published in the Federal Register by the executive departments and agencies of the federal government. The Federal Register and The Code of Federal Regulations are used in tandem to determine the latest version of any rule or regulation.
- Administrative power expands as the power and responsibilities of government expand. An industrialized, urbanized, interdependent society requires a more active role for government.
- Rulemaking and adjudication are not the same. Rulemaking is general and focuses on the future. Adjudication is particular, focusing on the present or the past. Administrative agencies interpret vagueness, ambiguity, and generality of laws; public administrators, as implementers of regulatory law, interpret rules. The terms rules and regulations are synonymous. There are four types of agency rules: legislative, or substantive, rules; interpretative rules; procedural rules; and general policy statements.
- Administrative responsibility entails the ideas of accountability, competence, fairness, and responsiveness. Executive control, pluralism, professionalism, and representative bureaucracy are especially important for achieving administrative responsibility. There are four types of accountability: bureaucratic, legal, professional, and political.
- Professionalism, participation, and publicity contribute significantly to administrative responsibility and provide a sound basis for better public management.

## Videos, Films and Talks

Please visit *The Craft of Public Administration* at www.millenniumhrmpress.com for up-to-date videos, films, talks, readings, and additional class resources.

What is Administrative Law? [6 min]
Tech Policy Lab, University of Washington
https://www.youtube.com/watch?v=ow5hZmU7Yfw

Is it Time to Update the Administrative Procedure Act? [3 min]
Christopher J. Walker
https://www.youtube.com/watch?v=WGrcnbe38R0

Ethical Leadership [5 min]
Notre Dame Deloitte Center for Ethical Leadership
John Heiser, President & COO of Magnetrol
https://www.youtube.com/watch?v=gbtVmR5WHUo

Whistleblower Protection and the Truth:
Linked intimately [18 min]
Tom Michael Devine, TEDxWilmingtonSalon
https://www.youtube.com/watch?v=WXUrYIFEZ08

## Suggested Readings

**Implementing the ASPA Code of Ethics: Workbook and Assessment Guide**
https://www.aspanet.org/ASPADocs/Membership/Ethics_Assessment_Guide.pdf

**Practices to Promote the ASPA Code Of Ethics**
https://www.aspanet.org/ASPADocs/ASPA%20Code%20of%20Ethics-2013%20with%20Practices.pdf

**Guide to the Federal Rulemaking Process**
https://www.federalregister.gov/uploads/2011/01/the_rulemaking_process.pdf

**Administrative Procedure Act**
https://www.archives.gov/federal-register/laws/administrative-procedure

## Notes

1. Jerre S. Williams, "Cornerstone of American Administrative Law," *Administrative Law Review* 28 (1976): v–xii.

2. Florence Heffron and Neil McFeeley, *The Administrative Regulatory Process* (New York: Longman, 1883), pp. 347–371.

3. Williams, "Cornerstone," pp. v–xii.

4. Kenneth F. Warren, *Administrative Law in the American System* (St. Paul, MN: West, 1982), pp. 111– 122.

5. Dwight Waldo, *The Enterprise of Public Administration: A Summary View* (Novato, CA: Chandler & Sharp, 1980). See especially Chapter 6, "Bureaucracy and Democracy: Reconciling the Irreconcilable," pp. 81–98.

6. Bernard Schwartz, *Administrative Law* (Boston: Little, Brown, 1976), p. 2.

7. Stanley A. Reigel and P. John Owen, *Administrative Law: The Law of Government Agencies* (Ann Arbor, MI: Ann Arbor Science, The Butterworth Group, 1982), pp. 4–5.

8. Lief H. Carter, *Administrative Law and Politics: Cases and Comments* (Boston: Little, Brown, 1983), p. 60.

9. *Richardson v. Perales,* 402 US 389 (1971).

10. "The 'Hidden Judiciary' and What It Does," *U.S. News & World Report,* November 1, 1982.

11. "Administrative Law and Procedure—Continued," *West Legal Directory,* July 4, 2002, http://www.wld.com/conbus/weal/wadmin2.htm.

12. Alexander Hamilton, John Jay, and James Madison, *The Federalist Papers* (New York: Modern Library, n.d.), p. 337.

13. Ralph Nader, Peter Petkas, and Kate Blackwell, eds., *Whistle-Blowing* (New York: Bantam Books, 1972).

14. Ibid., pp. 39–55.

15. Quoted in George E. Berkley, *The Democratic Policeman* (Boston: Beacon Press, 1969), pp. 159–160.

16. Hamilton, Jay, and Madison, *The Federalist Papers*, p. 337.

17. "Why Regulation Matters," The Regulation Home Page, regulation.org, http://www.regulation.org/ whyregs.html.

18. Daniel J. Gifford, *Administrative Law: Cases and Materials* (Cincinnati: Anderson, 1992), pp. 1–9.

19. Florence Heffron with Neil McFeeley, *The Administrative Regulatory Process* (New York: Longmans, 1983), pp. 1–23.

20. Robert Longley, About.com: US Government Info; see http://usgovinfo.about.com/library/ weekly/ blfedregs.htm?

21. Murray Weidenbaum, *A New Approach to Regulatory Reform* (St. Louis, MO: Center for the Study of American Business, 1998), pp. 2–3. See also Thomas D. Hopkins, *Regulatory Costs in Profile* (St. Louis, MO: Center for the Study of American Business, 1996).

22. Susan Dudley and Melinda Warren, "Regulatory Response: An Analysis of the Shifting Priorities of the U.S. Budget for Fiscal Years 2002 and 2003," Mercatus Center, Arlington, VA, and the Murray Weidenbaum Center on the Economy, Government, and Public Policy, St. Louis, MO, 2002, www.mercatus.org & www.wc.wust.edu.

23. Hopkins, *Regulatory Costs,* pp. 3–12; Weidenbaum, *A New Approach*, pp. 2–8.

24. Douglas R. Wholey and Susan M. Sanchez, "The Effects of Regulatory Tools on Organizational Populations," *Academy of Management Review* 16, no. 4 (October 1991): 743–767.

25. Wholey and Sanchez, "The Effects of Regulatory Tools," pp. 743–767.

26. Heffron with McFeeley, *The Administrative Regulatory Process,* pp. 347–371.

27. James T. O'Reilly, *Administrative Rule Making: Structuring, Opposing, and Defending Federal Agency Regulations* (New York: McGraw-Hill), pp. 4–6.

28. Lief H. Carter, *Administrative Law and Politics: Cases and Comments* (Boston: Little, Brown, 1983), pp. 14–39.

29. Administrative Procedure Act, P.L. 404, 60 Stat. 237(1946), 5 U.S.C.A. 551.

30. William F. West, *Administrative Rule-Making: Politics and Processes* (Westport, CT: Greenwood Press, 1985), p. 17.

31. Darlene Superville, "*Federal Register* Celebrates 70th Birthday," *Boston Globe*, March 14, 2006.

32. Walter Lippman, *The Public Philosophy* (Boston: Little, Brown, 1955), p. 42.

33. Glendon A. Shubert, Jr., *The Public Interest* (New York: Free Press, 1952), p. 223.

34. Carl Friedrich, "Public Policy and the Nature of Administrative Responsibility" in *The Politics of the Federal Bureaucracy,* ed. Alan A. Altshuler (New York: Dodd, Mead, 1968), p. 417.

35. Ibid.

# Integrate Theory with Practice: Bringing Public Administration to Life

- **Introduction:** The Case Study Method
- **Case 1:** Darn Tootin' Environmental Impact
- **Case 2:** Kaizen Goes Public
- **Case 3:** Community and Economic Development

# INTRODUCTION: The Case Study Method

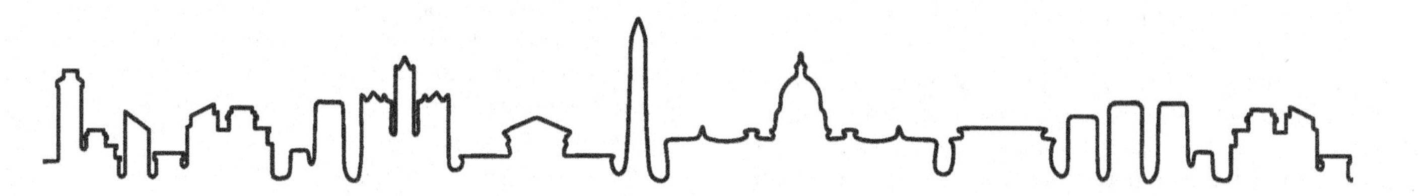

The cases provided in this module enable class participants to confront a number of complex administrative and public policy issues and make decisions or recommendations on how they believe the dilemmas, issues, and problems should be handled. In the processes surrounding the case (incident) analysis, the participants should be asked to assume a variety of specific roles such as the role of administrative consultant, program director, department head, policy analyst, staff analyst, administrative colleague, etc., in relation to the specific problems of the case. Typically, in a small group situation, the learners will analyze the problems and present their respective recommendations and evaluations.

Each case was developed to emphasize a particular administrative idea, notion, concept, or theory related to effective managerial performance. In dealing with unfamiliar problems, the class participants will gain experiences in differentiating the important or salient characteristics from the unimportant or irrelevant facts of the case. In turn, a systematic way of analyzing administrative realities will be encouraged throughout the course. This disciplined approach to thinking and analysis will assist participants in identifying the nature or root causes of the problem, the kind of problem for which a resolution is sought, the type of analytical or administrative techniques that would be appropriate to the solution of the problem, and the alternatives available to the public decision-maker. Also, the consequences and potential impacts of a decision on the organizational and political environment will be assessed.

## Introduction to the Case Study Method

The use of cases in facilitating the learning process is a well-established one, especially in the study of medicine, law, nursing, public administration and management. Cases are increasingly becoming a staple learning tool in the study of pharmacy, information systems, statistics, accounting, public relations, and marketing. In the discipline of public management, we have historically valued the many contributions that Syracuse University and Harvard University, among many others, made to the case study methodology over the past 80 years. While case studies themselves do not technically form a "research methodology," they represent a choice by the authors of this work to use a single case or story to bring together learners and have them focus their attention on a set of particular facts, situations, and questions. The case study method uses a single story, incident, or slice of organizational life to explore the nature of administration, management, and public policy making. This method enables the student to follow an argument in a forum in which additional ideas and counterclaims are made by one's colleagues, and

then collectively scrutinized and evaluated in class. In using the case study approach to learning, one will frequently hear the following overgeneralized argument—"One case does not create a theory or set of practices that can be used in all other situations." Overall, this claim is accurate. Case studies cannot claim to result in the development of a uniform theory or practice that can be generalized to subsequent, or for that matter, even similar situations. It is not the purpose of these cases to develop a generalizable statement that would be true in all situations—this is even difficult to do under the most carefully controlled environment in which the experimental scientist labors. Instead, the goal here is simply to discover methods by which we can more clearly understand situations that impact our organizational and life experiences. If, in the final analysis, continued research and discussion leads those of us who are actively engaged in analyzing the case studies to have an expanded and continuing conversation, and if this conversation leads us to the conclusion that the notions and theories developed as a result of these cases are sound, then the argument of generalization related to this research and method of study will have been sufficiently satisfied.

Although it is not proposed here that case analysis replace the more traditional models of academic learning, it is suggested that the case approach adds a needed dimension to the learning of public-management concepts. Further, teaching and learning through experiences provide a framework in which analytical and communication skills can be developed. In this structured milieu, the pupil shares with the instructor both the responsibility and the control of the learning processes. It is a process in which learning is active rather than passive; an approach that uses both problem-centered as well as theory-based types of learning. The primary goal of the case study approach; therefore, is to enable the maximum transfer of learning to take place in terms of knowledge acquisition, attitude change, problem solving and interpersonal skill development, and knowledge retention, by integrating theory with active participation and action (decision-making). Laurence E. Lynn, Jr., of the John F. Kennedy School of Government suggests that the case study approach helps fulfill this goal, and as a learning mechanism facilitates the development of these desired managerial, human relations, and effective communication attributes and skills.

In using the case study method, the learner becomes the "centerpiece and essential target" of the learning process. Unlike the more prescriptive types of learning characterized by textbook material and lecture formats, professionals are recognized as coming into the classroom milieu from many different backgrounds, coupled with a wealth of different managerial and administrative experiences. In the case study methodology, these experiences are valued and serve as a reservoir of empirical observations that participants have learned about the behaviors of individuals, groups, organizations and institutions and how they individually or collectively respond to different dilemmas or situations. As such, the student brings to each case study a set of perspectives—some well-developed and others less well formulated. In the aggregate, however, these viewpoints help to shape their attitudes, values, beliefs, and opinions about organizational and human behavior and their conceptualization of the basic nature of people in terms of what motivates them (external or internal), how they respond to authority, and, in the final analysis, whether they can be trusted. Of course, the theoretical perspective (philosophy) that learners have about the nature of people will influence the variety of managerial techniques that will seem appropriate to them in dealing with opportunities, problems, or threats that they face in real organizational living. That is, philosophy impacts the techniques of management.

The overall success of the case study methodology is predicated on the assumption that participants will come to each class meeting well prepared. This methodology can be utilized in various pedagogical approaches including flip-classroom and problem-based situational learning systems. The instructor can adjust the methodology to best suit the learners and the learning environment. That means, they will have read and analyzed the case study assigned for the class period. As such, the main administrative and policy issues need to be identified, and the student needs to ascertain the relevance of the various administrative concepts, ideas, theories, notions, and

techniques, as they pertain to managing organizations today. In addition to identifying the major issues, learners should attempt to isolate what the facts are in each case study. As we know, facts are elusive at times, and we are reminded that what we see can be influenced by the position we have in the organization. It is also important to note here what social psychologists have formulated in theory long ago: "assumptions affect perceptions;" that is, what we see is pretty much determined by what we wish or want to see. Further, learners need to know who the major actors are in the incidents that they analyze. This requires that they identify the key persons, departments/units or agencies, and discern if the case study involves a variety of customers—both internal and external—and identify the plethora of stakeholders who normally have an interest in the outcome of public choices. It also requires that participants understand the business of making public policy and administering the people's business is both complicated and messy. This sentiment is reinforced by the often-cited maxim of public policy: "We are not making sausage; rather, we are making public choices." This means, by definition, that judgments of worth be made—that is, what is "right, best, optimal, efficient, necessary," and what is valued. The magnitude and type of value or worth assigned to any issue, problem, relationship, or possible outcome is related to the repertoire of experiences and beliefs that the administrator holds, and this, is certainly influenced by one's formal education, and of course, the composite of one's life experiences.

In addition, learners are asked to identify if any rules or regulations, etc., need to be changed to implement their decisions, or to discern if there is precedence for the action that they wish to take. Participants also should attempt to discern if the case study presents any clues that will help identify the interests, needs, motivations, and personalities of the actors involved in the case. In the final analysis, participants are asked to engage in a learning assessment. That is, what do the concepts, theories, notions, etc., identified in the case study mean to each student? What do these concepts and theories mean to the student in the role of a manager and how can this learning be put to use outside the classroom? Learners are asked to assess if there are any difficulties that one would expect to encounter during the implementation or evaluation phase associated with their decisions or choices. Finally, participants are asked to reflect upon how they might enhance the learning value received from the group discussion and analysis of the case studies, and how personally they might in subsequent cases learn more by making additional contributions to the case analysis and discussion.

Also, if the learner wishes to maximize the learning acquired and retained, sharpen their decision making and problem-solving skills, and enhance their interpersonal skills, it is necessary that they take each case study seriously, assume the role called for in the Questions and Instructions portion of each case study, are prepared for the case discussion, participate in the case analysis and discussion, and encourage their colleagues to become similarly engaged. They also should look at the discussion as an opportunity to achieve a heightened awareness of their own values, ideologies, and beliefs—thereby achieving a better self-understanding of the merits and limitations of their own managerial philosophies. In the final analysis, it would be desirable if everyone engaged in the analysis of the case studies developed a better understanding and appreciation of their own managerial philosophy. It also would be laudatory if everyone could better discern and appreciate the natural linkages that exist between "theory and practice"—a connection that all too frequently gets lost in the academe and the workplace.In the processes associated with critical thought and reflection on the issues associated with the case studies, participants will be encouraged to share their personal experiences and perspectives with the other participants in the class. When experiential learning is utilized in an open, honest and safe environment, the learning is usually more effective, and the experiences encountered become more memorable and meaningful. As the cases get discussed, the richness of the collective background of the course participants will become apparent. The variety and magnitude of your colleagues' collective leadership experiences will reveal—whether they have occurred in the more traditional public, nonprofit, or private organizations or in a diverse "hybrid" community-based organization, the general workplace, the family or other organizations—an impressive array of observations and examples. For instance, in dealing with valuing differences or diversity (pluralism), specific discussions might take place on how the scenarios presented in the cases affect African-Americans, Asians, Latinos, gay/lesbian, bisexual, transgender, questioning, and persons with disabilities. But diversity goes well beyond these traditional areas of interest and includes veteran status, socio-economic status, age, ways of thinking, appearance, national origin, gender, and lifestyle.

When the critical components of the cases are analyzed and discussed, many divergent perspectives will emerge and personal beliefs, values, and ideologies will reveal their sometimes "passionate" and not so easily compromised or resolved perspectives or choices. During this hopefully vigorous exchange between members of the group, new interpersonal relationships will be formed. How the class participants deal with these newly formed relationships will affect the overall course effectiveness and be associated with the zeal, enthusiasm, or reluctance in which the learners take on the various challenges presented in the case studies.

It is known by writers of case studies, that cases that reflect real-world scenarios often require input from many different sources. Such is the case with the cases contained in this edition of *The Craft of Public Administration* since these cases are based on the collective experiences of the authors and their associates. The names and identities of the key actors or their organizational affiliations are not revealed in some cases, and sometimes the cases represent a composite of multiple similar situations, issues, dilemmas, problems that require analysis, interpretations, and purposive decision-making. We wish to again emphasize that any names or organization identities used are constructed to conceal the actual identities of those portrayed.

The hidden secret—if there is one—in making the case studies presented in this book come to life, is to know what is needed to spark "zeal and enthusiasm" for the cases and the major and minor concepts embedded in them. Thus, the class truly belongs to the participants, and it is their primary responsibility, augmented by the class moderator or facilitator, to see that communication is multi-directional. It is important that class participants actively participate in the case under examination, do what is suggested in the questions and instructions portion, listen actively to their colleagues and cognitively and emotionally try on for themselves the solutions and remedies offered by others, and come to class prepared having read the case, analyzed the situations, and developed responses to the selected questions which they can defend in class. By doing this, we have found over the years, that the instructional technique that most helpfully links proficiency and knowledge with the general areas of administrative-management practices and human relations has been the case study. Lastly, it is important to realize that most case problems do not easily submit to simple solutions and there are many potential answers or solutions to the problems presented. That means, there is simply no one best answer for each question; instead, there are many ways to deal with a problem or issue satisfactorily—the principle of equifinality. The operations of governmental agencies, private businesses and nonprofit organizations are complex and when we touch the work of those employed in these environments we actually "...touch their lives." Overall, it is necessary that we keep focused on our analyses and place the problems and issues discussed within a broader societal context with its competing economic, social, psychological, political, ideological, legal and technological interests and demands.

The authors believe it is important to formalize the individual learning assessment so that pre-class reading, and analysis can be integrated and synthesized with the in-class learning experience. Often the course facilitator or instructor will ask that individual assessments be submitted as part of the course and learning requirements for further evaluation purposes or shared with members of a team or group for peer review and comment. To encourage and facilitate teamwork, a number of cases are well suited by issues, problems, complexity, and length. These cases may be assigned early on in the course and the analysis presented at the end of course. Although the actual format used for presentation of the case study analysis, such as executive summations, simulations, to PowerPoint presentations, etc., may vary, the class will normally be broken into sub-groups or teams of four to five learners. Since these cases are more comprehensive, the issue identification, critical thinking, and problem-solving skills required are more demanding.

Group or teamwork is by its nature collaborative learning. This kind of learning involves engagement, inclusion, listening, analyzing, investigating, reflective thinking and, of course comprehension. It is a form of active versus passive learning. Studies show that active learning increases retention, comprehension, integration and synthesis of theory and practice. The authors of this casebook have used group learning and problem-solving methods in many diverse courses, which they have facilitated over the years: human resource management, urban management, state and local government, research methods and statistics, public policy analysis, etc., and ethics in public administration. A note of caution is in order, if group learning is to reach its highest objectives it should be based on a well-developed design, plan, system, or carefully reasoned approach. If the overall design is poorly focused, then the results will be difficult to evaluate or assess (measure). With this "yellow light" on focus, our collective experience with cases assigned to different groups has resulted in higher levels of understanding and an increased ability to lead and relate to peers. In the end, skills associated with evidence and data presentation are sharpened, communication skills are augmented, and the ability to make cogent arguments are refined. As we related in *Solving Public Management Problems*, team learning enables peers to motivate one another, earn how to delegate and develop a profound sense of accountability, and of course throughout this complicated process have time for laughter, fun, and joy.

It is important to note that the analysis of the many concepts and issues embedded in these cases will require careful planning if they are to be confidently and professionally presented to their counterpart peer groups.

In the processes associated with critical thought and reflection on the issues associated with the case studies, participants will be encouraged to share their personal experiences and perspectives with the other participants in the class. When experiential learning is utilized in a honest and safe environment, the learning is usually more effective, and the experiences encountered become more memorable and meaningful. As the cases get discussed, the richness of the collective background of the course participants will become apparent. The variety and magnitude of the collective leadership experiences will reveal whether they have occurred in the more traditional public, nonprofit, or private organizations, or in diverse "hybrid" community-based organizations, the general workplace, the family or other organizations.

Last, the authors have consulted with many instructors and students who have used the case studies they have researched and written. One theme expressed frequently, is the overall efficacy of the learning process, especially the transferability of what has been experienced in the cases analyzed to other real-life situations. Although we have emphasized the case study methodology is particularly useful in integrating experiential knowledge with its substantive counterpart, one limiting factor is the adequacy and completeness of the literature reviewed and how it informs the analysis. The concepts embedded in the case studies, such as communication style, organization and motivation theories, leadership style, etc., serve as natural, substantive areas that should be reviewed when bringing the questions to their full exploration and analysis.

*Source: Excerpted and adapted, in part, from C. Kenneth Meyer, et al, "Introduction to the Case Study Approach," in C. Kenneth Meyer, et al, Managing America's Organizations, Des Moines: Millennium HRM Press, 2006. Reprinted with permission.* 

# CASE 1:
## Darn Tootin' Environmental Impact

By C. Kenneth Meyer, Leah Hutchinson, Jeffrey A. Geerts, and Lance Noe

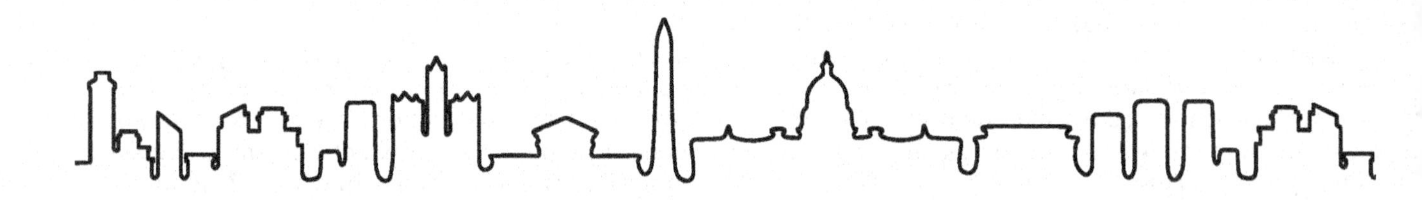

Uncle Timothy Plano, as he is affectionately called by his nieces and nephews, has ranched in Elk County, Kansas, for the past 50 years. As such, he often recounts the "worst to the best years" in his run at making a living off the "fat of the land." His 4,000-acre ranch has been in his family for several generations, and he hopes it will someday become a legacy farm as defined by state law.

As a child, he grew up on the ranch helping out where he could, and then, as he grew older, eventually upon the death of his father, took over the family brand—Barr Double Zero Ranch. Tim, as an agricultural aficionado, often waxes eloquently to those in his presence, about the cattle business, and all those who have patiently endured his long, and folksy tales, come away with realization that ranching is an uncertain and sometimes tumultuous life! In a typical encounter, Tim talks about the work beginning at the break of dawn, and arduously, coming to a close as the moon begins to rise in the East. Tim reminiscences about how his brothers and sisters endured many hardships growing up on the isolated ranch, knowing, and begrudgingly accepting the fact that there would be good times and bad times—but not fully comprehending how the number of bad times would eclipse the good times, especially with the financial problems associated with the occurrence of drought after drought. In the narrative that Tim painted, the unforeseeable and unchangeable environmental factors played a role in the agricultural success for farmers and ranchers of the Great Plains.

Now, Tim is all too ready to recount his concerns about the over regulation and monitoring by state government agencies of his cow-calf business, but mostly about what he terms the "intrusive laws and regulations" emanating from the federal level of government. And this is how he tells the story.

The U.S. Department of the Interior (USDOI), Bureau of Land Management (USBLM) was established to protect the long-term health and productivity of the rangelands. Cattle grazing, everyone realized, can cause damage to soil, plants, streams, springs, and wildlife. The BLM required that all cattle ranchers obtain a grazing permit for land use. As such, they must then uphold the stipulations and guidelines in their contract, established by federal statutory law. A grazing fee is required per cattle calculated by a formula set by Congress in the Public Rangelands Improvement Act of 1978 (PRIA, 1978). On top of that, cattle operators must adhere to the mandates of the Taylor Grazing Act of 1934 (TGA, 1934), that established grazing districts, the National Environmental Policy Act of 1969 (NEPA, 1969), Federal Land Policy and Management Act of 1976 (FLPMA, 1976), and the Endangered Species Act of 1973 (ESA, 1973). These environmental protective stipulations require pricey construction. For example, fences, cattle guards, facilities and structures are mandated to be constructed. Grants are available; however, and most of the cattle operators are held responsible for 100 percent of all labor and construction costs. Tim Plano soon realized he had little say in how to manage the land he inherited, the land he grew up on and worked his entire life! As he often has stated, "The land belongs to me but is controlled by the feds."

Tim Plano has researched the environmental standards and knows about some of the empirical studies pertaining to environmental impact statements. In the past, the United States Environmental Protection Agency (USEPA) introduced methane as one of the main greenhouse gases (GHG) to be regulated. Second only to carbon dioxide (85 percent), methane (CH4) accounts for 10 percent of GHG emissions in the atmosphere that is emitted by human related activities. According to Tim, the EPA data show that cattle emit methane from a digestive process called *enteric fermentation*—a process that occurs in the multi-chambered stomachs or digestive systems of ruminant animals, such as cattle, buffalo, camels, and sheep. As the microbial enzymes are produced in their digestive system and course food (grass, hay, silage, etc.) is broken down, methane is released outside their body as a by-product. This potent, atmospheric damaging gas is either exhaled or belched from the mouth, or well, expelled as flatulence, as shown in **Figure 1**.

The EPA acknowledged, according to Tim, that the cow-calf sector of the industry is the main culprit. Beef cows are responsible for the most emissions because they are large animals; their diets, consist mainly of forages of varying quality, and they are generally poorer than in the dairy or feedlot sectors; the level of management is typically not as good; and mainly because of the sheer number of cow-calf medium sized farms in the Midwest. The EPA estimates that methane emissions from beef and dairy cattle in the U.S. are distributed accordingly: feedlots and stockers, 19 percent; dairy, 23 percent; and cow-calf operations, 58 percent. Tim knows his laws and regulations and indicates that since the Clean Air Act of 1965 (CAA, 1965), the EPA has established Greenhouse Gas Regulations and reporting processes for large corporations. Businesses with over 29,300 head of cattle are required to report. This applies to large feedlots; yes, they are only responsible for 19 percent of total emissions.

**Figure 1. U.S. Methane Emissions by Source**

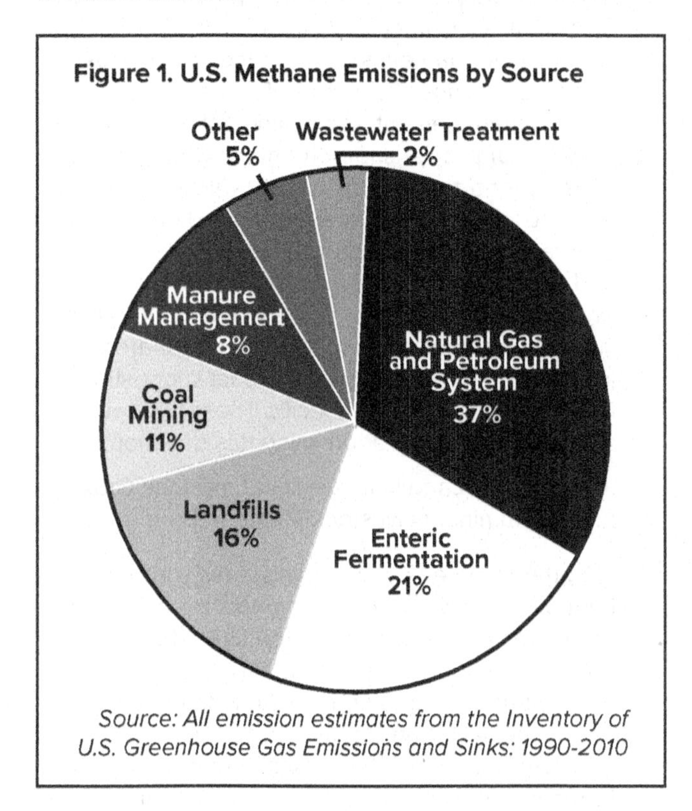


*Source: All emission estimates from the Inventory of U.S. Greenhouse Gas Emissions and Sinks: 1990-2010*

At a local Grange meeting, Tim learned that he EPA and environmental lobbyists were advocating stronger reporting standards, with accompanying taxes on methane emissions. As he was told, on the average, each rancher would have to pay $175 per cow if legislation passed muster. The tax commonly referred to as the "cow tax" angered Tim and others at the meeting—especially Western ranchers. Although the EPA issued a public statement denouncing the accuracy of the official tax proposal, ranchers were worried about the future, especially if the desire to curb greenhouse gases gained interest in the "liberal Obama administration."

On top of all the taxes, regulations, and bureaus that mandate Timothy Plano, he wonders if he will have any discretion on how he will manage his privately-owned cattle business in the future. He now has added a new line to his cowboy story: "The cow tax will make it hard to stay in business and taxing his cow's flatulence is 'just root'n tootin' ridiculous!"

## Questions and Instructions

1. Timothy Plano considers himself a steward of the land. He is sensitive and supportive of the many management practices that can improve a livestock operation's production efficiency and reduce greenhouse gas emissions. Some of the most effective practices he knows of include improving grazing management; soil testing, followed by the addition of proper supplements and fertilizers; supplementation of cattle diets with needed nutrients; development of a preventive herd health program; provision of appropriate water sources and protecting water quality; and improvement of genetics and reproductive efficiency. Do these suggestions have any remedial affects, or are they just "untested" environmental impact suggestions? Please elaborate and be specific. These two sources should be of help in addressing this question.
   a. Bureau of Land Management Livestock Grazing
   b. EPA Ruminant Livestock Methane Program
2. Timothy Plano enjoyed reading in his youth, Aldo Leopold's *A Sand County Almanac*. He embraced the ideas of Leopold and often cites this wise adage: "That land is a community is the basic concept of ecology, but that land is to be loved and respected is an extension of ethics." Do you think Tim's concern about excessive government intrusion in his business life is consistent with Leopold's dictum as stated here? Please present a cogent defense for your opinion.
3. In your opinion, should the Obama Administration, in an effort to decrease pollution, use the Clean Air Act to establish a tax on methane emissions for cow-calf businesses? Please explain.
4. Please consult either the department of agriculture or natural resources in your state and get their reactions to the Granges "hypothetical of an impending cow tax." What if any kinds of government programs could be established to decrease the amount of methane produced by cow-calf industries? Please elaborate.
5. Would it be fair to offer incentives or a tax credit to farming operations who agree to replant their pastures, modify their cow's diets, or alter genetics? If yes, why? If not, why not?
6. During the last twenty years or so, there has been a robust discussion about greenhouse gases and how they are or are not connected to climate change and the associated issues of rising sea levels, coral reef bleaching, uncontrollable wildfires, coastal housing values, changing (worldwide) migration patterns, severe storms, prolonged draught, hurricanes, and warming trends in Alaska to the Midwest, and the impact which humans, in general, have on their environment. Given your own understanding of methane emissions from the various sources as presented in **Figure 1**, how might these emissions be reduced without severely hurting economic growth and development in the United States? Please explain. Useful reference for addressing this question is found in 4th National Climate Assessment (see sources).
7. Much has changed over the last decade in the development of plant-based "meat" alternatives in the laboratories of nutritionists and food scientists. The meat alternatives are now amply available in grocery stores, food markets, and several international chain restaurants and touted as being environmentally safe since they are comprised of plant products or from animal cells grown in a laboratory. Please research the meat alternative movement and its estimated impact on food production in the United States and especially the economic and political pros and cons to this movement. Please be specific.

*Adapted and reprinted with permission, American Society of Business and Behavioral Sciences (ASBBS). Hutchison, Leah, Meyer, C. Kenneth, & Geerts, Jeffrey (2020). Darn Tootin' Environmental Impact. Journal of Business and Educational Leadership, Vol. 10, No. 1; Fall 2020.*

# CASE 2: Kaizen Goes Public

By Jeffrey A. Geerts, C. Kenneth Meyer and Lance Noe

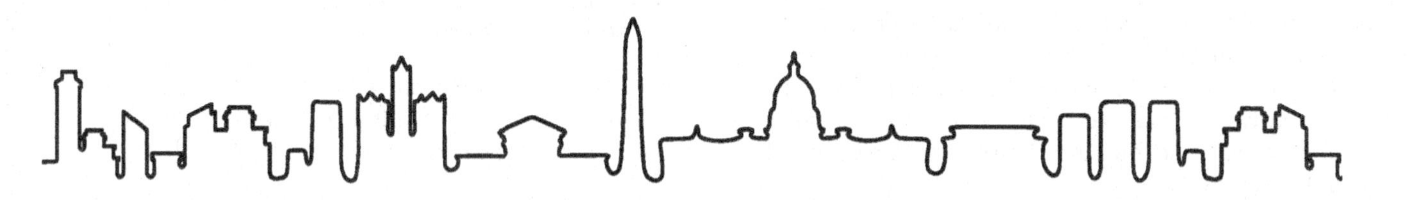

## PART ONE

Steve Anderson worked for the Department of Air Quality since the early 1970s. He was known by his colleagues as a tireless worker and, as such, as his tenure grew, so did his rank. In his younger years, when he had just completed college, he worked as a lab specialist and conducted air emissions tests throughout the state. Over three decades of working in the department, his responsibilities increased as his knowledge of air quality standards and regulations grew. He was fond of saying that he went to CHK for his education—the "College of Hard Knocks." In instances where the tension would rise in important meetings, he was always quick to be self-deprecating when it came to his understanding of bureaucracy and public policy, and now, there was no one in the department who questioned his expert knowledge or authority in the field of air monitoring sciences.

When asked to speak about air quality and environmental protection to business, industry, or manufacturing groups he did so eloquently. After all, no one in the state had a better grasp of the many standards associated with emission control and his knowledge was encyclopedic when it came to understanding the synergistic effects associated with combining different chemical emissions.

He would often say to those he was meeting for the first time, "I'm in the air business and we all need clean air for healthy living!"

When Steve Anderson was earning his business degree, he never thought his professional life and career employment would be so inextricably connected with monitoring and improving the quality of life for the state. Earlier on in his academic studies, he was exposed to quality of life and social indicator research, and then, like now, found it to be an intriguing field of study. He loved the measurement side of the field, especially when it came to the operationalization of concepts, such as poverty, health, civic enhancement, crime, social disintegration, and air and water quality, and he kept a portfolio of indices, formulas, and equations that might prove to be useful in assessing quality of life in general. As an undergraduate student, he studied business administration and marketing and he did everything that he could to hone his administrative skills. Now he had finally reached the position of supervisor for the air quality permitting program. His colleagues not only enjoyed working with him but among themselves they would frequently say that his knowledge and expertise are above reproach.

Anderson had seen a lot of changes in state government and air quality regulations during his years of governmental service. One of the biggest changes he experienced in state government was the passage and implementation of the national Clean Air Act. With the passage of the Clean Air Act, the state Department of Air Quality's workload increased tremendously. The number of companies needing air quality permits exploded from literally a handful to several thousand, but Anderson's staff didn't expand with the growth.

In commenting to those less experienced in the field, he would often say that, "New state rules had to be written and adopted, permitting procedures had to be developed and put into practice, and major industries with political clout wanted their permits yesterday." In a way, he wished he could have simply "boiler-plated" the federal manuals for the state.

He often reminisced in public conversation, "At least the Clean Air Act came with a funding source. It was not one of those pesky unfunded mandates."

The funding necessary to hire qualified staff to implement the Clean Air Act in the states came from the regulated industries that required the state program services. In the world of public administration, then as now, the trend of charging user-fees made sense to many in the legislature and in the department. Some industries, as expected, wanted reasonable standards and a fair fee structure; others argued with passion that, everyone benefits from clean air so everyone should contribute to funding the program. Some industrial representatives conceded that industry would in the final analysis be obligated to pay, but that the fee structure should be fair and equitable across the playing field, regardless of the type, kind, size or location of the regulated organization.

The riskiest political part of Anderson's job was to establish a fee structure that would be used by the state Department of Air Quality. Anderson and his staff had to determine a precise formula that could be used in its calculation. That is, they had to develop a high level of confidence in their expense and revenue estimates, and that would not be an easily accomplished task. Anderson knew that if they estimated revenue that would be excessive, that the legislative "movers and shakers" would not be happy, and, conversely, if the permitting expenses were underestimated, they would have to go back to the industry for higher fees in the future. Anderson was politically astute and savvy enough to realize that those industries with political clout and acumen to leverage it, would not appreciate a ratcheting-up of the permitting fees for air quality monitoring.

Anderson, when reflecting about the untenable position in which he found himself, would state, "It was if one was between the devil and a hard spot!"

As difficult as it might seem at first glance, the state and the regulated industries were able to reach agreement on a fee structure, however, along with industry payments came the corollary issue of industry expectations. In administrative parlance, Title V air permits were implemented as a function of the Clean Air Act, and these permits cost companies up to several thousands of dollars to obtain. In addition, in order to secure a permit, large amounts of paperwork had to be meticulously completed and this process was time consuming. Further, the permitting instructions were often confusing, filled with jargon and "bureaucratese," and difficult to follow. Some industries did not feel that they had the engineering expertise required to complete the application forms and, therefore, were required to hire specialized consultants at an additional cost.

As one industry CEO stated, "It cost us a tidy sum to have an outside engineer come in and serve as a consultant. We were required to fill out several thousand pages of documented material and translate the instructions into a common, understandable language. The instructions should have been written for the average consumer in the first place."

Other industry spokespersons noted, and they were correct in their assertion, that an air permit was required even before a new industry could begin plant construction and that a new permit was even required prior to making any modifications in the operation of an existing plant.

For the first two to three years of operation under the new federal law, the state Department of Air Quality issued air permits in approximately 120 days or four months. Thus, for one-third of a year, affected industries could not begin construction or make any plant modifications. As one might reasonably expect, the extensive waiting period became a very tense and stressful time for the applicants, as well as for Steve Anderson and his staff. As a new start-up program, Anderson and his staff had to learn the new program's requirements and, simultaneously, field questions and respond to pressures from the state legislators, various industries, environmental groups, residents and economic development officials.

After a few years passed, Anderson told a colleague during a private conversation, "It was a most trying time for all parties concerned—I never realized what a steep learning curve the department and industries would have to ascend. It was hard for all parties concerned and I actually felt empathy for those firms that were trying to act in a legal and socially responsible manner!"

As the "...regulations, standards, and specifications matured," Anderson frequently noted, "... the department lowered the turnaround time on air permits to only 65 to 80 days. This reduction in permitting time was largely associated with a larger staff that had eventually acquired the needed experience required to fully implement the law, augmented by a continuous quality improvement process that the department used."

In the long journey to proficiency, the staff and the department felt reasonably good about their ability to cut the permitting time by almost 50 percent, while at the same time developing and maintaining a good working relationship with the regulated industries.

Anderson noted in his monthly staff meetings that the fee for permits had not gone up during the past few years and that monthly client meetings were essential to keeping industries informed on department activities and pending federal regulatory measures. It came as a surprise to Anderson, when several industry leaders approached the department and stated that "much more process improvement was needed."

Henry Lopez, general manager for Consolidated Energy the state's largest private utility, and Jill Evans, director of lobbying for the State Association of Businesses, approached the Department of Air Quality about assisting it in some process improvement initiatives. Lopez and Evans were vehement when they argued that the 65 to 80-day turnaround for permits was too long. They stated that the delay in issuing permits was costing their companies money, put them at a competitive disadvantage, and placed the state at a disadvantage in attracting new businesses. They further asserted that the delay, especially in a couple of cases that they had firsthand knowledge of caused some businesses to consider out-of-state relocations.

Lopez and Evans further suggested to Steve Anderson that the air permitting staff go through a continuous quality improvement process called *Kaizen*. Evans and Lopez reported that the Kaizen process was used frequently in their companies and with great success.

Steve Anderson listened intently to what they had to say but expressed reservations. He explained that he first learned of continuous quality improvement practices in his college days and that his staff had put some of these efforts to work reducing the time it took to obtain a permit nearly in half. He expressed skepticism about how much more improvement would be possible.

"I think we have streamlined the permitting process and have removed nearly all bottle-necks and obstacles," said Anderson. "I don't believe further improvement is possible at this time."

He further informed Lopez and Evans that the members of his staff already had a full schedule trying to complete the permits in a timely fashion and that to implement the Kaizen process now would not only cost a lot of time and money, but it would negatively impact the timely response that industry had come to expect from his office.

Not to be dissuaded by obstacles to reform themselves, Lopez and Evans countered Anderson's objection by agreeing to fund the installation of the Kaizen process with private dollars. In addition, Lopez indicated that he knew about a change agent who was recognized internationally as a tremendous facilitator for the process, and Evans upped the already attractive proposal by offering to provide assistance from her own experienced staff who had successfully installed the Kaizen process in the business association.

Anderson thought about the determined attitude of the two prominent members of the business community and said he needed time to think about the offer, to do some research and to talk to other members of the department. "Thanks for the generous offer," Anderson stated to Lopez and Evans. "I know you are both convinced about the process and believe it will improve our operations as it has improved yours. I'll get back to you in two weeks."

Several weeks later, Steve Anderson invited Lopez and Evans to his office. He informed them that the Department of Air Quality would take them up on their generous offer, and that the staff was eager to be briefed and acquire the needed training. Anderson also asked that Lopez and Evans notify the industrial community that this effort would take place and to ask them for their patience as some delays in permitting might be expected to occur – especially with the large amount of time needed to initially learn and use the Kaizen process.

## Questions and Instructions

1. Does a 65-day to 80-day permit turnaround time seem like an acceptable length of time for this governmental service? What about other types of governmental services?
2. Is an industry-based fee or "polluter-pays" fee system appropriate for this example? Why or why not?
3. How much more influence on the Department of Air Quality do you think the user-pays fee system provides the industry? Why?
4. What other kinds of funding mechanisms could be used instead of the industry-paid permitting fee? What are the advantages and disadvantages of these other mechanisms?
5. Is it ethically responsible for the applicant industry to pay for the Kaizen process? Why or why not?
6. Does your answer to question number five change depending on whether just a few industry members provide the funding versus an industry association? If a donation or sponsorship is in order, should it be anonymous for the industry donors? Please explain.

## PART TWO

The big week has arrived! Steve Anderson has gathered his staff along with Henry Lopez, Jill Evans and her staff and the Kaizen consultant. For the last month, Steve Anderson's staff has been closely scrutinizing the current operations for opportunities for improvement. Also, job-related tasks and responsibilities have been reviewed and time and motion studies completed. Some members of the staff have researched the Kaizen process and Anderson attended a Kaizen process improvement program at a local industry.

During the span of a week, participants in the Kaizen process put in more than 60 hours. On the first day they learned about the Kaizen process and how and why it works. They also learned what was expected of them individually; as a group; and how the process would have to be fully embraced on an everyday basis, now and in the future if dividends were to be expected on their investment.

The second day was spent analyzing the current permitting process step-by-step, from the moment the application entered the building to the moment it left.

"No stone or cubicle was left unturned," as one staff assistant explained. Additional time and motion studies were done. All members of the staff were interviewed, including engineers, permit writers, administrative-support staff, custodial staff, information technology staff, and industry members. At the end of day two, it was determined that: of the 65 to 80 days it takes to issue a completed permit, only five hours was actually spent working on each permit from beginning to end. This was an astonishing revelation to the training participants. As iterated and reiterated many said, "Only five hours per permit! Unbelievable!"

On the third and fourth days, the participants were still somewhat stunned and amazed that only five hours went into each permit. The facilitator inspired and challenged them to work together and further identify ways to improve the process.

"We have tasted success already and the process has only begun," said the facilitator. "We can do better, and we will! We must now savor the success associated with the use of this powerful process."

Smiling and nodding toward the participants with an accepting approval, he asked them to fully explore and use the data collected on day two. The participants then began their journey of examining everything possible that would enhance the speed and accuracy of the permitting process. They constructed a document checklist that would be provided to the applicant and would ensure that a fully completed permit had been submitted. They designed a new electronic database and process tracking system; and they reassigned staff responsibilities in the permitting process that they now found to have caused delays. In the final analysis, they had been able to shorten the 65-day to 80-day permitting process to only eight days.

On the fifth day, the process of implementing the recommended process improvements began in earnest along with a celebration of their accomplishments. They laughed with one another as the facilitator asked them to burn the outdated rules and regulations in a Weber kettle that he had prepared for this purpose. The steps and obstacles that had impeded effective permitting were now gone forever and there was reason to celebrate!

They could have rested, but as one member noted, "They had experienced joy in improving the efficiency, and the effectiveness of the permitting process. Their journey had just begun and they were going to enjoy the ride."

## Questions and Instructions

7. Knowing now that the permitting process was reduced from as much as 80 days down to eight days, does this change any of your answers to questions 1, 5, and 6? In what ways? Please explain.

8. What, if anything, do you believe will need to be addressed before the Department of Air Quality will be able to fully implement all the necessary changes and lessen the permitting turnaround time to eight days? Keep in mind such issues as staff reassignment, office space configuration, and union contract issues. Please explain.

9. Name three or more additional continuous quality improvement processes or strategies and at least one of their strengths and weaknesses.

10. Knowing the dramatic turnaround that the department realized when it implemented the Kaizen process, would you recommend the process be tried on other public programs? Why or why not?

11. Are there any other ways to get workers involved in continuous quality improvement processes, especially since some employees and unions may fear loss of jobs if the process gets too efficient and if all redundancy is eliminated? Please explain.

12. Can you think of any advantage to building in a slight delay in the permit granting process? Please elaborate.

PART THREE

The Department of Air Quality's Kaizen process received substantial positive attention in the state's major newspaper and it even garnered several awards nationally and internationally. Within a year, the department had completed more than a dozen additional Kaizens covering several air quality programs, as well as programs in land quality, water and solid waste. The proof of the Kaizen process success was evident by the facts of the 60 percent reduction in the time required for permit processing and in the financial and technical assistance required, while simultaneously protecting the environment. As a result of the successful Kaizens, many additional staff members of the department were trained to facilitate future Kaizen processes. Kaizens were also conducted to improve internal departmental operations.

The adage that "...nothing sells like success," was most apropos and the reputation of the department rapidly spread to many other state agencies. The department became ever more entrepreneurial and began to "sell" its Kaizen facilitators to other state bureaus, commissions and agencies who in turn became valuable "home grown" specialists on the process.

Although the Kaizen process was initially approached with suspicion and measured acceptance, its successful implementation went well beyond anyone's wildest imagination. Today, the department and its programs are more efficient, customers report a higher level of satisfaction with the permitting process; and the department has objectively demonstrated an increase in effectiveness without increasing the cost of its operations. Of course, the department rightfully promotes, with pride, the many productivity improvements it has achieved. Indeed, as if fate would have its own revenge, perhaps it celebrated its many accomplishments too vigorously! Anderson was a cautious administrator, but he had enough administrative and political savvy to know that with successful ventures, there is a strange irony that often accompanies them.

As the "rest of the story" is now revealed, the legislators showed how much they valued the Kaizen success in the department when they singled it out for even greater financial scrutiny. The state's Legislative Audit Service was charged with the task of closely examining and auditing the department's operational budget. The completed audit report revealed no major operational deficiencies, and their analysis demonstrated that the department had realized substantial improvements in efficiency and productivity over the previous fiscal year. With the audit in hand, the legislators argued that the department did not require the previous higher level of funding due to their efficient and effective operations, and, therefore, reduced the departments appropriated budget by $700,000 for the next fiscal year.

The departmental administrators and staff faced this "twisted turn of fate" with a feeling of disbelief. They could not fathom what had just transpired before them and they let their feelings gush out concerning the fairness of the legislative process. In short, their hard work, innovativeness and success had been rewarded with punishment—and that made no sense at all.

## Questions and Instructions

13. What are your thoughts about the agency's legislative budget cut for becoming more efficient?
14. Does it make any political or administrative sense to reduce the department's budget as its level of efficiency and effectiveness improved? Please justify your response.
15. Who should decide how to invest or utilize savings accrued from increased productivity or improved efficiency? Would "gainsharing" be an appropriate administrative technique to be used in this instance? If yes, why? If no, why not?
16. What impact will the legislature's decision have on future Kaizen events and process improvement efforts? Please explain.
17. Do you think the department or other state agencies will be prone to use the Kaizen processes in the future given the legislature's action?
18. Should the agency have expected a reduction in its budget as its efficiency increased? Please explain.

# CASE 3: Community & Economic Development

By C. Kenneth Meyer and Jeffrey A. Geerts

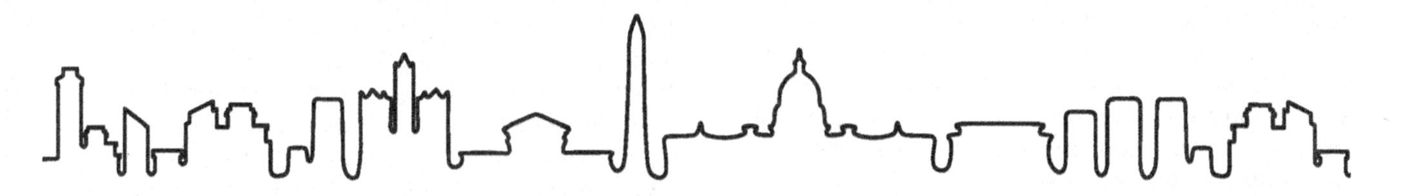

Jasper Stretch, the head of Green Isle's economic development department, prided himself of having his finger on the pulse of the Southeastern regional economy, and he was knowledgeable and conversant on national and global economic trends. Stretch was not a novice when it came to the management and development of things "economic" and his experience as an economic analyst, urban planner and former economics professor was transparent in the manner and ease that he conducted staff meetings, met with potential businesses and industries, and talked about the opportunities for Green Isle's economic and community growth and development. Over the years, Stretch had mastered many of the topics that had become the mainstay of professional conferences dedicated to learning the essential tools of the economic development business. Although he had a fault finding personality, he wondered why so much time at the conferences he attended was devoted to topics that were already reasonably known to those like himself her were already steeped in their careers and why so little training was given to "best practices," "collaborative management," and the philosophy associated with creating the sustainable community.

Green Isle was known as a regional economic center and served as a magnet for commerce in a five county area. It had sustained a steady population of about 630,000 persons and had witnessed the overall decline of its industrial, commercial, and financial base within the first several concentric zones that were immediately adjacent to its urban core. However, it had recently experienced growth in businesses, residential, and service areas in the outer rings of its jurisdiction and had witnessed a sizeable population and development shift most commonly connected with urban sprawl—estate homes, gated communities, Planned Unit Developments (PUDs), high density condominium, townhouses and apartments, and, of course, the ever growing strip malls with their low slung buildings rooted on a cement slab with an average life expectancy of thirty-five years.

As Jasper Stretch drove his car toward City Hall where his department was housed, he once more was reminded that many parts of Green Isle's "urbanscape" were undeveloped, underutilized, or were lying dormant. He fully recognized the effect of having housing and other parts of the built environment in derelict or run-down condition. He also noticed that some vacant or abandoned lots were located immediately adjacent to new immigrant settlements; others were in areas of the city that were in the process or had recently undergone urban redevelopment or as some affectionately called "gentrification;" and, still other parcels of land or lots were randomly scattered among a variety of different land use types: high density, residential, commercial, light industrial and varying combinations of mixed-land uses. As he motored in the city, he pondered on how unsightly the underutilized property and land had become and how it "showcased" the "aesthetics" of urban blight and decay in a city that was considered by most of its residents in an earlier time as having been reasonably well planned and groomed.

Today, however, Jasper Stretch would experience an ecological shock! He would experience the effect of letting his imagination trump his otherwise carefully guarded rational and cognitive style of thinking. In fact, Stretch could not believe what was beginning to flash through his mind. Mentally, he saw the blemishes on Green Isle's land cover as opportunities for "greening." Familiar by means of academic education and on-the-job experience, the visions of what might be possible raced by and he was now clearly beginning to see only a small number of the creative uses that had been unleashed. He questioned how the land that was underused and valued only for building development had taken on an entirely new worth. As he gave permission for his creative juices to bubble-up and out, he thought about how these vacant lots could be seen and understood as a blessing in disguise.

Green Isle had been mainly seen as a built environment and the vast majority of the structures still had some social, economic, and even architectural value. Stretch, however, was now beginning to see the blighted areas as representative "green spots" that could be used as basic resources in stabilizing and revitalizing neighborhoods and building a sustainable community. Stretch was zealous about his newly found discovery—even if it was only a mental abstraction at this time and wondered why he had not previously been privy to seeing or comprehending the natural, essential relationship between under used urban spaces and his deeply held values associated with creating sustainable leadership, sustainable organization, sustainable economy, and a sustainable environment.

Stretch met the new revelations and mental pictures he had of Green Isle with excitement and a sense of urgency. He let his mind roam more freely now and what he began to envision took on a picture of what might be possible, of a newly found reality—a city that would look quite different in the future and represent the latest social and economic values in their character and expressions. He thought about marshalling the resources needed to create a community garden program that would enable his community to better understand land as an essential resource that had economic, social and environmental value. He saw a changing landscape dotted with multiple gardens dedicated to unique neighborhood interests and needs. Some of the niche gardens would be predominantly used for mixed food production and in those plots, eggplants, tomatoes, pickles, onions, and vegetables unique to specific ethnic backgrounds of the residents would be grown. Alternatively, he saw other gardens that would be highly specialized due to the interest of the neighbors in growing flowers, exotic trees, ferns and shrubs that would be grown and then readied for replanting on residential and public lands. Additionally, he saw the possibility of having one or more gardens devoted to the planting and harvesting of medicinal herbs and foods. Further, he could think of no reason why lots located next or near public buildings would not be ideally suited for fostering programs related to food education, production, preservation and consumption—workshops and training programs that would be geared toward local youth organizations, schools (K-12), and even meeting some tertiary (college/university) education. He believed in his heart that "...when you touch the people's food, you have touched the heart of their culture."

The more Jasper Stretch engaged in "internal" brainstorming, the more disappointed he was with himself. He wondered why he had not been able to see earlier on in his career the potential for community enhancement, development and environmental sustainability. He had always had a passion for the quiescent, not too quiet farmer's markets where organically grown fruits, vegetables, produce, flowers, a variety of meats and the ever present pastries and zucchini, and banana bread were on display. In addition, although less pervasive, were the tables of preserved black current, blueberry, and gooseberry jams and jellies, and the dried tomato paste and canned seafood chowder. Together, these commodities produced a symphony of sights and smells with a cacophony of the grower's voices eager to sell their fanciful products and wares in the background.

"Now it was all coming together," he silently muttered, "and how people use the land relates not only to their understanding of the total ecology, but to how they might individually contribute to the current themes of reducing global warming, reducing the carbon footprint, and simultaneously increasing food awareness and security. The greening of Green Isle would not only be valued from an aesthetic perspective, it would also enable residents to get their hands "dirty" when they grew some of their own food, taught basic planning and management principles to gardeners, and cemented the emotional and intellectual relationships between concepts as varied as buying-local, farmers' markets, land stewardship, food dependency, natural interdependencies and the Four P's: People, Planet, Production, and Profitability. Later on, Stretch saw himself arguing that this new community glue would become as valuable in the field of community development—if understood, supported, and properly mixed—as the cement that was used to define the concrete jungle and urban infrastructure. He began to realize that there was more to think about than the complex and entangled maze that many in the field of economic development saw as synonymous with profit maximization and economic sustainability.

Jasper arrived at his office filled with a continuing sense of wonderment and puzzlement. He had to put this flurry of creative thoughts on the back burner for the time being, but the relationships and opportunities that he had felt were still fermenting in his mind. He had to become focused again on the scheduled events of the day and at 10:00 a.m. he was scheduled to meet with the local planning commission and deal with some zoning variances that had been requested and were essential if two new business ventures were to be attracted to Green isle.

The planning meeting would not be a routine one. Jasper Stretch was prepared to tell a new and different story and present a new picture of economic and community development to his colleagues. He said, "It is amazing to see how the land is used and used up in Green Isle. It is analogous to going to an expensive, posh restaurant that reeks with ambience. The maître d' seats you comfortable at a table with a great view and one adorned with elegant crystal, silver, and china. The tale is covered with a pristine, white line that has been perfectly prepared and ironed and the chairs are appropriate for comfortable, relaxed dining. Everything seems perfect until you realize that the table is for some reason unstable. You gently pull the table toward yourself in an attempt to level it, desperately trying to keep your efforts unnoticed and careful not to upset the water and wine goblets, but the table becomes more unsteady. Your guest detects your irritation and suggests that the waiter be called to level the table. A waiter is summoned, and a book of matches is placed under one of the table legs. The table rather than becoming stabilized now wobbles uncontrollably. In frustration, your party is moved to another table that is solid, but the ambience and view have been lost. This scenario is similar to what happens environmentally when the table legs of sustainability are not in sync and the social, cultural, economic and environmental pillars of the community become imbalanced. It is my hope that the decisions we make today will be based on the acknowledgement that these four factors must be considered."

Although Stretch was passionate about his new vision, he was also a realist in every sense of the word. He sensed that his vision of the city might not be widely shared by all of the political, economic, and social "movers and shakers" in Green Isle. If history were a prologue to the present, Stretch Jasper felt that the present time was probably not the best suited for broad proposals, especially with the impending slump in the housing market brought about by a complex combination of factors such as housing speculation, variable interest rates, zero-down payments, interest only mortgages, sub-prime lending mechanisms. In his gut he felt that the housing bubble would eventually be deflated or actually burst—not unlike the dot.com surge and bust that occurred earlier. As such, the vacant lands and run-down areas might not be assets now in the sense of new buildings or major refurbishment of old ones. He worried about how reductions in housing starts generally in Green Isle would affect his city's coffers.

With a serious decline in new housing starts, history dictated that there would be an accompanying decline in property tax revenue; reduction in revenue from building permit fees, tax revenue due to foreclosures; loss of real estate transfer tax revenue, and even some effect on Green Isle's ability to borrow money due to the overall weakness in the municipal bond market. Of course, other problems would kick in such as the increased costs associated with having vacant property (code enforcement, mowing, building and property maintenance, inhabitation by "squatters," and reduced aesthetics), the decline in value of housing in areas besieged with foreclosures and mortgage defaults, and the ever gnawing problems of having to potentially downsize staff, freeze or at least have a "slush" on vacant positions—except those which were deemed as emergency or essential.

## Questions and Instructions

1. What does sustainability as a concept mean to you? Please explain.
2. Do you think that Jasper Stretch's vision for Green Isle is a realistic one or is it a mere fantasy? Please elaborate on the pros and cons of his vision.
3. If you were on the planning commission, how would you have received the opening statement proffered by Stretch? Please explain your reactions and the basis for your decision making.
4. If you were to tell a story about how to achieve balance in nature, what "story" would you tell and what do the symbols and actors used in the story tell us about managing in an urban setting. Please elaborate.

## ESSENTIAL VIEWS:

### ACADEMICS/PRACTITIONERS AT THE STREET LEVEL

**Professional Portfolios: Showcasing Your Experience**
By Thomas E. Poulin

Demonstrating educational accomplishments is relatively easy with diplomas and transcripts. It is more difficult to demonstrate relevant professional experiences and capacities, creating challenges when seeking greater opportunities in the future. One means of addressing this is the development of a professional portfolio.

A professional portfolio is a collection of materials showcasing your competencies in a concrete fashion. These materials may support your future, professional pursuits. When creating a portfolio, do not fret about excess; you will be selective when presenting relevant materials with applications. For now, collect a wealth of materials from which to make later selections. Potential portfolio materials might include:

- Reports where you were the primary author or where you made a major contribution as a team member,
- Documentation on official letterhead describing your accomplishments.
- Performance appraisals and course evaluations.
- Tangible artifacts of your work such as programs, job aids, or course syllabi (excluding any which are proprietary).
- Certifications, awards, or plaques.
- Public information on organizations where you have worked (working for organizations with strong reputations increases your credibility).

When seeking professional advancement, especially when doing so in another organization where your performance is an unknown, a professional portfolio serves as a means of showcasing your talents. It is one thing to claim an experience in an interview or a resume; it is far more powerful to validate and illustrate this experience through the contents of a professional portfolio with evidence of your capabilities.

Public administration largely revolves around problem-solving, moving from project to project, program to program. This contributes to a work history difficult to document retroactively. Consequently, public-sector professionals would be prudent to begin early in their careers to document their work history, skills set, and professional development. Both the leadership and human resource management professionals of public-sector agencies should stress this to "newbies" in any discipline, at any level.

Letters of reference might be included in your professional portfolio, but they differ from documentation letters. Letters of reference hold greater value when targeted towards a specific position -- they are current. Letters of documentation might be older, but their value lies in being written at the time. For example, if assigned to a special project, a documentation letter describing your role written immediately after captures your competencies in "real-time." This might be of great value should the individual to whom you reported no longer be with the organization, as it was written during their official tenure on agency letterhead.

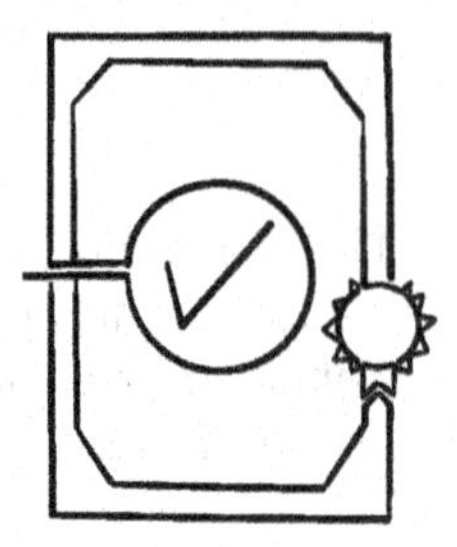

Many professional certifications exist based on general or specialized experiences. When seeking greater professional opportunities, these certifications might be the critical difference between you and other candidates. Many of these certifications require documented experience to support your application, and a professional portfolio is a valuable tool in this endeavor. If you are considering seeking greater opportunities in the future, the time to start seeking these certifications is now, developing your portfolio proactively.

When you submit a portfolio, you should organize it based upon the competencies and areas of expertise for a particular role, and these shall be unknown until you apply for a specific position. Consequently, do not concern yourself now with how to organize the materials in the present - you just need to ensure you are collecting them. However, when you do apply for a position, you must organize and present your portfolio materials in the most suitable, most powerful manner to support your application, not just as a loose collection of items.

Throughout your public-sector career, moving from role to role, and perhaps from agency to agency, you will collect many valuable competencies, preparing you for future challenges and opportunities. A professional portfolio is a powerful means to document and present your competencies, increasing the likelihood you will be afforded the opportunity to engage in future challenges by demonstrating your capacity and your professional growth over the arc of your career. If you have not yet done so, you should begin creating your portfolio, and you should begin to do so today.

*Source: Abridged version of "Professional Portfolios: Showcasing Your Experience," PA Times Online, November 28, 2020.*

# Index

## A



## B

## C



## D

## E



## F

## G



## H



## I

## J



## K



## L



## M

## N



## O



## P

## R

## S



## T

**U**



**V**



**W**



**Y**



**Z**